Essays in Public Economics

Essays in Public Economics

The Kiryat Anavim Papers

Edited by
Agnar Sandmo
Norwegian School of Economics
and Business Administration

Lexington Books
D.C. Heath and Company
Lexington, Massachusetts
Toronto

Library of Congress Cataloging Publication Data

Main entry under title:

Essays in public economics.

"Contains papers presented at a conference on public economics held at Kibbutz Kiryat Anavim, Israel, in June, 1975."

1. Finance, Public—Congresses. 2. Public goods—Congresses. I. Sandmo, Agnar.

HJ113.E77 336 77-7

ISBN 0-669-01424-9

Published simultaneously in Canada.

Printed in the United States of America.

International Standard Book Number: 0-669-01424-9

Library of Congress Catalog Card Number: 77-7

Contents

Preface

The present volume contains papers presented at a conference on public economics held at Kibbutz Kiryat Anavim, Israel, in June 1975. Many of the papers have already appeared in the professional journals; however, several of them are published here for the first time.

The following contributions have something more in common than the fact that they were originally presented at the same conference. All of them are written in the spirit of the "new public economics," which is in many ways very different from the traditional approach to public finance. Some of the characteristics of the new approach are greater reliance on methods of general equilibrium analysis, more attention to problems involving second best solutions, and the broadening of the field of study into areas traditionally occupied by other disciplines, notably law and political science. All of these characteristics are evident in the following collection, and it should therefore be a useful one both to students and to scholars who wish to explore the modern literature in this area.

The conference was sponsored by Israel's National Council for Research and Development. It was one in the fifth series of Scientific Research Conferences organized by the Council. All participants in the conference are indebted to the Council and its head, Mr. Eliezer Thal, for financial support, and to Dr. Shabtai Gairon and his staff for their expert handling of practical matters of organization in the pleasant atmosphere of Kibbutz Kiryat Anavim. The scientific program of the conference was drawn up by an organizing committee with Professor Eytan Sheshinski as chairman; needless to say, their work contributed decisively to the success of the conference. I am particularly indebted to Professor Sheshinski for his assistance in preparing for the publication of this volume and to the various publishers and organizations who granted permission to reprint previously published articles.

Essays in Public Economics

1 Public Safety

Serge-Christophe Kolm

All measures taken by the public sector have some influence upon the occurrence of human deaths and other bodily injuries. And to diminish these risks is the essential or unique aim of a number of them, which include both expenditures and regulations. What is the optimum for these measures? Is the present situation close to it?

A very strong negative answer to the latter question has often been suggested by the observation of the marginal costs incurred to save lives in various sectors by various measures (or, equivalently, of the marginal efficiency of life saving expenditures). The information is plentiful for several countries; in English, let me just mention the studies by William Gorham and Dan Usher and the references they give. The result is always of the same order of magnitude: according to sectors and measures, these marginal costs or efficiencies can be multiplied by factors up to thousands. Can we conclude that human life, the most important commodity, the only one which is an indispensable complement to the enjoyment of any other, is also the one produced with the grossest misallocation and waste?

Several arguments have been and could be advanced to justify discrepancies in these marginal costs and efficiencies. Their general presentation and discussion can be found in my paper (1975). One of them is by far more important than the others, and I focus on it here. It will give results such that, most of the time, the number of dollars spent to avoid a marginal casualty must be higher the more "collective," or "public," the danger is in some sense. And, it will turn out that computations from purely technical observable data can tell us whether safety has received too little or too much emphasis in any given sector.

1.1. Assumptions

Unavoidably, a number of simplifications must be accepted. In some cases, my model and results will be directly applicable. In others, the model must be completed by other considerations, and the role of this study then is to show the way toward important phenomena and conclusions. The main simplifications are as follows. I shall explicitly consider only death, but the same analysis applies to other bodily injuries; more generally, it is the theory of optimum allocation of

Reprinted, with permission of the American Economic Association, from the *American Economic Review*, vol. 66, June 1976, pp. 382-387.

nontransferable consumptions produced by both private and public inputs (education and recreation are other cases). There is only one period, short enough so that everyone's probability of dying during this period is small. The main problem considered will be to allocate public safety funds between several uses, and the only valuable effect is to reduce casualties; I assume no effective nonnegativity constraints on these different amounts. Finally, there will be no externalities, an assumption which has four main applications here. 1) There are no Pareto-irrelevant (distributional) price externalities, which means that either the considered variations affect too small a sector of the whole economy to influence prices, or that price effects are compensated. 2) There is no externality in consumption: individuals are not directly affected by the consumption-work choices of others, be it through their tastes or their choices' nonbudget constraints. 3) As a special case of 2), individuals are not so affected by the probability of death of others. 4) The death probability of individuals is not affected by the others' choices, i.e., we exclude manslaughter. (Accidents as "congestion externalities" are analyzed in my book (1970).)

The last three cases require an explanation. For individuals' choices about consumption, work, safety, etc., for both the decision and the evaluation, the biological "individual" is not, in fact, the right social unit. To consider "the family" as the unit would be far better. This term is, however, ambiguous. Every biological individual is the center of concentric circles of individuals who are more or less directly (i.e., not through markets) concerned by, and participating in, "his" choices: himself, the nuclear family, relatives, friends, acquaintances, etc. They, more or less, have a feeling for the individual's situation and influence the corresponding choices. Then, the absence of interindividual externality means that, in some sense, their influence is "proportional to" their feeling. This participation in choice is through suasion, "reciprocity" exchange, vicarious choice, an individual's desire to please another, etc. This chapter is not the place to develop this analysis. Let me just mention its application to the question of risks of death. Who is concerned by an individual's survival probability? First, himself. Then his closest family, first for affective reasons, often with the same intensity as the individual himself, and for material and economic reasons. Then his friends, relatives, etc. Then members of the social communities to which he belongs (neighborhood, church, region, nation, mankind), with a spectrum of degrees of intensity. We are assuming here that the influences on the individual's choices which affect his death probability (as well as on other aspects of his well being) internalize the corresponding feelings, especially at the intrafamily level where they would be impossible to ignore.

1.2. Optimality Conditions

Turning now to traditional economic concepts, let i be an individual, p^i his death probability, v^i his marginal willingness to pay for p^i, s^i the social marginal value of his wealth. We assume "normal" individuals and society, so that $v^i < 0$, $s^i > 0$, and all the s^i are equal if "distribution is optimal." The term y^i is the set of parameters describing i's "situation" (commodities consumed, work, location, etc.); x_j is the amount of public money spent to reduce risk of type j; and x is the vector of x_j. From the assumptions, p^i is a function of x and y^i only: $p^i = p^i(x, y^i)$, where $p^i_j = \partial p^i/\partial x_j$ is the "direct" marginal effect of x_j on p^i; we shall normally have $p^i_j < 0$. The individual i chooses y^i in a possibility set Y^i (which includes in particular its budget constraint but does not directly depend upon $p^{i'}$, and $y^{i'}$ for $i' \neq i$), so as to maximize his utility function $u^i[y^i, p^i(x, y^i)]$. It is shown in the Appendix that an optimality condition for x_j is that $\Sigma s^i v^i p^i_j$ is the same for all j. This condition holds if Σx_j is given, but it also holds if we explicitly consider how this sum is obtained, for instance through taxation of any kind, as long as the x_j enter in the problem's constraints only by their sum. The result can be applied to any set of risks j (containing at least two j's).

1.3. Direct and Indirect Effects

With given functions u^i and Y^i, the y^i chosen by individual i, y^{i*}, depends upon x: $y^{i*} = y^{i*}(x)$. We assume that this function is differentiable for the present exposition, although it is not necessarily so in this field (decisions to incur or shun some kind of risk). The sensitivity (total derivative) of p^i for x_j is

$$P^i_j = \frac{dp^i}{dx_j} = p^i_j + \sum_k \frac{\partial p^i}{\partial y^{i*}} \frac{\partial y^{i*}}{\partial x_j}$$

where the y^i_k are the components of y^i. In the normal case $0 > P^i_j > p^i_j$, meaning that the increment in income received by the gift in safety through an increase in x_j is redistributed among several items of consumption, including some left in safety.

It is usually possible to distinguish for each x_j a subset of y^i_k, say those with $k \in K_j$, which are parameters chosen by the individuals and having some influence on their risk which is affected by x_j; thus, $\partial p^i_j/\partial y^i_k = 0$ for $k \notin K_j$; we then call

$$\pi^i_j = p^i_j + \sum_{k \in K_j} \frac{\partial p^i}{\partial y^{i*}_k} \frac{\partial y^{i*}_k}{\partial x_j}$$

The normal case seems to be such that $0 \geqslant \pi^i_j \geqslant p^i_j$. The case $\pi^i_j = p^i_j$ generally implies that the individual has no influence on the risk affected by x_j. Ordinary behavior seems also to suggest that $\pi^i_j = P^i_j$ is not infrequent.

We now have three candidates for measuring the marginal efficiency of x_j in number of lives saved: $\Sigma_i |P^i_j|$, $\Sigma_i |\pi^i_j|$, and $\Sigma_i |p^i_j|$. The "right" one may seem to be the total marginal number of lives saved, $\Sigma_i |P^i_j|$. However, the one which is given by the above mentioned statistics is the number of lives saved in the considered activity, $\Sigma_i |\pi^i_j|$. One may consider the individuals' adjustments as their own responsibility, implying that the marginal efficiency which should count for allocating x_j is the marginal number of lives "directly" saved, $\Sigma_i \mid p_j^i \mid$. According to which number of deaths we would like to minimize, it is the equality for all j of one of these three numbers which are the corresponding first-order conditions. None is, however, a priori the true optimality condition.

1.4. Whe Must We Save As Many Lives As Possible?

There are, however, nonfortuitous cases when $\Sigma_i p_j^i = \Sigma_i p_k^i$ is the condition for optimal allocation between x_j and x_k. One is when x_j and x_k are such that, necessarily, p_j^i is the same for all i and p_k^i is the same for all i. We call the corresponding risks "pure public risks." Practically, this happens for risks which are common to the whole population under consideration. The case also practically requires that individuals cannot modify this risk for themselves, and thus that $p_j^i = \pi_j^i$ and $p_k^i = \pi_k^i$. In such cases, if statistics show $\mid \pi_j^i \mid \neq \mid \pi_k^i \mid$, or if engineering computation concludes that $\mid p_j^i \mid \neq \mid p_k^i \mid$ in the actual situation, there is misallocation from the less to the more efficient use.

Another case, at the extreme opposite, is when x_j and x_k actually affect the safety of only one and the same individual. That is, $p_j^{i'} = p_k^{i'} = 0$ for all $i' \neq i$. The corresponding risks are "purely private risks" for individual i. We then note that the condition $p_j^i = p_k^i$ does not depend upon the fact that individual i may be more able to shun one risk than the other one by his own choices, i.e., does not depend upon the differences in individual responsibility in risks.

These two cases are subcases of the one where x_j and x_k affect in a purely public way the safety of the individuals of some subsociety, and do not affect the others. That is, there is a set I of i such that $p_j^i = p_k^i = 0$ for $i \notin I$, and p_j^i are the same for all $i \in I$ and p_k^i are the same for all $i \in I$.

A third case would be when all $V^i = v^i s^i$'s are equal: then $\Sigma_i p_j^i$ must be the same for all j. But this certainly does not hold. Even apart from inequalities in s^i, the v^i are far from equal, due to differences in individuals' situations and tastes (some people never take a plane, others play Russian roulette).

In all these cases but the last, the result does not depend upon the V^i, and therefore not on the v^i or s^i. Thus it is independent of the income distribution, of individual tastes, and of costs of raising public funds. The most significant of these cases is that of pure public risks: the allocation of safety funds among risks must save as many lives as possible.

1.5. The Technological Optimality Condition

With $s^i v^i = V^i$, the optimality conditions are $\Sigma_i V^i p_j^i = \lambda$. We write p_i for optimum p_j^i when j is a pure private risk for i. The condition gives $V^i p_i = \lambda$.

Then, for any general risk j, the condition is $\Sigma_i p_j^i/p_i = 1$. The interest of this formula is that p_j^i/p_i is the rate of substitution of purely private safety costs to x_j in p^i. In particular, it may be a purely private safety expenditure in the same field where x_j intervenes. Then, p_j^i/p_i are often computable through engineering data or from casualty statistics. We would generally conclude that x_j is too small or too large from the fact that $\Sigma_i p_j^i/p_i$ is larger or smaller than one.

1.6. Pure Public and Private Risks

Let us now call p_0 the optimum p_j^i for any pure public risk j. The above optimality condition gives $1/p_0 = \Sigma 1/p_i$. Or, n being the number of persons in the society,

$$\frac{1}{np_0} = \frac{1}{n}\Sigma\frac{1}{p_i}$$

$n\,|\,p_0\,|$ is the direct marginal efficiency of purely public safety in number of lives saved. It must thus be the harmonic mean of the like efficiencies of purely private safety, $|\,p_i\,|$. Thus, if $m = Min_i\,|\,p_i\,|$ and $M = Max_i\,|\,p_i\,|$ $m \leqslant n\,|\,p_0\,| \leqslant M$ must hold. Furthermore, from an easy application of Cauchy's inequality, one must have $n\,|\,p_0\,| \leqslant (1/n)\,\Sigma\,|\,p_i\,|$, that is to say, one extra dollar must save more lives if it is equally shared between purely private safeties than if it is used for pure public safety; both allocations are "egalitarian" in some sense. It may seem surprising that equal sharing, which is arbitrary from efficiency viewpoints, is nevertheless the most efficient way of saving lives. Schweitzer's and Sisha-Mond's inequalities furthermore show that

$$\frac{1}{n}\Sigma\,|\,p^i\,|\,/n\,|\,p_0\,| \leqslant (M+m)^2/4Mm$$

and

$$\frac{1}{n}\Sigma\,|\,p^i\,| - n\,|\,p_0\,| \leqslant (M^{1/2} - m^{1/1})^2$$

The equalities hold everywhere if and only if p_i were equal, which is unlikely since it would also imply the equality of all V_i at the optimum. Thus, if a nonpure public risk j is close enough to a pure public risk in the sense that the dispersion of the p_j^i is low enough, the same inequalities must hold when $\Sigma_i\,|\,p_j\,|$ replace $n\,|\,p_0\,|$. In particular, $\Sigma_i\,|\,p_j^i\,| \leqslant (1/n)\Sigma\,|\,p_i\,|$. It is, however, the comparison between general $\Sigma_j\,|\,p_j^i\,|$ and $n\,|\,p_0\,|$ which is the most interesting one: this is the topic of Section 1.8.

1.7. Public or Private Provision

Before leaving purely private risks, we must note a difference between two kinds of safety expenditures according to who decides about them: the public sector or the individual. There are publicly provided pure private safety and privately provided pure private safety. We considered the former. For the latter, the individual's choice does not necessarily conform to the social optimum: if we call p_i' the derivative of p_i for any safety expenditure chosen by individual i, this choice is such that $v^i p_i' = 1$. This private choice would coincide with what would be the optimum one if the public sector were in charge of this decision if $s^i = \lambda$ giving $p_i' = p_i$ at optimum. This would happen if lump sum transfers between individual i's wealth and the public safety fund Σx_j were possible. Otherwise, generally $p_i' \neq p_i$. More precisely, at optimum $p_i'/p_i = s^i/\lambda$, which means that the marginal rate of substitution of publicly provided to privately provided purely private safety funds for i must be equal to the social marginal value of i's wealth measured in public safety dollars. Now, statistics sometimes provide p_i' more easily than p_i; for instance, in the case of road traffic safety, accident statistics based on cars (a private choice) give p_i', whereas statistics based on the condition of roads (a public safety choice) give p_j^i. If "income distribution is optimal," s^i is the same for all i by definition, and the first-order optimality condition for the allocation of the x_j is that $\Sigma_i p_j^i/p_i'$ is the same for all j. If, furthermore, there can be lump sum transfers between individuals' incomes and the public safety fund, these conditions become that $\Sigma_i p_j^i/p_i' = 1$ for all j. And the actual discrepancies between these values indicate how the x_j must be reallocated.

1.8. General and Pure Public Risks

Optimum allocation between purely public and general safety imply

$$p_0 = \sum_i \frac{V^i}{\Sigma V^i} p_j^i = \sum_i \frac{1/p_i}{\Sigma 1/p_i} p_j^i$$

and the marginal number of lives saved by x_0 is

$$n\,|p_0| = \sum_i \frac{V^i}{\overline{V}} |p_j^i|$$

where $\overline{V} = \Sigma V^i/n$ is the average V^i. Therefore $n\,|p_0| < \Sigma_i\,|p_j^i|$ if the p_i and the p_j^i are similarly classified by i, and the reverse inequality holds if they are inversely classified by i (i.e., $(p_i - p_{i'})(p_j^i - p_j^{i'})$ for all pairs i, i' is positive in the former case and negative in the latter one).

Let π^{ij} be the probability that the cause of risk j kills individual i. It is an additive part of p^i. It depends upon x_j the amount of public money which diminishes this risk for all i, and upon y_j^i the sum spent to diminish this risk for individual i only, x_j and y_j^i influence p^i through π^{ij} only. We also assume that $\pi^{ij} = \pi^j(x_j, y_j^i)$; i.e., the only reason why π^{ij} depends upon i that the y_j^i differ. This is a frequent situation which only means that the effect of x_j and y_j^i on π^{ij} is a purely technical matter, general and not dependent upon other individual characteristics; π^j is a decreasing function of both its arguments. But, being a probability, it is constrained by $\pi^{ij} \geqslant 0$. It is small by assumption, and in ordinary cases very small. We consider the situation at the optimum. We certainly have $\partial^2 \pi^j / \partial y_j^{i2} > 0$ because of π^j's positivity and smallness; this indicates a point of decreasing returns to scale of y_j^i expenditure on safety. But $\partial \pi^j / \partial y_j^i = p^i$ and $\partial \pi^j / \partial x_j = p_j^i$. Thus p_i is an increasing function of y_j^i, and therefore p_i, y_j^i, $-\pi^{ij}$ are similarly ordered by i. Also p_j^i is similarly ordered or, on the contrary, inversely ordered, by i, depending on whether it is an increasing or a decreasing function of y_j^i, i.e., on whether $\partial^2 \pi^j / \partial x_j \partial y_j^i$ is positive or negative, i.e., on whether x_j and y_j^i are substitutes or complements in providing safety.

To conclude, *a public expenditure on a general public safety must marginally save more or fewer lives than one on a pure public safety depending on whether it is a substitute or a complement to private safety measures* (i.e., the marginal cost of saving a life must be lower or higher in this manner than from pure public risks depending on this condition).

In most cases, public and private safety measures happen to be substitutes rather than complements. This is for instance the case for most road (public) and car (private) safety improvements, for firemen and private fire protection (extinguishers, use of fireproof material, exits), for police and private watchmen or systems preventing entry, for most home and hospital cures, for vaccination and public sanitation, for public air pollution prevention and private air filters, etc. There are however cases when they are complements: for instance, various aspects of health care, or car lights and road signals, or, generally, private alarm systems (things or men) and the public service they call (fire, police, accident rescue).

The most common case thus is $n \,|p_0| < \Sigma_i |p_j^i|$ at the optimum, i.e., an extra dollar must save fewer lives from a pure public risk than from nonpure public risks, or, we must pay more to save an extra life from a pure public risk than elsewhere. The reason for it as shown above is that the nonpure public safety measure saves on the average "cheaper" lives than the purely public one because the more valuable ones are more sheltered from this risk by specific protection—a discrimination which is not possible for purely public risks.

The difference in death's marginal costs may have to be substantial. If risk averters (i.e., high $|v^i|$ people) completely shun risk j so that $p_j^i = 0$ for these i, whereas other people care little (low $|v^i|$), then $\Sigma_i (V^i/\overline{V}) \,|p_j^i| = n \,|p_0|$ may be much smaller than $\Sigma_i |p_j^i|$.

1.9. General Risks

Now calling ρ_j the correlation coefficient between V^i and p_j^i, we have

$$\sum_i V^i p_j^i = \overline{V} \cdot (1 + \rho_j) \cdot \sum_i p_j^i$$

which shows that the marginal cost of saving a life by x_j must be proportional to $1 + \rho_j$ ($\rho_j = 0$ for a pure public risk and the above argument is that $\rho_j < 0$ for most of the other cases). It is also possible to distinguish the factors in $V^i = s^i v^i$ and analyze the effect on the optimum marginal costs of life of the correlations between s^i (income distribution), v^i (individual risk aversion), and p_j^i.

1.10. Conclusion

Given its importance, the economic value of human life has received little attention. It is hoped that this chapter sheds some light on some of these important aspects, in particular on the question of the inequality of values for different sectors and decisions, especially public decisions. Among the results are the following: There generally must be inequalities. An exception is the case of purely public risks where as many lives as possible must be saved by the appropriate allocation of safety funds. For other safety measures, life must generally be cheaper or more expensive than for purely public safety depending on whether this expenditure is a substitute or a complement to purely private safety; most often, it must be cheaper. Finally, it has been shown how statistical or engineering data may indicate whether safety is too low or too high in any given sector.

References

C. Abraham, Goldberg, and J. Thédie, "Le choix des investissements routiers," *Transports*, Nov. 1960.

C. Abraham and J. Thédie, "Le prix d'une vie humaine dans les décisions économiques," *Revue Française de Recherche Opérationnelle,* 3ème trimestre 1960.

J. Drèze, "L'utilité sociale d'une vie humaine," *Revue Francaise de Recherche Opérationnelle,* 2ème trimestre 1962.

G. Fromm, "Comment" on Schelling's paper, in S.B. Chase, Jr., ed., *Problems in Public Expenditure Analysis*, Washington 1968.

W. Gorham, "Some Use of Quantitative Analysis to Improve the Allocation of Public Funds," in J. Paelinck (ed.), *Programming for Europe's Collective Needs*, Amsterdam, 1970.

J.H. Jones, *Road Accidents–Report submitted to Minister of Transport*, London 1946.

M. Jones-Lee, "Valuation of Reduction in Probability of Death by Road Accident," *Journal of Transport Economics and Policy*, Jan. 1969.

S. Ch. Kolm, "Concernements et décisions collectifs, une contribution à l'analyse économique des sociétés," *Analyse et Prévision*, 1967.

_______, *Le Service des Masses*, Paris 1970.

_______, "Connaissance des coûts et valeurs d'environnement," in *Estimation des dommages d'environnement*, O.C.D.E., 1972-74; English translation (O.E.C.D.)

_______, "L'inégalité des valeurs des vies humaines," *Cahiers du Séminaire d'Econométrie*, 1975.

R. McKean, "Comment" on Schelling's paper, in S.B. Chase, Jr. (ed.), *Problems in Public Expenditure Analysis*, Washington 1968.

E.J. Mishan, "Evaluation of Life and Limb: A Theoretical Approach," *Journal of Political Economy* 79 (July-Aug. 1971):687-705.

G. Morlat et al., "Recherches sur les coûts de protection de la vie humaine," Centre de Recherche Opérationnelle, Institut de Statistique des Universités de Paris.

D.J. Reynolds, "The Cost of Road Accidents," *Journal of the Royal Statistical Society* 119, pt. 4 (1956):393-408.

T. Schelling, "The Life you Save May be Your Own," in S.B. Chase, Jr., ed., *Problems in Public Expenditure Analysis*, Washington 1968.

J. Thédie, "Valeur économique de la sécurité routière," *La Route*, 1958.

D. Usher, "An Imputation to the Measure of Economic Growth for Changes in Life Expectancy," in M. Moss, ed., *The Measurement of Economic and Social Performance*, National Bureau of Economic Research *Studies in Income and Wealth*, Vol. 38, New York 1974.

CERMAP, "Le dépistage précoce du cancer du col de l'utérus. Etude économique," juillet 1968.

Appendix 1A

The usual notations are used for the derivatives for vectors and of vectors. We call v^i_y the vector of individual i's willingness to pay for the components of y^i when p^i is given. We note p^i_y for $p^i_{y^i}$. Given x, individual i chooses an y^i, $y^{i*}(x) \in Y^i$. Either $v^i p_y + v^i_y = 0$, or $y^{i*}(x)$ is on the border of Y^i and the vector $v^i p_y + v^i_y$ for $y^i = y^{i*}(x)$ is within the cone of normals to Y^i at this point. Thus, when x differentially varies, we have

$$(v^i p^i_y + v^i_y)\Big|_{y^i = y^{i*}(x)} \cdot y^{i*}(x) \cdot dx = 0$$

Therefore, individual i's marginal willingness to pay for a change dx in x is the value at $y^i = y^{i*}(x)$ of

$$[v^i p^i_x + (v^i p^i_y + v^i_y)\, y^{i*}_x] \cdot dx = v^i p^i_z \cdot dx$$

whence the mentioned optimality condition. The same result can be shown to hold when $y^{i*}(x)$ is not differentiable, a not unimportant case (choices to incur or not some risk—for instance, to take a plane or not).

2 Distribution of Tastes and Skills and the Provision of Local Public Goods

Eitan Berglas

2.1. Introduction

The theory of public goods has recently been used as an explanation for the distribution of a nation's population among different fiscal jurisdictions. All these studies follow the classical Tiebout (1956) paper in which individuals select the community that best satisfies their private preferences.

In recent studies it is possible to distinguish two major different approaches. In the first approach it is assumed that the public goods are of the nonpure type, i.e. public goods for which costs of maintaining a given level of service depend on the size of community. In this case the minimization of cost of providing public services determines the optimal community size.[1] In the second approach it is assumed that each community has some resource which is fixed locally–say land. Then public goods are used to explain the optimal distribution of the one movable factor–identical labor–between communities. These models enable an interesting analysis of the optimality of competition and the need for intercommunity grants.[2] Once diversity of tastes is appropriately introduced in these models they lead to the result that identical individuals will tend to concentrate in homogeneous communities.

Thus the two approaches fail to explain the formation of mixed communities and therefore are inappropriate to the study of alternative tax structures. It is the purpose of this paper to analyze the conditions that lead to the formation of mixed communities, to analyze the efficiency of competition of these cases and to analyze the appropriate tax structure.

The analysis of mixed communities is made possible by the assumption that, in addition to the difference in preferences, individuals differ in their productive skills. It is the interaction between the distribution of tastes and skills that leads to different community patterns. It is further shown that when intercommunity trade is allowed for, it will have a considerable effect on the size, population mix and the level of public services in different communities.

Throughout the analysis it will be assumed that the movement of people between communities is costless and, furthermore, when intercommunity trade is allowed for, it is assumed that transportation of commodities is costless. It is

Reprinted, with permission of North-Holland Publishing Company, from the *Journal of Public Economics*, vol. 6, November 1976, pp. 409-423. This paper was written during the author's stay as a Xerox Visiting Professor at the University of Rochester.

not intended to imply that these are realistic assumptions. The location of different communities, their production activities and their population mix cannot generally be explained without references to many other important considerations such as geography, climate, distribution of natural resources, past changes in technology as well as transportation and individual transfer costs. Models such as the one suggested in this study may be helpful in explaining the economic forces that affect the size of communities, their composition, the across community divergence in public services, and may also be helpful in explaining changes in communities through time.

The model to be used in this chapter is introduced in the next section. In this section the properties for Pareto optimal communities are derived. In section 2.3 the possible competitive equilibria are studied. It is shown that in order to achieve equilibrium the taxing freedom of communities is very restricted. If redistribution of income is desirable, a central government is necessary. A taxing agreement between communities will not be stable. The Pareto optimality of competition with various tax structures is analyzed.

In section 2.4 the diversity of tastes is increased and independence of the distribution of skills and preferences is allowed. It is shown that in this case different type communities can coexist, all of them mixed, and provide different levels and composition of public services. The tax system appropriate for this case is derived. The results of this model are compared with the Tiebout (1956) results and it is shown that although a tendency of similar people to group together still exists, other effects are important in the determination of population mix.

In section 2.5 trade among communities is allowed. It is shown that the effect of trade is similar to the effect of allowing independence between the distribution of tastes and productive skills. Trade will increase diversity between communities, will lead communities to specialize in production and will lead to different wage rates for the same factors in various communities. Trade is not an efficient substitute for factor mobility in this case. The optimal community patterns and the taxation implications are analyzed. Following this section the main conclusions are summarized in section 2.6.

2.2. The Model

Assume that the population is composed of two types of individuals. Each type is homogeneous with respect to tastes and productive capacity. There are N individuals of type a and M individuals of type b. The respective utility functions are

$$u = \tilde{u}(x^a, y), \tag{2.1}$$

$$v = \tilde{v}(x^b, y),$$

where y denotes the public good and x^a and x^b denote the private good consumption of individuals type a and b. The production function of x is given by

$$x = \tilde{x}(n, m), \tag{2.2}$$

where n, m are the number of type a and b individuals employed in the production of x. Let partial derivatives be denoted by subscripts, i.e., $x_1 = \partial x/\partial n$. We assume that the production function of x is homogeneous of the first degree in n and m, and $\tilde{x}_1, \tilde{x}_2 > 0; \tilde{x}_{11}, \tilde{x}_{22} < 0$ and $\tilde{x}(n, 0) = \tilde{x}(0, m) = 0$.

In section 2.5 below it is shown that when the number of private goods exceed one the results of the analysis are unaffected as long as the different goods cannot be traded between communities. In this case teachers, bus drivers, accountants and unskilled workers can be regarded as complementing skills.

The production function of the public good y is given by

$$y = \tilde{y}(x^y, n + m), \quad \tilde{y}_1 > 0, \tilde{y}_2 < 0, \tag{2.3}$$

$$\partial x^y/\partial(n + m)\,|_{y=\text{constant}} > 0, \; \partial^2 x^y/\partial(n + m)\,|_{y=\text{constant}} > 0.$$

x^y is the quantity of x used in the production of the public good.

The definition of the public good may have two alternative interpretations. The first is that all people enjoy the same level of service—exclusion is impossible—but the utility derived is affected by the number of people using the service. In this interpretation $\partial y/\partial(n + m)$ represents congestion costs. The second interpretation is a good the consumption of which involves significant externalities and the service provision of cost increases as community increases as in the case of education, fire and police protection.[a]

The requirement that the marginal cost of producing the same level of y when n is increased will be positive and increasing will generally hold only beyond a certain level of population. When population is small no congestion cost need exist. The restrictions on the derivatives are assumed in order to guarantee that beyond a certain population level an equiproportionate increase in the two types of individuals will result in a smaller proportionate increase in

[a]Equation (2.3) is restrictive in two respects. It implies that congestion effects of the two type individuals are the same. Suppose individual type a has more children or travels more than individual type b then congestion effects may differ, or $\partial y/\partial n \neq \partial y/\partial m$. This case is analyzed in section 2.3. Another restriction is that each type individual has the same aversion towards congestion. This restriction could be eliminated by introducing $n + m$ into the utility functions. It can be shown that this formulation does not affect the results.

the output of the two commodities. If this were not the case the optimal community size will be indeterminate or infinity.

In the following optimization analysis we shall assume that identical individuals will have the same utility. This is regarded as one of the rules of equity (horizontal equity) and will facilitate comparison of optimization results with competitive results. We start by deriving the rules for an optimal community defined as a community in which the utility levels of individuals type a is maximized for a given utility v^0 of individuals type b. The necessary conditions can be derived by differentiation of the following Lagrangian expression,

$$L = \tilde{u}(x^a, y) - \lambda_1 [\tilde{v}(x^b, y) - v^0] - \lambda_2 [\tilde{x}(n, m) - nx^a - mx^b - x^y]$$

$$- \lambda_3 [y - \tilde{y}(x^y, n + m)]. \tag{2.4}$$

Differentiating with respect to x^y, x^a, x^b, y, n and m, we get

$$n\tilde{u}_2/\tilde{u}_1 + m\tilde{v}_2/\tilde{v}_1 = 1/\tilde{y}_1, \tag{2.5}$$

$$\tilde{x}_1 - x^a = -\tilde{y}_2/\tilde{y}_1, \tag{2.6}$$

$$\tilde{x}_2 - \tilde{x}^b = -\tilde{y}_2/\tilde{y}_1. \tag{2.7}$$

Equations (2.5)-(2.7) together with the three constraints in equation (2.4) are sufficient to solve for the six variables. Equations (2.5)-(2.7) have a simple economic interpretation. Equation (2.5) is the well-known Samuelson (1954) criterion for pure public good. It is important to note that this equation is necessary regardless of size and composition of the community. In examining equation (2.6) observe that by the implicit function theorem $-\tilde{y}_2/\tilde{y}_1 = \partial x^y/\partial(n + m)|_{y = \text{constant}}$. It is meaningful to define $-\tilde{y}_2/\tilde{y}_1$ as the marginal social cost per individual while $\tilde{x}_1 - x^a$ (marginal product minus personal consumption) is the marginal social contribution of individual type a. Equation (2.6) thus can be interpreted as equating marginal social contribution to marginal social cost of individual type a and equation (2.7) applies the same rule to individual type b. If $\tilde{x}_1 - x^a > \partial x^y/\partial(n + m)$ then the utility of everybody could be increased by adding individual type a to the community, since then the level of y can be increased without any reduction in private consumption.[b]

[b]As suggested by a referee, equation (2.3) can be replaced by a cost function $c = \tilde{c}(y, n + m)$, where $c = x^y$. At the optimal solution $\tilde{c}/(n + m)|_{y=y^*}$ must be at a minimum, otherwise by changing community size utility of everybody can be increased. Finite optimal community size requires that such a minimum exist hence the restrictions on the derivatives of equation (2.3). Given this formulation the tax per capita is c_2. At the minimum point total taxes equal $(n + m)c_2 = c$, or, the budget is exactly balanced.

The Pareto optimum defined by these equations is relative to v^0. As we increase v^0, u must fall. The optimal size, the mix of the community and the consumption of y, will change. The direction of change will depend on the relative preference for public goods of the two type individuals.[c]

Suppose now that there exists a v, denoted by v^*, for which the optimal population mix is n^* and m^* such that $n^*/m^* = N/M$. Then a Pareto optimal solution for the population as a whole is divide total population into N/n^* identical communities composed of n^*, m^* people of the two types with identical production and consumption.[d]

If the u^*v^* distribution is undesirable according to some national social welfare function, it is possible to derive Pareto optimal conditions for any distribution of utility. This can be done by adding another constraint to equation (2.4) requiring $n/m = N/M$. In this case the resulting conditions are equation (2.5) while equations (2.6) and (2.7) are replaced by

$$N(\bar{x}_1 - x^a + \bar{y}_2/\bar{y}_1) + M(\bar{x}_2 - x^b + \bar{y}_2/\bar{y}_1) = 0. \tag{2.6'}$$

For v^* and u^* the expressions in the brackets of (2.6′) vanish and the constraint is of course not binding. But suppose now that the expressions in the brackets do not vanish, then

$$(\bar{x}_1 - x^a + \bar{y}_2/\bar{y}_1) \overset{\text{sign}}{=} -(\bar{x}_2 - x^b + \bar{y}_2/\bar{y}_1).$$

Suppose that the left-hand side expression is positive, then the welfare of the nation (of all individuals) can be increased by stimulating immigration (out migration) of type a (b) individuals. This will, of course, affect the distribution of income in the rest of the world.

2.3. Competition and Alternative Tax Schemes

Given the model of the earlier section we shall analyze the possible competitive equilibria for this nation. Throughout the section it will be assumed that wages are equal to marginal products. People are shopping for the best community. Costs of movement between communities are zero. New communities can be created at no cost.

[c]In a situation where private goods constitute a large share of total consumption it is plausible to assume that a rise in v/u is positively associated with a rise in n/m. This condition is necessary for the stability of the competitive equilibrium that will be discussed later.

[d]There exists the problem raised by Pauly (1970) if $N/n^* \neq$ integer. Throughout the paper we shall assume that either N/n^* is an integer or alternatively that the number of communities is sufficiently large and that small variations around the optimal ratio do not meaningfully affect the utility of the two types of individuals.

Case I

Consider the case where the population is divided into N/n^* communities. Each community is composed of n^*, m^* people of the two types. Each community provides the quantity y^* of the public good which is financed by equal per capita taxes. It is clear that this case, which corresponds to our Pareto optimal solution with no income redistribution, is also a competitive equilibrium. All identical people enjoy the same utility and it is not possible to design a community in which the two type individuals will be better off.

The implication of this example for the freedom of communities to write their own tax laws needs further elaboration. Suppose that one community changes the tax pattern by taxing relatively heavily the type a individuals (assume they are richer). As a result u falls below u^* and v rises above v^*. This will cause an out migration of type a people and an in migration of type b persons. However, since the rules for optimal taxation [equations (2.6)-(2.7)] are violated, the community cannot reach an equilibrium with $v \geqslant v^*$ and $u \geqslant u^*$. Therefore by our zero cost of transfer assumption it will have either to conform to the optimal tax rule or it will be empty. (For a similar analysis see Oates (1972, p. 7).) Another way to interpret this result is to say that local government can follow independent distributional objectives only when the costs of migration are high. By the same considerations it is easy to show that local benefit (Lindahl) taxes are inefficient.

It should be emphasized that the formula of taxing everyone the same is a direct result of the way equation (2.3) was defined. Allowing for the case where different people will have a different congestion effect (in our notation $\partial x^y/\partial n \neq \partial x^y/\partial m$—see footnote a) then each type should pay a different tax; type a persons should each pay $\partial x^y/\partial n$ and type b $\partial x^y/\partial m$, or each should pay according to his marginal social cost. Furthermore, if a community provides several public goods then the tax should equal the sum of the marginal social costs. When there are several public goods, some may be of the pure type. However, it is necessary in this case that the derivative restrictions imposed on equation (2.3) will hold for the sum of derivatives for all public goods.

Case II

Suppose that all communities agree on the same redistribution policy. This can reflect a general adoption of the principle of ability to pay, or alternatively, the adoption of the principle of benefit taxation. Denote the tax on individuals a and b by t^a and t^b respectively. Let t^a and t^b be the same across communities and $t^a > t^b$. As has been shown, Pareto optimal solution requires that equations (2.5) and (2.6′) hold. Suppose the population is divided into Pareto optimal communities consistent with t^a and t^b. Given this situation it is optimal for each community to adopt policies that attract type a individuals and discourage type b individuals. Alternatively if we allow into the model developers that can control the size and the mix of community then, by setting in their project $n/m > N/M$ developers can attract people from other communities, increase their utility somewhat and make profit. Thus this tax system leads to instability.[3]

Case III

Suppose instead that there exists a central government which is collecting a tax of t^a and t^b from type a and type b individuals respectively. The tax proceeds are distributed to local governments on a fixed per capita basis. The transfer per capita is $t = (Nt^a + Mt^b)/(N + M)$. Solving for optimal community we have to rewrite the allocation of x constraint in the Lagrangian (2.4) in the following form:

$$\tilde{x}(n, m) - nx^a - mx^b - x^y - nt^a - mt^b + (n + m)\tilde{t} = 0. \tag{2.8}$$

By differentiation and rearranging terms, we get equation (2.5) as before and the following equations instead of equations (2.6) and (2.7):

$$\tilde{x}_1 - x^a - t^a = -\tilde{y}_2/\tilde{y}_1 - \tilde{t}, \tag{2.9}$$

$$\tilde{x}_2 - x^b - t^b = -\tilde{y}_2/\tilde{y}_1 - \tilde{t}. \tag{2.10}$$

This means that it is still optimal to tax every individual according to his marginal social cost redefined as $\partial x^y/\partial(n + m) - \tilde{t}$. It can easily be shown that equations (2.9)–(2.10) and the central government budget constraint guarantee that equation (2.6′) is satisfied. Thus we may conclude that using this method the central government can redistribute income efficiently.

Contrary to a lump-sum redistributive tax an income tax (even a proportional income tax) will not be nondistorting. This is true although in our model there are no leisure-work or saving-consumption choices which are the usual causes for distorting effects of income tax. In order to show this substitute in equation (2.8) $\tau\tilde{x}_1$ and $\tau\tilde{x}_2$ for t^a and t^b respectively, where τ is the common proportional tax rate. The necessary conditions for a Pareto maximizing community are:

$$\tilde{x}_1 - x^a - \tau\tilde{x}_1 = -\tilde{y}_2/\tilde{y}_1 - \tilde{t} + n\tau\tilde{x}_{11} + m\tau\tilde{x}_{21}, \tag{2.9′}$$

$$\tilde{x}_2 - x^b - \tau\tilde{x}_2 = -\tilde{y}_2/\tilde{y}_1 - \tilde{t} + m\tau\tilde{x}_{22} + n\tau\tilde{x}_{12}. \tag{2.10′}$$

Thus it is optimal for communities in defining their own tax rates to take into account their effect on the taxes that will be paid to the central government.

Given this behavior of communities the national income tax is compatible with competitive equilibrium but is not Pareto optimal. As we further develop the model we show that the national income tax has additional distorting effects.

Concluding this section it is interesting to emphasize the factors that in this model lead to mixed communities. It is clear from the analysis that if we allow for separation between the production and consumption activity, then individuals will prefer to join homogeneous consumption groups by residing in suburbs or by forming clubs [see Buchanan (1965) and Berglas (1975)]. But when there are economies of scale to the total community, then it may be worthwhile for people with different tastes to combine in the consumption of public good. Thus, the advantages in production activities, together with the cost of separating into smaller consumer units, explain the creation of mixed communities.

It turns out that in the Tiebout (1956) analysis the (artificial) assumption that income (received in the form of dividends) is independent of location is crucial for the result that individuals will prefer to join homogeneous communities. In the following sections we shall allow for greater variability in tastes and for intercommunity trade. Each of these factors will allow some separation between the size of income and locality and thus will result in more (though not completely) homogeneous communities. Therefore, these models can be viewed as general equilibrium extensions of Tiebout's analysis.

2.4. Diversity of Tastes with Identical Skills

An interesting means of introducing Tiebout-type effects into the model is to allow independence between the distribution of tastes and the distribution of productive skills. The simplest way of analyzing this case is to assume a third type of individual (c) who has the same productive skills as (say) individual b but a different utility function. Without loss of generality assume that individual c, the utility function of whom is denoted by h, shows a stronger preference for the public good; in our notation, $\tilde{v}_2/\tilde{v}_1 < \tilde{h}_2/\tilde{h}_1$ for all bundles of x and y.

Divide the population into identical communities composed of the three types of individuals by the same proportion as they have in total population. Allocate production and consumption in a way that all the necessary conditions derived in section 2.2 will hold. This allocation will not be Pareto optimal. Take any two communities, by transferring, say, one individual type b to community one and one individual type c to community two the same level of individual and public consumption is possible in the two communities. But the existing allocation is no longer optimal because the provision of the public good and therefore the utility of everybody can be improved in the two communities. Suppose we maximize v (h) in community one (two) holding u, h, (u, v) and the respective populations constant. As a result the welfare of type b (c) people will rise in community one (two) with all other utilities unaffected. Thus a further movement of type b people to community one and type c people to community two is beneficial until we arrive at specialized communities (to be denoted, hereafter, by L^{ab} and L^{ac}).[e]

Pareto optimal conditions, recognizing that the optimal solution requires that type b and c individuals will join separate communities, can be derived in the following way. For community type L^{ab} maximize u relative to an arbitrary level of v^1. This will result, of course, in conditions (2.5)-(2.7). Denote the solution to this problem by superscript one. Now maximize h for community type L^{ac} subject to u^1, by forming a Lagrangian type (2.4) with the appropriate changes in notation. This will result in the following conditions:

$$n^2\tilde{u}_2^2/\tilde{u}_1^2 + k^2\tilde{h}_2^2/\tilde{h}_1^2 = 1/\tilde{y}_1^2, \tag{2.11}$$

$$\tilde{x}^2 - x^{2a} = -\tilde{y}_2^2/\tilde{y}_1^2, \tag{2.12}$$

$$\tilde{x}^2 - x^{2c} = -\tilde{y}_2^2/\tilde{y}_1^2. \tag{2.13}$$

In these equations the superscript 2 denotes the solutions for community type L^{ac}; and x^{2a} and x^{2c} denote the consumption of x by individuals a and c in community L^{ac}; k^2 denotes the number of type c individuals in community L^{ac}. The total number of type c individuals will be denoted by K.

Divide total population into M/m^1 communities type L^{ab} and into K/k^2 communities type L^{ac}. If there is an excess (insufficient) number of type a individuals, repeat the same procedure with higher (lower) v^1. This procedure continues until the total population is divided among communities. The result is both Pareto optimal and a competitive equilibrium. The iteration procedure can be regarded as a description of the path by which competition will converge to equilibrium.[f]

It is important to note that, in this solution, the marginal productivity of each type worker is different in the two communities. This can be demonstrated using figure 2-1. In this figure we present the demand curves of each type individual in optimal community L^{ab} by $\tilde{u}_2/\tilde{u}_1$ and $\tilde{v}_2/\tilde{v}_1$ respectively. Construct the average demand curve D^{ab} as follows for any point A: $AC = ABm^*/(n^* + m^*) + AFn^*/(n^* + m^*)$. Construct the supply curve $1/\tilde{y}_1(n^* + m^*)$ where along this curve n^* and m^* are held constant. E^{ab} will be the equilibrium point since at this point equation (2.5) is satisfied. Assume for a moment, that the number of type a individuals and total population in community L^{ac} is the

[e]The complete specialization is easy to visualize if the number of b and c type people is equal. If this is not the case complete specialization implies that the numbers of L^{ac} and L^{ab} communities may differ.

[f]Stability considerations require that the assumption in footnote c holds for the two communities.

same. Let $\tilde{h}_2/\tilde{h}_1$ be located between $\tilde{v}_2/\tilde{v}_1$ and $\tilde{u}_2/\tilde{u}_1$. Then the average demand curve D^{ac} will be above D^{ab} and below $\tilde{u}_2/\tilde{u}_1$. Observe that at the point E^{ac} utility of type a individuals is above that of point E^{ab}. The utility of type a individuals in L^{ac} communities will be further increased if we optimize for community size holding the ratio of type a and c individuals unchanged. This means that in order to guarantee equality of utility of type a individuals across communities the wage (fraction) of type a individuals in community L^{ac} must be smaller (higher) than in community L^{ab}. This can be generalized in the following way: when workers with the same skills are divided into groups according to their preference patterns, then those whose preferences are closer to the preferences of the workers who complement them in production are likely to receive higher wages.

The results of our tax discussion in section 2.3 apply to this case with one important addition. Income, now, is a poor measure of personal welfare. While competition equalizes utility of type a people across communities, their incomes (both before and after local taxes) differ. Thus even a proportional income tax will cause type a people to move from communities L^{ab} to communities L^{ac}. It may be further noted that in this case, wage is not sufficient to identify groups of homogeneous types. Though we started with three homogeneous types of people we observe in the market four groups with different wages and consumption patterns.

It is interesting to compare the results of this section to those of the Tiebout (1956) model. The comparison may be summarized as follows. (1) Like

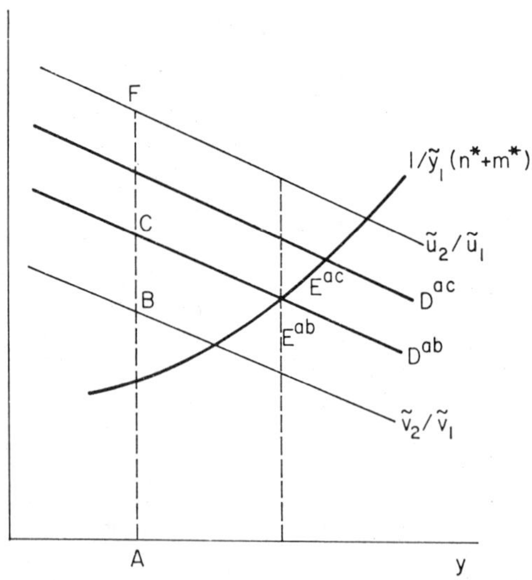

Figure 2-1. Marginal Productivities in Equilibrium.

the Tiebout case, costless shopping for the best community will insure optimal provision of local public goods. (2) People with higher preferences for public good will tend to concentrate in communities which provide relatively more public services. But the converse does not necessarily hold, e.g. individuals of type a will be found in the two community types. (3) Consumption preferences affect the distribution of before tax income. This possibility was ruled out by assumption in the Tiebout original analysis and in many recent interpretations of it. (4) While in the Tiebout analysis the pattern of communities depends on the distribution of individual preferences and communities tend to be composed of homogeneous population, in the current model the interaction of the distributions of preferences and productive skills will determine the pattern of the different communities, and communities will consist of mixed populations. In the following section intercommunity trade is introduced. It will be shown that the introduction of trade will not alter the differences between results of the models in this paper and the results of a pure Tiebout model.

2.5. Trading Communities

In order to allow for trade it is necessary to add a second private good and it is sufficient to assume only two types of individuals. Thus we are essentially in the model of sections 2.2 and 2.3 except that production and utility functions are expanded by introducing a second private consumption good z. More specifically we introduce the following changes: $u = \tilde{u}(x, y, z)$; $v = \tilde{v}(x, y, z)$ and $z = \tilde{z}(n, m)$. The production function $\tilde{z}$ has the same characteristics assumed for $\tilde{x}$. All notations and other functions remain as in section 2.2 and 2.3.[g]

Following the same procedure as in section 2.2 we derive the optimal conditions when intercommunity trade is not allowed. To save space, we shall not write the necessary conditions explicitly. They include equations (2.5)-(2.7) unchanged and an additional condition that the marginal rates of substitution between the private goods be equal for every individual and equal to the marginal rate of transformation.

Since all communities are identical, all relative prices, including relative factor prices, are equalized between communities. Nevertheless, it is possible to show that allowing for trade with no transport costs this solution is not Pareto efficient.

Assume that, in the maximization above, x and z are produced by inputs n^x, m^x, n^z, m^z respectively. Without loss of generality assume $n^x/m^x > n^z/m^z$.[h] Take any two communities–it is possible now to move some type a individuals, say from the second community to the first community, and some type b persons from the first community to the second. As long as communities do not

[g]We have the same Lagrangian expression as in (4) with an additional constraint for the production and distribution of z which may be written, $\tilde{z}(n, m) - n\bar{z}^a - m\bar{z}^b = 0$.

specialize in production, population transfer can be made without any effect on the production of the local public goods as well as the total production of x and z and the marginal product of any individual. The only change will be that more x will be produced in the community with relatively more type a individuals.[4] Thus over a range we have a situation where income is independent of location; this allows for gains from diversified communities. It is possible to show that these advantages are maximized as we move towards completely specialized communities.[i]

In the appendix we use the result that trading communities will specialize in production of one commodity to derive the necessary conditions for Pareto efficiency. The results are given by equations (2A.1)-(2A.7), and can be summarized as follows: (1) marginal rates of substitution between private goods will be equalized among individuals and across communities (2A.1); (2) the Samuelson public good criterion holds for every community (2A.2)-(2A.3); (3) within each community taxes per capita will be the same and equal the marginal social cost (2A.4)-(2A.7).

It is important to note that these conditions are consistent with different values of marginal productivities in the two communities. In the community that specializes in the production of x individuals type a constitute a larger share of the population and the provision of public goods will be more responsive to their preferences. Thus in order to equalize utilities, the value of marginal product of type a (b) individuals must be lower in the community that specializes in the production of x (z).

In this case utility equalization of the same type individuals implies that factor prices are not equalized. It should be emphasized that this equal utility solution is not a constrained Pareto efficient solution, in the sense that it is impossible to make everybody better off by dividing utility otherwise. Furthermore trade in this model is not a perfect substitute for movement of factors. The gains from trade among communities arises not from increase in productivity but from increase in consumption efficiency, by making it possible for more homogeneous communities to exist.

The results of the previous section pertaining to taxation carry over without modification. It is interesting to note that although we have now only two types of individuals (with the same level of utility), we have four different wages

[h]The assumption $n^x/m^x \neq n^z m^z$ facilitates the explanation. It will become clear later that this is not a necessary condition.

[i]The outline of the proof is the following. Move one type b individual from community one to two and one type a from community two to one. Every individual can consume the same bundle of x, y, z as before. Let the planner optimize now for utility of b holding the utility of a unchanged. In doing so he is allowed to make interpersonal transfers necessary to guarantee that the utility of the same type individuals will remain equal. The necessary conditions for this stage require production efficiency and that the public good supplied in community one (two) will be more preferable to individual a (b). Thus, as long as x and z are produced in the two communities further transfer of type a (b) into community one (two) is beneficial. From the optimal conditions for completely specialized communities (see appendix) it can be shown that in this case equalizing transfers are not necessary.

which means that, compared with section 2.4, wage is even a weaker measure of individual welfare. Furthermore, the existence of a national income tax will have further dislocative effects once trade exists. It may be useful to note that these arguments do not necessarily imply that an income tax should not be introduced. All known taxes cause inefficiencies, and the selection of a proper tax system is thus necessarily a second best type of problem. The existence of these dislocation effects should be taken into account in devising tax systems.

In reality, trade and diversity of skills coexist, which means that the effects discussed in both sections 2.4 and 2.5 occur simultaneously. Since we have shown that they each increase diversity of communities, it may be concluded that together they will result in a still larger diversity of communities. We shall have more (mixed) community types, larger diversity in wages, and it will be possible to benefit even further from the Tiebout diversification effects.

2.6. Concluding Remarks

This paper introduces into the Tiebout model the possibility that individuals may differ in skills in addition to their differences in tastes, while still allowing individuals to move freely between communities. It is shown that Tiebout type benefits will exist if either (1) the distribution of skills is independent of the distribution of tastes or (2) intercommunity trade is allowed for. In each case the competitive allocation is Pareto optimal.

There is a tendency of people with similar tastes to concentrate in separate communities but this tendency is not pushed to completely homogeneous communities. Thus the observation that an individual is located in equilibrium in a community with a relatively large public sector is not an evidence that he prefers this allocation. Wages for persons with the same skills and tastes will vary between communities in a way which will guarantee equal utility of identical persons across communities.

Competition with free movement of people imposes severe restrictions on the taxation structure of communities. Everyone is required to be taxed according to his marginal social cost. When these are equal for different people, the taxes should be equal per capita. Redistribution policy which will be Pareto efficient can be carried out only by a central government. An intercommunity agreement on progressive taxation cannot substitute a central government.

Redistributive taxation will be efficient only if performed by lump sum taxes and subsides. Although in this model no work–leisure or consumption–saving choices exist, an income tax is shown to be Pareto inefficient and will result in nonoptimal community patterns.

Notes

1. For recent studies using this approach see Oates (1972) and McGuire (1974).

2. For this approach see Buchanan and Wagner (1970), Flatters, Henderson and Mieszkowski (1974) and Stiglitz (1974).

3. In a paper that was published after this study was completed Wheaton (1975) derives the same results from a more restrictive model.

4. This is a straightforward application of the Rybczynski (1955) theorem.

References

Berglas, E. "On the Theory of Clubs," *The American Economic Review Papers and Proceedings* 66 (1975):116-121.

Buchanan, J.M., "An Economic Theory of Clubs," *Economica* 32 (1965):1-14.

Buchanan, J.M. and R.E. Wagner, "An Efficiency Basis for Federal Fiscal Equalization," in *The Analysis of Public Output*, J. Margolis (ed.), New York: Columbia University Press, 1970.

Flatters, F., V. Henderson and P. Mieszkowski, "Public Goods Efficiency and Regional Fiscal Equalization," *Journal of Public Economics* 3 (1974):99-112.

McGuire, M., "Group Segregation and Optimal Jurisdictions," *Journal of Political Economy* 82 (1974):112-132.

Oates, W.E., *Fiscal Federalism*, New York: Harcourt Brace Jovanovich, 1972.

Pauly, M., "Cores and Clubs," *Public Choice* 9 (1970):53-65.

Rybczynski, T.N., "Factor Endowments and Relative Commodity Prices," *Economica New Series* 22 (1955):336-341.

Samuelson, P.A. "The Pure Theory of Public Expenditure," *Review of Economics and Statistics* 36 (1954):387-389.

Stiglitz, J.E., "The Theory of Local Public Goods," *Technical Report No. 144*, The Economic Series Institute for Mathematical Studies in the Social Sciences, Stanford University, 1974.

Tiebout, C.M., "A Pure Theory of Local Expenditure," *Journal of Political Economy* 64 (1956):416-424.

Wheaton, W.C., "Consumer Mobility and Community Tax Bases: The Financing of Local Public Goods," *Journal of Public Economics* 4 (1975):377-384.

Appendix 2A

In this appendix we derive the optimal conditions for the case of trading communities. In order to simplify notation we assume that all advantages of diversification can be utilized by trade between two communities. This implicitly assumes that the number of the two community types will be equal. The maximization conditions derived do not depend on this assumption. The following notation is adopted: x^{ij} is variable x in community i consumed by individual j. Whenever there is only one superscript it denotes community, e.g. y^1 is the consumption of y in community 1. All other variables were defined in text. Using these notations we form the Lagrangian expression

$$
\begin{aligned}
L = {} & \tilde{u}^1(x^{1\mathrm{a}}, y^1, z^{1\mathrm{a}}) \\
& -\lambda_1 [\tilde{v}^1(x^{1\mathrm{b}}, y^1, z^{1\mathrm{b}}) - v^0] \\
& -\lambda_2 [\tilde{u}^1(\cdot) - \tilde{u}^2(x^{2\mathrm{a}}, y^2, z^{2\mathrm{a}})] \\
& -\lambda_3 [\tilde{v}^1(\cdot) - \tilde{v}^2(x^{2\mathrm{b}}, y^2, z^{2\mathrm{b}})] \\
& -\lambda_4 [\tilde{x}(n^1, m^1) - n^1 x^{1\mathrm{a}} - n^2 x^{2\mathrm{a}} - m^1 x^{1\mathrm{b}} - m^2 x^{2\mathrm{b}} - x^{y1} - x^{y\mathrm{b}}] \\
& -\lambda_5 [\tilde{z}(n^2, m^2) - n^1 z^{1\mathrm{a}} - n^2 z^{2\mathrm{a}} - m^1 z^{1\mathrm{b}} - m^2 z^{2\mathrm{b}}] \\
& -\lambda_6 [y^1 - \tilde{y}^1(x^{1y}, n^1 + m^1)] \\
& -\lambda_7 [y^2 - \tilde{y}^2(x^{2y}, n^2 + m^2)] .
\end{aligned}
$$

The formation of the Lagrangian has the following interpretation. The first constraint restricts the level of utility of individual type b. The next two constraints guarantee that the level of utility of the same type individuals will be the same across communities. The next two constraints equate the production and consumption of commodities x, z. The last two constraints are the production functions of the public goods. Differentiating this Lagrangian we derive necessary conditions for optimal production, consumption and population patterns for the two communities. These necessary conditions are all the constraints and

$$\tilde{u}_1^1/\tilde{u}_3^1 = \tilde{u}_1^2/\tilde{u}_3^2 = \tilde{v}_1^1/\tilde{v}_3^1 = \tilde{v}_1^2/\tilde{v}_3^2, \tag{2A.1}$$

$$n^1 \tilde{u}_2^1/\tilde{u}_1^1 + m^1 \tilde{v}_2^1/\tilde{v}_1^1 - 1/\tilde{y}_1^1 = 0, \tag{2A.2}$$

$$n^2\tilde{u}_2^2/\tilde{u}_1^2 + m^2\tilde{v}_2^2/\tilde{v}_1^2 - 1/\tilde{y}_1^2 = 0, \tag{2A.3}$$

$$\tilde{x}_1 - \tilde{x}^{1a} - z^{1a}\tilde{u}_2^1/\tilde{u}_1^1 + \tilde{y}_2^1/\tilde{y}_1^1 = 0, \tag{2A.4}$$

$$\tilde{x}_2 - x^{1b} - z^{1b}\tilde{v}_3^1/\tilde{v}_1^1 + \tilde{y}_2^1/\tilde{y}_1^1 = 0, \tag{2A.5}$$

$$(\tilde{z}_1 - z^{2a})\tilde{u}_3^2/\tilde{u}_1^2 - x^{2a} + \tilde{y}_2^2/\tilde{y}_1^2 = 0, \tag{2A.6}$$

$$(\tilde{z}_2 - z^{2b})\tilde{v}_3^2/\tilde{v}_1^2 - x^{2b} + \tilde{y}_2^2/\tilde{y}_1^2 = 0. \tag{2A.7}$$

These conditions are compatible with competitive equilibrium provided ν^0 is adjusted to the level where $n^1 + n^2/m^1 + m^2 = N/M$, and communities tax their residents on an equal per capita basis and provide services in quantities which maximize the welfare of their inhabitants.

As we increase the number of private commodities while maintaining the number of individual types, we increase the number of community types respectively where each will specialize in the production of one tradeable private good and each will have different wages.

3 The Theory of Clubs: A Technological Formulation

Arye L. Hillman

In a seminal paper James Buchanan [1965] proposed the idea of an economic club as a sharing arrangement enabling consumers to capture the potential gains from the collective provision of public goods. Buchanan added to the usual goods specification of consumer preferences attendant sharing preferences for each good, and the necessary conditions for individual utility maximization consequently solved for both commodity demand functions and desired sharing arrangements. Crowding was accordingly a subjectively evaluated phenomenon determined with respect to an individual's preferences by his choice of equilibrium club size. In this chapter we present a theory of clubs which has as its beginning the alternative hypothesis that the crowding characteristics of a good may be portrayed as the objectively determined attributes of a sharing technology. In taking this point of departure we are able to provide a perception of clubs which follows in many key respects the line of development of the partial equilibrium theory of the firm.[1]

We shall begin in section 3.1 by introducing a sharing technology as a description of technologically feasible sharing arrangements for rival collective goods. We then consider in turn the nature of deployment of such a technology by a nonprofit club and a profit maximizing, monopolistic collective. Section 3.2 derives from the sharing technology the cost and supply functions for a nonprofit club. The latter's supply function is defined such that for each level of collective consumption the inputs into the sharing technology are chosen to minimize average cost per club member. Price discrimination is not allowed, and the club neither receives subsidies nor pays taxes, so output is priced at a common average cost per member.

In section 3.3 we employ a complementary club demand function representative of club willingness to pay to describe supply-demand equilibria. In establishing such equilibria, we complete the positive component of the analysis of the nonprofit club: equilibria may be derived from a knowledge of the technology, demand, and the market price of marginal units of the facility capacity employed by the club. We then confront in section 3.4 the question of ascertaining the normative characteristics of a supply-demand equilibrium. As a

I wish to express my gratitude for their helpful comments to Henry Tulkens, Mark Pauly, Elhanan Helpman, and Shlomo Maital. I retain the usual responsibility. Financial support from the Foerder Institute for Economic Research, Tel-Aviv University, is gratefully acknowledged.

normative frame of reference we employ the club version of the Samuelson [1954, 1969] collective good rule. Contrary to other analyses of the club problem (e.g., Buchanan [1965], Litvak and Oates [1970], Borcherding and Deacon [1972], Bergstrom and Goodman [1973]), our club equilibrium is not necessarily first-best. Second-best aspects arise because we assume nondiscriminatory average cost pricing to consumers who are not necessarily identical, and because of diverse possible scale characteristics of the sharing technology. A club supply-demand equilibrium is, however, shown to be a constrained first-best outcome via its correspondence to the pricing, output and sharing solution that obtains when the club maximizes output subject to the technology, its zero-profit budget constraint and a predetermined expression of marginal willingness to pay governing expenditures on the common club facility.

In section 3.5 we consider provision of the collective good by a monopolistic, profit maximizing collective and compare the solution that thereby obtains with the output maximization solution of the nonprofit club. The usual higher monopoly price and lower output obtain, but with respect to sharing the inference is that the higher monopoly price and lower output do not generally translate into a less crowded facility. We obtain as a necessary condition for profit maximization a precise relation between the average rate of profit and a measure of the difference in crowding between profit maximizing and nonprofit club equilibria. This permits the departure of the profit maximizing equilibrium from that of a nonprofit club to be gauged, and it follows readily as a limiting case that if competition among profit maximizing collectives dissipates profits to zero, the profit maximizing equilibrium corresponds to that of the nonprofit club. Our analysis differs from other analyses of the private provision of collective goods in its comparative focus on monopolistic as against nonprofit collective good provision. For example, Thompson [1968], Demsetz [1970] and Berglas [1976] have all considered the private provision of public goods assuming competition. Thompson further allowed discriminatory Samuelson psuedo-pricing which we do not, and both he and Demsetz assume pure public goods so that the objective is to sell to all consumers. We, on the other hand, are concerned with establishing, simultaneously with profit maximizing price and output, the profit maximizing number of consumers to whom sales will be made. That is, we seek the monopolists' profit maximizing level of exclusion which we compare with the exclusion policy of the nonprofit club.

We conclude with some brief comparative remarks on clubs and firms.

We view the club in a partial equilibrium setting. In a manner suggestive of the theory of the firm, and following Buchanan's club analysis, we relate to a representative club.[2] Consequently, our equilibrium conditions are independent of consumers excluded from club participation. Other authors have investigated the club problem with reference to a given population which is to be allocated among clubs. Pauly [1967, 1970], McGuire [1974], and Berglas [1976] have treated the number of clubs among whom the population is to be assigned as a decision variable, while Buchanan and Goetz [1972], Flatters, Henderson and Mieszkowski [1974], Stiglitz [1974], Ng [1973, 1974], and Helpman and Hillman [1977][3] have assumed the number of clubs to be predetermined. Ng has pointed out the need to account for excluded consumers when describing desired sharing arrangements and has argued that whereas Buchanan's clubs (and by implication, the clubs we formulate below) maximize average net benefit per club member, the appropriate objective to be sought is the maximization of total net benefit. The conflict between the objectives of average net benefit and total net benefit maximization pointed out by Ng is, of course, resolved if the number of clubs is a variable chosen such that no consumers are excluded.[4] As a background to our discussion of the nonprofit club, we implicitly suppose as the analogue of a competitive firm environment that there exist many clubs, each insignificantly small in numbers relative to the total population. There are no interclub externalities and no individuals are disadvantaged by a lack of alternatives if excluded from the club. When we consider the profit maximizing collective as contrasted with the nonprofit club, the objective of profit maximization precludes a concern with the welfare of excluded consumers.

3.1. Sharing Technology

We begin with the specification of a sharing technology for the single collective good, g, provided equally and exclusively[5] to a club membership N from a club facility of capacity, G:

$$g = \tilde{g}(G, N) \tag{3.1}$$

The distinction between g and G is characteristic of the discussion of rival collective goods.[6] All variables are measured continuously and cardinally, and the function $\tilde{g}(.)$ is assumed to be continuous and at least twice differentiable, with

$$\frac{\partial \tilde{g}}{\partial N} < 0; \qquad \frac{\partial \tilde{g}}{\partial G} > 0$$

$$N \geqslant 1; \qquad g, G \geqslant 0$$

$$\forall \bar{g}, \qquad \{g / \tilde{g}(G, N) \geqslant \bar{g}\} \quad \text{strictly convex} \tag{3.2}$$

Strict monotonicity between g and $\tilde{G}$ permits the sharing technology to be expressed as

$$G = \tilde{G}(N, g) \tag{3.3}$$

for which strict convexity and differentiability imply

$$\frac{\partial \tilde{G}}{\partial N} > 0, \qquad \frac{\partial^2 \tilde{G}}{\partial N^2} > 0 \tag{3.4}$$

Figure 3-1 depicts in two dimensions a sharing technology satisfying equations (3.1)-(3.4).

We may view the sharing technology as an analogue to a strictly convex production technology with N entering "production" as a negative input having the general connotation of "crowding." The technology exhibits two related measures of marginal crowding. The slope of an iso-facility contour in $\{g, N\}$ space measures locally marginal congestion as the fall in g when N is marginally enlarged; and the slope of an iso-g contour in $\{G, N\}$ space provides a local measure of what we term "rivalry" by indicating the marginal facility expansion required to maintain a given level of the collective good when N is enlarged. Let us define the unit-free partial elasticities of the sharing technology[7]

$$\gamma(\overline{G}, g, N) < 0, \qquad \eta(\overline{g}, G, N) > 0, \qquad \xi(\overline{N}, g, G) > 0 \tag{3.5}$$

where $\gamma(.)$ is the point congestion elasticity for a given facility capacity G; $\eta(.)$ the point rivalry elasticity for the maintenance of a given level of collective consumption g; and $\xi(.)$ the point scale elasticity when, for a given number of participating consumers N, the facility is marginally enlarged. Logarithmically differentiating (3.1) and (3.3) and substituting yields the relationship among these three characteristic elasticities,

$$\eta(\overline{g}, G, N) = -\gamma(\overline{G}, g, N) \Big/ \xi(\overline{N}, g, G) \tag{3.6}$$

which implies

$$\eta(.) \gtreqless |\gamma(.)| \text{ as } \xi(.) \lesseqgtr 1. \tag{3.7}$$

Accordingly, congestion and rivalry yield symmetrical measures of crowding if there are (locally) constant returns to facility expansion.[a]

A sharing analogue to production efficiency obtains at points on each of the three frontiers in figure 3-1. A point on an iso-G contour is efficient in that there is no means of increasing g without reducing the numbers sharing the facility; at a point on an iso-N contour no means exists of increasing g without increasing facility capacity; and at a point on an iso-g contour, there is no means of increasing the population with access to the facility without increasing the dimension of the facility itself. We assume that club notice of $\{g, N, G\}$ is as such always efficient.

[a] γ and η also yield identical measures of crowding in the pure public good case, where then $\eta \equiv \gamma \equiv 0$.

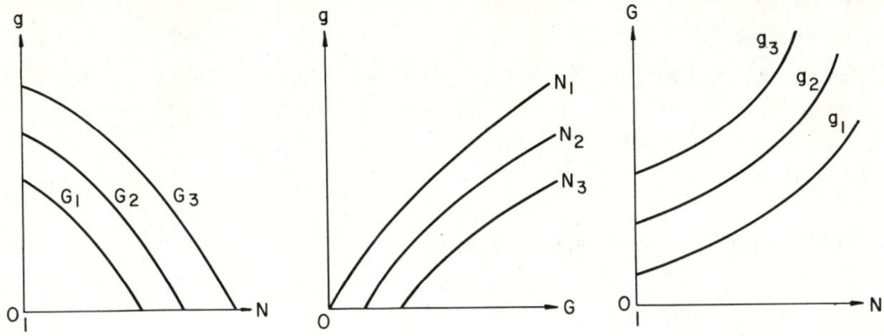

Figure 3-1. A Sharing Technology Satisfying Equations (3.1)-(3.4).

A special case is the polar pure public good. To define a pure public good, we assume in place of (3.2) and (3.4)

$$\frac{\partial \tilde{g}}{\partial N} \equiv \frac{\partial \tilde{G}}{\partial N} \equiv 0 \qquad \text{or} \qquad \gamma \equiv \eta \equiv 0 \tag{3.2a}$$

which yields as an example figure 3-1a.

We shall place some restrictions on the values of the characteristic elasticities of the sharing technology. With respect to crowding we assume that for each g $\eta(.)$ takes on values between zero and infinity; this will be seen to guarantee existence of equilibria. Further, with respect to the scale elasticity $\xi(.)$, it is evident that an equilibrium application of a sharing technology would exhibit $\xi(.) < 1$ only in the presence of a constraint prohibiting the provision of collective output from separate facilities; for with decreasing returns to facility expansion $g_1 = g(G_1, N_1)$ and $g_2 = g(G_1/2, N_1) > g_1/2$ and hence for any population N_1 there are gains from employing two facilities of capacity $G_1/2$

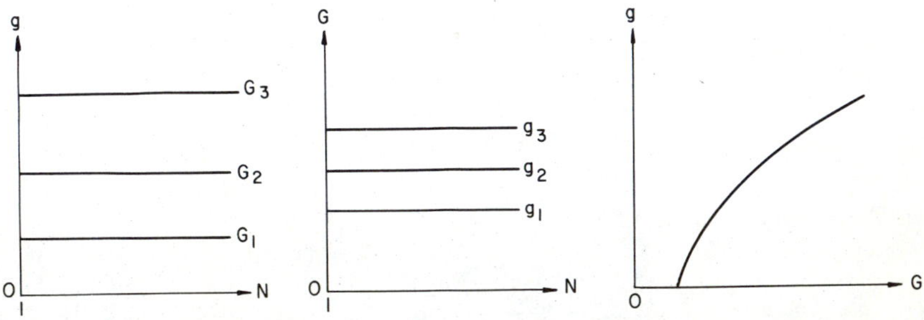

Figure 3-1a. A Sharing Technology for a Pure Public Good.

rather than a single facility of capacity G_1. Whereas jurisdictional constraints may preclude arrangements entailing access to more than one facility for a given consumer, nevertheless the general statement of the problem suggests that while the technology may exhibit $\xi(.) < 1$ locally, in the neighborhood of an equilibrium it should exhibit $\xi(.) \geqslant 1$.

3.2. The Nonprofit Club: Costs and Supply

Consider now a nonprofit club whose sole expenses are incurred in providing facility units at a given price π per unit of time. Total costs are therefore πG, and denote the club's average cost by

$$AC \equiv c = \pi G/g \tag{3.8}$$

We constrain the club to nondiscriminatory pricing, which in conjunction with the zero-profit constraint implies the pricing of g at average cost per man. Total club receipts are accordingly cg and (3.8) may be expressed as the zero-profit budget constraint

$$\phi \equiv cg - \pi G = 0 \tag{3.8a}$$

Define a point on the club supply function as a price-output pair $\{\rho^*, g^*\}$ such that, via (3.3) and (3.8),

$$\rho^* \equiv \min_N \frac{c(g^*, N, \pi)}{N} = \min_N \left\{\frac{\pi \cdot \tilde{G}(g^*, N)}{g^* N}\right\} \tag{3.9}$$

That is, for each g the club applies the information of its sharing technology to minimize average cost per man, c/N. The first-order condition for (3.9) is

$$\frac{d\rho}{dN} = \frac{1}{N}\left\{\frac{\pi}{G} \cdot \frac{\partial \tilde{G}}{\partial N} - \frac{c}{N}\right\} = \frac{c}{N^2}\left\{\eta(.) - 1\right\} = 0 \tag{3.10}$$

which implies

$$\eta(g^*, G, N) = 1 \tag{3.11a}$$

Or alternatively, substituting

$$\frac{\partial c}{\partial N} = \frac{\pi}{g^*} \frac{\partial \tilde{G}}{\partial N} > 0 \tag{3.12}$$

into (3.10) yields

$$\frac{\partial c}{\partial N} = \frac{c}{N} \tag{3.11b}$$

The solutions to (3.9) yielded by (3.11a) and (3.11b) respectively indicate that average cost per man is minimized if a facility-membership combination yields a unitary rivalry elasticity (Inman [1973]); or equivalently, if the familiar requirement is satisfied that average cost per man equals the marginal change in average cost when membership is marginally enlarged (see, for example, Pauly [1970], McGuire [1974]).[8] Strict convexity of the technology ensures that (3.11a) yields a globally minimal c/N in the manner of figure 3-2 (assuming existence).

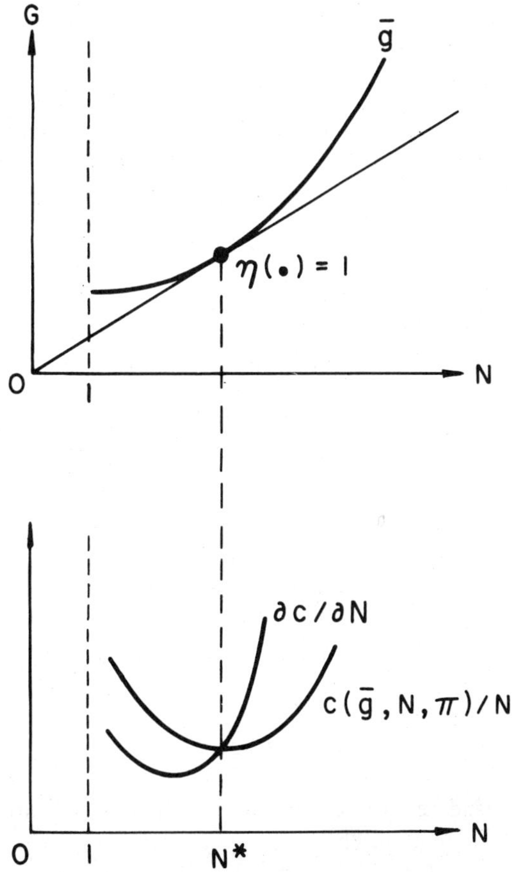

Figure 3-2. Globally Minimal c/N.

Denoting now cost minimizing club membership by $\bar{N}$ permits us to express the nonprofit club, least cost per man supply function over the range of g as

$$\rho = S(g, \pi) = s(g, \bar{N}, \pi) \equiv \min_{N} \left\{ \frac{c(g, N, \pi)}{N} \right\} \tag{3.12}$$

We obtain the elasticity of supply by first totally differentiating (3.12):

$$d\rho = \frac{\partial s(.)}{\partial g} \cdot dg + \frac{\partial s(.)}{\partial N} \cdot dN + \frac{\partial s(.)}{\partial \pi} \cdot d\pi \tag{3.13}$$

Setting $d\pi = 0$ and noting that $\bar{N}$ minimizes $s(.)$ so that $\partial s(.)/\partial N = 0$, we reduce (3.13) to

$$\frac{d\rho}{dg} = \frac{\partial s(g, \tilde{N}, \pi)}{\partial g} = \frac{\rho}{g}\{\xi^{-1}(.) - 1\} \tag{3.14}$$

so that the elasticity of club supply obtains in terms of the scale elasticity of the sharing technology as

$$\frac{d\rho}{dg} \cdot \frac{g}{\rho} = \xi^{-1}(.) - 1 \gtreqless 0 \text{ as } \xi \lesseqgtr 1 \tag{3.15}$$

Via (3.7), since $\eta(.) = 1$ along the supply locus, we may also express the supply elasticity in terms of the congestion elasticity of the sharing technology by simply substituting $\xi(.) = -\gamma(.)$ in (3.15).

The supply function is accordingly the locus over the range of g that obtains in (ρ, g) space as a consequence of choosing (G, N) combinations in the manner of figure 3-2 for all g: whether there are locally increasing, constant, or decreasing supply costs depends on whether there are locally respectively decreasing, constant, or increasing returns to the expansion of facility capacity to serve the club population designated at a point on the supply function; or an equivalent alternative means of evaluation of the supply elasticity is in terms of the crowding elasticity exhibited by the attendant facility capacity.

3.3. Nonprofit Club Supply-Demand Equilibria

Let consumer demand be given by the partial equilibrium, continuous, at least once differentiable, monotonically declining function

$$g = D(P) \tag{3.16}$$

where P denotes a nondiscriminatory price which has been determined via (3.9) for the case of the nonprofit club as[9]

$$\rho = P_i \qquad i = 1 \ldots N^* \tag{3.17}$$

A supply-demand equilibrium, when it exists, is described by a price output combination satisfying

$$\rho^* = S(g^*, \pi) = D^{-1}(g^*) = P^* \tag{3.18}$$

with G^* and N^* in the equilibrium sharing arrangement determined via (2.4).[10]

3.4. Normative Aspects of the Nonprofit Equilibrium

Let us consider now the normative aspects of the equilibrium described by (3.18). Since we are dealing with collective goods, we are immediately led to inquire into the relationship of the Samuelson [1954, 1969] equilibrium condition to the above supply-demand equilibrium. Rearrangement of the zero-profit constraint yields

$$NP = AC\ (\equiv c = \pi G/g)\ \forall\, N \tag{3.19}$$

and if $\nu(g)$ is the common partial equilibrium marginal evaluation function of any and all consumers in the equilibrium club we have

$$N \cdot \nu(g) = AC \equiv c\ \forall\, N \tag{3.20}$$

However, the Samuelson condition requires that for a given N the sum of marginal evaluations be equal to marginal cost (MC); i.e.,

$$N \cdot \nu(g) = MC\ \forall\, N \tag{3.21}$$

Differentiation of total cost $\pi \cdot G(g, N)$ partially with respect to g yields

$$MC = AC \cdot \xi^{-1}(.) \tag{3.22}$$

and hence (3.20) and (3.21) are compatible only if $\xi = 1$. Otherwise, with $\xi(.) < 1$, MC pricing violates the zero-profit constraint by not generating sufficient revenue to meet expenses of facility provision.

If all potential club members are identical, then the above marginal evaluation function simply obtains as the inverse

$$P = \nu(g) = D^{-1}(g) \tag{3.23}$$

and provisional on $\xi(.) = 1$ in the neighborhood of equilibrium, (3.20) is satisfied. But if individuals are perceived as different, no common $\nu(g)$ function exists to invert and the demand function $D(P)$ must then be viewed as an exogeneous club characteristic willingness to pay on the basis of which club decisions are made. With the personalized prices of a Samuelson pseudo-equilibrium consequently replaced by nondiscriminatory pricing and with a dictatorship in the imposition of preferences governing marginal willingness to pay, any individual who joins the club is guided by the personal combatibility of his preference in a Tiebout (1956) manner with characteristic club demand.[12]

Let us suppose that equation (3.16) is indeed a given representation of club willingness to pay, and further, let us not constrain the scale elasticity to unity in equilibrium, so the nonprofit club equilibrium does not satisfy the Samuelson equilibrium condition and hence the equilibrium described by (3.18) is second-best, relative to an equilibrium wherein personalized prices are charged and wherein centralized lump-sum tax subsidy policies permit marginal cost pricing to be reconciled with the need to cover the costs of facility provision. The club optimization problem is then that of maximizing the output of the collective good subject to the club characteristic willingness to pay, the conditions of feasible sharing described by the sharing technology and the condition that profits be zero:

$$\max_{N} \quad g \tag{3.24}$$

subject to:

$$g = D(P) \tag{3.16}$$

$$cg - \pi G = 0 \tag{3.8a}$$

$$G = \tilde{G}(g, N) \tag{3.3}$$

Substituting we obtain the simple problem

$$\max_{N} g = D\left\{\frac{\pi \tilde{G}(g, N)}{Ng}\right\} \tag{3.25}$$

for which the first-order condition may be expressed in elasticity terms as

$$\frac{dg}{dN} \cdot \frac{N}{g} = \frac{\alpha\,\{\eta(.) - 1\}}{1 - \alpha\,[\xi^{-1}(.) - 1]} = \frac{\alpha\,\{\eta(.) - 1\}}{\beta} \tag{3.26}$$

where α is the finite, nonzero (not necessarily constant) elasticity of club demand. $\eta(.) = 1$ reappears as a necessary condition and the sign of β governs whether a maximum or minimum obtains. In the neighborhood of the supply-demand equilibrium described by (3.3), let the club behave according to the adjustment rule $dE(.)/DP < 0$ where $E(.)$ is excess demand for g. It can then be shown that

$$\text{sign } \beta = -\text{sign} \frac{dE(.)}{dP} \tag{3.27}$$

so that $\beta > 0$ corresponds to a stable supply-demand equilibrium and also a local maximum in g; and conversely, $\beta < 0$ corresponds to an unstable equilibrium and a local minimum in g.

We may summarize the above as:

Proposition 1: With the first-best (Samuelson) collective good equilibrium not necessarily attainable because of nondiscriminatory pricing and an absence of tax subsidy intervention, a unique, stable nonprofit club supply-demand equilibrium as described by (3.18) yields a global maximum in the level of collective consumption provided to an equilibrium club membership, given the sharing technology, the budget constraint, and a club characteristic willingness to pay for marginal availability of the collective good.

We have made no reference to utility functions. The introduction of any monotonic transformation on g in (3.23) as an ordinal utility index does not alter the outcome of the club's output maximization problem; for if all individual $v(g)$ functions are positive valued, then under the given technological, financial and willingness-to-pay constraints, the best possible outcome for each club member is that the availability to him of g be maximized.

3.5. The Profit Maximizing Collective

Consider now a profit maximizing monopolist confronting the same technology and demand as the nonprofit, mutual benefit club. Total revenue and total cost functions are respectively

$$R(g, N) = NPg = N \cdot D^{-1}(g) \cdot g \tag{3.28}$$

$$C(g, N, \pi) = \pi G = \pi \cdot \tilde{G}(g, N) \tag{3.29}$$

and the profit function is then

$$\begin{aligned} \phi(g, N, \pi) &= R(g, N) - C(g, N, \pi) \\ &= N \cdot D^{-1}(g) \cdot g - \pi G(g, N) \end{aligned} \tag{3.30}$$

At an interior solution, necessary conditions for a profit maximizing choice of g and N are:

$$\frac{\partial \phi}{\partial g} = NP(1 + \frac{1}{\alpha}) - c\xi^{-1}(.) = 0 \tag{3.31}$$

$$\frac{\partial \phi}{\partial N} = Pg - \pi \cdot \frac{\partial \tilde{G}}{\partial N} = 0 \tag{3.32}$$

The former condition indicates that in equilibrium $N \cdot MR = MC$, and is thus the profit maximization analogue of the Samuelson competitive allocation rule; the latter condition describes profit maximizing exclusion, and indicates that the marginal revenue from the admission of a marginal consumer is equal to the congestion-incurred cost of maintaining equilibrium output.

Assume the profit maximization equilibrium described by (3.31) and (3.32) to yield positive profits.

Equation (3.31) in conjunction with the nonprofit club average cost per man pricing rule yields the familiar higher monopoly price and lower monopoly output.

Equation (3.32) may be rewritten as

$$NPg - \pi G\,\eta(.) = R(.) - C(.) \cdot \eta(.0) = 0 \tag{3.32a}$$

which yields the result that in the profit maximizing equilibrium $\eta(.)$ is equal to the ratio of total revenue to total cost. That is,

$$\eta(.) = R(.)/C(.) \gtreqless 1 \qquad \text{as} \qquad \phi(.) \gtreqless 0 \tag{3.32b}$$

Further denoting the average rate of profit by $r \equiv \phi/C$ we obtain the profit-maximization condition

$$r = \eta - 1 \tag{3.32c}$$

The above permits the comparative statement that:

Proposition 2: Assume common technology and demand, and let their respective unique equilibria be stable. Then a profit maximizing monopolistic collective earning positive equilibrium profits provides a smaller output at a higher price compared to the nonprofit club and by the crowding measure η the monopolistic equilibrium is necessarily more crowded than the nonprofit club equilibrium with the measure of excess monopoly crowding $(\eta(.) - 1)$ equal to the average rate of equilibrium monopoly profit.

For an alternative crowding comparison, we may employ the measure of congestion, $\gamma(.)$. From (3.7) it follows that in their respective equilibria the monopolist and nonprofit clubs have congestion elasticities respectively given by $-\gamma^0 = \eta^0\xi^0$ and $-\gamma^* = \eta^*\xi^*$. Since with positive profits $\eta^0 > 1 = \eta^*$, we obtain the comparative crowding effects,

$$\begin{aligned} |\gamma^0| &> |\gamma^*| & \quad \xi^0 &\geqslant \xi^* \\ |\gamma^0| &\gtreqless |\gamma^*| & \quad \xi^0 &< \xi^* \end{aligned} \tag{3.33}$$

which implies:

Proposition 3: If in the neighborhood of their respective equilibria the monopolist's scale elasticity for a marginal expansion of output is not less than that of the nonprofit club, then by the crowding measure $\gamma(.)$ the monopolist earning positive profits congests his facility capacity relative to facility usage in the nonprofit club equilibrium; and if the condition on the relative magnitudes of scale elasticities does not obtain, the monopolist's facility may nevertheless be more congested. By implication, for all constant scale elasticity sharing technologies, the monopolistic equilibrium facility is more crowded.

In figure 3-3 we depict nonprofit and profit maximizing equilibria for the case of the constant unitary scale elasticity sharing technology

$$G = \overline{G}(N) \cdot g \tag{3.34}$$

η is then independent of g and so the cost functions over the range of N for different levels of g collapse into a single average cost per man function

$$c/N = \pi\overline{G}(N)/N \tag{3.35}$$

Because $\xi \equiv 1$, average cost and marginal cost per man for any given N are equal and constant over the range of g. The nonprofit club provides an output g^* at $P^* = \min(C/N)$ and chooses facility size G^* and membership N^* so that $\eta^* = 1$. The profit maximizing monopolist provides the output g^0 at price P^0 with $MR = (c/N)^0 > \min\,(c/N)$, which derives from $\eta^0 > 1$. The monopolist's profits are $N^0 g^0\,[P^0 - (c/N)^0] > 0$.

In making the above comparisons, we have associated a nonprofit equilibrium with a competitive equilibrium. This association follows as an implication of competition among profit maximizing collectives and free entry and exit. Zero profits imply via (3.32b) employment of the sharing technology at $\eta(.) = 1$, so that a competitive profit maximizing equilibrium corresponds to a nonprofit club equilibrium.

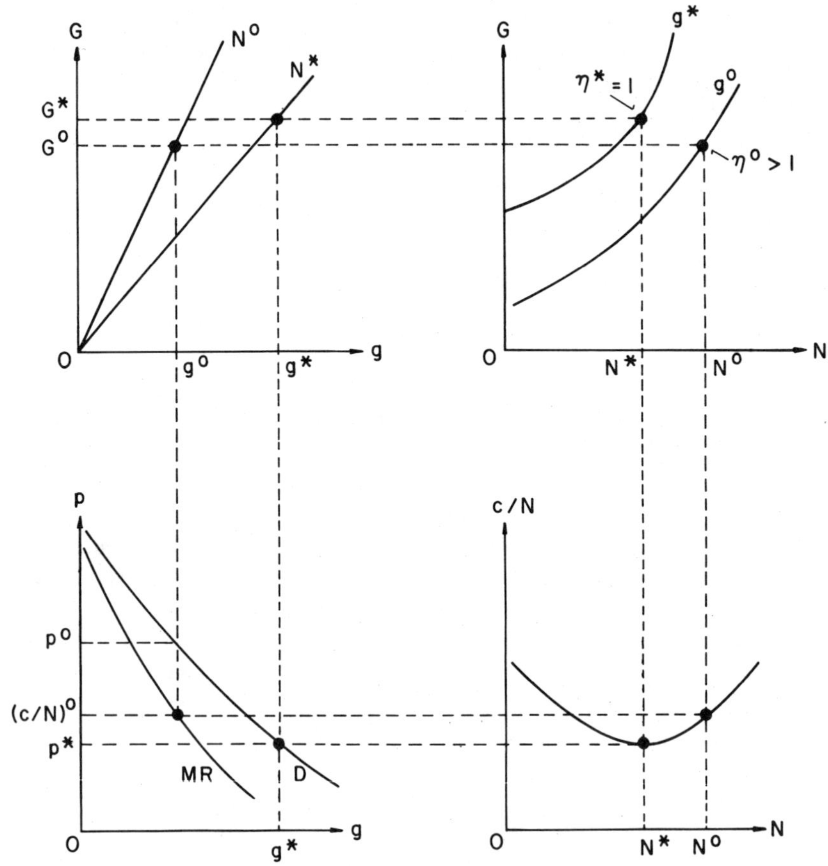

Figure 3-3. Nonprofit and Profit Maximizing Equilibria for Constant Unitary Scale Elasticity Sharing Technology.

3.6. Clubs and Firms

We have developed in this paper a theory of clubs in which the club, like the firm, employs a technology and confronts a demand for its output. Our procedure has been to develop the nonprofit club model and then compare it with the provision of a collective good by a profit maximizing monopolist. For the nonprofit club we have systematically developed from a sharing technology cost and supply functions whose features are expressed in terms of a characteristic crowding and scale elasticities of the technology. By complementing supply with demand we could establish a supply-demand equilibrium as a positive description of the pricing, output and sharing solution that obtains if the club maximizes output subject to the technology for the provision of the collective good, the zero-profit budget constraint and a preconceived club willingness to pay.

The structure of the club model differs from that of the firm in some significant respects. The club variable, membership size, for example, links the nonprofit club's technology and its financial constraint in a manner to which there is no analogue in the theory of the firm. Besides being an argument in the club's technology, membership size also determines club expenditures by determining receipts. When the firm, on the other hand, chooses the arguments of its technology to maximize output, total potential factor market expenditures are generally predetermined.

The nonprofit club further differs from the neoclassical firm in that the club internalizes both transacting components of the market. Club members form a cooperative to which supply is monopsonistic: that is, only club members are purchasers of the club's output. So although confronted with a less than perfectly elastic demand function as a constraint on its choice of output, the club nevertheless has no reason to exploit the implied monopoly power to charge other than a "competitive" price and to supply other than a "competitive" output. The profit maximizing, monopolistic collective on the other hand makes sales in the sense of the firm, and given the common profit maximizing objective, the symmetry is stronger between the firm and it.

We have refrained throughout the course of the chapter from referring to the profit maximizing collective as a firm in order to maintain a distinction which permits us to relate Coase's [1937] definition of the firm to clubs. Coase perceived the firm as internalizing factor market transactions within a production technology, and similarly the club, be it nonprofit or profit maximizing, may be viewed as internalizing via its sharing technology product market transactions for collective goods. The conceptual symmetry between the firm and the club is complete with the realization that in both cases collectives are formed to internalize market failures. Whereas the firm segments factor supply into cooperating coalitions of productive inputs, the club segments market demand for rival collective goods into consumer coalitions.

Notes

1. There are certain obvious symmetries between clubs and firms which have been noted previously. See, for example McGuire [1974].

2. Buchanan's equilibrium conditions related to a single consumer, the presumption being that there are enough compatible consumers to form an equilibrium club. We likewise assume that the equilibrium membership is forthcoming.

3. Buchanan-Goetz, Flatters-Henderson-Mieszkowski and Stiglitz view the congestion characteristics of a jurisdiction as not derived primarily from the properties of the collective good which is assumed pure, but from the diminishing marginal productivity of labor as migration takes place into a jurisdiction with a given fixed factor.

4. See Helpman and Hillman [1977].

5. That is, we do not allow for individual variations in consumption of g, as might be introduced via a variable such as "time spent in a facility" (see Berglas [1976]), nor do we allow spillover effects among clubs (see Pauly [1970]).

6. An extensive analysis of the properties of a shared good technology is found in Inman [1973]. Bradford, Malt (Maital) and Oates [1969] provide a discussion of the problems entailed in measuring g as distinct from G for education, health and hospital, police and fire protection, and public welfare services. Borcherding and Deacon [1972] and Bergstrom and Goodman [1973] avoid the potential difficulty of dealing explicitly with g by proceeding from the specification of sharing technologies to the estimation of expenditure functions. In Buchanan's [1965] model the cardinal measurement problem for g is not confronted, since g is subjectively evaluated via the ordinal utility index $U(G, N)$ as contrasted with the technology $\tilde{g}(G, N)$ (our notation).

7. We introduce elasticities here for notational simplicity and also to provide unit-free measures for characteristic values of the technology. The elasticities defined in (3.5) are of course variable. Borcherding-Deacon and Bergstrom-Goodman employ constant elasticity sharing technologies of the form $g = G N^{\gamma}$ $(\gamma < 0)$. Inman provides other functional forms satisfying the convexity condition.

8. Pauly develops his results in a cooperative game theoretic context by examining the conditions under which stable clubs will form from a given population. The correspondence between (3.11a) and (3.11b) may be imputed from McGuire by introducing into McGuire's model a sharing technology as underlying the derivation of his stated cost functions. Employing our notation, McGuire's "normative supply function" is

$$C(g, N) - N \cdot \partial C(.)/\partial N = 0,$$

where $C(.)$ denotes the total cost function. Since $C(g, N) = \pi \cdot \tilde{G}(g, N)$, we have $\partial C(.)/\partial N = \pi \cdot \partial \tilde{G}/\partial N$ so that substituting into the normative supply function yields

$$C(g, N) - \eta(.)\, C(g, N) = 0,$$

which implies $\eta(.) = 1$.

9. The preference revelation problem in assigning discriminatory prices to nonidentical individuals is well known. Recent preference evoking mechanisms proposed by Groves [1973] and Green and Laffont [1974] offer answers to the free rider problem, and Sandmo [1973] and Hori [1975] have considered public good preference revelation via complementarity with private goods within a consumption technology (to be distinguished from the above sharing technology). Our assumption of nondiscriminatory pricing is not intended to indicate a belief that none of the above preference evoking mechanisms is useful. It is more intended to reflect the real-life fact that discriminatory pricing for a common, collectively consumed output on the basis of diverse individual preferences does not occur.

10. An alternative to (3.16) is the specification of club demand as defined by the preferences of the median voter in the club (see Bowen [1943], Barlow [1970], Borcherding-Deacon [1972], Bergstrom-Goodman [1973]). Then the equilibrium requirement is the more complex condition that the equilibrium population's median voter have preferences underlying the representation of equilibrium club demand.

11. The assumption of identical individuals has, however, more merit in the case of clubs than in instances where it is commonly adopted, as for example, in international trade to characterize the inhabitants of a country, and in urban economics to characterize the inhabitants of a city. Moreover, as Ng [1975] has recently pointed out, the notion of identity of individuals is in effect an analytical approximation up to a threshold in the perception of individual differences, and it may not matter much for analytical purposes if individuals are not exact replicas of one another: for example, Roberts [1974] has recently shown that theorems on the gains from international trade proven under an identical individual's assumption carry over when individuals are assumed "nearly" identical; and perhaps more pertinently, Wheaton [1975] has demonstrated the inherent instability of coalitions when club members are *not* identical.

References

1. Barlow, R., "Efficiency Aspects of Local School of Finance," *Journal of Political Economy*, 78 (Sept./Oct. 1970):1028-39.

2. Berglas, E., "On the Theory of Clubs," *American Economic Review*, Papers and Proceedings, 66 (May 1976):116-121.

3. Bergstrom, T.C., and Goodman, R.P., "Private Demand for Public Goods," *American Economic Review* 63 (June 1973):280-296.

4. Borcherding, T.E., and Deacon, R.T., "The Demand for the Services of Non-Federal Governments," *American Economic Review*, 62 (Dec. 1972): 891-901.

5. Bowen, H.R., "The Interpretation of Voting in the Allocation of Economic Resources," *Quarterly Journal of Economics*, 58 (Nov. 1943):27-48.

6. Bradford, D.F., Malt(Maital), R.A., and Oates, W.E., "The Rising Costs of Local Public Services: Some Evidence and Reflections," *National Tax Journal* (June 1969):185-202.

7. Buchanan, J.M., "An Economic Theory of Clubs," *Economica*, 32 (Feb. 1965):1-14.

8. Buchanan, J.M., and Goetz, C.J., "Efficiency Limits of Fiscal Mobility: An Assessment of the Tiebout Model," *Journal of Public Economics*, 1 (Apr. 1972):25-43

9. Coase, R.H., "The Nature of the Firm," *Economica*, 4 (1937):386-405.

10. Demsetz, H., "The Private Production of Public Goods," *Journal of Law and Economics*, 13 (Oct. 1970):293-306.

11. Flatters, F., Henderson, V., Mieszkowski, P., "Public Goods, Efficiency and Regional Fiscal Equilibrium,"*Journal of Public Economics* 3 (May 1974):99-112.

12. Green, J., and Laffont, J.J., "On the Revelation of Preferences for Public Goods," Technical Report No. 140, *Institute for Mathematical Studies in the Social Sciences, Stanford University*, 1974.

13. Groves, T., "Incentives in Teams," *Econometrica*, 41 (July 1973):617-631.

14. Helpman, E., and Hillman, A.L., "Two Remarks on Optimal Club Size," *Economica* 44 (1977); forthcoming.

15. Hori, H., "Revealed Preference for Public Goods," *American Economic Review*, 65 (Dec. 1975):978-91.

16. Inman, R.P., "The Specification of a Shared Good Technology," paper read before the *Econometric Society*, Winter Meeting, Dec. 1973.

17. Litvak, J.M., and Oates, W.E., "Group Size and the Output of Public Goods: Theory and an Application to State Local Finance in the United States," *Public Finance*, 25 (March 1970):42-58.

18. McGuire, M., "Group Segregation and Optimal Jurisdictions," *Journal of Political Economy*, 82 (Jan./Feb. 1974):112-132.

19. Ng, Y.K., "The Economic Theory of Clubs: Pareto Optimality Conditions," *Economica*, 40 (Aug. 1973):291-98.

20. Ng, Y.K., "The Economic Theory of Clubs: Optimal Tax Subsidy," *Economica*, 41 (Aug. 1974):308-21.

21. Ng, Y.K., "Bentham or Bergson? Finite Sensibility Utility Functions and Social Welfare," *Review of Economic Studies*, 42 (Oct. 1975):545-570.

22. Pauly, M., "Clubs, Commonality and the Core: An Integration of Game Theory and the Theory of Public Goods," *Economica*, 34 (Aug. 1967):315-34.

23. Pauly, M., "Cores and Clubs," *Public Choice*, 9 (Fall 1970):53-65.

24. Pauly, M., "Optimality, 'Public Goods', and Local Governments: A General Theoretical Analysis," *Journal of Political Economy* 78 (May/June 1970):572-85.

25. Roberts, J., "Continuity in the Gains from Trade with Similar Consumers," *Journal of International Economics*, 4 (1974):25-36.

26. Samuelson, P.A., "The Pure Theory of Public Expenditure," *Review of Economics and Statistics*, 36 (Nov. 1954):387-89.

27. Samuelson, P.A., "Pure Theory of Public Expenditure and Taxation," *Public Economics*, Margolis and Guitton, (eds.), New York: St. Martins Press, 1969.

28. Sandmo, A., "Public Goods and the Technology of Consumption," *Review of Economic Studies*, 40 (Oct. 1973):517-28.

29. Stiglitz, J., "The Theory of Local Public Goods," *Technical Report No. 144. Economics Series,* Institute for Mathematical Studies in the Social Sciences, Stanford University, Oct. 1974.

30. Tiebout, C.M., "A Pure Theory of Local Expenditures," *Journal of Political Economy*, 64 (Oct. 1956):416-24.

31. Thompson, E.A., "The Perfectly Competition Production of Collective Goods," *Review of Economics and Statistics*, 50 (Feb. 1968):1-12.

32. Wheaton, W.C., "Consumer Mobility and Community Tax Bases: The Financing of Local Public Goods," *Journal of Public Economics*, 4 (Nov. 1975):377-83.

4 Pure and Local Public Goods: A Game-Theoretic Approach

Joseph Greenberg

Introduction

The application of game theory to economics is achieved through the notion of the "market-game." This game consists of a set N of traders, $N = [1, 2, \ldots n]$, and of m commodities. For each trader $i \in N$ there is a vector $w^i \in E^n_+$ which represents the initial endowment of the ith individual. Each trader i, has a binary relation $>_i$ defined on E^m_+ called the preference ordering. Moreover, for every collection S of traders, $S \subset N$, there is a set $Y(S) \subset E^m$, which generally represents the technology of the coalition S. Formally:

Definition 1: A *market* is composed of a natural number n, and a natural number m, an n-tuple of elements in E^m_+, and n-tuple of relations on E^m_+ and a function Y from 2^N into E^m.

The preference ordering satisfies the requirements of Debreu's theorem for the existence of a utility function [7]. We may therefore assume that every individual i has a utility function, u^i, defined over all possible consumption bundles for this individual, that is, it is defined on E^m_+.

Definition 2: An allocation a^S is called S-feasible if $(\sum_{i \in S} a^S_i - \sum_{i \in S} w^i) \in Y(S)$.

That is, if a^S is an S-feasible allocation, then the members of S can unite, produce and trade in such a way that individual $i \in S$ receives the bundle a^S_i. $Y(S)$ usually represents the production possibilities of S, as well as the laws and conditions of the trade, or any other such constraint. In order to discuss the market game, we have to write down its characteristic-function representation (Def. 13).

Definition 3: A market game is given by the following characteristic function:

$$V(S) = [u \in E^S_+ \mid u_i \leqslant u_i(x_i) \forall i \in S, \sum_{i \in S} x_i = x$$

where x is S-feasible].

In order to prove that a market game is indeed a game, one has to ensure that $V(S)$ satisfies requirements (i)-(iii) in Definition 13, for which some

This is part of the author's Ph.D. thesis, supervised by Professors E. Sheshinski and M. Yaari, to whom he is indebted.

generally accepted assumptions are needed. By the continuity of the utility functions and the fact that $Y(S)$ is closed, we have that $V(S)$ is closed. The boundedness of $V(S)$ follows from that of the transformation curve and the nonsatiation in consumption, which are fundamental assumptions in economics. Thus $V(S)$ is compact and satisfies (i). Assuming $0 \in Y(S), \forall S \subset N$, (a very reasonable assumption if $Y(S)$ is interpreted as the technology set), $V(S)$ is nonempty, since $\sum_{i \in S} w_i$ is an S-feasible allocation. Free disposal in $Y(S)$ for all $S \subset N$, the continuity and monotonicity (i.e., all goods are wanted) of the utility functions ensure (ii). Condition (iii) is the normalization of the utility functions so that $u^i(w^i) = 0$, $i \in N$. All the above requirements are needed to establish, for example, the existence of a competitive equilibrium. It should be noted, however, that $V(S)$ need not be convex in Definition 13, and hence neither the utility functions nor the production functions need to be concave—an essential requirement in proving the existence of a competitive equilibrium.

In economics, the most frequently used solution concept is the concept of the core (Def. 20), which is borrowed from game theory. It can easily be shown that every competitive equilibrium is in the core (of the market game) and furthermore, Debreu and Scarf have proved [8] that the core of an economy shrinks to the set of all competitive equilibria as the number of consumers becomes infinite. A similar result was shown by Aumann [1], who considered a market with a continuum of traders and established the "equivalence theorem," i.e., "The core coincides with the set of equilibrium allocations."

It is only natural, therefore, that the core has also been investigated in economies with pure public goods. Foley proved [11] that every Lindahl equilibrium lies in the core, (thus, from the existence of Lindahl equilibrium, the core is not empty), and he proposed the hypothesis, analogous to the case where there are no externalities, that the core shrinks to the set of Lindahl allocations. Counterexamples to this conjecture have been offered by both Milleron [15] and Muench [16]. Muench considered an economy with a continuum of traders, while Milleron gave an example in which the number of individuals tends to infinity. Another theorem dealing with the existence of a core for economies with beneficial externalities (of which public goods is a special case), was proved by Shapley and Shubik [21]. It states that if the economy meets suitable conditions which, except in the presence of externalities, ensure the existence of a competitive equilibrium, the core of the economy is nonempty.

While these results are encouraging, when it comes to dealing with economies with public goods (or with beneficial externalities), there is a problem in defining the core, or, more precisely, the concept of the characteristic function. Aumann [2] presents two alternative definitions for the characteristic function of a game:

$V_\alpha(S)$ = The set of all payoff S-vectors x, such that S can guarantee that each of its members receive at least x_i.

$V_\beta(S)$ = The set of all payoff S-vectors x, such that $N\backslash S$ cannot prevent members of S from getting at least x.

Aumann also comments that "the α notion seems to be intuitively more appealing," and indeed the α notion is more in the spirit of blocking coalitions (Def. 18) and hence of the core.

In the market game generated from an economy without externalities, $V_\alpha(S) = V_\beta(S)$ for all $S \subseteq N$, since the behavior of the coalition $N\backslash S$ does not effect the production or consumption possibilities in S. Therefore, the utilities that S can ensure its members, are independent of the actions of the players not in S. Indeed, if S forms, its members will receive precisely that level of utility ensured in $V_\alpha(S)$. Clearly, this is not the case if pure public goods exist, since by definition, the public goods produced by $N\backslash S$ cannot be barred to members of S. As expressed by Johansen: "Pure public goods are goods which are of such a nature that they cannot be split up and sold to some individual buyers, while other people are excluded from consuming these goods." Thus, S can guarantee a higher utility level than that which would be achieved from any S-feasible allocation, provided the members of S are convinced that $N\backslash S$ will produce public goods. We no longer have that $V_\beta(S)$ coincides with $V_\alpha(S)$, but rather, that $V_\alpha(S) \supsetneq V_\beta(S)$. (For some attempts to overcome this difficulty see [19] and [22]). Note that all the above cited results, involving the core of an economy with public goods, were established when the core was defined as $V_\beta(S)$.

Interest has been growing lately in economic systems involving local public goods. Local public goods are pure public goods for members of the region (or organization), but do not influence the welfare of nonmembers. As defined by McGuire [14], these are "goods which cannot readily be supplied and priced on a variable unit-of-service basis, but which are best provided communally at the same level to all members of the association, in such a way that nonmembers are excluded from enjoying them altogether." The difficulties which arise in the analysis of pure public goods—the problem of defining the characteristic function—disappear when we focus our attention on local public goods, since consumers outside the local area can be excluded from the use of the local public goods, and therefore the characteristic function is unambiguously defined, i.e., $V_\alpha(S)$ coincides with $V_\beta(S)$. Thus, the core of the market game with local public goods may be defined as in the case of an economy with no externalities and this definition is consistent and leads to no difficulties.

Clearly, the utility derived by an individual from the consumption of a public good depends upon the number of people with whom he must share its benefits. In particular, due to congestion, utility may diminish as the number of individuals sharing the public good increases. On the other hand, it is also conceivable that the benefit obtained from a public good might increase with the number of people sharing it, within a certain range. For example: being alone on the beach, in a park, on a highway, at the cinema, etc. may be less pleasant than being in these places with others. However, in these same examples, utility begins to decrease when these public places become overcrowded. The addition of one more person to the community will on the one hand increase the number of tax payers contributing to the purchase of the local public goods, but due to congestion it will, beyond a certain point, tend to decrease utilities of members of the region. In such cases there exists an optimal number of individuals sharing the costs and benefit of a given public good. Indeed, this might be a reason for the fact that people do settle in different "regions" (countries, cities, social institutions, etc.). The dimensions and characteristics of the region depend on the nature of the local public good under consideration.

In the extreme case, that of a private good, the optimal number of individuals in the "region" may be taken as one. It might be argued that marriage (housing services, etc. [4]) is a case of a public good, where the optimal size of the "region" is two. The case on which this chapter focuses is one where the "region" might be thought of as a city (or a settlement) and where the local public goods are various types of the municipal services. When considering national defense or foreign policy, the region is to be interpreted as the whole country.

Formally, we employ Buchanan's model [6], in which the utility to individuals does not depend solely on the goods they consume, but on the number of co-consumers. That is, for each individual i, we have a utility of the form

$$u^i = u^i[(x^1, N^1), (x^2, N^2), \ldots, (x^n, N^n),$$

where N^k represents the number of people sharing in the consumption of commodity k, whose quantity is given by x^k. As we have observed (see also [6]), this kind of utility function brings about the formation of different regions, having populations of various sizes and producing different public goods. The notion of a coalition structure (Def. 15) from game theory arises naturally in this context.

Before we proceed to the problem of how a particular coalition structure forms, and what payoffs will prevail within a given coalition structure, it should be noted that in the case where all public goods are pure public goods, the only efficient coalition structure (Def. 21) is $\{N\}$. On the other hand, with local public goods, the efficient coalition structure will generally differ from $\{N\}$ due to congestion. To prove this, suppose that $B = [B_1, \ldots, B_k]$, $k > 1$, is an efficient coalition structure for the case of pure public goods. Let x_j denote the quantity of public goods produced in the city B_j, $j = 1, \ldots, k$. Obviously, if all individuals unite and form the grand coalition N, each individual can consume, in addition to the bundle of private goods he consumes in B, the amount $\sum_{j=1}^{k} x_j$ of public goods. Each player thus increases his utility, which depends only on the amount of goods consumed and not on the number of co-consumers. Hence, B is inefficient. In particular, a game generated from an economy with pure public goods is super-additive, whereas local public goods generate a game which may be sub-additive for sufficiently large coalitions, as a result of congestion. It is evident, then, that with local public goods the core of the coalition structure $\{N\}$ is empty, in contrast with the results that are known for economies with pure public goods.

The purpose of this chapter is to study equilibrium concepts for economies with local public goods, when:

(1) Mobility is allowed, i.e., individuals may choose the city in which they would reside.
(2) Each individual's preferences depend on the amount of private and public goods he consumes as well as on the members of his city, thus, the personalities (names) of his co-consumers effect his benefit from consumption.

In section 4.2, we investigate the notion of an equilibrium for a coalition structure where each city has its market price system for the private goods and levies lump sum taxes on its residents to finance the purchase of those private goods used as production factors for the public goods it offers. We also observe that the model remains valid if transaction costs exist, costs induced by the migration of an individual from one city to another.

In section 4.3, we define a "structural equilibrium," which is a new solution concept in game-theory, much in the spirit of ψ-stability the core, and pure competition. The main result in this section is the equivalence of the set of competitive allocations (defined in section 4.2) and the set of equilibrium payoffs. We also investigate the existence of such allocations. We show that, while for every game there exists a coalition structure for which equilibrium payoffs exist, there are games (even games with side payments) for which no efficient coalition structure B has an equilibrium payoff. Thus, we are led to a "broader" solution concept, namely, that of the stable set (Section 4.4). For this purpose, we modify the classical concept of the bargaining set for cooperative games without side payments, a modification which seems to be essential in any context of game theory. The main result in this section is that for every coalition structure B there exists a stable payoff. The proof of this result is based on Billera's theorem.

The relevant definitions from game theory appear in the appendix to this chapter.

4.2. Equilibrium with Lump Sum Taxes

In the sequel, a coalition structure B denotes the partition of individuals into cities. (The entire discussion remains valid for any other interpretation of the characteristic of the coalitions in the coalition structure). In each city, public goods are produced and taxes are levied on individuals in order to finance production costs of these goods. In a competitive equilibrium each unit views the price as given, despite the fact that cooperation among some of the units might allow greater gains, for example by bringing about price changes, as in the case of a monopoly. We shall make an analogous assumption here, namely that individuals take the structure of the cities as given and that their only alternative is to move to another existing city. In particular, they cannot form a new city.

Let there be n individuals $N = \{1, 2, \ldots, n\}$. Each individual $i \in N$ has an initial endowment $w^i \in E^l_+$ with $\sum_{i \in N} w^i > 0$, (for notation see the appendix to this chapter), a utility function $u^i(x, y^i, S)$, where $x \in E^q_+$ is the vector of public goods, $y^i \in E^l_+$ denotes the bundle of private goods consumed by individual i, and $S \subseteq N$ is the coalition to which i belongs. As in Buchanan's model, we may assume as a special case that the utility function depends only on the number of people in the city, disregarding individual bias based on ethnic origin, social stratification, and the like, which render an individual different levels of utility from different persons. For each S, u^i is strictly monotonic in x and in y^i, continuous and quasi-concave. To each S there is associated a technology $Y^P(S) \subset E^l$ for private goods, which is a closed convex cone including the origin and satisfying the free disposal property. (The fact that $Y^P(S)$ is a convex cone ensures that there are no profits in the private sector, so that no share system is required to divide the profits.) The production function of the public goods is given by the technology $Y^G(S) \subset E^q_+ \cdot E^l$, a closed convex set with $\underline{0} \in Y^G(S)$, for all $S \subseteq N$. Moreover, given a sufficiently large quantity of production factors, every public good can be produced in a positive quantity. We denote this set of assumptions by H.

Definition 4: An *S-feasible allocation* is an allocation $z^S, x^S, \{y^i\}_{i \in S}$ such that:

$$(x^S, -z^S) \in Y^G(S) \qquad \text{and} \qquad (\sum_{i \in S} y^i - \sum_{i \in S} w^i + z^S) \in Y^P(S)$$

Definition 5: Let $B = [B_1, \ldots, B_k]$ be a coalition structure. The allocation $\{x^j\}_{j=1}^k$, $\{z^j\}_{j=1}^k$, $\{y^i\}_{i \in N}$ is *B-feasible* if x^j, z^j, $\{y^i\}_{i \in B_j}$ is a B_j-feasible allocation for all $B_j \in B$.

Definition 6: An *equilibrium for* $\mathrm{B}_m \in \mathrm{B}$ consists of a B-*feasible allocation,* $\{x^j\}_{j=1}^k$, $\{z^j\}_{j=1}^k$, $\{y^i\}_{i \in N}$, a price system $\{p^j\}_{j=1}^k$, $p^j \in E^l_+$, $\|p^j\| = 1$ and a tax system $\{t^i_j\}$ $j = 1, \ldots, k$, $i = 1, \ldots, n$ such that:

$$p^m z^m = \sum_{i \in B_m} t^i_m \qquad \text{(a)}$$

$$\pi_0^m = p^m(\sum_{i \in B_m} y^i - \sum_{i \in B_m} w^i + z^m) \geqslant p^m y_m \forall y_m \in Y^p(B_m) \qquad \text{(b)}$$

$\forall i \in B_m$, (x^m, y^i, B_m) is the solution for:

$$\text{Max } u_i(x^j, \bar{y}^i, B_m) \text{ s.t. } p^j \bar{y}^i \leqslant p^j w^i - t^i_j, \qquad B_j \in B \qquad \text{(c)}$$

There is no $\bar{z}^m$, $\bar{x}^m$, $\{\bar{t}^i_m\}_{i \in B_m}$ with

$$p^m \bar{z}^m = \sum_{i \in B_m} \bar{t}^i_m, \qquad (\bar{x}^m, -\bar{z}^m) \in Y^G(B_m)$$

such that for all $i \in B_m$ there is $\bar{y}^i$ satisfying

$$p^m \bar{y}^i \leqslant p^m y^i + t^i_m - \bar{t}^i_m$$

and

$$u_i(\bar{x}, \bar{y}^i, B_m) > u_i(x^m, y^i, B_m) \qquad \text{(d)}$$

Condition (a) requires that the net taxes collected in a city will suffice to finance the production of the public goods x^m, by the purchase of the production factors z^m at the competitive prices p^m and by the use of technology $Y^G(B_m)$. It should be noted that taxes can be redistributed, and in particular, that negative taxation may occur, i.e., transfers among individuals can exist since there is no requirement that

$$\sum_{i \in B_m} | t^i_m | = p^m z^m .$$

Due to the convexity of private technology, condition (b) guarantees that the production in city B_m is efficient and maximizes profits. Condition (c) reflects the assumption that an individual takes the city's structure as given, and that he maximizes his utility over the possibilities of moving to other existing cities. If the individual migrates to another city, B_j, he enjoys the public goods produced in that city, x^j, a quantity he takes as given, and he has to pay taxes (an entrance fee) in the amount of t^i_j. The fourth requirement pertains to the distribution of taxes in a city B_m. It entails that no proposal to change taxes can be such that at the existing prices p^m, it is possible to produce $\bar{x}^m$ by buying $\bar{z}^m$, and furthermore, that every individual–within his new budget set stemming from the change in municipal taxation–is able to purchase private goods $\bar{y}^i$, at the existing prices, in such a way that his utility from the bundle $(\bar{x}, \bar{y}^i, B_m)$ will exceed his utility under the allocation of equilibrium for B_m.

This definition coincides for the case that $B = \{N\}$ with the definition of public competitive equilibrium. In this case, as the utility function of an individual is independent of the number of coconsumers of the public goods, we can define $\hat{u}_i(x, y^i) = u_i(x, y^i, S)$, and, indeed, when dealing with pure public goods the utility functions do not include the number of people in the city.

Definition 7: A *pseudo-equilibrium for B* is an equilibrium for all $B_j \in B$. Whereas an equilibrium for $B_m \in B$ requires that no individual in B_m would want to migrate to another city, a pseudo-equilibrium condition ensures, in addition, that no individual outside B_m would prefer B_m to his present coalition. Therefore, in a pseudo-equilibrium there is no migration of individuals from one city to another, so that this notion pertains to stable solutions. We seek conditions for the existence of a pseudo-equilibrium for any given coalition structure B, and wish to characterize pseudo-equilibrium allocations.

Definition 8: An allocation $z^s, x^s, \{y^i\}_{i \in S}$ is called *pareto-optimal* in S if it is S-feasible and there exists no other S-feasible allocation $\bar{z}^s, \bar{x}^s, \{\bar{y}^i\}_{i \in S}$ such that:

$$u_i(\bar{x}^s, \bar{y}^i, S) > u_i(x, y^i, S), \forall i \in S.$$

Theorem 1: Under the assumptions H, every B-feasible allocation which is pareto-optimum in the city $B_m \in B$, is an equilibrium allocation for B_m.

Proof: In [9] it is proved that for every pareto-optimal allocation z^m, $x^m, \{y^i\}_{i \in B_m}$ in B_m there exists a price system p^m and a tax system $\{t^i_m\}_{i \in B_m}$ satisfying conditions (a), (b) and (d) of Definition 6 with

$$u_i(x^m, y^i, B_m) = \text{Max}\, u_i(x^m, \bar{y}^i, B_m) \qquad \text{s.t.} \qquad p^m \bar{y}^i \leqslant p^m w^i - t^i_m$$

It thus remains only to show that no individual $i \in B_m$ would want to move to another city $B_j \in B$, so that requirement (c) holds as well. Let e be the unit vector in E^m (i.e., $e = (1, 1, \ldots, 1)$), and let

$$T = e \sum_{i \in N} w^i + 1$$

Since $e \geqslant p^m$ we have:

$$p^m w^i \leqslant e \sum_{i \in N} w^i < T$$

Thus, for every $i \in B_m$ and $j \neq m$ we define $t_j^i = T$. Hence

$$\{x^j\}_{j=1}^k, \{z^j\}_{j=1}^k, \{y^i\}_{i \in N}, \{p^j\}_{j=1}^k, \{t_j^i\}_{j=1}^k \qquad i \in N$$

is an equilibrium for $B_m \in B$, where p^m and $\{t_j^i\}_{j=1}^k$ for $i \in B_m$ are defined above, the allocation being the B-feasible allocation pareto-optimal in B_m, and where $\{p^j\}$ for $j \neq m$ and $\{t_j^i\}$ with $i \notin B_m$ are arbitrary. *Q.E.D.*

Corollary 1: Every allocatin which is pareto-optimal in each city $B_j \in B$, under assumptions H, is a pseudo-equilibrium allocation for B.

Theorem 2: Every allocation of an equilibrium for B_m is pareto-optimal in B_m.

Proof: This is easy to verify. A detailed proof is given in [9].

Corollary 2: Under assumptions H, the set of allocations of a pseudo-equilibrium for B coincides with the set of allocations which are pareto-optimal for every $B_j \in B$.

From the proof of theorem 1, it is clear that in pseudo-equilibrium the prevention of individuals from migrating from their cities can be achieved by imposing artificially high taxes which no individual could sustain. However, there is no reason to assume that such taxes will be imposed. A city B_j levies entrance fees on nonresidents based on the benefits it will derive. It is unjustified to assume that a city is never interested in absorbing migration. We therefore seek a concept which incorporates a city's will to receive nonresidents. In other words, we wish to construct an equilibrium in which taxation is rational, so that it becomes a function of the utilities derived by the cities from the various individuals and does not stem merely from considerations of stability.

Let $B_l \in B$ and let $i_0 \in B_m$, $m \neq l$. Without loss of generality we assume: $B_l = \{1, 2, \ldots, q\}$. Define:

$$B_{k+1} \equiv [n+1, \ldots, n+q+1]$$

where the individual $n+i$ is identical to individual i for $i = 1, \ldots, q$, and i_0 is identical to $n+q+1$. Individuals are identical if they share the same utility function, the same initial endowment and are treated alike by all cities. Moreover, for all S, $i \in S$, $Y^P(S) = Y^P(S \setminus \{i\} \cup \{n+i\})$, and similarly for $Y^G(S)$. Consider the coalition structure $\hat{B} = [B_1, \ldots, B_k, B_{k+1}]$ for the $n+q+1$ players: $\hat{N} = [1, 2, \ldots, n+q+1]$, i.e., we now assume that in addition to the existing cities (in B) a new city, B_{k+1}, forms.

For each $B_j \in B$ the tax t_j^i levied on an individual $i \in N$, $i \notin B_j$, is based not on the city from which he comes, but on the utility the coalition B_j can derive when this individual is joining it. In particular, identical individuals will pay identical entrance fees. Thus, the tax $\tilde{t}_j^{n+i}$, levied on individual $n + i$, $i = 1, \ldots,$ q, in the city B_j, $j \neq l$, is equal to $\tilde{t}_j^i$. Similarly, for $m \neq j$ we have: $\tilde{t}_j^{n+q+1} = \tilde{t}_j^{i_0}$. We shall require, in addition, that the tax levied on $n + i$, $i = 1, \ldots, q$ in the city B_l will be equal to that levied on individual i. Analogously, the tax levied on i_0 in B_m coincides with that levied on $n + q + 1$ in this city. The rationale behind this requirement will be clarified in the sequel.

Let

$$R \equiv [\{t_j^i\}_{j=1}^{k}\ i \in N, \{z^j\}_{j=1}^{k}, \{x^j\}_{j=1}^{k}, \{y^i\}_{i \in N}, \{p^j\}_{j=1}^{k}]$$

be a pseudo-equilibrium for B, and let

$$A(R, B_l \cup \{i_0\}) = [x^{k+1}, \{y^i\}_{i \in B_{k+1}} \mid \{x^j\}_{j=1}^{k+1},$$

$$\{z^j\}_{j=1}^{k+1}, \{y^i\}_{i \in N}, \{p^j\}_{j=1}^{k+1}, \{t_j^i\}_{j+1}^{k+1} \qquad i \in \hat{N}$$

be an equilibrium for B_{k+1}, where

$$t_j^{i_0} = t_j^{n+q+1}, \qquad t_j^i = t_j^{n+i}, \qquad j = 1, \ldots, k,\ i = 1, \ldots, q]$$

Define:

$$V_l^{i_0}(R) = \begin{cases} U_{i_0}(X_1^m, y^{i_0}, B_n) - 1 & \text{if} \quad A(R, B_l U \{i_0\}) = \phi \\ \text{Max}\ u_{i_0}(x^{k+1}, y^{n+q+1}, B_{k+1}) & \text{otherwise} \end{cases}$$

Lemma 1: $V_l^{i_0}(R)$ is well-defined.

Proof: Under assumptions H, the set of all pareto-optimal allocations for B_{k+1} is a closed and bounded set [21]. By theorem 2, A is a subset of this set, so that A is bounded. It follows readily from Definition 6 that A is closed. Hence A is compact. u_{i_0} being a continuous function on A, we have that the maximum is attained, provided $A \neq \phi$. *Q.E.D.* The intuitive interpretation of $V_l^{i_0}(R)$ is as follows: Let us assume that i_0 joins the coalition B_l. We thus avoid the case in which the tax $t_l^{i_0}$, which individual i_0 might possibly be unable to pay, hence prevents him from moving to B_l (e.g., as when $p^l w^{i_0} < t_l^{i_0} = T$).Coalition B_l, on its part, will agree to i_0's entrance only if its residents' welfare will not decrease as a result. It follows from the requirement that the projection of the equilibrium for B_{k+1} onto B is R, and from the requirement that the entrance tax levied by B_l on individual $n+i \in B_{k+1}$ is equal to t_l^i, that every $i \in B_l$ has the option of resisting any change in the status quo. That is, every $i \in B_l$ can remain in this city and enjoy the utility to be derived from the allocation R, which is $u_i(x^l, y^i, B_l)$, and veto the acceptance of i_0 to the city. As far as i_0 is concerned, he can obtain maximal utility provided the members of B_l consent to his entrance, i.e., he can enjoy the maximum utility over all allocations in A. This maximum is $V_l^{i_0}(R)$. To clarify this point we prove:

Theorem 3: If $A(R, B_l \cup \{i_0\}) \neq \phi$ then for all $i \in B_l$ and for all $(x^{k+1}, \{y^{n+i}\}_{n+i \in B_{k+1}}) \in A(R, B_l \cup \{i_0\})$ we have:

$$u_{n+i}(x^{k+1}, y^{n+i}, B_{k+1}) \geqslant u_i(x^l, y^i, B_l)$$

Proof: Let $x^{k+1}, \{y^{n+i}\}_{n+i \in B_{k+1}}$ be an allocation in $A(R, B_l \cup \{i_0\})$. Hence there exists an equilibrium for

$$B_{k+1}, \{z^j\}_{j=1}^{k+1}, \{x^j\}_{j=1}^{k+1}, \{y^i\}_{i \in \hat{N}}, \{p^j\}_{j=1}^{k+1}, \{t^i\}_{j=1}^{k+1}, \qquad i \in \hat{N}$$

such that for all $n+i \in B_{k+1}$

$$u_{n+i}(x^{k+1}, \bar{y}^{n+i}, B_{k+1}) \geqslant u_{n+1}(x^j, \bar{y}^{n+i}, B_j)$$

with $B_j \in B$ and $p^j \bar{y}^{n+i} \leqslant p^j w^i - t_j^{n+i}$.

In particular, the inequality holds for $B_j = B_l$. From the definition of B_{k+1}, for all $i \in B_l$:

$$u_{n+i} = u_i, \qquad w^{n+i} = w^i \qquad \text{and} \qquad t_l^{n+i} = t_l^i$$

Moreover, since R is a pseudo-equilibrium for B:

$$u_i(x^l, y^i, B_l) = \text{Max}\, u_i(x^l, \bar{y}^i, B_l) \qquad \text{s.t.} \qquad p^l \bar{y}^i \leqslant p^l w^i - t_l^i$$

Hence, for all $i \in B_l$:

$$u_{n+i}(x^{k+1}, y^{n+i}, B_{k+1}) \geqslant u_i(x^l, y^i, B_l) \qquad Q.E.D.$$

By definition, $B_l \cup \{i\} = B_l$ for all $i \in B_l$. We introduce the notation:

$$v^i(R) = \underset{B_j \in B}{\text{Max}}\ V_j^i(R)$$

This maximum exists, since there is a finite number (k) of coalitions within the structure B, and from lemma 1, for each coalition $B_j \in B$, $V_j^i(R)$ is well-defined.

Definition 9: An *equilibrium for B* is a pseudo-equilibrium, R, for B satisfying:

$$u_i(x^m, y^i, B_m) \geqslant V^i(R) \forall i \in N, i \in B_m$$

In the allocation of an equilibrium for B, no $i \in N$ gains by moving from his city, since the maximum utility an individual may derive when joining another of the existing cities which accept him (i.e., the utilities of the individuals of that city will not decrease as a result of his joining), does not exceed the utility he enjoys in his present coalition under the structure B.

Proposition 1: For any $i \in B_m$, for any $B_m \in B$, and for any pseudo-equilibrium R for B, the inequality

$$V^i(R) \geqslant u_i(x^m, y^i, B_m)$$

always holds.

Proof: Let $i \in B_m$. Since R is a pseudo-equilibrium for B, the allocation $x^m, \{y^i\}_{i \in B_m}$ is an equilibrium for B_m and hence for $B_m \cup \{i\} = B_m$ as well. Therefore, $(x^m, \{y^i\}_{i \in B_m}) \in A(R, B_m \cup \{i\})$, implying

$$V_m^i(R) \geqslant u_i(x^m, y^i, B_m)$$

Since $V^i(R) \geqslant V_m^i(R)$, the proposition is proved. *Q.E.D.*

Corollary 3: If R is an equilibrium for B, then

$$\forall i \in N, \quad i \in B_m: \qquad u_i(x^m, y^i, B_m) = V^i(R)$$

An alternative way of defining an equilibrium for B, is by adding one more constraint on the pseudo-equilibrium for B. The minimal requirement for an individual $i \in B_j$ not to join B_m, is that there exists at least one "democratic" welfare function, (i.e., one which takes into account the welfare of every individual), for which the welfare of $B_m U_{i_0}$ under the given allocation is not less than that which would be derived if i joins B_m.

Formally:

An equilibrium for B is a pseudo-equilibrium that fulfills, in addition to conditions (a)-(d) of Definition 6, the condition:

For all $i_0 \in N$, $\quad i_0 \in B_1$, $\quad i_0 \notin B_m \in B$, there exists $\lambda^{im} \geqslant 0$ such that:

$$\sum_{i \in B_m} \lambda^{im} U_i(x^m, y^i, B_m) + \lambda^{i_0 m} U_{i_0}(x^1, y^{i_0}, B_1) \geqslant \sum_{i \in B_1 U i_0} \lambda^{im} U_i(\bar{x}, \bar{y}^i, B_m U_{i_0}) \tag{e}$$

for all $\bar{x}$, $\{\bar{y}^i\}$ $(B_m U_{i_0})$ feasible allocations.

Under assumptions H, using the separating hyper-plane theorem, it can be shown that the two definitions are equivalent.

Remark 1: Suppose that individual i incurs cost c_{il} in moving to the city B_l. Since different prices $\{p^j\}$ prevail in every city, these costs (unlike taxes) have no "monetary value," especially as prices reflect only the exchange rates in the city while money does not exist in this model. We shall therefore assume that c_{il} is a vector representing the quantity of physical commodities (time, food, etc.) involved in the migration of an individual i to the city B_l. Clearly, the transaction costs $\{c_{il}\}$, $i \in N$, $B_l \in B$ are a function of the coalition structure that is formed, since the costs i incurs in moving to city B_l depend on the city in which i initially resides. For example, one can require that for $i \in B_l$, $c_{il} = 0$. All the above definitions and results remain valid for the case in which transaction costs do exist, provided we alter the initial endowment w^i of individual i to $w^i - c_{il}$, if the individual moves to B_l. For example, in Definition 6 of an equilibrium for $B_m \in B$, condition (c) thus becomes:

For all $i \in B_m$, (x^m, y^i, B_m) is the solution for:

$$\text{Max } u_i(x^j, \bar{y}^i, B_j) \qquad \text{s.t.} \qquad p^i \bar{y}^i \leqslant p^i(w^i - c_{ij}) - t^i_j,$$

$$B_j \in B, \qquad \text{and} \qquad w^i - c_{ij} \geqslant 0. \tag{c'}$$

We shall also modify the definition of the set $A(R, B_l \cup \{i_0\})$ by imposing the additional requirements:

$$c_{n+i,j} = c_{ij}; \qquad c_{n+i+1,j} = c_{i_0,j} \forall B_j \in B \qquad i \in B_l,$$

and

$$c_{i,k+1} = c_{il} \forall i \in \hat{N}$$

If the inequality $w^i - c_{il} \geqslant 0$ fails to hold, this means that the individual i cannot move to B (e.g., in the given technology the time needed is more than a lifetime). In particular, it can be argued that the formation of new cities is barred due to exceedingly high transaction costs, by requiring, for example, that for all $i \in N$, $S \subseteq N$, $S \notin B$, the inequality

$$c_{is} \geqslant \sum_{i \in N} w^i$$

holds. We should nevertheless emphasize that the individual only considers joining one of the existing cities as a result of its size relative to that of existing cities, rather than as a result of the transaction costs involved in forming a new city.

4.3. Structural Equilibrium

Having defined the notion of equilibrium for B, it is natural to ask whether such equilibria exist for any coalition structure B, whether there is a B for which an equilibrium exists or whether there is an equilibrium for any efficient B. In approaching these problems it is convenient to pursue a game theoretic approach. From Corollary 2 it is clear that no price or tax systems are required in characterizing allocations of a pseudo-equilibrium for B. Moreover, passing from a pseudo-equilibrium to an equilibrium for B, we actually circumvented the tax problem and disregarded taxes levied on an individual i_0 upon joining B_l, and this was achieved by forming coalition $B_{k+1} = B_l \cup \{i_0\}$ and considering $\hat{B}$. The only restrictions imposed on equilibrium for B were feasibility constraints which are precisely the specifications of A. It is a very reasonable conjecture, then, that the allocations of equilibrium for B may be characterized without using tax and price systems which serve merely as a mechanism bringing about these allocations. In the case of pure competition for a continuum of traders, the competitive allocations may be characterized without using prices; this is achieved via the notion of the core. Analogously, we shall prove that it is possible to characterize allocations of equilibrium for B as a (new) solution concept in game theory.

Definition 10: A *structural equilibrium* for a game $(N; V)$ is a pair (u, B), where $B = [B_1, \ldots, B_k]$ is a coalition structure and u is a payoff satisfying:

$$u \in X(B) \tag{i}$$

$$\forall i \in N \nexists \quad a \in V(B_l \cup \{i\}) \quad i \notin B \in B^{ii}$$
$$\text{s.t. } a_t \geqslant u_t \quad t \in B_l, \quad a_i > u_i \tag{ii}$$

u is called an *equilibrium payoff.*

That is, (u, B) is a structural equilibrium if the equilibrium payoff u is pareto-optimal in every coalition in the structure B (Def. 17), and no individual $i \in N$ can increase his payment by joining any of the existing coalitions, while ensuring its residents a payment which will at least match the one they receive under u.

The definition of a structural equilibrium is not restricted to market games with local public goods; it is valid for any game. This notion incorporates the concept of the core and that of competition. The core of a coalition structure B, $B = [B_1, \ldots, B_k]$ (Def. 19) can be defined as the set of all payoffs u such that:

$$u \in X(B) \tag{i}$$

$$\nexists\, a \in V(S), \quad S \subset N \quad \text{s.t. } a_t > u_t \forall t \in S \tag{ii}$$

It is easily verified that under the assumption that each player can, by decreasing his utility, increase the utility of any other player, the core and the structural equilibria differ only in the blocking possibilities players face. If, as we shall assume, this hypothesis holds, every payoff in the core is also an equilibrium payoff.

In most solutions in game theory, the basic threat available to a player i against the payoff he receives, u_i, is in forming any blocking coalition, S_0 (Def. 18). That is, every individual can (even if he does not choose to do so) form any group combination from among the given set of players N. When applying the game-theoretic approach to economics, one should question whether this is a reasonable assumption for an economy. It seems that the answer depends on the nature of the regions considered. If the regions include only a few persons (as in the case of marriage), it is sound to assume that every individual can form any S_0, and hence the game-theoretic analysis applies with the solutions carrying over unchanged. Let us consider the case of clubs, cities or countries, where the number of individuals is large. Here it is unreasonable to assume that one person can threaten his city residents by forming another city, S_0. This is due to the lack of information and communication among the individuals, or to the high transaction costs (Remark 1). Hence a new city cannot serve as a blocking coalition.

Very little has been written on the subject of restricting the set of blocking coalitions, with the exception of the notion of ψ-stability [13], which was investigated for games with side-payments. Luce and Raiffa describe the idea behind this notion as follows:

> Intuitively one senses that there are constraints in society limiting changes in coalition structures, and that these are to a large degree nonrational. Nonetheless, one may conjecture that these constraints are a source of considerable social stability. Of course, one wonders what there is about society that introduces them, particularly if everyone is free to bribe or, to be less evaluative, to compensate others for their cooperation. It is doubtful that there is a single answer, but we would argue that one factor must be the expense and difficulty of complex communication which prevents players in a game from considering at one moment any but the simplest modifications of their alliance structures. Roughly speaking, society seems to exhibit a form of "friction." If such is the case, the problem then becomes one of formalizing these limitations on coalition

changes, so that the resulting model is both somewhat realistic and at the same time mathematically tractable.

The authors' strongest criticism of this concept is given in [13]: "There seem to be at least two major objections to postulating such a function ψ; first, we have no theory to justify it; and, second, we have no idea how it is to be determined in particular cases." It should be noted, as well, that although a mathematical treatment has been provided as to the existence of ψ-stable solutions for certain games with side payments (namely, for k-stable games), there is no such treatment of the subject for games without side payments. Moreover, the definition of k-stability does not coincide with that of structural equilibrium, though as explained above, the principle of restricting the set of blocking coalitions is common to both definitions. In this chapter the restrictions are due to economic factors; namely, the individuals take the coalition structure as given, and they are too small to form a new city by themselves. This was our assumptions in investigating the problem of competitive equilibrium for a coalition structure.

We now prove an equivalence theorem for the structural allocations and allocations of equilibrium for B. To this end, we must interpret the game $(N; v)$, having a structural equilibrium, as the market-game generated from an economy with local public goods, namely the characteristic function is given by:

$$V(S) = [u^S \mid \exists \text{ an } S\text{-feasible allocation } x^S, \{y^i\}_{i \in S}$$

with

$$u_i^S \leqslant u_i(x^S, y^i, S), \forall\, i \in S].$$

In the discussion following Definition 3 above, we have seen that under assumption H, a market game is a game.

Theorem 4: If $\{x^j\}_{j=1}^k, \{y^i\}_{i \in N}$ is an equilibrium allocation for B, then (u, B) is a structural equilibrium for the market game, where:

$$u_i = u_i(x^m, y^i, B_m)\, \forall\, i \in N,\ i \in B_m.$$

Proof: An equilibrium allocation for B is, in particular, an allocation of a pseudo-equilibrium for B. Hence, by Corollary 2, it is pareto-optimal for $B_j \in B$. Therefore, $u^{B_j} \in \overline{V}(B_j)$ for all $B_j \in B$, whence $u \in X(B)$. Suppose to the contrary that (u, B) is not a structural equilibrium for the market game. That is, suppose there exists $i_0 \in B_m \in B$, $i_0 \notin B_l \in B$, and $a \in \overline{V}(B_l \cup \{i_0\})$ with $a_t \geqslant u_t$ $\forall t \in B_l$ and $a_{i_0} > u_{i_0}$. Since v is the characteristic function of the market game, it follows from $a \in \overline{V}(B_l \cup \{i_0\})$ that there exists an allocation

$\hat{x}, \{\hat{y}^i\}_{i \in B_l \cup \{i_0\}}$ pareto-optimal for $B_l \cup \{i_0\}$ and satisfying:

$$a_t = u_t(\hat{x}, \hat{y}^t, B_l \cup \{i_0\}) \forall t \in B_l \cup \{i_0\}$$

Consider

$$\hat{B} = [B_1, \dots, B_k, B_{k+1} \equiv B_l \cup \{i_0\}]$$

Since $\hat{x}, \{\hat{y}^i\}_{i \in B_{k+1}}$ is pareto-optimal for B_{k+1}, and since $\{x^j\}_{j=1}^k, \{y^i\}_{i \in N}$ is an equilibrium allocation for B, and therefore pareto-optimal for all $B_j \in B$, the allocation $\hat{x}, \{\hat{y}^i\}_{i \in B_{k+1}}, \{x^j\}_{j=1}^k, \{y^i\}_{i \in N}$ is pareto-optimal for all $B_j \in \hat{B}$. By Corollary 1, it is a pseudo-equilibrium allocation for $\hat{B}$. Moreover, as

$$u_t(\hat{x}, \hat{y}^t, B_l \cup \{i_0\}) = a_t \geqslant u_t = u_t(x^l, y^t, B_l)\ t \in B_l,$$

$$u_{i_0}(\hat{x}, \hat{y}^{i_0}, B_l \cup \{i_0\}) = a_{i_0} > u_{i_0} = u_{i_0}(x^m, y^{i_0}, B_m)$$

we have $(\hat{x}, \{\hat{y}^i\}_{i \in B_{k+1}}) \in A$. Hence,

$$v^{i_0} \geqslant v_l^{i_0} \geqslant u_{i_0}(\hat{x}, \hat{y}^{i_0}, B_{k+1}) > u_{i_0}(x^m, y^{i_0}, B_m)$$

implying that $\{x^j\}_{j=1}^k, \{y^i\}_{i \in N}$ is not an equilibrium allocation for B. Contradiction. *Q.E.D.*

Theorem 5: Under assumptions H, if (u, B) is a structural equilibrium for the market game, there exists an equilibrium allocation $\{x^j\}_{j=1}^k, \{y^i\}_{i \in N}$ for B such that:

$$u_i(x^j, y^i, B_j) = u_i \forall i \in N, i \in B_j$$

Proof: Since (u, B) is a structural equilibrium, we have in particular that $u^{B_j} \in \bar{V}(B_j)$ for all $B_j \in B$. That is, there exists an allocation $\{x^j\}_{j=1}^k \{y^i\}_{i \in N}$ which is pareto-optimal in every $B_j \in B$. By Corollary 1, under assumptions H, it is also a pseudo-equilibrium allocation for B, satisfying:

$$u_i = u_i(x^j, y^i, B_j) \quad \forall \quad i \in B_j, \quad \forall \quad B_j \in B$$

It remains to show that this is also an equilibrium allocation for B. Suppose the contrary, i.e., assume there exists an $i_0 \in B_j$ with $V^{i_0} = V_l^{i_0} > u_{i_0}(x^j, y^{i_0}, B_j)$. Hence, there is an allocation $\hat{x}, \{\hat{y}^i\}_{i \in B_l \cup \{i_0\}}$ in A, and therefore it is pareto-optimal for $B_l \cup \{i_0\}$ and satisfying:

$$u_i(\hat{x}, \hat{y}^i, B_l \cup \{i_0\}) \geqslant u_i(x^j, y^i, B_l) \quad \forall \quad i \in B_l$$

and

$$V_l^{i_0} = u_{i_0}(\hat{x}, \hat{y}^{i_0}, B_l \cup \{i_0\}) > u_{i_0}$$

Define:

$$a_i = u_i(\hat{x}, \hat{y}^i, B_l \cup \{i_0\}), \ \forall \ i \in B_l, \quad \text{and} \quad a_{i_0} = \bar{V}^{i_0}$$

Then

$$a \in \bar{V}(B_l \cup \{i_0\}), \qquad a_t \geqslant u_t \ \forall \ t \in B_l \qquad \text{and} \qquad a_{i_0} > u_{i_0}$$

whence (u, B) is not a structural equilibrium. Contradiction. *Q.E.D.*

Corollary 4: Under assumptions H, (u, B) is a structural equilibrium for the market game if and only if there exists an equilibrium allocation for B such that for all $i \in N$, $i \in B_m$, we have $u_i = u_i(x^m, y^i, B_m)$.

It is clear from Corollary 4 that a structural equilibrium for a market game with public goods can exist even if an equilibrium for B does not. That is, it is not necessary that all the assumptions H hold in the economy, but only those that ensure that the market game is a game. In particular, here we need to assume neither the concavity of the utility functions nor the convexity of the sets $Y^P(S), Y^G(S)$, which were essential assumptions in proving the existence of a pseudo-equilibrium for B. Moreover, structural equilibrium is a meaningful notion also outside the context of markets or economies with public goods. However, under assumptions H, the existence of a structural equilibrium for a market game implies the existence of an equilibrium for B. It is, therefore, convenient to investigate the problem of the existence of an equilibrium for a coalition structure by examining the existence of a structural equilibrium.

Proposition 2: Not for every B does a payoff u exist such that (u, B) is a structural equilibrium for the game $(N; v)$.

Proof: Consider, for example, the game in which $V(\{i\}) \times V(\{j\}) \subsetneqq V(\{i, j\})$ i.e., $\underline{0} \in \text{Int. } V(\{i, j\})$, for all $i, j \in N$, $i \neq j$. There can be no equilibrium payoff for the coalition structure $B = [\{1\}, \{2\}, \ldots, \{n\}]$, since every $i \in N$ fails to satisfy condition (ii) in Definition 10. *Q.E.D.*

Although the proof was given for a game $(N; v)$ and not for a market game, we can easily define a market game for which v will fulfill the above requirement. For this purpose we have to require that the utility of every individual increases with the number of people with whom he shares the consumption of the public good, in the domain of 1 to 2 individuals. This is a frequent situation as exemplified above: being alone in a park or a theater is less pleasant that being there with another individual. Moreover, a market game with a characteristic function like the one in the proof of Proposition 2 can be achieved by changing the technology sets for different numbers of individuals. Even in case there are no externalities in consumption, if we assume increasing returns to scale in management (the number of players in the coalition), we shall obtain the required characteristic function. It thus follows as a corollary from Proposition 2 that not for every coalition structure B does an equilibrium exist. On the other hand, we have

Proposition 3: For every game $(N; v)$ there exists a structural equilibrium.

Proof: For the coalition structure $B = \{N\}$, every payoff $u \in \bar{V}(N)$ is an equilibrium payoff. *Q.E.D.*

From Proposition 3 it is clear that, under assumptions H, there exists a B for which there is an equilibrium. In particular, the set of all pareto-optimal allocations for $\{N\}$ coincides with the set of equilibria for this coalition structure. This is precisely the result in [9], which deals with pure public goods, a case in which $\{N\}$ is also the efficient coalition structure.

Aumann and Dreze [3], in attempting to explain why the groups B_k of the coalition structure would form (for games with side payments), state: "In particular, if B were the only efficient coalition structure our question would be readily answered. One could say that the formation of the groups B_k is explained by efficiency considerations, which receive logical precedence over the bargaining for the payoff." The following proposition shows that this is not the case when the solution is achieved by a competitive mechanism.

Proposition 4: There are games $(N; v)$ for which no efficient coalition structure B has an equilibrium payoff.

Proof: Consider the example in the proof of Proposition 2 when $N = 3$ and $v(N) = \prod_{i \in N} v(\{i\})$. *Q.E.D.*

Proposition 5: The core of an inefficient coalition structure is empty.

Proof: Let B be an inefficient coalition structure, and let $u \in X(B)$. There exists another coalition structure $\tilde{B}$ and payoff $y \in X(\tilde{B})$, with $y \geqslant u$; there also exists $S_0 \in \tilde{B}$ for which $y^{S_0} > u^{S_0}$. Thus, S_0 is a blocking coalition for the payoff u. *Q.E.D.*

Corollary 5: There are games for which the core is empty for every coalition structure.

Proof: By Proposition 4, there are games for which there is no equilibrium payoff for an efficient B, so that, in particular, the core is empty for efficient coalition structures. By Proposition 5, the core is empty for every B which is inefficient. Hence for every B the core is empty. *Q.E.D.*

Corollary 5 justifies the definition of structural equilibrium, since by Proposition 3, a structural equilibrium always exists, which is not the case for the core.

4.4. Stable Payoffs

In view of the fact that not every coalition structure has an equilibrium payoff, and that possibly no efficient coalition structure might have an equilibrium payoff, we must seek another solution concept if we wish to maintain efficiency. There is no need to relinquish requirement (i) in Definition 10 and doing so is also impossible if efficiency in the solution is to be preserved. A wider solution concept will thus violate requirement (ii), giving rise to the question of why, then, has the coalition structure B formed if there is an i_0 who can better his situation and that of each member of the coalition he is joining? In general, the question posed is how can we accept a solution concept (such as the bargaining set or the kernel) for which there exists a blocking coalition? There are a number of solutions to this problem in game theory, yet all offer more of a justification than a true explanation for this phenomenon.

The easiest answer is provided by assuming administrative rules and regulations forbidding an individual to move from his present coalition as given by the coalition structure B. Hence the threat cannot be actualized, but can be used only for the sake of bargaining. If it is known, however, that the individual will not carry out his threat because he is either unable or forbidden to do so, why should such a threat be considered seriously by any of the other individuals? Another argument proposed in explaining the above question points to the high transaction costs involved in forming a blocking coalition. Though this answer seems convincing, and such costs indeed undoubtedly exist, the definition of the characteristic function $V(S)$ has to include these costs, returning us to the starting point.

The best argument, in my opinion, was given by Aumann and Dreze [3]. In bargaining over the tax burden or the benefits derived from a certain good, it may be the case that each individual would actually prefer to stay within the given coalition structure B, taking into account his true utility (i.e., *all* benefits received). Yet, for the sake of bargaining, he can employ blocking coalitions specific to the subject on hand. To illustrate this point further, consider the following example: Let the coalition structure B represent the cities formed by the population. A coalition here means a group of people forming a settlement for itself. It is true that very high transaction costs are involved in this case, but as we have said, the characteristic functions are discounted from these costs. The problem facing the people is how to apportion the burden of the expenditures in producing the local public goods, and which goods are to be produced. Assuming that the individuals have chosen to settle in the different cities, for whatever reasons, the bargaining is restricted only to the previous issue. Factors such as sentimentality, loyalty and patriotism do not enter into the bargaining over the tax burden of the individual. We can further say that the fact that individual i prefers city A, lying near the sea (which, in itself is a local public good) over city C, which is in the mountains (again a local public good of C), is immaterial when bargaining, for example, over the tax burden and the level of the city's educational system. For this issue, individual $i \in A$ can maintain that if he moves to city C, he will enjoy a higher educational level and pay less taxes. Nevertheless, even the status quo remains, he will not leave city A. It should be emphasized that this argument does not answer the question of why B forms or which B will be formed. It merely explains the possibility that a solution may be stable despite the existence of blocking coalitions. This is in contrast to the case of administrative regulations regarding migration, for here the individual *can* carry out his threat, yet he does not *desire* to. Since complete information about the utilities of other individuals is not available, and since many important factors influencing a person's decision cannot be measured or compared with those of other players, individuals can make threats while having no intention of carrying them out. The fact that the bargaining is over only one specific issue permits us to concentrate on only one coalition structure. An individual belongs to a specific coalition in this structure only for one specific issue, though he generally belongs simultaneously to different coalitions (labor unions, cities, clubs, colleges, marital status, etc.). We can thus argue that each individual i has a "real" utility function u_i^R, representing the real benefits the individual derives from the bundle of private and local public goods and from the members of his city. On the other hand, he may present a "fictitious" utility u_i^F, in which he does not disclose all of the benefits for the sake of bargaining. A complete equilibrium should be an allocation which is a structural equilibrium for the utility u_i^R, and the payoff in each coalition would be in some sense stable for the preferences represented by u_i^F.

Thus the need for the following discussion arises because the set of structural equilibria is too "sparse," and hence does not exist for certain coalition structures, from which we may conclude that our requirements of a structural equilibrium are too strict. Alternately, even should a structural equilibrium exist, if it is possible to conceal benefits, an individual can, for the sake of bargaining, threaten to form a blocking coalition which will seemingly increase his utility, but will actually not.

Since such a problem is not considered in game theory, we shall present the formal model and motivate the various definitions. However, the underlying approach is borrowed from game theory.

Definition 11: Let $B = [B_1, \ldots, B_k]$ be a coalition structure with $\emptyset \in B$. We say that individual i is *more powerful than* individual j for the payoff x, and denote $i \succ j$, if $i, j \in B_l \in B$ and:

$$\exists\, a \in V(B_t \cup \{i\}), \quad t \neq l, \quad B_t \in B \quad \text{s.t. } a_n > x_n \quad \forall\; n \in B_t \cup \{i\} \tag{i}$$

$$\exists\, \bar{a} \in V(B_m \cup \{j\}), \quad l \neq m \neq t \quad \text{s.t. } \bar{a}_n \geqslant x_n \quad \forall\; n \in B_m \cup \{j\} \tag{ii}$$

$$\nexists\, \hat{a} \in V(B_t \cup \{j\}) \quad \text{s.t. } \hat{a}_n \geqslant a_n \quad \forall\; n \in B_t \quad \text{and} \quad \hat{a}_j \geqslant x_j \tag{iii}$$

$$\text{For all } \hat{b} \in V(B_t \cup \{j\}) \quad \text{for which } \hat{b}_n \geqslant x_n \;\forall\; n \in B_t \cup \{j\}, \tag{iv}$$

$$\exists\, b \in V(B_t \cup \{i\}) \quad \text{with} \quad b_n > \hat{b}_n, \;\forall\; n \in B_t \quad \text{and} \quad b_i > x_i$$

This definition extends the notion of "stronger" (Def. 25), which was introduced in defining the bargaining set (Def. 26), for the particular case we are investigating. Here player i may threaten player j only by joining one of the existing cities or else by living in seclusion on his own. For the second possibility we assume that $\emptyset \in B$. Condition (iv) is not to be found in the definition of "justified objection" (Def. 24). This condition guarantees that the binary relation "more powerful than" be asymmetric (we prove this below), i.e., we cannot have i more powerful than j with j simultaneously more powerful than i Were this so, we could not expect i to have a justified threat against j.

By definition, i is more powerful than j if both belong to the same city and if i can threaten to move to another city $B_t (t \neq l)$, and ensure each of its members, himself included, a higher utility level than they presently have $(a_n > x_n)$. In this case, j cannot join another city B_m (distinct from B_t), and ensure its citizens and himself a payoff which is not worse than the present one, so that they will not oppose j's joining their city. Moreover, j cannot join B_t, the city with which i threatened, and offer each individual there a utility level which is greater than or equal to that offered by i, and also guarantee himself the payoff x_j. This is the content of parts (i)-(iii) of the definition. Requirement (iv) is an additional condition nonexistent in the literature of game theory. It provides that every proposal offered by j to the members of B_t, which involves no loss in utility level to any resident and to himself, can be bettered by i. That is, i can guarantee each member of B_t, a payoff exceeding j's offer, while also increasing his own utility were he to join B_t. The motivation behind (iv) is that for i to be able to threaten j via B_t, j should be incapable of joining B_t and bribing some of its members in order to prevent i's acceptance.

Theorem 6: For games with side payments, conditions (i)-(iii) in Definition 11 imply condition (iv).

Proof: Denote $a_i - x_i$ by ϵ. From (i), $\epsilon > 0$, and by (iii)

$$\mu(B_t \cup \{j\}) - x_j < \mu(B_t \cup \{i\}) - (x_i + \epsilon)$$

which is equivalent to condition (iv). *Q.E.D.*

Since historically the bargaining set was initially defined for games with side payments, it seems to me that condition (iv) was not imposed in defining the bargaining set for games without side payments, a notion which is a trivially formal extension of that for games with side payments. To illustrate why such a condition is intuitively called for, consider the following game:

$$N = \{1, 2, 3, 4\}, \quad V(i) = 0 \quad i \in N, \quad V(1, 2) = V(2, 3)$$

$$= [(x_i, x_j) \mid 0 \leqslant x_k \leqslant 1 \quad k = i, j].$$

Let the coalition structure formed be $B = [(1, 2), (3, 4)]$ and the payoff $x = (1, 1, 1, 1)$. In figure 4-1, OAB represents the projection of $V(1, 3, 4)$ for $y_1 = 1$. Similarly, OCD represents the projection of $V(2, 3, 4)$ for $y_2 = 1$. If condition (iv) were absent, we would have that player 1 is more powerful than player 2, using the coalition (3, 4) and the payoff α and also that 2 is more powerful than 1, using (3, 4), again, and the payoff β. When dealing with public goods such phenomena are very frequent. For example, players 1 and 4 may belong to the same ethnic or religious group, while 2 and 3 to another, and hence player 3 prefers that player 2 join the city (3, 4) over player 1, while player 4 has the

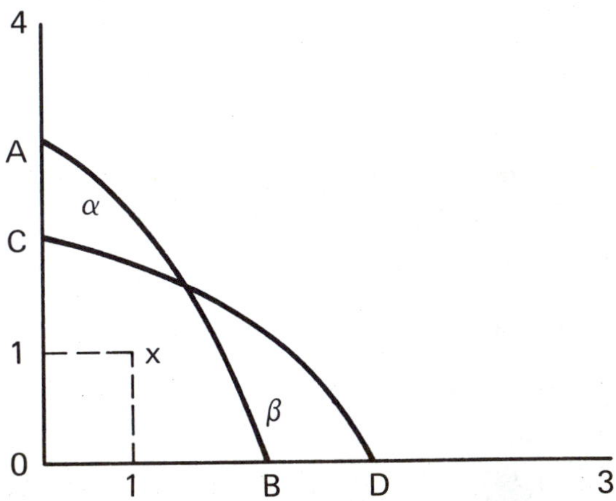

Figure 4-1. Illustration of the Necessity of Condition (iv).

opposite preference. Even if we disregard social differences, it may still be the case that 1 and 4 have similar preferences as to which public goods should be produced, while players 2 and 3 have different preferences. Since all public goods are desired by all players, both 3 and 4 gain if either 1 or 2 joins them. Yet, the utility 3 and 4 receive differ in quantity, depending on which individual joined their community.

Definition 12: x is called a *stable payoff* for the coalition structure B if no player is more powerful than any other.

By Definition 11 a player cannot counter-object by staying in his original coalition. That is, if i threatens j with a move to B_t, $i, j \in B_l$, $l \neq t$, it may be argued that j can remain in $B_l \setminus \{i\}$ and if j can thereby ensure all members of this last coalition a payoff not worse than the one suggested, (by x), i should not be more powerful than j. From an economic point of view this counter-threat is acceptable. Yet, as $B_l \setminus \{i\}$ is not a coalition in B, by Definition 11, j cannot use this coalition as a counter-threat. We shall prove that for every coalition structure B there exists a stable payoff, so that if we also permit the above counter-threat (i.e., if we allow that j can stay in the original city, B_l, even if i leaves), the result still holds. This is true because we thereby enlarge the number of counter-threats, thus decreasing the number of justified ones. In other words, if i is more powerful than j when the use of $B_l \setminus \{i\}$ is allowed to j as a counter-threat, i is also more powerful than j according to our definition. Therefore, if, by Definition 11, there exists a payoff under which i is not more powerful than j (for all i and j), this payoff is also stable if we allow the above modification.

Theorem 7: For every coalition structure B there exists a stable payoff. In order to prove this theorem we need the following lemmas:

Lemma 2: The binary relation "more powerful than" is transitive.

Proof: Let $\{1, 2, 3\} \subset B_0 \in B$, and suppose that 1 is more powerful than 2 and 2 is more powerful than 3. We have to prove that 1 is more powerful than 3. Since 1 is more powerful than 2:

$$\exists\, a \in V(B_1 \cup \{1\}) \quad \text{s.t.} \quad a_t > x_t \quad \forall \quad t \in B_1 \cup \{1\} \tag{i}$$

$$\nexists\, \bar{a} \in V(\bar{B}_1 \cup \{2\}), \quad \bar{B}_1 \neq B_1 \quad \text{with}\, \bar{a}_t \geqslant x_t \quad \forall \quad t \in \bar{B}_1 \cup \{2 \tag{ii}$$

$$\nexists\, \bar{a} \in V(B_1 \cup \{2\}) \quad \text{s.t.} \quad \bar{a}_t \geqslant a_t \quad \forall \quad t \in B_1 \quad \text{and} \quad \bar{a}_2 \geqslant x_2 \tag{iii}$$

$$\text{For every}\, \alpha \in V(B_1 \cup \{2\}), \quad \alpha_t \geqslant x_t \quad \forall \quad t \in B_1 \cup \{2\},$$

$$\exists \hat{\alpha} \in V(B_1 \cup \{1\}) \quad \text{s.t.}\ \hat{\alpha}_t > \alpha_t \quad \forall \ t \in B_1 \quad \text{and} \quad \hat{\alpha}_1 > x_1 \tag{iv}$$

Since 2 is more powerful than 3:

$$\exists b \in V(B_2 \cup \{2\}) \quad \text{s.t.}\ b_t > x_t \quad \forall \quad t \in B_2 \cup \{2\} \tag{v}$$

$$\nexists \bar{b} \in V(\bar{B}_2 \cup \{3\}) \quad \bar{B}_2 \neq B_2 \quad \text{with} \quad \bar{b}_t \geqslant x_t \quad \forall \quad t \in \bar{B}_2 \cup \{3\} \tag{vi}$$

$$\nexists \bar{b} \in V(B_2 \cup \{3\}) \quad \text{s.t.}\ \bar{b}_t \geqslant b_t \quad \forall \quad t \in B_2 \quad \text{and} \quad \bar{b}_3 \geqslant x_3 \tag{vii}$$

$$\text{For every } \beta \in V(B_2 \cup \{3\}), \quad \beta_t \geqslant x_t \quad \forall \quad t \in B_2 \cup \{3\},$$

$$\exists \hat{\beta} \in V(B_2 \cup \{2\}) \quad \text{s.t.}\ \hat{\beta}_2 > x_2 \quad \text{and} \quad \hat{\beta}_t > \beta_t \quad \forall \quad t \in B_2 \tag{viii}$$

Suppose 1 is not more powerful than 3. Obviously, 1 can object by using B_1, the city with which he threatened player 2. Yet 3 has a counter-objection. Thus, at least one of the following three cases will hold:

$$\exists c \in V(B_3 \cup \{3\}), \quad B_3 \neq B_1 \quad \text{s.t.}\ c_t \geqslant x_t \quad \forall \quad t \in B_3 \cup \{3\}) \tag{ix}$$

$$\exists c \in V(B_1 \cup \{3\}), \quad c_3 \geqslant x_3 \quad \text{and} \quad c_t \geqslant a_t \quad \forall \quad t \in B_1 \tag{x}$$

$$\exists \gamma \in V(B_1 \cup \{3\}), \quad \gamma_t \geqslant x_t \quad \forall \quad t \in B_1 \cup \{3\}$$

$$\text{s.t.} \nexists \hat{\gamma} \in V(B_1 \cup \{1\}) \quad \text{which satisfies: } \hat{\gamma}_1 > x_1 \quad \text{and} \quad \hat{\gamma}_1 > x_t \quad \forall \quad t \in B_1 \tag{xi}$$

Suppose (ix) holds. In particular $B_1 \neq B_3$. We distinguish two cases:

(a) If $B_3 \neq B_2$, by choosing $\bar{B}_2 = B_3$ we get a contradiction to (vi).
(b) If $B_3 = B_2$, by choosing $\bar{B}_1 = B_2$, we have that (ii) contradicts (v).

Assume, therefore, that (x) holds. Again we distinguish between the two cases:

(c) If $B_1 \neq B_2$, let $\bar{B}_2 = B_1$. From (1) $a_t > x_t$ for all $t \in B_1$ and hence, by (x), $c_t \geqslant x_t$ for all $t \in B_1 \cup \{3\}$ contrary to (vi).
(d) Suppose $B_1 = B_2$. By (viii) there exists $\hat{\beta} \in V(B_2 \cup \{2\})$ such that $\hat{\beta}_2 > x_2$ and $\hat{\beta}_t > c_t \geqslant a_t$ for all $t \in B_2$. This is a contradiction to (iii).

The only remaining possibility is (xi). Again we distinguish the two cases:

(e) If $B_1 \neq B_2$, let $\bar{B}_2 = B_1$ and let $\bar{b} = \gamma$. Then (xi) contradicts (vi).

(f) If $B_1 = B_2$, by (viii) there exists a $\hat{\beta} \in V(B_2 \cup \{2\})$ such that $\hat{\beta}_2 > x_2$ and $\hat{\beta}_t > \gamma_t \geqslant x_t$ for all $t \in B_2$. From (4), then, there is an $\hat{\alpha} \in V(\bar{B}_1 \cup \{1\})$ such that $\hat{\alpha}_1 > x_1$ and $\hat{\alpha}_t > \bar{\beta}_t$ for all $t \in B_2$. By choosing $\hat{\gamma}$ to be $\hat{\alpha}$, we arrive at a contradiction to (xi). Hence 1 is more powerful than 3. *Q.E.D.*

Lemma 3: The binary relation "more powerful than" is acyclic.

Proof: The relation is by definition irreflexive (i.e., *i* is not more powerful than *i*). By transitivity (lemma 2) it is therefore acyclic. *Q.E.D.*

For each individual *i*, $i \in B_l \in B$, we introduce the set:

$E_i = [x \in X(B) \mid j \not\succ i, \forall j \in B_l \setminus \{i\}]$, *i.e.*, E_i is the set of all payoffs for which there is no player *j* more powerful than *j*.

Lemma 4: The set E_i is closed in $X(B)$ for all $i \in N$.

Proof: We shall show that the set $A_{i,j} = [x \in X(B) \mid i \succ j, \quad j \in B_l \setminus \{i\}]$ is an open set of $X(B)$ for all $i \in N$. Let $x_0 \in X(B)$ and let α be a justified threat of *i* against *j* (i.e., a threat fulfilling conditions (i)-(iv) in Def. 11), $\alpha \in V(B_t \cup \{i\})$. It is clear that $K = [x \in X(B) \mid \alpha_n > x_n \quad \forall \quad n \in B_t \cup \{i\}]$ is an open set, since it is defined by a strong inequality. Similarly, the set $\bar{R}_m = [x \in X(B) \mid \exists\ \bar{a} \in V(B_m \cup \{j\} \quad a_n \geqslant x_n \quad \forall \quad n \in B_m \cup \{j\}]$ is a closed set for each $B_m \in B$, since if $x^k \to x$ and $\bar{a}^k \to \bar{a}$ by the closedness of $V(B_m \cup \{j\})$ it follows that $a \in V(B_m \cup \{j\})$. Since limits preserve weak inequalities and since $X(B)$ is closed, $\bar{R}_m$ is a closed set for all B_m. Hence $\bigcup_{\substack{B_m \in B \\ l \neq m \neq t}} \bar{R}_m$ is also a closed set, whence the complementary set:

$$R = [x \in X(B) \mid \nexists \bar{a} \in V(B_m \cup \{j\}) \quad t \neq m \neq l \quad \text{s.t.}$$

$$\bar{a}_n \geqslant x_n \quad \forall \quad n \in B_m \cup j \ ]$$

is open. By the same reasoning, the set $\bar{Z}$ is also closed, where

$$Z = [x \in X(B) \mid \exists\ a \in V(B_t \cup \{j\})$$

$$\hat{a}_j \geqslant x_j, \quad \hat{a}_n \geqslant \alpha_n \quad \forall \quad n \in B_t]$$

Hence

$$Z = [x \in X(B) \mid \nexists \hat{a} \in V(B_t \cup \{j\})$$

$$\hat{a}_j \geqslant x_j, \quad \hat{a}_n \geqslant \alpha_n \quad \forall \quad n \in B_t]$$

is an open set. The set:

$$F = [x \in X(B) \mid \forall \hat{b} \in V(B_t \cup \{j\}), \quad \hat{b}_j \geqslant x_j, \quad \hat{b}_n \geqslant x_n$$

$$\forall n \in B_t \quad \exists \quad b \in V(B_t \cup \{i\}) \quad \text{s.t.}\, b_n > \hat{b}_n \quad \forall \quad n \in B_t, b_i > x_i]$$

is clearly also open. Therefore, $A_{i,j}$ is an open set, since $A_{i,j} = K \cap F \cap R \cap Z$. It now follows that there exists an open subset M of $X(B)$ such that $x_0 \in M$ and such that if $z \in M$, i is more powerful than j for the payoff z, the justified threat being obtained through α.

Hence $\bigcup_{j \in B} A_{i,j}$ is open. Since $E_i = X(B) \setminus \bigcup_j A_{i,j}$, the lemma is proved. *Q.E.D.*

Lemma 5: For all $i \in N$, $E_i \supset [x \in X(B) \mid x_i = 0]$.

Proof: By Definition 11, $\emptyset \in B$. Hence i can always ensure himself the payoff 0 by living in seclusion on his own, since $V(i) = 0, \forall i \in N$. There is no j, therefore, more powerful than i. *Q.E.D.*

Lemma 6: For all $x \in X(B)$ and for all $B_l \in B$, there exists $i \in B_l$ such that $x \in E_i$.

Proof: Suppose the lemma is false. There exists $x_0 \in X(B)$ and $B_p \in B$ such that $x_0 \notin E_i$ for all $i \in B_p$. That is, for all $i \in B_p$ there is $j \in B_p$ more powerful than i. This is in contradiction to the acyclicity of the binary relation (lemma 3). *Q.E.D.*

Proof of theorem 1: From lemmas 4, 5, 6, the conditions of Billera's theorem [5] are satisfied, and hence $\bigcap_{i \in N} E_i \neq \phi$. In particular, there exists $x_0 \in \bigcap_{i \in N} E_i$. For this payoff, no player is more powerful than any other player, i.e., x_0 is a stable payoff. *Q.E.D.*

Remark 2: It should be noted that, in general, the bargaining set is empty [18].

References

1. R.J. Aumann, "Markets with a Continuum of Traders," *Econometrica* 32 (1964):39-50.

2. _______, "A survey on Games without Side Payments," *Essays in Mathematical Economics*, M. Shubik (ed.), Princeton University Press, 1967, 3-27.

3. R.J. Aumann and J. Drèze, "Solutions of Cooperative Games with Coalition Structures," CORE discussion paper 7334, Sept. 1973.

4. G.S. Becker, "A Theory of Marriage," *Journal of Political Economy*, 81 (1973):813-876, 82 (1974):S11-S26.

5. L.J. Billera, "Existence of General Bargaining Sets for Cooperative Games without Side Payments," *Bulletin of the American Mathematical Society* 76: 375-379.

6. J.M. Buchanan, "An Economic Theory of Clubs," *Economica* 32 (1965):1-14.

7. G. Debreu, *Theory of Value*, New York: Wiley, 1959.

8. G. Debreu and H. Scarf, "A Limit Theorem on the Core of an Economy," *International Economic Review* 4 (1963):235-246.

9. J. Greenberg, "Efficiency of Tax Systems Financing Public Goods in General Equilibrium Analysis," *Journal of Economic Theory*, forthcoming.

10. D.K. Foley, "Resource Allocation and the Public Sector," *Yale Economic Essays*, Spring 1967.

11. ______, "Lindahl's Solution and the Core of an Economy with Public Goods," *Econometrica* 38 (1970):66-72.

12. L. Johansen, *Public Economics*, Amsterdam: North Holland, 1965.

13. R.D. Luce and H. Raiffa, *Games and Decisions*, New York: Wiley, 1967.

14. M. McGuire, "Group Segregation and Optimal Jurisdictions," *Journal of Political Economy* 82 (1974):112-132.

15. J.C. Milleron, "Theory of Value with Public Goods: A Survey Article," *Journal of Economic Theory* 5 (1972):419-477.

16. T.J. Muench, "The Core and the Lindahl Equilibrium of an Economy with Public Goods: An Example," *Journal of Economic Theory* 4 (1972):241-255.

17. J. Nash, "Noncooperative Games," *Annals of Mathematics* 54 (1951):286-295.

18. B. Peleg, "Bargaining Sets of Cooperative Games without Side Payments," *Israel Journal of Mathematics* 1 (1963):197-200.

19. R.W. Rosenthal, "External Economies and Cores," *Journal of Economic Theory* 3 (1971):182-188.

20. P.A. Samuelson, "The Pure Theory of Public Expenditure," *Review of Economics and Statistics* 36 (1954): 387-389.

21. L.S. Shapley and M. Shubik, "On the Core of an Economic System with Externalities," *American Economic Review*, 1969, 678-684.

22. L.G. Telser, "Externalities and Public Good in the Core Theory," August 1973. Unpublished manuscript.

23. C.M. Tiebot, "A Pure Theory of Local Expenditures," *Journal of Political Economy* 64 (1956):416-424.

Appendix 4A: Definitions

Let N be a finite nonempty set, and let S be a nonempty subset of N. An S vector x^S is a real function defined on S whose value at $i \in S$ is x_i^S. The superscript N will be omitted. E_+^S denotes the nonnegative orthant of the Euclidean space E^S of all the S vectors. Let x^S and y^S be two S vectors. $x^S \geqslant y^S$ if $x_i \geqslant y_i$ for all $i \in S$ and $x^S > y^S$ if $x_i > y_i$ for all $i \in S$.

Definition 13: An *n person cooperative game without side payments* is a pair $(N; v)$ where N is a set with n members, and v is a function which assigns to each nonempty subset S of N a nonempty subset $V(S)$ of E_+^S so that:

(i) $V(S)$ is compact.
(ii) If $x^S \in V(S)$ and $0 \leqslant y^S \leqslant x^S$ then $y^S \in V(S)$.
(iii) $V(i) = 0$ for all $i \in N$.

N is the set of *players* of the game and v is its *characteristic function.*

Definition 14: A cooperative game with side payments is the pair $(N; \mu)$ which is a cooperative game without side payments where v is given by: $V(S) = [x^S \in E_+^S \mid \sum_{i \in S} x_i^S \leqslant \mu(S)]$. $\mu(S)$ is called the *value of the coalition S.*

Definition 15: The collection $B = [B_1, \ldots, B_m]$ is called a *coalition structure* if it is a partition of N. That is, $\bigcup_{j=1}^{m} B_j = N$ and for all $1 \leqslant i,\ j \leqslant m,\ i \neq j$, $B_i \cap B_j = \emptyset$. We shall assume, unless otherwise stated, that $\emptyset \notin B$.

Definition 16: x^S is called a *payoff for the coalition S* if $x^S \in \overline{V}(S)$ where

$$\overline{V}(S) = [y^S \in V(S) \mid \nexists\, z^S \in V(S) \quad \text{s.t. } y^S < z^S]$$

Definition 17:,x is called a *payoff* (for the coalition structure B), if $x \in X(B)$ where $X(B) = \prod_{B_l \in B} V(B_l)$.

Definition 18: Let B be a coalition structure and x a payoff. Coalition S_0 is called a *blocking coalition* if there exists $y \in V(S_0)$ such that $y_i > x_i$ for all $i \in S_0$,

Definition 19: The *core* of the game $(N; v)$ for the coalition structure B, is the set of all payoffs for which there is no blocking coalition. That is x is in the core if $x \in X(B)$ and for all $S \subseteq N$, $y^S > x^S \Rightarrow y^S \notin V(S)$.

Definition 20: The *core* of the game $(N; v)$ is the core of the game for the coalition structure $B = \{N\}$.

Definition 21: A *coalition structure B is efficient* if there exists an $x \in X(B)$ such that for all other coalition structure $\tilde{B}$, there is no $y \in X(\tilde{B})$ with $y \geqslant x$ and $y_i > x_i$ for all $i \in \tilde{B}_l \in \tilde{B}$.

Definition 22: Let x be a payoff for the coalition structure, B, and $i, j \in B_l \in B$, $i \neq j$. An *objection of i against j* is a Q-vector y^Q that satisfies: $i \in Q$, $j \notin Q$, $y_k > x_k$ for all $k \in Q$ and $y \in V(Q)$.

Definition 23: Let x be a payoff for the coalition structure B, and y^l an objection of player i against player j. A *counter-objection* of j against i is an R vector z^R that satisfies: $j \in R$, $i \notin R$, $z_k \geqslant x_k$ for all $k \in R$, $z_k \geqslant y_k$ for all $k \in R \cap Q$ and $z^R \in V(R)$.

Definition 24: An *objection is justified* if it cannot be countered.

Definition 25: If i has a justified objection against j, *i is stronger than j.*

Definition 26: The set of all payoffs for which no player is stronger than another player is called the *bargaining set.*

5 The Incentives for Correct Revelation of Preferences and the Number of Consumers

John Roberts

5.1. Introduction

While questions of incentives and self-interested behavior have always been at the heart of economics, it is only recently that these phenomena have begun to be modeled formally and studied systematically.[1] A central result of the literature that has developed from this work is a fundamental impossibility theorem. This theorem states that if consumer preferences are not directly observable, then it is impossible to design a mechanism for allocating resources which always selects a Pareto optimal allocation preferred by each consumer to his initial endowment and which is individually incentive compatible in the sense that no agent by misrepresenting his preferences can ever cause the mechanism to select an allocation which he prefers to the one which would have resulted if he had revealed his preferences correctly. It is important to note that this impossibility theorem holds in the nicest of private goods economies, as well as when public goods are present. Indeed, Hurwicz (1972) first obtained the result for the pure exchange case, and it was only later extended to situations with public goods by Ledyard and Roberts (1974).

The fact that the same impossibility theorem is true whether or not public goods are present would seem to suggest that their presence or absence has no fundamental effect on the nature of the incentive problem of obtaining from consumers the information about their characteristics that is necessary to achieve efficient resource allocation. This suggestion is, of course, in direct contrast to the position argued by Samuelson (1954) and often repeated since that even though agents may have an incentive to misrepresent their interests in public goods, the competitive price system will elicit correct information about preferences between private goods. Of course, it has long been recognized that as long as there are only a small set of agents any one of them typically would be able to influence price formation by deviating from perfectly competitive behavior and that self interest would lead him to do so. The competitive

Reprinted, with permission of North-Holland Publishing Company, from the *Journal of Public Economics*, vol. 6, November 1976, pp. 359-374.

This work was done while I was a visiting faculty research fellow at CORE. I would like to thank Andrew Postlewaite for his many helpful suggestions, the members and staff of CORE for their kind hospitality, the referees for the *Journal of Public Economics* for their comments, and the National Science Foundation for its support of my work under Grant No. SOC 74-04076.

assumption is held to be applicable only when there is a 'large' number of agents. Further, this same large numbers case has been recognized as the one where incentive problems with public goods are the most acute. These ideas would lead one to expect that increasing the number of agents would improve the incentives to abide by the rules of the competitive mechanism but simultaneously would worsen the incentives to reveal correctly one's willingness to pay for public goods.

Recently, Roberts and Postlewaite (1976) have analyzed the first part of this suggestion. They show that the utility gain to a consumer from departing from price-taking behavior typically will go to zero as the economy grows, so that one may say that the incentives under the competitive mechanism for allocating private goods do improve. In this chapter we address the second half of the idea, arguing formally that the incentives on the public goods side cannot be expected to improve and may well worsen as the number of agents increases. What then emerges is that there is indeed a difference between private and public goods from the point of view of incentive problems, but that this difference does not manifest itself in situations with a fixed, finite number of agents. Rather, it emerges only in the case of a very large number of agents and in the effect of increasing the numbers on the incentives for correct revelation.

5.2. The Model: Public Goods and Numbers

We consider economies whose commodity space is $\mathbf{R}^{M+N}$, where the first M coordinates of a commodity space vector refer to private goods and the last N to public goods. A K-person economy E is specified by the characteristics (preferences and endowments) of the K consumers and by the production set Z. We take the preferences $\succsim$ of each consumer k to be defined over the non-negative orthant $\mathbf{R}_+^{M+N}$, and assume that the endowment vectors are of the form $(\omega_k, 0)$, where $\omega_k \in \mathbf{R}_+^M$, so that there is no endowment of public goods. An allocation for such an economy is represented by a vector $(x_1, \ldots, x_K, y)$ in $\mathbf{R}_+^{KM+M}$. It is feasible if $(\Sigma_{k=1}^K x_k - \omega_k, y) \in Z$.

We will assume throughout that the preferences of all possible consumers are monotonic in the private goods, i.e. that if $(x, y) \in \mathbf{R}^{M+N}$ and $x' \gg x$, then $(x', y) \succ (x, y)$.

Our interest is in studying how the incentives facing a consumer with given characteristics would depend on the total number of other agents with him in the economy. This leads us to consider sequences $\{E_h\}$ of economies where the number of consumers in E_h, denoted by $\# E_h$, goes to infinity and where an agent with given specified preferences $\succsim$ and endowment ω belongs to each E_h. Further, we will be concerned with sequences made up of economies which are basically similar except for the number of consumers, so that we can hope to isolate the effect of this factor. We must thus specify what we mean by sequences of 'similar economies,' and this brings up several problems.

In the context of private goods economies there is a well-established methodology for examining questions of the effect of the number of agents.[2] Specifically, one defines a notion of similarity of consumers by defining a metric space of consumer characteristics, i.e. a distance function on preferences and endowments, so that two consumers are similar if they have preferences and endowments that are close in the sense of these distances. One can imagine many such distance functions: for example, one plus the usual Euclidean distance on endowment vectors if the preference orderings are in any way different and simply the distance between the endowments if the preferences are identical. The most commonly used metrics are ones that lead to similar consumers having similar competitive demand functions (as they would under this example) but which are less sensitive to differences in preferences than is the metric. These metrics are usually based on looking at the preferences as sets of ordered pairs, where a pair (z, z') belongs to the set representing the preferences $\succsim$ iff $z \succsim z'$, and then defining a distance between such sets (for example, the Hausdorff metric or a metric inducing the topology of closed convergence). Given such a setup, the consumption sector of an economy can be described in terms of the distribution it induces on this space of consumer characteristics. One then says that two economies are similar if they lead to similar distributions (in the sense of the concept of weak convergence familiar from probability theory) and have similar production sets.

The simplest example in this context is that in which the sequence is one of pure exchange economies generated by replication, so that in the economy E_h there are h consumers with preferences and endowments identical to those of each one of the consumers in the base economy $\{E_1\}$ (where $\# E_1 = K$ and $\# E_h = hK$), while the production set is always $Z = \{0\}$. In this case, each E_h corresponds to the same distribution of agents' characteristics. Further, the economies are, in fact, 'similar' in an intuitive sense. For example, they have the same sets of attainable allocations in per capita terms, if preferences are convex they have the same competitive equilibrium prices, and with strict convexity of preferences, the consumption bundles received by an agent with given preferences and endowment at the individually rational Pareto optima which treat equals equally are unaltered by replication.

However when we introduce public goods things are less clear-cut. The problem can be indicated by considering a sequence generated by replicating an economy in which there is one public good and one private good, two agents, each of whom is endowed with one unit of private good, and a production set $Z = \{(z, y) \in \mathbf{R}^2 \mid z \leqslant 0,\ z + y = 0\}$. In the economy E_h there are then $2h$ consumers, a total endowment of $2h$ units, and a production set $Z_h = Z$. Thus, the allocation $((\sqrt{(2h)} - 1)/\sqrt{(2h)}, \ldots, (\sqrt{(2h)} - 1)/\sqrt{(2h)}, \sqrt{(2h)})$ is feasible in E_h. But, *even in per capita terms*, this sequence is unbounded, with the public goods level going to infinity while the per capita cost of the public good, $1/\sqrt{(2h)}$, goes to zero.

We usually take it to be a distinguishing characteristic of a pure public good that the total cost of providing a given amount of the good is independent of the number of people to whom it is provided, so that the per capita cost is inversely proportional to the size of the group consuming the good. However, this modeling arose in considering situations where the total number of potential consumers was more or less fixed. The question is whether it should be maintained when we want to consider economies with radically different numbers of agents, or whether instead costs should increase with the size of the economy. Maintaining constant costs has a certain appeal, but the problem that it brings is that illustrated in the example: the per capita productivity in producing public goods of an economy with $2K$ consumers is twice that of an economy with K consumers, and, in this crucial respect, replica economies, although having the same distribution of agents' characteristics, are significantly dissimilar.

Casual empiricism would not seem to offer any definite basis for choice between maintaining the constant cost assumption or introducing crowding, although, if anything, it might seem to support the latter. For example, it would seem it should be more expensive to provide national defense to twice as many people than it is for a given number if population densities are the same in the two cases. In any case, the implications of both possibilities should be explored. However, as noted earlier, we are concerned here with sequences of 'similar' economies. For this reason, we will (more or less implicitly) limit consideration to sequences where per-capita productivity levels between economies are similar, so that we will effectively be assuming that the total costs of a public good increase with the size of the economy.

As the need arises, we will make more specific the structure of the economies being considered. For example, in some of the later results we will require that the production set Z_h in E_h is of the form $(z, y) \in Z_h$ if and only if $(z/F(\# E_h), y) \in Z$, where Z is some given production set and $F:\mathbf{R}_+ \to \mathbf{R}_+$ is such that $K/F(K)$ is bounded for $K \geqslant 1$. Thus, as the economy grows, F imposes increasing total input costs in such a way that if the per capita endowment stays bounded, so too do the production possibilities. At the same time, within the context of a given number of consumers the effect of F washes out and we have the usual pure public goods setup. A particular example is $F(K) = K$, so that per capita (rather than total) costs are independent of the number of agents.[3] For the early results, however, we will simply assume that the sequence of public goods levels being provided is convergent. Still, this assumption is probably most readily interpreted in terms of the feasible sets remaining bounded, as they would if increasing costs are imposed.

One should note that the imposition of increasing costs between economies does not at all automatically imply that the level of public goods that will be provided will ultimately go to zero, even though the total costs become arbitrarily large. This fact is illustrated by a simple Cobb-Douglas example which is given in section 5.4.

After this rather lengthy build-up, we can now finish our basic specification of the model. In particular, we will assume that we have a metric d which gives us a distance between pairs of economies. One particular d could be obtained using the measure-theoretic techniques indicated in connection with private goods economies. In fact, all we will require is that if we consider two sequences $\{E_h\}$ and $\{E'_h\}$, where $\# E_h = \# E'_h \to \infty$ and where E'_h is obtained from E_h by replacing the preferences $\succsim$ of one specified agent with given characteristics belonging to each E_h by another given set of preferences, $\succsim^*$, then $d(E_h, E'_h) \to 0$ as $h \to \infty$. This property would, by the way, hold under the particular specification obtained by adapting the techniques used by Hildenbrand (1974) in treating exchange economies.[4]

We will call a sequence $\{E_h\}$ of economies such that $\# E_h \to \infty$ and such that all economies E_h have the same commodity space $\mathbf{R}^{M+N}$, $N > 0$, an *expanding sequence of public goods economies.* If there is a consumer with given, specified preferences $(\succsim, \omega)$ in every one of the E_h, we say that the sequence *contains* $(\succsim, \omega)$.

5.3. The Model: Mechanisms and Incentives

A resource allocation rule Φ is a function which specifies for each economy E in some domain a feasible allocation $\Phi(E)$ for E. Such a rule specifies the outcomes of the complex process of communication, decision and action (the description of which is involved in the full specification of a resource allocation mechanism) which results when agents follow the behavior prescribed by the mechanism. We take Φ to be a function since if Φ has multiple values then the allocation problem is not completely solved: there still remains a choice to be made among allocations. Moreover, single-valuedness of Φ simplifies the arguments to be made, although it is not essential to all of them.

If for each E in its domain of definition $\Phi(E)$ is Pareto optimal, then we say that Φ is *nonwasteful*. If the allocation $\Phi(E)$ is weakly preferred by each agent in E to the initial endowment allocation, then we say that Φ is *utility-respecting.*

In the context of a resource allocation mechanism, the incentive question is that of whether the agents in the economy will find it in their self-interest to abide by the behavioral rules of the mechanism or whether, instead, they will find it advantageous to depart from the specified behavior. In examining this question, it is often interesting to limit the forms of misbehavior open to the agents. One such restriction which is particularly interesting in the context of public goods is to limit misbehavior to misrepresentation of preferences, that is, an agent with preferences $\succsim$ may act as if he were following the rules but that his preferences were some $\succsim'$. Such misbehavior would be undetectable as such to an outside agency charged with enforcing the rules but unable to observe preferences directly.

With this restriction, a particularly simple formalization of the incentive question is possible. Given an economy E, let $\mathscr{E}(E, k)$ be the set of economies E' which can be obtained from E by replacing the preferences $\succsim_k$ of the kth consumer in E by some other preferences $\succsim'$. Then $\mathscr{E}(E, k)$ consists of those economies which, given the other agents' preferences, the kth consumer can make appear to be the true economy by misrepresenting his preferences. Define a consumption vector $(\bar{x}, \bar{y})$ as achievable under Φ by the kth consumer in E if there exists some E' in $\mathscr{E}(E, k)$ such that $(\bar{x}, \bar{y})$ is the consumption he receives at $\Phi(E')$. Then the resource allocation rule Φ is said to be *individually incentive compatible* in E if for each agent k in E the consumption vector received by that agent in E is preferred or indifferent to any other consumption vector achievable by him in E under Φ. Thus, individual incentive compatibility requires that, given the preferences revealed by the other agents, no agent can profitably misrepresent his preferences.[a]

Hurwicz (1972) showed that if the resource allocation rule Φ is utility-respecting and nonwasteful then it cannot be individually incentive compatible in the simple two-good, two-person exchange economy E where each consumer has Cobb-Douglas preferences with equal exponents, $\omega_1 = (1, 0)$ and $\psi_2 = (0, 1)$. Ledyard and Roberts (1974) extended Hurwicz's argument to establish the incompatibility of these three conditions in public goods economies by the same procedure: they give an example of a very simple, two-good, two-person economy with identical consumers in which no rule which selects individually rational Pareto optima can be individually incentive compatible.[b] Thus, self-interested behavior and the achieving of individually rational Pareto optima by decentralized means are not in general consistent, whether or not public goods are present.

However, an interesting difference appears if we consider the impact of the number of consumers on the incentives for correct revelation of preferences.

[a]In the language of game theory, Φ is individually incentive compatible in E if correct revelation of preferences constitutes a Nash equilibrium of the game in which the strategies are defined by the choice of preferences to reveal and the payoffs are the true utility values of the outcomes under Φ.

[b]The preferences of the two agents in this example are given by the homothetic utility function whose indifference curves have slope of -1 for $x > y$ and -3 for $x < y$. Each consumer holds one unit of private good, and the production set is given by $z + y \leqslant 0$. The individually rational Pareto optima are the union of the sets

$$P_1 = \left\{(x_1, x_2, y) \mid x_1 + x_2 + y = 2, x_2 = y, 4/10 \leqslant x_1 \leqslant 2/3\right\},$$

$$P_2 = \left\{(x_1, x_2, y) \mid x_1 + x_2 + y = 2, x_1 = y, 4/10 \leqslant x_2 \leqslant 2/3\right\}.$$

If the allocation selected belong to P_i, then correct revelation is not a Nash equilibrium, since consumer i can, by misrepresenting his preferences, shift the set of apparently individually rational Pareto optima so that it lies entirely in his upper contour set to the point (2/3, 2/3), the best point for him in P_i. For example, if consumer 1 announces preferences given by $U(x, y) = 3x + y$, the individually rational Pareto optima are

$$\left\{(x_1, x_2, y) \mid x_1 + x_2 + y = 2, x_2 = y, 4/5 \leqslant x_1 \leqslant 1\right\}.$$

Consider the competitive mechanism in a pure exchange economy. If the number of participants is small, then the demand of any one agent is typically a significant portion of the aggregate. By altering his offers to buy and sell from their competitive values, an agent could then have a significant impact on the final prices at which trade takes place. In such a case, the incentive to depart from such monopolistic behavior, from competitive price-taking behavior, as measured by the utility gain realizable would be quite strong if the other agents' demand functions can be considered as given. If, on the other hand, each consumer's demand and endowment were individually infinitesimal relative to the aggregate (as in the model of a nonatomic continuum of traders), no one agent could influence price formation by his actions. In this case, any deviation from price-taking would only harm the agent, and the competitive rule would be individually incentive compatible. Thus, in the small numbers case the competitive rule is not consistent with individually self-interested behavior, while in the idealized large numbers case it is. This suggests that, modulo some continuity, the incentives under the competitive mechanism would improve as the number of consumers increased. As each consumer's endowment and demand became small relative to the aggregate, his ability to influence prices and the consequent gain from doing so would correspondingly diminish. Thus, in very large economies, the possible gain from misbehavior would be very small, and, especially if we allow for differential costs in finding profitable misbehavior, we could well assume that consumers will act competitively.[5]

Now consider the situation with public goods. If there are but a very small number of consumers, then the contribution of any one of them towards the cost of producing the public good will typically be a substantial portion of the total. In considering revealing different preferences an agent will be deterred from attempting to go for a full free ride (contributing nothing) by the realization that if he were to do so, supplies of the public goods would be significantly decreased. In contrast, in the limiting case in which each consumer is infinitesimal his failure to contribute leads to no diminution in the supply, and so he has only a very weak incentive to reveal his true preferences if in doing so his private goods consumption would be in any way reduced.

These observations suggest that the incentives with public goods do not improve as the number of consumers increases, and may well worsen. The following propositions and example are intended to formalize this suggestion.

5.4. Numbers, Incentives and Public Goods

Given a sequence (E_h) of economies and a particular agent belonging to all of them, we say that a resource allocation rule Φ is *limiting incentive compatible* for this agent in this sequence if for any utility function U representing the agent's true preferences and any $\epsilon > 0$, there exists an h^* such that if $h > h^*$

then for any consumption vector $(\bar{x}, \bar{y})$ achievable by the agent in E_h there exists an allocation in $\Phi(E_h)$ yielding the agent a consumption vector (x, y) such that $U(\bar{x}, \bar{y}) < U(x, y) + \epsilon$. This definition is meant to capture, without appealing to cardinal utility, the idea that the gain from individual departures from the specified behavior rule goes to zero.[c] It is, of course, natural to think of $\{E_h\}$ as a sequence in which $\# E_h$ goes to infinity.

If Φ is a resource allocation rule, let Φ_y denote the mapping assigning to each E in the domain of Φ the public goods component of $\Phi(E)$. If E and E' are two economies with $\# E = \# E'$ and if the production sets in E and E' are the same, we will call E and E' comparable. Then, given a sequence $\{E_h\}$ we will say that Φ_y is *uniformly continuous* on $\{E_h\}$ if for any $\epsilon > 0$ there exists $\delta > 0$ such that for any $E_h \in \{E_h\}$ and for any E comparable to E_h, if $d(E, E_h) < \delta$ then $| \Phi_y(E) - \Phi_y(E_h) | < \epsilon$. Note that we are requiring the same δ to work, given ϵ, for all h, while we directly compare only economies of a given size.

Our first proposition considers the incentives facing a single agent in the case of one private good and any number of public goods.

Proposition 1. Let $\{E_h\}$ be an expanding sequence of public goods economies containing an agent with characteristics $(\succsim, \omega)$ and suppose $M = 1$. Let Φ be a utility-respecting resource allocation rule, let (x_h, y_h) be the consumption vector received under Φ by this agent in E_h, and suppose that Φ_y is uniformly continuous on $\{E_h\}$ and that $y_h = \Phi_y(E_h) \rightarrow \bar{y}$. Then, if lim inf $x_h \equiv \bar{x} < \omega$, *$\Phi$ cannot be limiting incentive compatible for this agent in $\{E_h\}$.*

Proof. Consider a subsequence along which $x_h \rightarrow \bar{x}$, and denote this subsequence by $\{E_i\}$. If the agent were to misrepresent his preferences by claiming his preferences were the ordering $\succsim'$ described by the utility function $U(x, y) = x$, then, since Φ is utility-respecting, the vector (x_i', y_i') he would receive under Φ in E_i must have $x_i' \geqslant \omega$. Thus, for any U representing his true preferences, $U(x_i', y_i') \geqslant U(\omega, y_i')$. Now, as $i \rightarrow \infty$, $d(E_i, E_i') \rightarrow 0$, where E_i' is the economy obtained from E_i by replacing the given agent's preference ordering $\succsim$ by $\succsim'$. Then the uniform continuity of Φ_y and the convergence of y_i imply $y_i' \rightarrow \bar{y}$. Thus, $[U(\omega, y_i') - [U(x_i, y_i)] \rightarrow [U(\omega, \bar{y}) - U(\bar{x}, \bar{y})] = B$. Since $\bar{x} < \omega$, this latter term is strictly positive. Thus, as $i \rightarrow \infty$, eventually $U(x_i', y_i') \geqslant U(\omega, y_i') \geqslant U(x_i, y_i) + B/2$, and Φ cannot be limiting incentive compatible for this agent.

---

[c] Since h^* may well depend on U as well as ϵ, this notion is perhaps not fully ordinal. An alternative approach might be to try to work in terms of the commodity space directly, formulating the limiting concept in terms of the metric on R^{M+N}. For example, one might define limiting incentive compatibility as 'for any $\epsilon > 0$ there exists h^* such that if $h > h^*$, then, for any (x, y) achievable by the agent in E_h, there is some (x', y') such that (x, y) is not preferred to (x', y') and (x', y') lies within an ϵ neighborhood of the consumption vector $(\bar{x}, \bar{y})$ the agent received at $\Phi(E_h)$.' We opt for the definition given in the text as being perhaps more intuitive.

Thus, given our continuity and convergence assumptions, limiting individual incentive compatibility can hold only if the agent's contribution of private good to public good production under correct revelation goes to zero. In fact, we actually showed that the very simple, fixed strategy of being a full free rider would give a gain that ultimately is bounded from zero unless the agent's implicit tax goes to zero.

It is not obvious how to extend this result in any interesting manner to arbitrary Φ in the context of economies with many private goods. However, one can do so for a special class of rules under which private goods are allocated through competitive market pricing with consumers purchasing private goods out of their (nonnegative) after-tax incomes. Suppose too that Φ has the property that if two consumption bundles differing only in their public goods coordinates are always indifferent for a given agent, then under Φ the allocation of private goods he receives always has value at the equilibrium prices at least equal to that of his endowment. Thus, those with no interest in public goods do not have to contribute any of their endowment for producing these goods. We call a Φ meeting these conditions a *property-respecting private market rule.*

For such a Φ, let $\Phi_{p,y}$ denote the mapping associating with each economy E the private goods prices and public goods quantities associated with the allocation $\Phi(E)$. The definition of uniform continuity of $\Phi_{p,y}$ on a family of economies is an obvious extension of that for Φ_y.

Proposition 2. Let $\{E_h\}$ *be an expanding sequence of public goods economies containing* $(\succsim, \omega)$, $\omega \neq 0$, *and let* Φ *be a property-respecting private market rule. Let* (x_h, y_h) *be the consumption bundle received by the given agent in* E_h *under* Φ. *Suppose* $\Phi_{p,y}(E_h) \to (\bar{p}, \bar{y})$, $\bar{p} \gg 0$, *and that* $\Phi_{p,y}$ *is uniformly continuous on* $\{E_h\}$. *Then* Φ *cannot be limiting individually incentive compatible for this agent if* $\liminf p_h(x_h - \omega) < 0$.

The proof is quite straightforward and is similar in spirit to that of the previous proposition in that the agent ultimately finds being a free rider beneficial. The idea of the proof is to consider preferences given by $V(x, y) = U(x, \bar{y})$, where U describes the agent's true preferences. We omit the details of the argument.

These results may be interpreted as saying that the only way that the incentives for an agent to reveal his true preferences for public goods could improve as the number of agents increases is if his implicit tax goes to zero. In this latter case, we cannot automatically rule out the attractiveness of being a free rider, since he is in fact ultimately a free rider even when he tells the truth. Yet it should be clear that there might well be rules Φ and sequences $\{E_h\}$ such that some agent might find that misrepresentation always will yield him a gain bounded from zero even though his tax goes to zero. Without placing more structure on Φ, we cannot be sure to rule out such possibilities. The following proposition gives one such restriction.

Proposition 3. Let $\{E_h\}$, $(\succsim, \omega)$ *and* Φ *be as in proposition* 1. *Suppose that* Φ_y *is uniformly continuous on* $\{E_h\}$, *that* $\Phi_y(E_h) = y_h \to y$ *and that* $x_h \leqslant \omega$ *for the agent in question, where* (x_h, y_h) *is his consumption vector under* $\Phi(E_h)$. *Then if* $t_h = (x_h - \omega) \to 0$, Φ *is limiting incentive compatible for this agent in* $\{E_h\}$.

Proof. Suppose to the contrary that Φ is not limiting incentive compatible for this agent. Then there exists $\epsilon > 0$, a function U representing $\succsim$, a subsequence $\{E_k\}$ and, for each E_k, a preference ordering the agent may employ such that

$$U(x'_k y'_k) > U(x_k, y_k) + \epsilon$$

where the consumption vector the agent receives when he misrepresents is (x'_k, y'_k) and that when he reveals his true preferences is (x_k, y_k). By hypothesis, the right-hand side of the inequality converges to $U(\omega, y) + \epsilon$. By the continuity and convergence assumptions, $y'_k \to y$. Further, if $x' = \lim\sup x'_k$, and $\{E_n\}$ is a subsequence along which $x'_k \to x'$, then the limit of the left-hand side along this subsequence is $U(x', y)$. But $x' \leqslant \omega$. Thus,

$$U(\omega, y) \geqslant U(x', y) \geqslant U(\omega, y) + \epsilon,$$

and this contradiction establishes the result.

In interpreting these results one must realize that the Φ_y or $\Phi_{p,y}$ functions cannot be expected always to enjoy the continuity properties assumed here. Nor, for that matter, can we always expect y_h to converge. But, as we discussed in section 5.2, this latter condition is not as unappealing as it might appear on first sight, and if we are willing to adopt the increasing cost assumption the convergence of y_h is not any serious additional restriction. Moreover, it is a reasonable requirement on Φ that continuity of $\Phi_{p,y}$ should hold in most situations (e.g. on an open dense set of economies), since otherwise a slight misspecification of the parameters of the economy could result in the determination of levels of p and y that are very far from their true solution values. This is clearly undesirable, especially in a planning context. Note that if we adopt the procedure of describing economies by distributions discussed in section 5.2, then the uniform continuity of $\Phi_{p,y}$ and the convergence of y_h can be replaced by an assumption that $\{E_h\}$ converges to a limit economy at which $\Phi_{p,y}$ is continuous. It is significant that it is precisely the fact that the Walras correspondence enjoys such continuity at most economies which permits showing in Roberts and Postlewaite (1976) that the competitive mechanism is limiting incentive compatible in most sequences of exchange economies.

With the regularity condition on productivity levels between the economies imposed by introducing increasing costs, as well as with some further regularity conditions on the set of consumers and the mechanism, we can derive a stronger implication of limiting incentive compatibility.

Specifically, we will say that a sequence of economies $\{E_h\}$ is a sequence of *types economies* if the preferences and endowments of each agent belonging to any of the E_h are drawn from a finite set $\{(\succsim_i, \omega_i) \mid i = 1, \ldots, I\}$. A sequence $\{E_h\}$, where Z_h is the production set in E_h, has *bounded productivity* if:

(1) there exists $F:\mathbf{R}_+ \rightarrow \mathbf{R}_+$ such that $K/F(K)$ is bounded for $K \geqslant 1$ and such that $(z, y) \in Z_h$ if and only if $(z/F(\# E_h), y) \in Z$, where Z is a closed set such that $Z \cap \mathbf{R}_+^{M+N} \subset \{0\}$; and

(2) the sequence $\{\overline{\omega}^h\}$ of per capital endowment vectors is bounded, where $\overline{\omega}^h = \Sigma_{k=1}^K \omega_k^h / K$, ω_k^h is the endowment of the kth agent in E_h and $K = \# E_h$.

Finally, a rule Φ has the *equal treatment property* is when two agents in an economy have the same preferences and endowments, Φ always assigns them consumption bundles which are indifferent.

Proposition 4. Let $\{E_h\}$ be an expanding sequence of public goods economies such that:

(1) $M = 1$ *(one private good)*;
(2) $\{E_h\}$ *is a sequence of types economies*;
(3) $\{E_h\}$ *has bounded productivity.*

Let Φ be a utility-respecting rule which has the equal treatment property and suppose that Φ_y is uniformly continuous on $\{E_h\}$ and that $\Phi_y(E_h) \equiv y^h \rightarrow \overline{y}$. Then, if Φ is limiting incentive compatible for each type of agent in the sequence, $\overline{y} = 0$.

Proof. Let E_h consist of K_i^h agents of type i, $i = 1, \ldots, I$, so that $\Sigma_{i=1}^I K_i^h = K^h \equiv \# E_h$. Let $\overline{x}_i^h$ be the amount of the private good allocated to agents of type i in E_h. Then, the total input to public goods production may be written in the form $z_h = \Sigma_{i=1}^I K_i^h(x_i^h - \omega_i)$. This term must be nonpositive and, if y^h has any positive component, it must be strictly negative. By proposition 1, limiting incentive compatibility and the equal treatment property imply that lim inf $(x_i^h - \omega_i) \geqslant 0$ for each i. Thus

$$\frac{\Sigma K_i^h(x_i^h - \omega_i)}{F(K^h)}$$

must go to zero, and so $\overline{y} = \lim y^h = 0$, since Z does not admit free production.

Thus, given the limiting form of crowding as expressed by the F function relating the production sets, limiting incentive compatibility of the type enjoyed by the competitive mechanism can obtain only if the solution levels of public goods under correct revelation go to zero. Thus, we cannot expect the incentives to improve in any interesting cases and especially if Φ is nonwasteful. In particular, suppose in the context of proposition 4 that $F(K) = K$, so per capita costs are constant, and that $K_i^h = 2^h K/I$, so that there are an equal number of each type in each economy. This is the situation considered in theorem 1 of Champsaur, Roberts and Rosenthal (1975), and it is an easy matter to adapt the argument there to show that the set of public goods levels corresponding to individually rational Pareto optima which treat equals equally is independent of E_h. Thus, unless $y = 0$ is Pareto optimal in E_1, no nonwasteful Φ could be limiting incentive compatible over such a sequence.

However, we suggested earlier that the incentives might actually in some sense worsen as the numbers increased. It is difficult to see how to formalize this idea without an assumption of cardinal utility which would permit meaningful computation and comparison of utility differences. We will thus simply limit ourselves to presenting an example in which, under any reasonable definition one might propose, incentives could be said to be worsening. In this example, the utility of the consumption vector received by any agent under correct revelation is constant over the sequence, so that we need only compare the outcomes when he misrepresents. These will form a sequence that is monotonically increasing under his preferences.

Specifically we consider a sequence $\{E_K\}$ of economies with one private and one public good. There are K identical consumers in E_K, each with preferences described by $U(x, y) = xy$ and endowment of one unit of the private good. The production set Z_K in E_K is such that $(z, y) \in Z$ if and only if $(z/K) + y = 0$. The mechanism Φ is assumed to be one which selects a Lindahl equilibrium in each E_K and in any economy in any of the $\mathscr{E}(E_K, k)$. Then $\Phi(E_K) = (x_1, \ldots, x_K, y) = (½, \ldots, ½, ½)$. (Note that although costs increases the public good level does not go to zero.) Now consider the possibility of one consumer misrepresenting his preferences while the others reveal their true preferences. If he is not allowed to claim that the public good is a 'bad' for him, then for $K \geqslant 3$ the best he can do is announce preferences given by $U(x, y) = x$. In this case, the allocation rule gives $y = (K - 1)/2K$, and he keeps his entire initial endowment. Thus, the consumption vector he receives if he tells the truth is a constant (½, ½), while that he receives if he pretends no interest in the public good in E_K is preferred to that in E_{K-1} since $(K - 1)/2K > (K - 2)/2(K - 1)$. Thus, if the other agents will not change their announced preferences, the gain from departing optimally from correct revelation (and from being a free rider) for any one agent increases in K.

5.5. Voluntary Financing of Public Goods

None of the techniques or arguments used here depend on the resource allocation rule being nonwasteful. This fact permits an interesting application of these arguments to a model of voluntary financing of public goods that has been discussed in the literature. In the process, we are able to answer some questions arising in the context of this model that previously have been open or treated only under quite restrictive hypotheses.

Consider the solution proposed by Malinvaud (1969) and extended by Castellan[6] of an equilibrium with subscriptions. Here market prices determine the allocation of private goods, while each consumer chooses an amount of purchasing power (money) to contribute to financing the provision of each public good. Given private goods input prices, these contributions define budgets for producing each public good, and the producer of each public good acts to maximize the output of that good subject to this budget. At an equilibrium markets clear, and, given the contributions to public goods production being made by the other agents, no one can alter his contribution–and thus the supply of public goods–so as to make himself better off.

The rule Φ that selects such an equilibrium is a utility- and property-respecting private market mechanism and has the equal treatment property. Further, it is clear that if (x, y) is the equilibrium consumption for an agent with endowment ω, then $x \leqslant \omega$. Equilibria of this type are typically not Pareto optimal, since they involve each agent who is making a positive contribution to public goods production equating his own marginal rate of substitution between public and private goods to the marginal rate of transformation.

Although the rule Φ corresponds to a Nash equilibrium, it is not incentive compatible in our sense. If an agent takes the others' contributions as given, he can do no better than follow the specified rules. On the other hand, if he recognizes that their contributions will ultimately depend on his through their reaction functions (as in the Stackelberg oligopoly model), he can gain by maximizing against these functions rather than against the contributions themselves.[7] Nevertheless, the equilibrium with subscriptions is still limiting incentive compatible under the conditions of proposition 4. To see this, consider an agent with given characteristics $(\succsim, \omega)$ who belongs to each E_h. Let (x_h, y_h) be his equilibrium consumption in E_h and let z_h be the public goods level that results when he contributes nothing to public goods production while the others follow the prescribed behavioral rules. If U is a utility function representing the preferences $\succsim$ we then have $U(x_h, y_h) \geqslant U(\omega, z_h)$. Since $z_h = \Phi_y(E'_h)$, where E'_h is obtained from E_h by replacing $\succsim$ by preferences for the agent which are flat in the public goods, the structure of the Z_h, the continuity of Φ_y, and the convergence of y_h to y together imply $z_h \to y$. Now suppose x_h does not converge to ω. Then, since $0 \leqslant x_h \leqslant \omega$, there is a subsequence $\{E_k\}$ along which $x_k \to x < \omega$. But then $U(x_k, y_k) \to U(x, y) < U(\omega, y)$, so for sufficiently large k, $U(x_k, y_k) < U(\omega, z_k)$–a contradiction. Thus, for any type of agent, $x_h \to \omega$, and so, by proposition 3, Φ is limiting incentive compatible for all agents.

A question that has been raised in the literature is that of how the public goods level under voluntary financing would be affected by increasing the number of agents.[8] This question is easily answered in our setup. By the arguments in the preceding paragraph, we know that the contribution made by any individual to public goods production must go to zero. Since we have equal treatment of equals under the equilibrium with subscriptions, this in turn means that the total input divided by $F(\#E_h)$ goes to zero (since $\#E_h/F(\#E_h)$ is bounded). Since we exclude free production and the production set is assumed closed, this means the public goods level must also go to zero as the number of agents goes to infinity. (This argument is, of course, just that of proposition 4.)

This implication in turn provides an approach to a second open question connected with the voluntary financing model. It is a simple matter to construct examples in which the Lindahl equilibrium is not unanimously preferred to the equilibrium with subscriptions. Castellan raised the question of whether the Lindahl equilibrium might eventually Pareto-dominate the equilibrium with subscriptions as the economy was replicated. Consider then a sequence of economies meeting the conditions in the previous paragraph, so that the amount of public good provided under voluntary financing goes to zero. If there is only one private good, this means the equilibrium consumption vectors converge to the initial endowment. Now suppose that the $F(K) = K$ and that the number of agents of each type in each E_h is a constant percentage of the total number of consumers. Suppose further that all consumers have strictly convex preferences. Together, these conditions imply that the consumption vectors assigned to any consumer of a given type at the Lindahl equilibria will be independent of the total number of consumers, while strict convexity means that any Lindahl equilibrium is unanimously strictly preferred to the initial endowment (and thus to anything in some neighborhood of the initial endowment). Since any equilibrium with subscriptions must eventually lie in any such neighborhood of the initial endowment, Castellan's conjecture is established for this admittedly special case.

5.6. Conclusion

These results serve to justify the usual contrasting of the incentive problem with private and public goods, provided it is interpreted as applying to the large numbers case or to the effect of increasing the number of consumers. They also point out the importance of the guarantee of not making anyone worse off, since Pareto efficiency of the outcomes was not required in the propositions shown here. Thus, even apart from the question of realizing full Pareto optimality, if we want to design a system for allocating resources which is even approximately incentive compatible and is capable of generating nonzero levels of public goods, we must either limit the possibilities for misbehavior more stringently than does the requirement of nonobservability or else be prepared to make some agents worse off than they would be if forced to live on their own resources. The first of these may be difficult to realize. The second means that individuals will not voluntarily agree to submit themselves to such a social system.

Notes

1. See, for example, Drèze and de la Vallée Poussin (1971), Hurwicz (1972), Groves and Loeb (1975), Groves and Ledyard (1975), Ledyard and Roberts (1974), Roberts and Postlewaite (1976), Gibbard (1972), Satterthwaite (1975) and the study by Green, Kohlberg and Laffont, in this issue.

2. For a detailed presentation of these methods and of the central results they have yielded, see Hildenbrand (1974).

3. Essentially this approach was employed by Champsaur, Roberts and Rosenthal (1975) in examining the core with public goods as the number of agents increases. Milleron (1972) has tackled the same problem by making the comparisons between economies where the individual preferences for public goods depend on the total number of agents.

4. In this setup, the consumption sector of an economy with K consumers would be described by a measure assigning weight $1/K$ to each of the K points in the space of agents' characteristics corresponding to the preferences and endowments of the K consumers. (Actually, one would take the Cartesian product of this space with some index set to allow for multiple consumers with the same preferences and endowments.) Then, changing a single consumer's preferences changes the measure only on a point whose weight goes to zero as $K \to \infty$.

5. As indicated earlier, Roberts and Postlewaite (1976) have formalized these arguments, showing that if sufficiently similar economies have equilibrium prices that are similar, then for any outcome any agent can achieve by manipulating prices there is a competitive outcome which is no worse than ϵ less in utility terms than the monopolistic outcome. The continuity condition on prices is known to hold for most economies, as is shown by Dierker (1974).

6. See Milleron (1972) for a presentation of Castellan's work.

7. This mechanism would, however, be incentive compatible in the sense used by Groves and Ledyard (1975) in their recent important contribution, since their agents take the messages (contributions) of the others as given. This illustrates the stringency of our notion of incentive compatibility.

8. See e.g. McGuire (1974).

References

Champsaur, P., D.J. Roberts and R.W. Rosenthal, "On Cores in Economies with Public Goods," *International Economic Review* 16 (1975):751-764.

Dierker, E., "Topological Methods in Walrasian Economics," *Lecture Notes in Economics and Mathematical Systems No. 92*, Berlin: Springer-Verlag, 1974.

Drèze, J., and D. de la Vallée Poussin, "A Tatonnement Process for Public Goods," *Review of Economic Studies* 38 (1971):133-150.

Gibbard, A., "Manipulation of Voting Schemes: A General Result," *Econometrica* 41 (1973):587-602.

Green, J., E. Kohlberg and J.-J. Laffont, "Partial Equilibrium Approach to the Free-Rider Problem," *Journal of Public Economics* 6 (Nov. 1976):359-374.

Groves, T., and J. Ledyard, "Optimal Allocation of Public Goods: A Solution to the Free Rider Problem," *Center for Mathematical Studies in Economics and Management Science, Discussion Paper No. 144*, 1975, Northwestern University, forthcoming in *Econometrica.*

Groves, T., and M. Loeb, "Incentives and Public Inputs," *Journal of Public Economics* 4 (1975):211-226.

Hildenbrand, W., "Core and Equilibria of a Large Economy," Princeton: Princeton University Press, 1974.

Hurwicz, L., "On Informationally Decentralized Systems," in *Decision and Organization: A Volume in Honor of Jacob Marschak* C.B. McGuire and R. Radner (eds.), Amsterdam: North Holland, 1972.

Ledyard, J., and D.J. Roberts, "On the Incentive Problem with Public Goods," *Center for Mathematical Studies in Economics and Management Science, Discussion Paper No. 116*, Northwestern University, 1974.

Malinvaud, E., "Lecons de la théorie microeconomique," Paris: Dunod, 1969.

McGuire, M., "Group Size, Group Homogeneity and the Aggregate Provision of a Pure Public Good under Cournot Behavior," *Public Choice* 18 (1974):107-126.

Milleron, J.C., "Theory of Value with Public Goods: A Survey Article," *Journal of Economic Theory* 5 (1972):419-477.

Roberts, D.J., and A. Postlewaite, "The Incentives for Price-Taking Behavior in Large Exchange Economies," *Econometrica* 44 (1976):115-128.

Samuelson, P., "The Pure Theory of Public Expenditure," *Review of Economics and Statistics* 36 (1974):387-389.

Satterthwaite, M., "Strategy-Proofness and Arrow's Conditions: Existence and Correspondence Theorems for Voting Procedures and Social Welfare Functions," *Journal of Economic Theory* 10 (1975):187-217.

6 A Sampling Approach to the Free Rider Problem

Jerry Green and
Jean-Jacques Laffont

6.1. Introduction

The problem of ascertaining the preferences of a group of individuals for a public good, or for governmental action in general, can be thought of as a special case of decision theory under imperfect information. The tastes of each individual are privately held pieces of data. In order to insure that an optimal action will be taken, the government must be able to elicit them without cost and without error. One cannot assume that individuals will correctly report their tastes if asked. Methods must be devised under which the correct elicitation of preferences is to the advantage of individuals in the context of the decision making mechanism.

In Green and Laffont [1977] we described the methods by which the true preferences would be willingly revealed by each individual independently of his beliefs concerning the true or professed preferences of others. The basic idea, originally due to Vickrey (1961), Clarke (1971) and Groves (1973) can be stated as follows:

Individuals are assumed to have preferences described by the following utility functions:

For each $i = 1, \ldots, n$:

$$
\begin{aligned}
u_i &= x_i + v_i && \text{if the public project is accepted} \\
&= x_i && \text{if the public project is rejected}
\end{aligned}
$$

where x_i is the amount of a transferable private good consumed by the individual i and v_i his true willingness to pay.

Let w_i be the agent i's stated willingness to pay, $i = 1, \ldots, n$:

A *mechanism* is a mapping, f,

$$f : R^n \to \{0, 1\} \times R^n$$

written as $f(w_1, \ldots, w_n) = (d, t_1, \ldots, t_n)$ where $d \in$ 0, 1 is the public decision taken (1 = accept project; 0 = reject project) and t_i is the transfer of the private good received by agent i.

The mechanisms defined by

$$d = 1 \quad \text{iff} \quad \sum_i w_i \geqslant 0$$

$$t_i = \sum_{j \neq i} w_j + h_i(w_{-i}) \qquad \text{if } d = 1$$

$$= h_i(w_{-i}) \qquad \text{if } d = 0$$

where $w_{-i} = (w_1, \ldots, w_{i-1}, w_{i+1}, \ldots, w_n)$ and h_i (.) are arbitrary real-valued functions, can be shown to have the property that setting $w_i = v_i$ is a dominant strategy for each agent, and therefore that a Pareto optimal outcome will always be found. Moreover, as we showed (Green and Laffont, 1977), this class of mechanisms exhausts all those with this attractive property.

If this mechanism could be costlessly applied, the "free rider" problem could be solved in this way—at least for environments with separable utility functions.[a]

However, as we will argue below, the use of such mechanisms entails auxiliary costs. It may therefore not be optimal to use these mechanisms, or to use them for eliciting the tastes of the entire population.

Ideally, the preferences of each individual should be accurately elicited before a public decision is taken. This is generally impossible, or undesirable, for two reasons. There may be costs of inquiring itself, and there may be problems in ascertaining individuals' true preferences once they have been solicited. Realistic decision making procedures must try to avoid these obstacles as much as possible, while taking the costs of doing so into account.

Typically, the number of individuals potentially affected by the public project is large—and this fact creates both problems and opportunities in the design of preference elicitation and decision making mechanisms.

Because individuals are numerous, it is natural to attempt to economize on information costs through random sampling. The sampled value, to be an accurate proxy for the tastes of the population, must be based on honest responses by individuals and must include a representative, unbiased selection of them. In a noncoercive society, one cannot, presumably, force some individuals to participate in the sampling process while others are left out. Thus, in addition to arranging the mechanisms for accurate elicitation of preferences and Pareto optimal decision making, the condition of universal willingness to participate must be regarded as an additional desideratum. In this way a purely random sample will be representative of the population.

The remainder of this paper is therefore organized as follows. In section 6.2

[a]In Green and Laffont (1977) we show that there are no mechanisms having this dominant strategy property when the class of allowable preference relations is extended beyond this. Problems with consumption sets for the private good that are bounded below can be easily handled however, see Green and Laffont (1976c), but some modification of this characterization theorem must be made.

we introduce the various reasons why drawing a random sample from the population might be desirable. This can be broken down into two major subheadings: First, (section 6.2.1) we consider random sampling procedures in which one of the mechanisms mentioned above is used to elicit the preferences of the sample precisely. Here the goal of sampling is to balance the associated costs, which are often increasing in the sample size with the risk that sampling variance will cause a nonoptimal decision to be taken. Second (section 6.2.2), we consider the cases in which a random sample from the population is taken in order to improve the accuracy of the responses given. In these cases we will ignore the associated costs mentioned above. Sampling will be designed to balance the accuracy of answers obtained against the sampling variance. Then, we see in which sense sampling can prevent coalitions from distorting their responses. Finally, in section 6.3 we take up the issue of participation and obtain the mechanisms which induce universal participation. The requirement of universal participation is then shown to be incompatible with even weak individual rationality.

6.2 The Use of Sampling to Improve Preference Revelation Mechanisms

6.2.1 Sampling to Reduce Direct Costs of Mechanisms

In this section we will consider the potential value of taking a random sample from the population, eliciting their tastes via a dominant-strategy mechanism as above, and making the decision for the entire group on the assumption that the sample's preferences are representative. We will be concerned with two questions in this regard: First we investigate properties of the optimal sample size. Second, we study whether and to what extent the resulting mechanism, whose outcomes and costs may be regarded as random functions of the true preferences, can be regarded as a solution to the free rider problem. More specifically, we compare the expected value of using this procedure, with the optimal sample size, to having perfect information or to being constrained to make the decision on the basis of the *a priori* beliefs of the planner. To the extent the imperfectness of information concerning tastes can be overcome by these methods, we can say that progress towards the solution of the free-rider problem has been made.

In this subsection we consider two obvious types of costs associated with the use of the dominant-strategy mechanisms. First, the process of elicitation of responses and their compilation might involve the expenditure of real resources. Letting N be the population size and n be the sample size, we assume that these costs are proportional to the latter, that is:

$$C = cn \tag{6.1}$$

where C is the direct cost of the mechanism.

A second type of cost is that which is due to the income transfers induced by the procedure. If we assume that the procedure is used on a population for which the existing income distribution is optimal, then a bound on the expected costs of the income transfers induced will be

$$C = \sum_{i=1}^{n} | t_i (w) | \tag{6.2}$$

These costs depend on the sample size both because the transfers are only distributed (collected) within the sample group and because the transfers received by each individual are dependent on the statements made by all others, and will vary according to the number of other agents in the sample.

The benefit of sampling is that we can reduce the risk of accepting or rejecting the project when the opposite action would have been superior. To quantify this value, it is necessary to suppose the planner has prior beliefs concerning the preferences of the population which will be modified in light of the sample. For mathematical simplicity we will suppose that he believes that the N individuals' willingness to pay, v_i, are independently and identically normally distributed

$$v_i \sim N(m, s^2)$$

Moreover he is uncertain about the mean, m, but (for simplicity) knows the variance. His prior on this parameter is described by

$$m \sim N(\mu, \sigma^2)$$

When a sample of size n is taken, the planner revises his beliefs about m according to Bayes theorem.

Letting $w = \sum_i w_i/n$ be the mean of the sample's responses, we have that the posterior distribution is described by

$$m \sim N\left(\frac{s^2 \mu + n\,\sigma^2 w}{s^2 + n\sigma^2}, \frac{\sigma^2 s^2}{s^2 + n\sigma^2}\right)$$

We will assume throughout that the planner is risk neutral. Thus the expected value of constructing the project is $(\mu s^2 + n\sigma^2 w)/(s^2 + n\sigma^2)$.

Recall that the rules under which the mechanisms operate are that the project is constructed only if the stated responses indicate that it is valuable. That is, in the process of eliciting the true preferences, the planner announces the mechanism to be used—including the rule for project acceptance,

$$\sum_{i=1}^{n} w_i \geqslant 0$$

It is the spirit of this analysis that the mechanism is then followed, even though this might not be optimal ex post, as would be the case if μ and w were of opposite signs but

$$|\mu| > \frac{n\sigma^2}{s^2} |w|$$

Thus, the expected value of adopting the project for each of the $(N-n)$ individuals who were not sampled is given by:

$$\int_0^\infty \left(\frac{s^2\mu + n\sigma^2 w}{s^2 + n\sigma^2} \right) f(w)\, dw$$

where $f(w)$ is the ex ante probability law of w:

$$w \sim N\left(\mu, \frac{s^2}{n} + \sigma^2\right)$$

For the sampled group, however, there is no residual uncertainty about their evaluations and, per capita, their expected willingness to pay for the decision that their responses induce is:

$$\int_0^\infty w f(w)\, dw$$

Thus the ex ante expected evaluation of the decision, when a sample of size n is drawn from a population of size N is

$$\int_0^\infty \left[(N-n) \frac{s^2\mu + n\sigma^2 w}{s^2 + n\sigma^2} + nw \right] f(w)\, dw$$

This can be evaluated (see Green and Laffont (1974, appendix)) as:

$$\frac{N\sigma^2 + s^2}{\sqrt{2\pi}\,(s^2/n + \sigma^2)^{1/2}} \cdot e^{-\frac{\mu^2}{2(s^2/n + \sigma^2)}} + \mu N \rho\left(\frac{\mu}{(s^2/n + \sigma^2)^{1/2}} \right)$$

where

$$\rho(x) = \frac{1}{\sqrt{2\pi}} \int_{-\infty}^{x} e^{-z^2/2} dz$$

We consider here only the case in which $\mu = 0$ (evaluation of the objective function when $\mu \neq 0$ is carried out in Green and Laffont (1974), by analogous methods). Thus the expected value of the decision becomes

$$\frac{N\sigma^2 + s^2}{\sqrt{2\pi}\,(s^2/n + \sigma^2)^{1/2}} \tag{6.3}$$

6.2.1.a. Sampling Cost Constant per Capita. We now consider the case of constant per capita sampling cost (6.1) and derive the optimal sample size. Let $V^{\mathrm{I}}(n, N)$ be the ex ante expected evaluation for this problem, which is (6.3) minus (6.1).

$$V^{\mathrm{I}}(N, n) = \frac{(N\sigma^2 + s^2) - cn\sqrt{2\pi}\left(\dfrac{s^2}{n} + \sigma^2\right)^{1/2}}{\sqrt{2\pi}\left(\dfrac{s^2}{n} + \sigma^2\right)^{1/2}} \tag{6.4}$$

Taking the derivative of this with respect to n:

$$\frac{dV^{\mathrm{I}}(n, N)}{dn} = \left(\frac{N\sigma^2 + s^2}{2}\right)\frac{s^2}{n^2} - c\sqrt{2\pi}\left(\frac{s^2}{n} + 2\right)^{3/2} \tag{6.5}$$

We are interested in computing the rate of growth of the optimal sample size. Therefore we set $n = N^{\delta}$ and look for the value of δ such that (6.5) is zero for large N. It is easy to show that the positive terms in (6.5) are increasing at the rate of $N^{1-2\delta}$, whereas all of the negative terms are nonincreasing as functions of N. Therefore, $\delta = 1/2$ is required for the first order condition. The sample size at the optimum will be proportional to the square root of the population size for large economies.

At this point we should pause to consider this somewhat puzzling result. Sampling theory teaches us that the accuracy of a sample is independent of the population size. One might therefore expect a bounded sample size to be optimal, rather than one growing like the square root of the total population. However, as the population size increases, a given degree of precision is no longer optimal. Any error made now affects a larger group of unsampled agents. Therefore a higher degree of precision becomes necessary.

6.2.1.b. Sampling Costs Proportional to Total Transfer Payments. We now neglect the cost of resources used in the sampling process and introduce the cost of distortions induced through the transfers mandated by the preference revelation mechanism. These transfers will, of course, depend upon the particular member of the class of preference revelation mechanisms being employed. In this section we consider two specific mechanisms; our choice is motivated by the results concerning the inducement of participation in the process presented in section 6.3. These mechanisms are defined by

$$h_i(w_{-i}) \equiv 0 \qquad \text{for all } i$$

and

$$h_i(w_{-i}) = \min\left(-\sum_{j \neq i} w_j, 0\right) \qquad \text{for all } i$$

(This second mechanism is referred to as the pivotal mechanism (see Green and Laffont, 1976).)

For the mechanism $h \equiv 0$, the transfer payments are $n(n-1)\, w$ if $w \geqslant 0$ and zero otherwise.

As a limiting hypothesis we regard the entire volume of these payments as a dead-weight loss. This is a very pessimistic viewpoint since we will be neglecting their beneficial effects on the welfare of the sample while fully counting the cost that their collection will impose on the unsampled group.

Thus the ex ante value of the procedure, defined as $V^{\mathrm{II}}(n, N)$ is

$$V^{\mathrm{II}}(n, N) = \frac{(N + n - n^2)\,\sigma^2 + (2 - n)s^2}{\sqrt{2\pi}\left(\frac{s^2}{n} + \sigma^2\right)^{1/2}}$$

Differentiating with respect to n and setting $n = N^\delta$ we can show that the derivative will be asymptotically negative whenever $\delta > 1/3$. Thus the largest local maximum of the objective function occurs when the sample size grows like the cube root of the population size (see Green and Laffont, 1974, for further details). This problem is not a concave one, however, and we cannot rule out zeros at smaller values of δ on purely theoretical grounds. Our computer simulations have shown, however, that over a wide range of the parameter values the zero of the order of the cube root of N is the global maximum.

Further analysis of this problem is necessary in order to show that the procedure is of positive information value. By this we mean that its optimal value exceeds what could be attained through the naive strategy that would accept or reject the project according to the sign of μ. This has an ex ante value of

$$N \max(\mu, 0)$$

since no transfers are required. The information value of the procedure depends on the parameters of the problem σ^2, s^2 and μ, as well as N and n. Let G be the informational value of the mechanism for a sample of size n.

$$G(n, N; \sigma^2, s^2, \mu) = V^{II}(n, N) - N \max(\mu, 0)$$

The following results can be demonstrated by using the approximation $n^*(N) = N^{1/3}$ which therefore provides a lower bound on G:

(1) For $\mu = 0$, G is always nonnegative.

(2) For $\mu \neq 0$, G may be negative for some N.

(3) However, $\lim_{N \to \infty} G(n^*(N), N; \sigma^2, s^2, \mu)$ is always nonnegative.

Moreover if $\sigma^2 \neq 0$ so that the decision problem is nontrivial, the above nonnegativity results can be converted into strict positivity.

Thus, in summary, the costs of this procedure, which grow like the square of the sample size, but only accrue when the project is accepted, account for the lower rate of growth of the optimal sample size than was derived in the constant per capita cost case. However, these costs are not so high as to cause us to revert to the naïve strategy. Nevertheless it would be incorrect to say that a complete solution to the free rider problem has been found—for it is easy to see that the value of the procedure does not approach that of perfect information, which is

$$\max\left(\sum_{i=1}^{N} v_i, 0\right)$$

In order to improve upon the solution given above we investigate the mechanism defined by

$$h = \min\left(-\sum_{j \neq i} w_j, 0\right)$$

This mechanism has the property that an individual is taxed whenever the social decision is altered on account of his statement. In this case he pays $|\sum_{j \neq i} w_j|$ since this is the cost that his participation and revealed preferences has imposed on the other members of the group. Note however that in those cases in which the project is overwhelmingly carried $-\sum_i w_i$ is larger than any of individual w_i—no taxes will be paid by anyone. This is to be contrasted with the situation for the $h = 0$ mechanism which would produce a total transfer of $(n-1)\sum_{i=1}^{N} w_i$.

Although it is not true that the

$$h = \min\left(-\sum_{j \neq i} w_j, 0\right)$$

mechanism involves less transfer payments in every case than $h = 0$ would,[b] it is

[b]Consider the three-person situation: $v_1 = +9$; $v_2 = -5$; $v_3 = -5$. A straightforward calculation reveals that under $h = \min\left(-\sum_{j \neq i} w_j, 0\right)^2$ the transfers received are: $t_1 = 0$, $t_2 = -4$, $t_3 = -4$, so that $\Sigma |t| = 8$; while under $h = 0$ they are $t_1 = 0$, $t_2 = 0$, $t_3 = 0$, so that $\Sigma |t| = 0$.

clear in an intuitive sense that the average payment would be lower in some statistical sense. This is made precise by the following theorem:

Theorem 6.2.1 (Green and Laffont, 1976b)

Let v_i be independently identically distributed according to $f(.)$, a distribution with finite variance. Then the mechanism defined by

$$h_i(w_{-i}) = \min\left(-\sum_{j \neq i} w_j, 0\right)$$

produces transfers t_i, $i = 1, \ldots, n$ always nonpositive such that $E\sum_{i=1}^{N} t_i/\sqrt{N}$ approaches a finite limit as $N \to \infty$.

Following our earlier procedure, we can define the ex ante expected value of using this mechanism on a sample of size n. In the normal case one can calculate

$$E_n = E\sum_{i=1}^{n} t_i\,(w_{-i})$$

exactly, not just its limit. This is (see Green and Laffont, 1976b):

$$E_n = \frac{s^2}{\sqrt{2\pi}}[n\sqrt{n-1} - (n-1)\sqrt{n}\,]$$

$$\approx \frac{s^2}{\sqrt{2\pi}}\left[\frac{\sqrt{n}}{2} - \frac{1}{8\sqrt{n}}\right] \quad \ldots$$

The ex ante value of the mechanism is therefore

$$V^{\text{III}}(n, N) = \frac{(N-n)\sigma^2}{\sqrt{2\pi}\left(\dfrac{s^2}{n} + \sigma^2\right)^{1/2}} - E_n$$

Calculations analogous to the ones described above give the order of the optimal sample size, namely

$$\frac{n^*(N)}{N^{2/3}} \to \text{constant}$$

The expected transfer costs are much smaller with the pivotal mechanism than with the mechanism associated to $h \equiv 0$. Consequently the optimal sample size is much higher.

Indeed, if we introduced simultaneously per capita sample costs and transfer costs with the pivotal mechanism, the per capita sample costs would dominate in the determination of the optimal sample size.

6.2.2. *Sampling to Improve the Accuracy of Responses*

When any of the dominant strategy mechanisms are used, the individuals sampled will respond with their true willingness to pay provided they act rationally and as individuals. However, we may expect to have difficulties with eliciting accurate responses if the individuals do not know their own willingness to pay precisely, or if they perceive that they can collude with others, jointly distorting their preferences.

6.2.2.a. The Strength of Incentives. Since the mechanisms may be used to decide on undertaking new public projects whose exact characteristics are unobservable ex ante, individuals may justifiably be uncertain about what their own ex post willingness to pay for the project are. The mechanism will thus bear a double burden. It should encourage individuals to ascertain their own true preferences and also to reveal them for use in the decision making process. What is the role of sampling in furthering these ends? It is a universal problem for any decision process concerning large groups that the strength of the individual's incentive is low. In majority rule the prospect that one's vote will be decisive is very minor.

In the process above, similarly, the utility of an individual is determined by the decision and by everyone else's stated willingness to pay. Thus since the probability that one's statement will change the sign of the aggregate is slight, there is little incentive to refine personal information about the true willingness to pay. In the language of statistical decision theory the regret function has its minimum at the truth, but it is very flat. If acquiring this exact information is costly, an individual may choose to respond to the mechanism on the basis of his prior beliefs alone. The decision is more likely to be nonoptimal if a larger proportion of the sample responds in this way. As the number of individuals grows, the severity of the problem will increase. It may thus be valuable to keep the sample size small in order to maintain the incentives for introspection or information acquisition, and accurate reporting of tastes.

This can be modelled as follows:

We first consider a typical agent who is one among $n + 1$ sampled individuals. It is assumed that the sample size is announced to the agents so that they know, with certainty, that there are n others. Let x denote the sum of the answers of these n others.

Let $B(v_i, w_i)$ be the agent's gain if he says v_i, the truth, instead of w_i. Clearly, $B(v_i, w_i)$ depends on x:

$$B(v_i, w_i) = 0 \qquad \text{if } v_i + x \geqslant 0 \text{ and } w_i + x \geqslant 0$$

$$\text{or if } v_i + x < 0 \text{ and } w_i + x < 0$$

$$= v_i + x \qquad \text{if } v_i + x \geqslant 0 \text{ and } w_i + x < 0$$

$$= -v_i + x \qquad \text{if } v_i + x < 0 \text{ and } w_i + x \geqslant 0$$

We assume that the agent believes that the n others will make statements such that the total is distributed according to a probability law $p_n(x)$. (We will see that this distribution will itself be determined endogenously.) The expected gain of saying the truth, v_i, instead of saying w_i is thus

$$\underset{x}{E}\, B(v_i, w_i) = \int_{\substack{w_i \leqslant -x < v_i \\ -w_i \leqslant x < -v_i}} | v_i + x | \, dp_n(x)$$

A typical individual is assumed to believe that his own v_i, initially unknown to him, is distributed normally with mean zero and variance r^2. At a cost c (in terms of the private good), he can learn v_i precisely. Moreover we assume that he knows that all other individuals are in exactly the same position, except for the fact that their discovery costs may be different from his. In any situation, he is therefore justified in assuming that those whose costs are low will ascertain their v_i and will correctly report them, whereas those with high costs will report zero. The cutoff value of costs will be denoted c^*; it will be determined endogenously as a function of n.

For any c^*, the typical agent is assumed to know the proportion of the sample whose value of c is below c^*, $F(c^*)$, where $F(.)$ is the distribution of costs in the population. We neglect the uncertainty that sampling will induce concerning the exact size of the group of agents whose values of c are below c^*. Hence the agent believes that $nF(c^*)$ individuals will respond according to their true v_i, drawn from a distribution $N(0, r^2)$ whereas $n(1 - F(c^*))$ will respond with zero. Thus his subjective distribution on x, $p_n(.)$ is $N(0, nF(c^*)r^2)$.

Before ascertaining his own v_i, the expected gain from doing so is

$$\underset{v_i}{E}\,\underset{x}{E}\, B(v_i, 0) = \underset{v_i}{E} \int_{\substack{w_i \leqslant -x < v_i \\ -w_i \leqslant x < -v_i}} | v_i + x | \, dp_n(x)$$

where the expectation over v_i is taken with the distribution $N(0, r^2)$. Thus, balancing the expected gain from information acquisition against cost, the individual will choose to learn his v_i only if

$$\underset{v_i}{E}\,\underset{x}{E}\, B(v_i, 0) \geqslant c$$

Thus an equilibrium value of c^* is one that gives rise to an equality in this relation. It can be shown (see Green and Laffont, 1976a) that $c^*(n)$ must satisfy

$$\frac{r}{\sqrt{2\pi}}[\sqrt{nF(c^*)+1} - \sqrt{nF(c^*)}] = c^*$$

and that the solution to this will be unique and decreasing in n. Thus as the planner chooses different values of n, he will obtain more accurate answers depending on the change in $nF(c^*(n))$.

As in section 6.2.1 we assume that the planner chooses the sample size to maximize the expected value of the outcome, net of costs, believing that the population is drawn from $N(\nu, \sigma^2)$ and that σ^2 is known but ν is unknown. His prior on ν is given by $N(0, p^2)$. In order to preserve the parity between the knowledge and beliefs of the planner and those of the individuals, it is natural to take $\sigma^2 + p^2 = r^2$. In this way the agents' beliefs about each other before ascertaining their own tastes are the same as the government's beliefs about each agent (before the sample's responses are known).

In a manner precisely analogous to that in section 6.2.1, we can therefore derive that the expected value of the public decision, ex ante is given by

$$\frac{(Np^2 + \sigma^2)}{(2\pi)^{1/2}\left(\dfrac{\sigma^2}{nF(c^*(n))} + p^2\right)^{1/2}} \tag{6.6}$$

The costs to be subtracted from this are the mean costs of private information acquisition incurred by individuals below the cutoff level of c^*.

$$\int_0^{c^*(n)} c\,dF(c) \tag{6.7}$$

The optimal value of n is that which maximizes the difference between (6.5) and (6.7). Because of the analytical complexity of $c^*(n)$ it is, in general, impossible to obtain results on the optimal sample size. However, by making further assumptions on the distribution of the information costs, such results can be attained. If $F(c)$ is of the form

$$F(c) = \frac{c^m}{K_m}$$

where $m \in [0, 1]$ and K_m is a constant, then a closed-form solution for c^* is

$$c^* = \left[\frac{r}{2\sqrt{2\pi}}\right]^{2/2+m} K_m^{1/2+m} n^{-m/2+m}$$

and the optimal sample size, $n^*(N)$, can be shown to grow at the rate $N^{(2+m)/2m+2-m^2}$ when N is large. Specifically, this means that when $m = 1$, so that c is distributed uniformly on $[0, K_1]$, that $n^*(N)$ is proportional to N, in large populations.

One can then ask whether the induced private information costs are worth the social value of information produced. It can be shown that the optimized value of the sampling procedure approaches $p/\sqrt{2\pi}$ per capita. The process is not only informationally valuable in large economies, but the value increases linearly with N.

6.2.2.b. Preventing Coalitions from Distorting Their Responses. In the studies mentioned above, eliminating the possibility of rational distortion of preferences by individuals was the only goal of the system of transfer payments used. It can be easily seen, however, that if a coalition of individuals could form and, tacitly or explicitly, could agree to alter their responses in the same direction, a superior result from their point of view could be achieved. A simple example of this can be seen in the three person economy with $v_1 = -3$, $v_2 = +1$, $v_3 = +1$. Using any Groves mechanism each person has an incentive to respond with $w_i = v_i$. The project would be rejected but if individuals 2 and 3 could agree to each say +3, then the pivotal mechanism would lead to acceptance of the project with no transfers, and this is better than they would achieve by telling the truth. However, they cannot be assumed to know the statement that will be made by the other individual; or more generally they will even be ignorant of how many other individuals there are. Distortions will involve some risks. For example if $w_1 = -5$, then the distortion mentioned above would lead to both individuals being taxed 2 units by the pivotal mechanism, which is more than their true willingness to pay for the project they have caused to be accepted. The larger their distortion, the surer they are of forcing their preferred social decision, but the more risk they must accept if their guess about the others' statements proves erroneous.

In Green and Laffont (1976d) we show that there is no successful mechanism that is capable of inducing truthful responses from coalitions as well as individuals. A related result was demonstrated by Bennett and Conn (1976).

The natural question then becomes: Given that there is no way to prevent cheating by coalitions in all circumstances, can we design systems with the property that coalitions will not find it very profitable to form? In this way, if there are any costs of collusion, communication or enforcement within the coalition, or if there are any problems of elicitation of preferences within the coalition itself, these will form a sufficiently strong barrier to their formation.

The prospect of sampling is a possible advantageous device in this regard—though the matter is not one of a simple optimization of the sample size as in the sections above. There are conflicting forces determining the optimal sample size, and some are difficult to quantify. On one hand a small random sample disbursed among the members of a large population may find it exceedingly difficult even to seek each other out and identify their common interests. On the other hand, since it is the variability and uncertainty concerning the responses of others that causes the risk of collusion, we should take a larger sample in order that each coalition perceives itself as facing a larger group of others in the sampled group. If they believe the statements to be independently and identically distributed, as we have assumed in other sections, then they will be less likely to try to distort their preferences.

We have shown (Green and Laffont (1976d)) that as the sample size grows, the expected profitability from cheating by the coalition for whom such distortion is potentially the most valuable falls to zero. This is done in several steps. We first study the optimal response by a coalition of agents whose willingness to pay have the same sign and who have made a binding agreement to share their taxes, if any, in a particular way. It is shown that the best joint response is to have all coalition members say the same thing, and for this to be approximately equal, for each individual, to the willingness to pay of the entire coalition.

Next, fixing the aggregate willingness to pay of the members of the coalition, it is shown that the expected gain to cheating compared to telling the truth, goes to zero with the number of agents in the sample. However, if the planner shares the individuals' beliefs about the distribution of willingnesses to pay, then as the sample size increases the probability that a coalition of a fixed size exists with an aggregated willingness to pay exceeding a particular quantity increases. Nevertheless, we show, by using the asymptotic theory of order statistics, that if these beliefs are normally distributed, the probability that a viable cheating coalition will exist with an expected per capita gain larger than some fixed positive number will approach zero as the sample size grows.

Of course the risks of collusion and the costs of eliminating it would have to be balanced against the other problems involved in the employment of these mechanisms. These more complex comparisons remain open questions that have not been studied thus far.

6.3. Participation

We have seen that it may be superior, for a variety of reasons, to elicit the preferences of only a sample from the whole population. In a noncoercive society, however, we cannot insure that all the members of the sampled group will respond by giving their true tastes. A reply of "no response" must be admitted as a valid individual strategy, in addition to the elements of the real line which form the allowable valuations for the project as we have posed the question thus far.

We are therefore faced with a choice of either designing mechanisms such that universal participation can be insured, or of specifying the outcomes that will arise in the event that the reply of "no response" is played by some of the agents. Because failures to respond may bias the outcome of the process, we have opted for the former possibility.

At this stage we must distinguish between alternative assumptions concerning participation. We might require, on one hand, that each individual should prefer to participate as a member of the sample instead of abstaining and leaving the decision making process to the others. This we term the requirement of *universal participation.* On the other hand, a more traditional approach is to require that no one can be hurt because of his participation–vis-à-vis the *status quo.* This is the requirement of *individual rationality.*

Due to the fact that no individually incentive compatible mechanism can balance the budget identically (see Green and Laffont 1976b) the members of the unsampled group will be paying or receiving transfers from the sampled group as a whole. This welfare will be further affected by the public decision taken. If a net subsidy to the sample is required the unsampled group is likely to contain at least some individuals who are made worse off by virtue of the use of this mechanism. We may ask, therefore, for mechanisms whose net transfer to the sample is always nonpositive, so that it will then be possible to treat the unsampled group in a welfare improving way, at least as far as monetary transfers are concerned. Indeed it is clear that it is impossible to design a mechanism which is individually rational for the whole population since an agent not in the sample may have an arbitrary (negative) evaluation.

We will say that a mechanism is *weakly individually rational* if it is individually rational for every member of the sample and generates a nonnegative transfer to the unsampled group.

Finally, the decision regarding participation, under either criterion, may depend on the individuals' beliefs regarding the statements made by other members of the sample. An interesting feature of the dominant strategy mechanisms in this regard is that the requirement of universal participation, independent of expectations, leads to a class of mechanisms defined by a set of functions $h_i(.)$ which are bounded below by the pivotal mechanism–which we found useful in section 6.2 in several contexts. Thus, if the government wants to minimize the total subsidies required by these procedures (or maximize the revenues they collect) then the pivotal mechanism should be selected within the class inducing universal participation. The pivotal mechanism would therefore have a very strong claim on our attention.

6.3.1. *Universal Participation*

Theorem 6.3.1

Let

$$h_i(w_{-i}) = \min(-\sum_{j+i} w_j, 0)$$

define the pivotal mechanism. Let

$$h'_i(\overline{w}_{-i}) < h_i(\overline{w}_{-i}) \text{ for some } w_{-i}$$

Then there exists $v_i \in R$ and expectations concerning $\overline{w}_{-i}$ such that an individual with these tastes and beliefs would refuse to participate if the mechanism were defined by $h'_i(.)$.

Proof

It suffices to consider $v_i = 0$, and expectations concentrated on $(\overline{w}_{-i})$. The expected payoff to such an individual will be

$$\sum_{j \neq i} w_{-j} + h'(\overline{w}_j) \qquad \text{if } \sum_{j \neq i} \overline{w}_j \geqslant 0$$

$$h'(\overline{w}_{-i}) \qquad \text{if } \sum_{j \neq i} \overline{w}_j < 0$$

Since $h'_i(\overline{w}_{-i}) < h_i(\overline{w}_{-i})$, we will have a negative quantity in either case, from the definition of $h_i(.)$. Hence the individual would be unambiguously worse off if he were to participate, as he would sustain a certain loss.

Thus any mechanism that gives lower transfers at any point than the pivotal mechanism will not necessarily induce universal participation.

We assume throughout this section that individuals are all risk-neutral. A mechanism induces participation by an individual, i, whose beliefs are given by $g(.)$, a distribution on $\overline{w}_{-i}$, only if the expected value of his payoff is nonnegative.

Theorem 6.3.2

For any distribution $g(.)$, an individual with $v_i = 0$ will choose to participate in the sampled group if and only if the mechanism would induce universal participation for any individual with these expectations.

Proof

The expected utility, given participation, can be written as:

$$\int_{\substack{\Sigma w_j = -v \\ j \neq i}}^{\substack{\Sigma w_j = \infty \\ j \neq i}} (v + \Sigma w_{-i})\, dg\,(w_{-i}) + \int_{-\infty}^{+\infty} h_i(w_{-i})\, dg\,(w_{-i})$$

Nonparticipation would induce the expected utility,

$$\int_{\substack{\Sigma w_i = 0 \\ j \neq i}}^{\substack{\Sigma w_j = 0 \\ j \neq i}} v_i\, dg\,(w_{-i})$$

The difference between them is, therefore,

$$\int_{\substack{\Sigma w_j = -v \\ j \neq i}}^{\substack{\Sigma w_j = \infty \\ j \neq i}} (v_i + \sum_{i \neq j} w_j)\, dg\,(w_{-i}) + \int_0^{+\infty} \sum_{j \neq i} w_j\, dg\,(w_{-i}) + \int_{-\infty}^{+\infty} h_i(w_{-i})\, dg\,(w_{-i})$$

Note that the first integral is nonnegative, whereas the second two are independent of v_i. Further, as $v_i \to 0$, the first integral converges to zero.

Therefore, if for some v_i the mechanism does not induce participation, then it will not induce participation by an individual whose $v_i = 0$. Moreover, if the second two integrals are nonnegative, then an individual for whom $v_i = 0$ will participate, and hence so will all individuals.

Corollary:

The set of all mechanisms that induce universal participation by all risk-neutral individuals is characterized by the set of all h_i (.) such that

$$h_i\,(w_{-i}) \geqslant \min\,(-\Sigma\, w_{-i}, 0)$$

Proof

For given expectations g (.), universal participation requires

$$\int_0^{\infty} \sum_{j \neq i} w_j\, dg\,(w_{-i}) + \int_{-\infty}^{+\infty} h\,(w_{-i})\, dg\,(w_{-i}) \geqslant 0$$

Since it must hold for any expectations g (.) it implies

$$h_i(w_{-i}) \geqslant \min\left(-\sum_{j\neq i} w_j, 0\right) \qquad Q.E.D.$$

6.3.2. Weak Individual Rationality

We have defined individual rationality to mean a welfare improvement for all members of the population as a result of using the mechanism. When a sample is taken, it is clear that this requirement can never be satisfied with certainty for individuals not in the sample. Some individuals can have a large, negative evaluation for the project while the sample can accept it. Therefore the best that can be hoped for is to have the nonsampled individuals receive a positive monetary transfer, albeit perhaps not enough to compensate them fully. It will be shown, however that even this more modest goal, is unattainable, if individual rationality for members of the sample is to be simultaneously insured. We demonstrate this in the following two theorems, which characterize the class of h functions required for the sampled and unsampled groups. It will then be shown that these are inconsistent.

Theorem 6.3.3

If h_i (.) are nonnegative for all i, then the mechanism is individually rational for the sampled group, and conversely.

Proof

If the project is rejected, $h_i \geqslant 0$ insures welfare improvement. If the project is accepted, individual i's change in welfare is

$$v_i + \sum_{j\neq i} w_j + h_i(w_{-i}) = \sum_j w_j + h_i(w_{-i})$$

Since $w_i = v_i$ by the dominant strategy property, and both terms are nonnegative.

If $h_i(\overline{w}_{-i}) < 0$ for some $\overline{w}_{-i}$, then letting

$$v_i = -\sum_{j\neq i} \overline{w}_j,$$

the project will be accepted ($\sum_j w_j = 0$) and the change in utility will be

$$v_i + \left(\sum_{j\neq i} \overline{w}_j\right) + h_i(\overline{w}_{-i}) = h_i(\overline{w}_{-i}) < 0.$$

Theorem 6.3.4

If

$$\iota_k (w_{-k}) \geqslant \min (-\sum_{j \neq k} w_j, 0) \text{ for all } k$$

and

$$h_i (\overline{w}_{-i}) > \min (-\sum_{j \neq i} \overline{w}_j, 0) \text{ for some } i \text{ and some } \overline{w}_{-i}$$

then there exists a number, $\hat{w}_i$, such that the sampled group will receive a positive subsidy if the statements are $(\overline{w}_1, \ldots, \overline{w}_{i-1}, \hat{w}_i, \overline{w}_{i+1}, \ldots, \overline{w}_N)$.

Proof

There are two cases according to the sign of $\sum_{j \neq i} \overline{w}_j$. If $\sum_{j \neq i} \overline{w}_j \geqslant 0$, take $\hat{w}_i$ large and positive. Then the transfer to i will be

$$\sum_{j \neq i} \overline{w}_j + h_i (\overline{w}_{-i}) > 0$$

By taking $\hat{w}_i$ sufficiently large, no other individual will be pivotal and hence no one else will have a negative transfer. Thus all transfers are nonnegative and their sum is strictly positive. The case of $\sum_{j \neq i} w_j < 0$ is handled analogously by taking $\hat{w}_i$ large and negative.

It may be, however, that we can have h functions above the pivotal one for some individuals while not for others and still maintain the nonnegativity of the transfer to the unsampled group in all situations.

However, if $h_i \geqslant 0$ is required for the individual rationality of the sampled group and $h_i \leqslant \min (-\sum_{j \neq i} w_j, 0)$ is required for positive transfer to the unsampled group, there is a clear contradiction as the two are incompatible wherever $\sum_{j \neq i} w_j > 0$. It is therefore impossible to maintain a weakly individually rational and incentive compatible mechanism under these definitions.

References

Bennett, E., and D. Conn, "The Group Incentive Properties of Mechanisms for the Provision of Public Goods," mimeo., 1976.

Clarke, E.H., "Multipart Pricing of Public Goods," *Public Choice*, 1971: 19-33.

Groves, T., "Incentives in Teams," *Econometrica*, 41 (1973):617-631.

Green, J., and J.J. Laffont, "On the Revelation of Preferences for Public Goods," Stanford Discussion Paper no. 140, 1974, to appear in *Journal of Public Economics.*

Green, J., and J.J. Laffont, "Characterization of Satisfactory Mechanisms for the Revelation of Preferences for Public Goods," *Econometrica*, 45 (1975): 427-438.

Green, J., and J.J. Laffont, "Uncertain Personal Information and the Demand Revealing Process: A Sampling Approach," to appear in *Public Choice*, 1976a.

Green, J., and J.J. Laffont, "Révelation des Préferences pour les Biens Publics: lère Partie: Caractérisation des Mécanismes Satisfaisants," Ecole Polytechnique, to appear in *Cahiers du Séminaire d'Econométrie*, 1976b.

Green, J., and J.J. Laffont, "Satisfactory Mechanisms for Environments with Consumption Lower Bounds." Unpublished manuscript. 1976c.

Green, J., and J.J. Laffont, "On Coalition Incentive Compatibility." Unpublished manuscript. 1976d.

Wickrey, W., "Counterspeculation, Auctions and Competitive Sealed Tenders," *Journal of Finance*, 16 (1961):8-37.

7 Equality, Complementarity and the Incidence of Public Expenditures

Michael Bruno

7.1. Introduction

Consider the observed distribution of a given type of public expenditure on private goods (such as education, health or development finance) and relate it to the associated distribution of income or wealth among individual receiving units. The implied regressivity or progressivity of expenditures is usually the result of two very different, and often conflicting, sets of forces, which cannot be read out of the data without further analysis. One is the technology that ties the public input together with some, often unobserved, individual attribute in the production of the observed income (or output). The other factor is the policy rule that explicitly or implicitly guides public decision-makers in the allocation of the given expenditure budget among different units. One helpful way is to think of the first set as a kind of reduced form production function, for each individual unit, while the second, policy rule, component can be represented as a social welfare function defined over the income distribution and characterizing the degree of importance society attaches to pure output efficiency or considerations of distributive justice.

If for some reason there is high complementarity between the government input and the individual endowment, even a potentially egalitarian policy may still bring about a regressive distributional outcome (e.g. education or investment finance). On the other hand pure output efficiency considerations may bring about an egalitarian outcome when there is high input substitutability (or negative interaction, as may be the case with health). The observed incidence of public expenditures can thus not be judged on welfare grounds without knowledge of the underlying component forces.

The starting point of this paper is the utilitarian approach outlined by Arrow (1971). The next section elaborates and extends that model for our present purpose. In section 7.3 it is shown how one could spell out the components of incidence in a quantifiable form that might, at least in principle, help one in interpreting positive distributional outcomes on the normative 'as if' assumption of optimum government behavior. Section 7.4 suggests a number of

Reprinted, with permission of North-Holland Publishing Company, from the *Journal of Public Economics*, vol. 6, November 1976, pp. 395-407. I am indebted to participants of the Conference and to two referees of the *Journal of Public Economics* for helpful comments on an earlier draft of this paper.

theoretical examples of input complementarity due to market imperfections (e.g. housing finance). The last section extends the model to include the effect of a progressive income tax and also considers the case of multiple government inputs.

7.2. Application of the Arrow Model

Assume a given distribution of economic units with density function $f(n)$, where $\int f(n)\,dn = 1$ and n stands for some measure of a given individual endowment. Next assume that for each unit the natural endowment (n) interacts with a government expenditure input (g) to form an objectively measurable income, wealth, or output (I), where

$$I = I(n, g), \tag{7.1}$$

and we assume positive marginal products[a] ($I_n > 0$, $I_g > 0$) and diminishing (or constant) marginal productivity of government expenditure ($I_{gg} \leqslant 0$). The case of $I_{gg} = 0$ is included in order to cover the case of a pure transfer (with no interaction) $I = b(n) + g$.

The government is assumed to allocate a given aggregate budget

$$\int g f(n)\,dn = \overline{G}, \tag{7.2}$$

among individuals so as to maximize an additive social welfare function defined over individual incomes (outputs):

$$W = \int U[I(n, g)]\, f(n)\,dn, \tag{7.3}$$

where the usual assumptions are made: $U' > 0$ and $U'' \leqslant 0$. The linear utility case ($U'' = 0$) is included here in order to consider the possibility of aggregate output maximization to which we shall subsequently refer as the 'pure efficiency' case. However, we shall not allow the simultaneous vanishing of I_{gg} and U''.

Constrained maximization of (7.3) subject to (7.2) leads to a form of the equal marginal benefit principle:

$$U_g = U' I_g = \text{constant}, \tag{7.4}$$

for all individuals n.

Before we proceed let us note that with some minor modifications this is

[a]One should in general think of equation (7.1) as the reduced form of a more detailed behavioral model (see section 7.4).

essentially the Arrow model. However, we have chosen to concentrate from the start on the case of an objectively measurable output I. This will help us articulate some of the implications for the present purpose. We also note that the function U need not be an individual utility level, but will be the implicit evaluation put on I by government (presumably from the point of view of society as a whole). U can, in principle, only be revealed from observation of resulting distributions. Next differentiate the optimality relationship (7.4) with respect to n. For the optimum allocation of g we find

$$\frac{\mathrm{d}g}{\mathrm{d}n} = \frac{U_{ng}}{-U_{gg}} = \frac{U'I_{ng} + U''I_nI_g}{-(U'I_{gg} + U''I_g^2)} = \frac{I_n}{aI_g}\left(\frac{1}{\rho}\right)\epsilon \qquad (7.5)$$

and

$$\frac{\mathrm{d}I}{\mathrm{d}n} = I_n + I_g\frac{\mathrm{d}g}{\mathrm{d}n} = U'\frac{(I_{ng}I_g - I_nI_{gg})}{-(U'I_{gg} + U''I_g^2)} = \frac{I_n}{aI_g}\left(\frac{I_g}{\rho} + \delta\right), \qquad (7.6)$$

where

$$\frac{1}{\rho} = I \cdot I_{ng}/I_nI_g,$$

$$\epsilon = -IU''/U' \geqslant 0,$$

$$\delta = -I \cdot I_{gg}/I_g > 0,$$

$$a = \delta/I_g + \epsilon > 0.$$

Equations (7.5) and (7.6) help to clarify the distinction between what is defined by Arrow as *input* progressivity (regressivity, equality) in terms of $\mathrm{d}g/\mathrm{d}n < (>, =) 0$ and what he calls *output* progressivity (regressivity, equality) in terms of $\mathrm{d}U/\mathrm{d}n = U'(\mathrm{d}I/\mathrm{d}n) < (>, =) 0$.[b]

First note that input regressivity (or equality) is a sufficient, though not necessary, condition for output regressivity.[c] As (7.6) shows, input regressivity ($\mathrm{d}g/\mathrm{d}n > 0$) always implies that the optimum distribution of public expenditure makes the final distribution of U (or I) in some sense less egalitarian than it would be in the absence of government intervention.[d]

[b]Note that the latter could also be defined in terms of $\mathrm{d}I/\mathrm{d}n$ which has the same sign as $\mathrm{d}U/\mathrm{d}n$. This will be used below.

[c]Cf. Arrow's proposition 3.

[d]This must here be represented by distributing the $\overline{G}$ equally among individuals, so that the initial reference point can be represented by $U'I_n$ (the slope U_n, holding g constant) and we have $U'(\mathrm{d}I/\mathrm{d}n) > U'I_n$.

Next note that the denominator of the right-hand side of the last equations in (7.5) and (7.6), respectively, is by assumption always positive.[e] Therefore the signs of dg/dn and dI/dn depend on the signs of the respective upper brackets only.

We can now proceed to study the implications in greater detail.

7.2.1. Input Progressivity

We have $dg/dn \gtreqless 0$ iff $1/\rho \gtreqless \epsilon$.

$\rho = I_n I_g / I \cdot I_{ng}$ is a measure of the degree of substitutability in production of I between the government input (g) and the endowed input (n). When $I(n, g)$ exhibits constant returns to scale in n and g, ρ is precisely the elasticity of substitution. Its reciprocal ($1/\rho$) is a measure of the degree of interaction of n and g. The more complementarity there is between the two inputs (or the more concavity in I), the lower is ρ and the higher is $1/\rho$. In the limit of fixed proportions we get $1/\rho \to \infty$. When there is zero interaction (the I isoquant is a straight line) $1/\rho = 0$. Note that here the interaction I_{ng} and therefore $1/\rho$ may be negative. $\epsilon = -IU''/U'$ measures the elasticity of the marginal utility schedule. Following Atkinson (1970) we can call it the parameter of 'relative inequality aversion.' The higher is ϵ the more concave is U and the more weight is put on an increase in the lower income groups. At the lower limit, when $\epsilon = 0$, only the total *sum* of I across the population matters. This case, therefore, corresponds to what one might call *pure efficiency*. At the upper extreme, letting $\epsilon \to \infty$, we get the *maximin* policy. In that case maximizing the lowest income bracket is the only thing that matters. In general one would expect ϵ to be somewhere between. We can summarize in the form of a proposition.

Proposition 1. The optimum policy is input progressive, input equal or input regressive according to whether $1/\rho < \epsilon, = \epsilon, or > \epsilon$.

This clarifies the separate role of the 'technological' and the welfare parameters in determining input progressivity (regressivity).[f]

We note two special cases.

(1) When there is negative input interaction $I_{ng} < 0$ $(1/\rho < 0)$ we get input progressivity no matter what the welfare objective is. Qualitatively (though not quantitatively) there will thus be no contradiction between efficiency

[e] This is one place where the nonvanishing of either I_{gg} or U'' plays an important role. It is of course, a reflection of the second-order condition for a maximum.

[f] Arrow's general proposition 1 ($U_{ng} \lesseqgtr 0$) of necessity hides the workings of the two separate components. Also note that unlike Arrow's proposition 6, which covers the case of an objectively measurable output, one does not have to assume additive separability in production.

and equity considerations. The same statement also applies to the limiting case of zero interaction $[I = b_1(n) + b_2(g)$, say)]. In this case $\epsilon = 0$ implies input equality.

(2) When there is complementarity or positive input interaction $(1/\rho > 0)$, which is the case in education and several other items of public expenditure (see below), pure efficiency $(\epsilon = 0)$ will always lead to input regressivity. Only a sufficiently high egalitarian objective may bring about input progressivity (or equality).[g]

7.2.2. *Output Progressivity*

From (7.6) we find that dI/dn, $dU/dn \gtreqless 0$ iff $I_{ng}I_g - I_nI_{gg} \gtreqless$ or iff $I_g/\rho + \delta \gtreqless 0$. An interesting aspect is the implication that output progressivity (regressivity) unlike input progressivity is independent of the form of the welfare maximand and depends only on the production relation.[h] This can be summarized in the following proposition.

Proposition 2. The policy will be output progressive, regressive, or equal according to whether I_{ng} is less than, greater than, or equal to I_nI_{gg}/I_g, which itself is nonpositive. This condition is independent of the properties of the welfare maximand as long as ϵ is finite.

Again let us mention two special implications.

(1) If the marginal product of government expenditure is constant $(I_{gg} = 0)$ output progressivity (regressivity) simply depends on the sign of interaction I_{ng} being negative (positive).
(2) If the interaction I_{ng} is positive one can never achieve full output equality (except in the extreme maximin case),[i] let alone output progressivity. For the latter, $I_{ng} < 0$ is a necessary (but not sufficient)[j] condition.

7.3. The Incidence of Government Expenditure

The above discussion may be of theoretical interest but need not, as it stands,

---

[g]E.g. if as in Becker (1964) $I = nI^0(S)$, where S = years of schooling, n is ability, and say $g = C(S)$, then $\rho = 1$ and we require $\epsilon > 1$. There is empirical evidence that ρ may in fact be considerably less than 1. Also note from (7.5) and (7.6) that as we let $\epsilon \to \infty$ we get $dg/dn \to -I_n/I_g < 0$ always. In the case $\epsilon \to 0$, $dg/dn \to I_{ng}/-I_{gg} \lesseqgtr 0$, according to whether $I_{ng} \lesseqgtr 0$

[h]Note that this is the same as input-normality or inferiority in production.

[i]In that case the denominator in (7.6) goes to infinity.

[j]Arrow's statement (p. 415) that for health we would expect output progressivity to be the norm thus has to be qualified.

lead to any empirically quantifiable results. Neither of the two progressivity (regressivity) concepts, as here defined, are necessarily observable in practice. What *may*, in principle, be observable and is often measured, with little theroetical foundation, is the degree of progressivity of public expenditures with respect to objectively measurable income. One can measure something like dg/dI or, in elasticity form, $\phi = I\ dg/g\ dI$. Call ϕ the incidence elasticity of public expenditure.[k]

Let us now take a somewhat heroic, though not rare, mental step. Suppose that the government (or society) could be attributed an underlying optimum behavior whose exact welfare parameter (ϵ) we do not know *a priori*, and suppose that there is an underlying production relationship $I(g, n)$ whose properties we can measure. What kind of ϵ–ρ interpretation could one give to an observed distributional outcome ϕ?

Going back to the analysis of the previous section we can divide equation (7.5) by equation (7.6) to get

$$\phi = \frac{I\ dg}{g\ dI} = \frac{1 - \epsilon\rho}{\alpha + \beta\rho}, \tag{7.7}$$

where $\beta = -gI_{gg}/I_g = \delta g/I$ and α = 'share' of g (or output elasticity of g) = $gI_g/I > 0$. In (7.7) all parameters with the exception of ϵ are in principle observable. In the special case in which $I(n, g)$ is homogeneous of degree γ in n and g we can replace the two parameters α and β in (7.7) by one (γ) since then $\alpha + \beta\rho = \rho + \gamma(1 - \rho)$.[l] We also obtain two special subcases: (a) if I is linearly homogeneous,

$$(\gamma = 1),$$

$$\phi = 1 - \epsilon\rho; \tag{7.7a}$$

and (b) if I is Cobb-Douglas of *any* degree of homogeneity ($\rho = 1$),[m]

$$\phi = 1 - \epsilon. \tag{7.7b}$$

Equation (7.7a) shows that in the constant-returns case the condition for input progressivity (regressivity, equality) is identical with $\phi < (>, =) 0$ and (7.7b) shows that under a Cobb-Douglas function this condition is in turn identical with $\epsilon > (<, =) 1$. Equations (7.7)-(7.7b) illustrate the kind of bias that may be involved in trying to read policy objectives into measured values of ϕ

---

[k]This is analogous to the concept of liability progression employed in taxation theory [see Musgrave and Thin (1948)].

[l]This follows from differentiating $gI_g + nI_n = \gamma I$ and substituting. We here assume $\rho > 0$.

[m]See note g above.

without recourse to the production constraint. Using any of these equations one could in principle estimate the implied value of ϵ for given observations on ϕ and independent estimates of the production parameters,

$$\epsilon = \frac{1 - \phi(\alpha + \beta\rho)}{\rho} = \frac{1 - \phi\gamma}{\rho} + \phi(\gamma - 1). \tag{7.8}$$

Probably the most widely mentioned example in this area is that of education. In principle, the source for the estimate of a production relation can be obtained from cross-section studies of income differences by ability and schooling (S). If, in addition, one knows the relationship between government expenditure (g) and the level of schooling (S) equation (7.1) can be written in the form[n] $I = I[n, S(g)]$, from which one obtains a modified expression for ϕ,

$$\phi = \frac{(1 - \epsilon\rho_s)\eta_1}{\alpha_s + \beta_s\rho_s + \rho_s\eta_2}. \tag{7.9}$$

Here ρ_s, α_s, β_s are the parameters of the production function, with S instead of g. η_1 is elasticity of g with respect to S and η_2 is the elasticity of g_s with respect to S. As a very rough illustration of possible orders of magnitude, consider the following example. Empirical estimates point to ρ_s values of between 0.2 and 0.4. Using rough data for the distribution of human capital among Israeli men one gets $\phi \simeq 0.7$ and η_1 between 2 and 3½. If the denominator in (7.9) is approximately unity, one gets an implied range for ϵ between 1½ and 4.

7.4. Examples of Positive Interaction between *g* and *n*

The discussion makes it clear that a crucial element in the possible regressivity of public expenditures is the existence of positive interaction (complementarity) between government expenditures and individual endowment n ($I_{ng} > 0$). For the case of education this is in the nature of the underlying production relation. We here mention additional examples where such interaction may come about as a result of various imperfections in the system.

In reality even the seemingly simplest system of welfare transfers may have that property. For example, suppose individuals differ in their access to information about pure transfers or in the government's ability to get transfers to them through the bureaucratic system. A way of representing such a

[n]This should be regarded only as a rough illustration. A more rigorous approach is to look at the reduced form as the outcome of a more detailed behavioral model.

Another paper of mine (1974) uses a life-cycle model for individual choice of S given the educational cost function and government tuition fee policy, to look at the implied optimal distribution of S and lifetime wealth across a cohort of individuals of varying ability (n).

constraint is to distinguish between the cost of the transfer at the government source (g) and the net transfer actually obtained by individuals ($\bar{g}$). Suppose the ability to earn income is correlated with the ability to gain access to transfers. We can write: $I = b(n) + \bar{g}(g, n)$, where $I_n = b_n + \bar{g}_n > 0$, $I_g = \bar{g}_g > 0$, and $I_{ng} = \bar{g}_{gn} > 0$. This would satisfy the conditions of the previous analysis and lead to a distribution of g that will not be fully progressive and may even become regressive if government objectives are not sufficiently egalitarian (i.e. if ϵ is not sufficiently high), and may even become regressive.

Two additional examples can be suggested based on the existence of imperfections in the capital market. Consider the partial public financing of private housing purchases (very common in Israel). Suppose each individual can use his fixed income (or wealth) $I(n)$ to buy consumer goods (C) or pay the cost of finance (R) for the purchase of his house (H), where $H = k + g$ and k = private borrowing or mortgage, g = government mortgage or grant, and costs are given by $R = R(k, g)$ with $R_k > R_g \geqslant 0$, $R_{kk} > 0$, and $R_{kg} < 0$. The last two assumptions reflect rising marginal cost for private borrowing and increasing risk to the lender when there is less complementary public financing available.

The individual is assumed to maximize utility $V(C, H)$ subject to the budget constraint $C + R(k, g) = I(n)$. The first-order condition, for any g, gives

$$V_c(C, k+g) \cdot R_k(k, g) = V_H(C, k+g). \tag{7.10}$$

Consider now the utility level (V) as a function of the two variables n (determining I) and g. We have $V_n = I_n V_C > 0$, $V_g = (R_k - R_g)V_C > 0$. To apply the above framework we have to work out the cross derivative V_{ng}. This is given by

$$V_{ng} = I_n \frac{\mathrm{d}(V_C)}{\mathrm{d}g} = I_n \left[V_{CC} \frac{\mathrm{d}C}{\mathrm{d}g} + V_{CH} \frac{\mathrm{d}H}{\mathrm{d}g} \right],$$

where

$$\frac{\mathrm{d}C}{\mathrm{d}g} = -\frac{\mathrm{d}R}{\mathrm{d}g} = -\left(R_k \frac{\mathrm{d}k}{\mathrm{d}g} + R_g \right),$$

$$\frac{\mathrm{d}H}{\mathrm{d}g} = \frac{\mathrm{d}k}{\mathrm{d}g} + 1 ,$$

and $\mathrm{d}k/\mathrm{d}g$ can be obtained by differentiating (7.10) totally with respect to g. We get:

$$\frac{\mathrm{d}H}{\mathrm{d}g} = \frac{1}{A} [(V_{CH} - R_k V_{CC})(R_k - R_g) + V_C(R_{kk} - R_{kg})],$$

$$\frac{dC}{dg} = \frac{1}{A}[(R_k V_{CH} - V_{HH})(R_k - R_g) - V_C(R_{kk}R_g - R_{kg}R_k)],$$

$$V_{ng} = \frac{I_n}{A}\{(V_{CH}^2 - V_{CC}V_{HH})(R_k - R_g) + V_C[V_{CH}(R_{kk} - R_{kg})$$

$$- V_{CC}(R_{kk}R_g - R_{kg}R_k)]\}\ , \tag{7.11}$$

where $A = -R_k^2 V_{CC} + 2R_k V_{CH} - V_{HH} + V_C R_{kk}$ and $A > 0$ from the usual concavity assumption on V.

Assuming that $V_{CH} > 0$ (housing and ordinary consumption are complementary goods) we have $dH/dg > 0$, while dC/dg may be positive or negative depending on the magnitude of the second derivatives of R. From equation (7.11) we can see that the expression multiplying V_C inside the square brackets will be positive while the first term is negative since $(V_{CH}^2 - V_{CC}V_{HH}) \leqslant 0$. Thus V_{ng} may in principle take any sign. However, if R_{kk} and $-R_{kg}$ are sufficiently large (or if $|V_{CH}^2 - V_{CC} - V_{HH}|$ is sufficiently small) we get $V_{ng} > 0$. In fact, one intuitively plausible sufficient condition for $V_{ng} > 0$ is $(R_{kg}V_C - V_{HH}) < 0$. Since $V_C = V_H/R_k$, this condition is satisfied if $\partial(\log R_k)/\partial g < \partial(\log V_H)/\partial H$, i.e. if the marginal cost of private borrowing falls more rapidly (with g) than the marginal utility of housing.

If the allocation of g is done on the basis of an additive welfare function (7.3) with $U = U(V)$ we can apply the previous framework, substituting V for I. With $V_{ng} > 0$ government housing policy may turn out regressive, as it often does in practice (again, assuming ϵ is not high enough).

A very similar phenomenon can be shown to occur in the case in which government allocates investment funds to individual family farms in a developing country or an international agency allocates foreign aid to individual countries. Suppose economic units produce output (Y) with the aid of a given fixed factor (N)[o] and capital K which can be borrowed at a cost $R(k, g)$. $K = k + g$ and R has the same properties as in the previous example. For each producing unit in equilibrium, $F_K(k + g, N) = R_k(k, g)$, where $Y = F(K, N)$ is the production function. We find

$$Y_{Ng} = F_{NK}\left(\frac{dk}{dg} + 1\right) = F_{NK}\left[\frac{R_{kk} - R_{kg}}{R_{kk} - F_{KK}}\right], \tag{7.12}$$

$Y_{Ng} \gtreqless 0$ iff $F_{NK} \gtreqless 0$ and the analysis proceeds as before, for $U = U(Y)$.

---

[o]N may be regarded as an aggregate index of natural resources or skills, etc., differentially distributed among units.

7.5. Multiple Tools

So far we have assumed, as in Arrow (1971), that there is only one input, i.e. one redistributive tool for which optimality is sought. Such an approach could be rationalized on the basis of what Tobin (1970) has called specific egalitarianism (i.e. 'equal education,' 'equal housing,' etc.). We accordingly consider two possible modifications in the analysis when there are supplementary or alternative redistributive tools available. First consider the effect of a progressive income tax. Later we discuss the case where there is more than one government input.[p]

Consider the model of section 7.2 modified to have disposable income equal to $I - T(I)$. $T(I)$ is a tax function satisfying $I > T' > 0$, $T'' \geqslant 0$. The government budget constraint (7.2) now becomes $\int [g - T(I)] f(n) \, \mathrm{d}n = \overline{G}$, and the equilibrium condition becomes

$$U' \frac{I_g(1 - T')}{1 - T'I_g} = \text{constant for all } n \, . \tag{7.13}$$

Repeating the analysis as before, one now obtains

$$\frac{\mathrm{d}g}{\mathrm{d}n} = \frac{1}{B}\left[\frac{1}{\rho} - (d + \epsilon)\right] , \tag{7.14}$$

where

$$B = \frac{I_g}{I_n}(d + \epsilon) - \frac{I \cdot I_{gg}}{I_n I_g (1 - T'I_g)} > 0 \, ,$$

and

$$d = \frac{IT''(1 - I_g)}{(1 - T')(1 - T'I_g)} \geqslant 0, \qquad (\text{assuming } I_g \leqslant 1).$$

The expression d is proportional to marginal tax progressivity (T'').

Comparing equation (7.14) with (7.5) we see that it is almost the same, with $(d + \epsilon)$ replacing ϵ. For a given ϵ the introduction of a progressive income tax makes for greater input progressivity (less regressivity) than otherwise. Alternatively we can say that d and ϵ act like substitutes. For output progressivity we now have $\mathrm{d}I/\mathrm{d}n \gtreqless 0$ iff $I_{ng} I_g - I_n I_{gg}/(1 - T'I_g) \gtreqless 0$, which is almost the same condition as before, and for the incidence elasticity (ϕ) we get [cf. (7.7)]

[p]Green and Sheshinski (1975) have produced an argument for greater regressivity when there is a by-product in the form of a public good.

$$\phi = \frac{I}{g}\frac{\mathrm{d}g}{\mathrm{d}I} = \frac{1-(d+\epsilon)\rho}{\alpha + \beta\rho/(1-T'I_g)}\,. \tag{7.15}$$

A given observed value of ϕ is thus consistent with a less egalitarian ϵ policy than in the absence of an income tax.[q]

Note that this analysis assumes that all of the income tax increment (or reduction) resulting from the particular government expenditure is earmarked for the finance of that expenditure item. Also we have ignored possible repercussions of the tax structure on the level of I.

Consider now the case of a policy package of two different inputs, g_1 and g_2, for which optimality is sought. We now assume[r] $I = I(g_1, g_2; n)$. Denote the derivatives with respect to the g's by index 1 and 2 respectively, and assume that

$$I_1 > 0, \quad I_2 > 0, \quad I_{12} \geqslant 0,^{s} \quad I_{11} \leqslant 0, \quad I_{22} \leqslant 0,$$

$$I_{11}I_{22} - I_{12}^2 \geqslant 0 \text{ (convexity).}$$

The government budget constraint now becomes $\int (g_1 + g_2) f(n)\,\mathrm{d}n = \overline{G}$, and the optimality condition becomes $U'I_1 = U'I_2 = \lambda = \text{constant}$ (and thus also $I_1 = I_2$). Differentiating totally by n, we obtain two equations for two derivatives, $\mathrm{d}g_1/\mathrm{d}n$ and $\mathrm{d}g_2/\mathrm{d}n$, which solve out to give for $\mathrm{d}g_1/\mathrm{d}n$,

$$\frac{\mathrm{d}g_1}{\mathrm{d}n} = \frac{1}{D}\left\{\frac{I_n}{I_1}\left[I_{22}\left(\epsilon - \frac{1}{\rho_1}\right) - I_{12}\left(\epsilon - \frac{1}{\rho_2}\right)\right] + (I_{n1} - I_{n2})\epsilon\right\}, \tag{7.16}$$

where

$$1/\rho_i = \frac{I \cdot I_{in}}{I_i I_n}, \qquad (i = 1, 2),$$

and

$$D = (-I_{11} - I_{22} + 2I_{12})\epsilon + \frac{I}{I_1}(I_{11}I_{22} - I_{12}^2) > 0.$$

Similarly, for the joint effect of g_1 and g_2 we get

---

[q]The factor d can be written in the form $d = \theta T'c$, where θ = elasticity of marginal tax schedule and $c = (1 - I_g)/(1 - T')(1 - T'I_g)$. For realistic orders of magnitude $\theta \simeq ½$, $T' \simeq ½$, and $c \simeq 1$, we get $d \lesssim ¼$.

[r]Consider n here to be a kind of composite index. The possibility of having different indexes of initial endowment (e.g. for health and education) is mentioned at the end of the paper.

[s]A positive I_{12} would imply that g_1 and g_2 are complementary inputs (e.g. housing and education or health and education).

$$\frac{d(g_1+g_2)}{dn}=\frac{I_n}{I_1 D}\left[(I_{22}-I_{12})\left(\epsilon-\frac{1}{\rho_1}\right)+(I_{11}-I_{12})\left(\epsilon-\frac{1}{\rho_2}\right)\right]. \quad (7.17)$$

Thus we have joint input-progressivity (regressivity) if ϵ is greater (smaller) than both $1/\rho_i (i=1, 2)$. On the other hand, as (7.16) shows, $\epsilon > 1/\rho_i$ is not a sufficient condition for each dg_i/dn to be negative. This, as could be expected, depends on whether $I_{n1} \lesseqgtr I_{n2}$. When the interaction between g_1 and n is greater than that between g_2 and n it pays to have g_1 less progressive (or more regressive) than otherwise, and conversely for g_2. Also, *ceteris paribus*, for the case $\epsilon > 1/\rho_1$, if I_2 is less steep, g_1 becomes more regressive.

The extreme polar case can be represented by having g_2 stand for a pure lump-sum transfer (or tax) so that I can be written in the form $I = I^0(g_1, n) + g_2$ (also allowing g_2 to be negative); in that case $I_2 = 1$ and $I_{12} = I_{22} = I_{2n} = 0$. In equation (7.16) above we get $dg_1/dn = -I_{1n}I_1/I_{11}I_n > 0$, which is the same as the regressive pure efficiency case, obtained from equation (7.5) by setting $\epsilon = 0$. Obviously if specific egalitarianism were not required and there existed a first-best redistributive device, there would be no need to impose a less than purely efficient allocation for g_1.

Next we have

$$\frac{dI}{dn}=I_n+I_1 d(g_1+g_2)/dn$$

$$=\frac{I_n}{D}\left[\frac{1}{\rho_1}(I_{12}-I_{22})+\frac{1}{\rho_2}(I_{12}-I_{11})+\frac{1}{I_1^2}(I_{11}I_{22}-I_{12}^2)\right].$$

Here too the sign of dI/dn is independent of the utility function (cf. section 7.2) and there is output regressivity if both I_{1n} and I_{2n} are positive. For the total incidence elasticity ϕ, we have

$$\phi=\frac{I}{(g_1+g_2)}\frac{d(g_1+g_2)}{dI}$$

$$=\frac{1}{\alpha}\frac{(I_{12}-I_{22})\left(\frac{1}{\rho_1}-\epsilon\right)+(I_{12}-I_{11})\left(\frac{1}{\rho_2}-\epsilon\right)}{(I_{12}-I_{22})\frac{1}{\rho_1}+(I_{12}-I_{11})\frac{1}{\rho_2}+\frac{I}{I_1^2}(I_{11}I_{12}-I_{12}^2)}$$

where $\alpha = (g_1 I_1 + g_2 I_2)/I$ = total 'share' of g_1 and $g_2 (I_1 = I_2)$. Again one can write ϵ as a function only of observable parameters.

The model could in principle be generalized to include any number of g_i. Using matrix notation it can be shown that

$$G_n = - U_{GG}^{-1} U_{Gn} = (\epsilon E - H)^{-1} \left(\frac{I_n}{I_1} \right) (h - \epsilon e) , \tag{7.18}$$

where:

$G_n = m \times 1$ column vector of dg_i/dn $(i = 1, 2, \ldots, m)$,

$U_{GG} = m \times m$ matrix of $U_{g_i g_j}$ and $U_{Gn} = (m \times 1)$ vector of $U_{g_i n}$,

$H = m \times m$ matrix of $1/\rho_{ij} = I \cdot I_{ij}/I_i I_j$ (and $I_i = I_j$ for all i, j).

$h = m \times 1$ vector of $1/\rho_i = I \cdot I_{in}/I_i I_n$,

$E = m \times m$ matrix of 1's,

$e = m \times 1$ vector of 1's,

ϵ, I_1, I_n are scalars defined as before.

Although the structure of (7.18) looks very simple, being a linear combination of factors $(1/\rho_i - \epsilon)$ (compare the cases $m = 1, 2$), it does not lend itself to any general statements on signs for the case $m > 2$. The inverse matrices $-U_{GG}^{-1}$ or $(\epsilon E - H)^{-1}$ need not in general be positive.

The very special case in which all off-diagonal elements in U_{GG} are nonnegative (leading to $-U_{GG}^{-1} > 0$), and U_{Gn} a nonnegative or nonpositive vector, leads to G_n being unambiguously nonnegative or nonpositive. This, however, requires that all g_i interact positively with each other to the extent that $1/\rho_{ij} \geqslant \epsilon$ for all $i \neq j$ (say we have an interdependent education, health, and housing program), and in addition all terms $(1/\rho_i - \epsilon)$ are of the same sign (for all i). Output progressivity is here measured by

$$\frac{dI}{dn} = I_1 e' G_n,$$

where e' is a row-vector of 1's. Finally, equation (7.18) can be further generalized to the case in which natural endowments appear as a vector $N(n_1, \ldots, n_R)$ instead of one scalar n. We then write $G_N = - U_{GG}^{-1} U_{GN}$, where G_N and U_{GN} become $(m \times k)$ matrices. Output progressivity must now be defined w.r.t. to each n_j separately—i.e. a vector $I_1 e' G_N$.

References

Arrow, K., "A Utilitarian Approach to Equality in Public Expenditures," *Quarterly Journal of Economics* 85, no. 3 (1971):409-415.

Atkinson, Anthony B., "On the Measurement of Inequality," *Journal of Economic Theory* 2 (1970):244-263.

Becker, Gary S., "Human Capital: A Theoretical and Empirical Analysis, with Special Reference to Education," *National Bureau of Economic Research General Series No. 80* New York: Columbia University Press, 1964.

Bruno, Michael, "Efficiency and Equity in Public Education Expenditures," *Falk Institute Discussion Paper 744*, forthcoming in IEA volume on the Economics of public services, M. Feldstein, ed.

Green, J.R., and E. Sheshinski, "A Note on the Progressivity of Optimal Public Expenditures," *Quarterly Journal of Economics*, Feb. 1975.

Musgrave, R.A., and T. Thin, "Income Tax Progression, 1929-48," *The Journal of Political Economy* 56 (1948):498-514.

Tobin, J. "On Limiting the Domain of Inequality," *Journal of Law and Economics* 13 (Oct. 1970).

8 Inequality as a Public Good: Unambiguous Redistribution and Optimality

Ephraim Kleiman

8.1. Introduction

The notion that some income redistribution may be Pareto-optimal has attracted considerable interest in recent years. But most of the literature on the subject has treated the redistribution effected by each individual as if it were independent of the behavior of all others (e.g., Hochman and Rodgers, 1969). This approach may be correct if we consider redistribution to be motivated by egalitarian sentiments which are *individual specific* (to parallel the *good specific* ones of Tobin, 1970). It is not applicable, however, to the case of redistribution motivated by attitudes towards equality "in the general." A single individual's contribution, however large in terms of his own income, may be too small to make any (to him) significant impact on overall inequality. Because of this (and ultimately to prevent free rides), he may make his contribution conditional on the participation of other members of the community. And, in fact, in the real world redistribution is not left to individual decisions, but is enforced through universally applied tax schemes. Yet this should not be taken to indicate that the resultant redistribution necessarily reduces the welfare of those individuals who pay a positive redistributive tax. On the contrary, as will be shown here, the amount which they are taxed may reflect their own preferences. The voluntary-redistribution literature assumed a certain behavior, derived from the utility function of individuals, and concerned itself with the overall redistributive pattern resulting from their unconcerted actions. In this chapter we invert the question. We take the overall redistributive pattern as given and ask how far an optimizing individual would wish to see it applied.

If individuals are "socially conscious," the degree of overall inequality enters directly into their utility function (Kolm 1969, Thurow, 1971). But inequality is a public good of a very special type: it is public in its consumption, because the degree of it prevailing at any given moment of time is the same for all members of society; but its production also generates externalities, in that it determines their individual incomes (Ng, 1973). In other words, when voting on a certain redistributive scheme, the individual is also voting on his own income.

The work on this paper was done during my stay at the Institute for International Economic Studies of the University of Stockholm. I wish to thank Jan Herin and Brian Hindley for, to me very fruitful, discussions; Reuben Gronau, Joram Mayshar, and Shlomo Yitzhaki for helpful comments on an earlier draft; and Uri Shainook for the programming of Figure 8-1.

Though the last-mentioned relationship is quite obvious, it does not, to my knowledge, appear to have been discussed in the literature.

An individual's reaction to changes in income inequality may thus be expected to vary with the way in which they affect his income, as well as with his taste for inequality in the general. And the former is determined not only by the extent of the change and by the individual's ordering in the income array, but also by the pattern of redistribution. To investigate the relationship between inequality and individual incomes, we will postulate a redistributive pattern consistent with the accepted definition of unambiguous changes in inequality. This will enable us to derive the income-inequality transformation functions for such changes, showing what they imply for the income of any individual. Assuming the individual to derive some positive utility from a reduction in inequality, we may then determine the degree of inequality which he will regard as optimal: that which equalizes his marginal rates of substitution of income for inequality in, so to say, its production and its consumption (compare Scott, 1972). Finally, we will examine how optimum inequality varies with income and, in particular, whether the optima of different individuals can coincide to yield a redistributive consensus.

8.2. Unambiguous, Gradual General Redistribution

We wish to discuss a redistribution pattern which fulfills the following conditions:

(i) It results in unambiguous changes in inequality.
(ii) It is general, affecting income differentials between all individuals.
(iii) It is not "revolutionary," preserving the individuals' ranking in the income array.

For condition (i) to be met irrespective of the utility function implied, the Lorenz curves corresponding to the different income distributions yielded by successive redistributions should not intersect (Dalton, 1920, Atkinson, 1971). This can also satisfy (ii) and (iii). Finally, to conform with reality, we also require that:

(iv) All the resulting income distributions should be positively skewed. Conveniently, a set of distributions yielding nonintersecting Lorenz curves can be generated by varying the parameters of any initial log-normal income distribution (Hart and Prais, 1956, Aitchison and Brown, 1957). There is, of course, no guarantee that redistribution will indeed preserve log-normality, but it seems to have generally done so. Both on the strength of the empirically established relationship and for the sake of convenience, we will, therefore, postulate the preservation of log-normality to be a characteristic of the redistribution scheme considered here. Alternative assumptions would, of course, yield different results.

Let the initial income distribution be such that the income logarithms are distributed normally, with a mean μ and a variance σ^2. An individual's position in the income array is given by λ, his "distance," in terms of σ, from μ. ($\lambda \gtreqless 0$ according to whether the individual is situated above or below the median.) His income is then:

$$y = e^{\mu + \lambda\sigma} \tag{8.1}$$

Both the Lorenz index and the Gini coefficient vary monotonically with σ (Aitchison and Brown, 1957). We may, therefore, identify changes in σ with changes in inequality. The mean income is

$$\bar{y} = e^{\mu + \sigma^2/2} \tag{8.2}$$

As we wish to consider changes in inequality only, we are restricted to those redistributions which allow the sum of the exponents in (8.2) to remain constant, so that

$$\mu + \tfrac{1}{2}\sigma^2 = c \tag{8.3}$$

Substituting from (8.3) into (8.1), we obtain

$$y = e^{c + \lambda\sigma - \sigma^2/2} \tag{8.4}$$

And the change in the individual's income with inequality, national income being kept constant, is then

$$\frac{\partial y}{\partial \sigma} = y(\lambda - \sigma) \tag{8.5}$$

Clearly, when $\lambda \leqslant 0$, this is negative for all values of σ. Starting from perfect equality, $\sigma = 0$, an increase in inequality reduces the incomes of the median-and-below individuals. For all above-median individuals, income will rise with inequality until $\sigma = \lambda$. But with inequality increasing beyond this point, the growing concentration of income in fewer and fewer hands requires more and more of the above-median ones also to fall. Thus, for each such individual there exists some value of σ at which both increases and decreases in inequality reduce his income:

$$\sigma_{\max y} = \lambda \tag{8.6}$$

Differentiating (8.5) again with respect to σ, we have

$$\frac{\partial^2 y}{\partial \sigma^2} = y[(\lambda - \sigma)^2 - 1] \tag{8.7}$$

This is negative or positive as, respectively, $|\lambda - \sigma|$ is smaller or greater than 1.[a]

The relationship between y and σ are illustrated in figure 8-1 for some selected values of λ.[b] The outstanding feature of the redistributive system described here is that, as far as above-median individuals are concerned, unambiguous changes in inequality do not affect income monotonically. Redistribution is commonly regarded as a movement from the "rich" to the "poor" or vice versa. However, under the conditions assumed here, the definition of "poor" and "rich," both in terms of income and in those of ranking, varies with inequality. Median-and-below individuals (those with $\lambda \leqslant 0$) are "poor" throughout. But the above-median ones (those with $\lambda \geqslant 0$) turn from "poor" into "rich" as inequality falls. The distribution being normal in its logarithms, values of λ can be translated into quantiles according to the ordinates of the normal curve corresponding to them. At $\sigma = 4$, all but 1 percent of the population (those with $\lambda > 4$) are "poor," in the sense that a decline in σ will increase their income. But

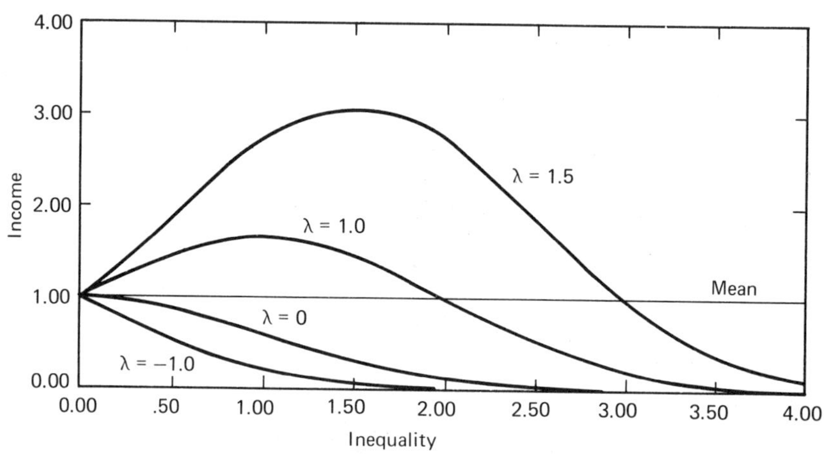

Figure 8-1. Relationship Between y and σ for various values of λ.

---

[a]We may note here that both (8.5) and (8.7) will be positive for $\lambda > \sigma + 1$. As $\sigma \geqslant 0$, this means that for any individual with $\lambda > 1$, there will be some segment of the trade-off curve of Figure 8-1 where the (positive) slope will be increasing, before it starts to decrease. See also below, in section 3.

[b]The diagram has been drawn for $c = 0$, so that $\bar{y} = 1$.

as income becomes more equally distributed they successively become "rich," that is, fall into the category of those from whom income is taken, so that at, say, $\sigma = 1$, nearly 16 percent of the population may be regarded as "rich." In other words, in the case of the above-median individuals ($\lambda > 0$), there is no one-to-one correspondence between σ and y: any one level of income, within the range $\bar{y} \leqslant y \leqslant y_{max}$, can be obtained at two different values of σ.

Inequality is sometimes implied to be reduced when income is transferred from above to below the median or the mean. We have seen the former to be only a necessary condition for general equalization, which requires transfers within the upper half of the population as well (and, depending on σ, may require also transfers within much higher quantiles). Figure 8-1 shows the same to be true of the mean: a reduction in σ may leave some above-mean income unchanged, and *raise* those between it and the mean. The basic concept, identifying equalization with movements around some pivotal individual whose income remains unaffected, is still correct. But neither the identity of this pivotal individual, nor the level of his income, are constant. More precisely, the roots of exponential in (8.4) are

$$\sigma = \lambda \pm (\lambda^2 + 2c)^{1/2} \tag{8.8}$$

This shows the trade-off curves of figure 8-1 to be symmetric around $\sigma = \lambda$. An individual will constitute the redistribution pivot only for transitions between the degrees of inequality which are equidistant from the one maximizing his income.[c] The transition between any two given values of σ can, thus, be defined in terms of the array position of the pivotal individual. As these positions can be translated into ordinates of the normal curve, we may prefer to speak of the quartile affected. Thus, for example, the transition from $\sigma = 1.0$ to $\sigma = 0.34$ requires transfers from all members of the upper quartile to the rest, while that to $\sigma = 0.68$ requires transfers from members of the upper quintile only.

From (8.8) we know also that for an individual to receive the mean income requires $\sigma = 2\lambda$. As the trade-off curves are symmetric around $\sigma = \lambda$, it follows, therefore, that the mean will constitute the pivotal income only in transitions from any existing σ to perfect equality. For any equalization stopping short of $\sigma = 0$, the pivotal income will exceed the mean one. A purely redistributive tax scheme, if it is to reduce inequality unambiguously, would therefore require that mean-income individuals receive a negative income tax!

8.3. Inequality Aversion and Optimality

Under the conditions postulated here, there exists for each individual some degree of inequality, $\sigma > \lambda$, at which a decrease in it will raise his welfare by

[c]As $\sigma \geqslant 0$, then, strictly speaking, a given individual can constitute the pivot only for redistributions from $\sigma \leqslant 2\lambda$ downwards; and at a given value of σ, an individual can constitute a pivot only if $\sigma \geqslant \lambda/2$.

increasing his income. But an individual may also derive a positive utility from a reduction of inequality directly, because of his benevolent attitude towards some other individuals (kinsmen, neighbors, the physically or mentally handicapped, etc.). He may also do so because it fits his image of the "good society": He may be averse so to say, to inequality "in the general"—reflecting "an aesthetic taste for equality . . . similar in nature to a taste in painting" (Thurow, 1971). In the latter case, some measure of inequality, either of income or of some transformation of it, enters directly the individual's utility function. Let us assume that the relevant measure is σ, the standard deviation of the income logarithms.[d] Then

$$U = U(y, \sigma) \tag{8.9}$$

and the individual's marginal rate of substitution of y for σ is

$$\frac{dy}{d\sigma} = -U_\sigma / U_y \tag{8.10}$$

y being a "good" and σ being a "bad" ($U_y > 0 > U_\sigma$), the individual's indifference curves are positively sloped: For an increase in inequality not to reduce his welfare, he has to be compensated by an increase in income. The curvature of the indifference curves is determined by

$$\frac{d^2y}{d\sigma^2} = U_y^{-3}(2U_{\sigma y}U_\sigma U_y - U_{yy}U_\sigma^2 - U_{\sigma\sigma}U_y^2) \tag{8.11}$$

It seems reasonable to assume that $U_{yy} < 0$, and that $U_{\sigma y} \leqslant 0$: the marginal disutility of inequality does not diminish as income rises (and the marginal utility of income does not increase with inequality). Then, for (8.11) to be positive—i.e., for the indifference curves to be concave with respect to the y axis—it is sufficient that $U_{\sigma\sigma} \leqslant 0$: the marginal disutility of inequality does not diminish as inequality rises.

Finally, as income rises:

$$\frac{\partial}{\partial y}\left(\frac{dy}{d\sigma}\right) = U_y^{-2}(U_{yy}U_\sigma - U_{\sigma y}U_y) \tag{8.12}$$

For an individual to be ready to pay more for a reduction in inequality as his income increases, it is sufficient that $U_{\sigma y} \leqslant 0$.

Equalizing the individual's trade-off rate of (8.5) with the marginal rate of

[d] Under the assumption of log-normality, the choice of the Lorenz or Gini indexes as measures of inequality would not affect the results to be obtained below.

substitution of (8.10), we obtain the first order condition for his welfare being maximized:

$$U_y(\lambda - \sigma)y + U_\sigma = 0 \tag{8.13}$$

This will hold for $0 < \lambda > \sigma$: the optimum for above-median individuals must obviously occur along the positively sloped part of the trade curve, where the trade-off is real, so that $0 < \sigma^* < \sigma_{\max y}$. For median and below individuals, whose incomes rise monotonically as inequality falls, perfect equality is obviously preferable to all other situations.

The second order condition is given by

$$U_y^{-2}(-2U_{\sigma y}U_\sigma U_y + U_{yy}U_\sigma^2 + U_{\sigma\sigma}U_y^2 + U_y U_\sigma^2/y$$
$$- yU_y^3) < 0 \tag{8.14}$$

The concavity of the indifference curves with respect to y–equation (8.11)–ensures the sum of the first three bracketed expressions to be negative. Furthermore, if the indifference curves are concave also in the ($\ln y$, σ) plane, the sum of the first four expressions is negative and, as $U_y > 0$, the condition of (8.14) will be fulfilled.[e]

As has been pointed out earlier, it follows from (8.7) that, for $0 < \lambda < 1$ the trade-off curve is convex to the y axis throughout its positively sloping part. As the indifference curves are assumed to be concave, the optimum in this case will be unique. For $\lambda > 1$, on the other hand, the positive part of the trade-off curve is first concave, than convex, to the y axis. In the case of each of the 16 upper percent of income recipients, therefore, there may exist two values of σ which fulfill the conditions of (8.5) and (8.6). In the discussion following we will, however, disregard the possibility of both multiple and corner equilibria and regard each $\lambda > 1$ individual as having only one optimal degree of inequality, which is not zero.

8.4. Changes in Optimum Inequality with Income

How does the optimal degree of inequality vary with income? Differentiating (8.13) implicitly, we obtain the change in σ^*, the optimal inequality, as income varies through changes in λ, the individual's ranking in the income array:

$$\frac{d\sigma^*}{dy} = \frac{1}{\partial y/\partial\lambda} \times \frac{d\sigma^*}{d\lambda}$$

$$= \frac{U_{yy}U_\sigma/U_y - U_{\sigma y} - U_y(\lambda - \sigma + 1/\sigma)}{U_y[\qquad\qquad\qquad\qquad]} \tag{8.15}$$

[e]I am grateful to J. Mayshar for pointing this out to me.

The empty brackets in the denominator stand for the second order optimum condition of equation (8.14). As shown there, if an optimum does exist this will be negative. The sign of (8.15) thus depends on that of the numerator (and will be the opposite of the latter). In particular, for $d\sigma^*/dy \leqslant 0$ it is required that

$$U_y^{-2}(U_{yy}U_\sigma - U_{\sigma y}U_y) \geqslant \lambda - \sigma + 1/\sigma \tag{8.16}$$

The left-hand side of (8.16) is identical with (8.12), the change in the slope of the indifference curves as y rises. By taking the derivative of (8.5) with respect to λ and dividing it by $\partial y/\partial\lambda$, the right-hand side can be shown to be the change with income in the slope of the trade-off curves. As in the relevant range, that of $\lambda > \sigma$, this is positive, (8.16) means that for σ^* not to rise with y, the increase in the slope of the indifference curves with income must not be smaller than that in the trade-off curves. For this to hold, it is a necessary condition that (8.12) be positive. In the preceding section this has been met by assuming $U_{\sigma y}$ to be nonpositive, i.e., that the marginal disutility of inequality is not negatively correlated with income. But even when $U_{\sigma y} > 0$, (8.12) will, and (8.16) may, hold, provided that

$$\frac{-U_{yy}}{U_y} > \frac{U_{\sigma y}}{-U_\sigma} \tag{8.17}$$

that is, if, as income rises, its marginal utility falls more rapidly than does the marginal disutility of inequality.

Were the "price" of reducing inequality the same for all individuals, (8.17) would be sufficient for them to vote for a lower inequality the higher their incomes. Under the redistribution pattern postulated here, however, this "price" (at any given value of σ) is higher the higher an individual's income. Thus, the shape of the optimal inequality path cannot be determined a priori, but depends on the actual form of the utility function. In particular, the possibility cannot be excluded of it being, as illustrated in figure 8-2:

(i) asymptotic,
(ii) horizontal–i.e., invariant to income, or even,
(iii) backwards bending.

In all three cases there exists some upper limit on σ^*, above which none of the individuals would wish the degree of inequality to rise. In case (ii) there will, in addition, exist a consensus of all individuals above a certain ranking, regarding the optimal degree of inequality. Case (iii) corresponds to the politically interesting situation in which some intermediate group of individuals prefer a higher degree of inequality than those ranked either below or above it. It should be noted that this case does not imply that the higher ranked individuals opt for

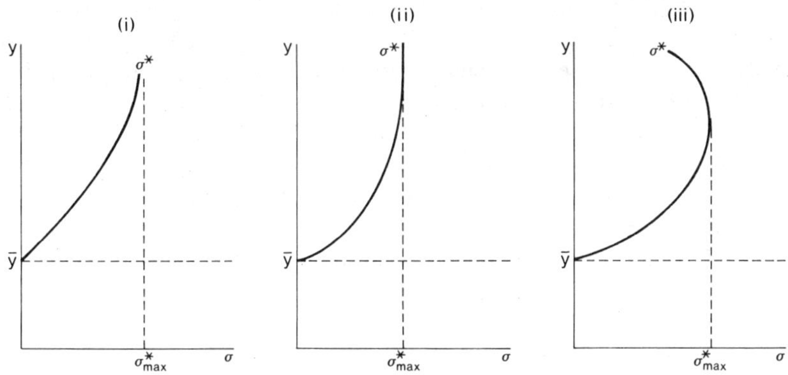

Figure 8-2. Possible Shapes of the Optimal Inequality Path.

a lower income than do those ranked below them: at the lower inequalities preferred by them, their incomes still exceed those which lower ranked individuals will receive at *their* optimal, higher inequality levels.

8.5. Optimal Inequality and Economic Growth

In the previous section we have examined the possible effect on σ^* of changes in an individual's income caused by changes in his ranking in the income array. We may now ask how does his optimal inequality change when, with ranking constant, his income is increased as a result of a general rise in the income level–i.e., of growth. Growth raises the level of the mean income, $\overline{y} = e^c$. Differentiating the first order optimality condition of (8.13) with respect to c, we obtain:

$$\frac{d\sigma^*}{dc} = \frac{y[(U_{yy}U_\sigma - U_{\sigma y}U_y) - U_y^2(\lambda - \sigma)]}{U_y^{-1}[\qquad\qquad\qquad\qquad]} \tag{8.18}$$

Here, again, the empty brackets in the denominator stand for the second order condition of (8.14). As this is negative, the sign of (8.18) will be inversely related to that of the numerator. Substituting in the latter from the optimality condition, we see that for $d\sigma^*/dc \leqslant 0$ it requires

$$yU_y^{-1}(U_{yy}U_\sigma - U_{\sigma y}U_y) + U_\sigma \geqslant 0 \tag{8.19}$$

As $U_\sigma < 0$, for (8.19) to hold it is, again, necessary that either $U_{\sigma y} \leqslant 0$, or that, as income rises, its marginal utility will decline more rapidly than does the marginal disutility of inequality.

This result is intuitively almost self-evident. Assuming economic growth itself to be "distribution-neutral"–that is, neither inducing inequality nor being induced by it–it causes an equiproportionate upward shift in the trade-off curves of all individuals. In the case of any given individual this means that, at a given value of σ, his marginal trade-off rate increases in the same proportion as income. However, if his utility function remains unchanged, his marginal rate of substitution also increases: having more income he is ready to sacrifice more of it in exchange for a marginal reduction in inequality. As illustrated in figure 8-3, if $-U_\sigma/U_y$ increases in the same proportion as the slope of the trade-off curve–that is, in proportion to income–the optimal degree of inequality will be unaffected by growth. On the other hand, if the marginal rate of substitution rises with income at a rate less than proportionate to the latter, growth will raise the degree of inequality optimal for the individual. But if it rises more than proportionately to income then, as the general level of income rises, individuals will acquiesce in more and more egalitarian redistribution schemes.

8.6. Summary and Discussion

In this paper we have considered the effect on redistribution of inequality being a public good not only in its consumption but also in its production. The "production function" postulated was one which yields unambiguous changes in equality, and at the same time preserves both the log-normality of the income distribution and the individuals' rankings in the income array. This enabled us to derive a set of income-equality trade-off curves for the various rankings. It has been shown that for each above-median individual there exists then some positive degree of inequality at which his income is maximized. If inequality "in general" has an adverse effect on such an individual's welfare, the degree of inequality optimal for him will fall short of that which maximizes his income. Furthermore, as the slopes of both the individual's trade-off curve and of his indifference curve rise with his ranking, the change in optimal inequality with income cannot be determined without further specification of the utility function. In particular, the degree of inequality optimal for different individuals may coincide. Such a consensus will never cover the majority of all individuals: for, as we have seen in section 8.2, the majority–i.e., all those with $\lambda \leqslant 0$, prefers perfect equality to any other position. But it may cover the majority of the potential "donors" to redistribution schemes–all those individuals whose incomes are maximized at positive values of σ. The possibility of the above result, as well as of the others mentioned above in section 8.4, depends, of course, on the slopes of the trade-off curves postulated here. It may be argued that the redistribution scheme generating them is unrealistic; that it is not what people have in mind when they think of redistribution. This may well be true; though if it is, it raises serious questions on the relevance of much of the literature dealing with the measurement of inequality, where similar assumptions

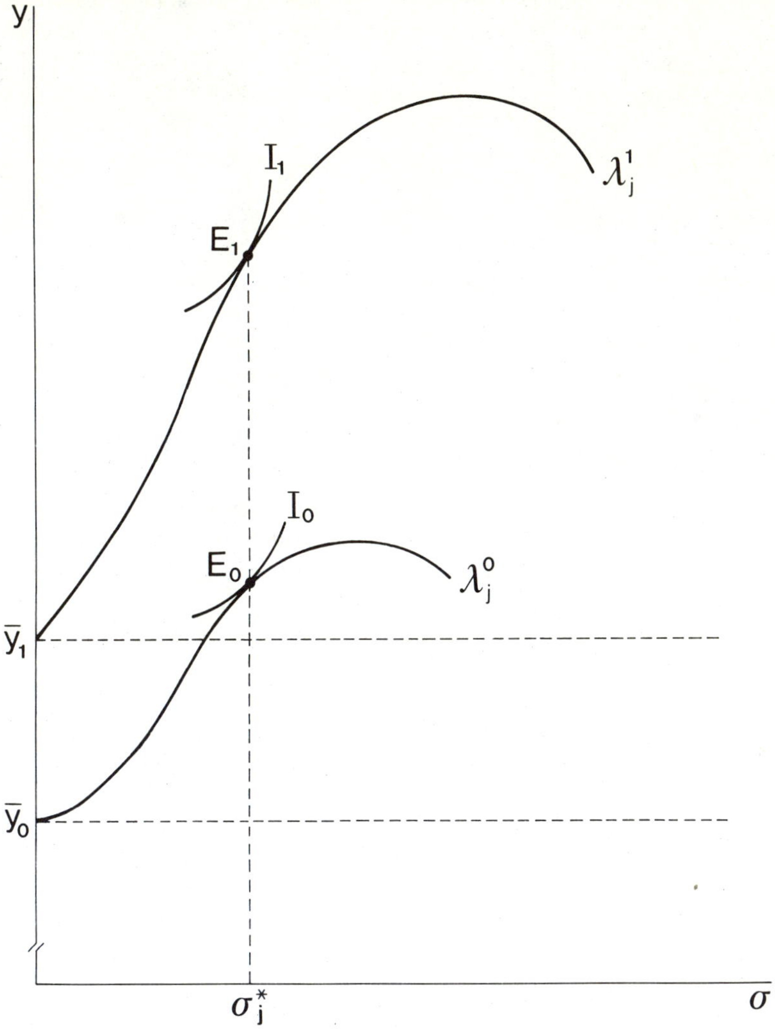

Figure 8-3. Distribution-Neutral Economic Growth.

are tacitly made.[f] But this objection does not invalidate the approach developed here: that of translating a proposed redistribution scheme into an explicit system of differential equality prices, and regarding the reaction to it of differently placed individuals as the result of choosing that degree of inequality which

[f]As manifest in the use of changes in the logarithmic variance to measure inequality changes.

maximizes their welfare.[g] The same approach can be applied to any other redistribution scheme. And it may also help to explain why, given the extent of the redistribution, different groups of individuals may prefer one redistributive scheme to another.

References

Aitchison, Y., and Y.A.C. Brown, *The Lognormal Distribution*, Cambridge: Cambridge University Press, 1957.

Atkinson, A.B., "On the Measurement of Inequality," *Journal of Economic Theory*, Sept. 1970.

Dalton, H., "The Measurement of the Inequality of Incomes," *Economic Journal*, Sept. 1920.

Goldfarb, R.S., "Pareto Optimal Redistribution: Comment," *American Economic Review*, Dec. 1970.

Hart, P.E., and S.J. Prais, "The Analysis of Business Concentration: A Statistical Approach," *Journal of the Royal Statistical Society*, (A), 1956.

Hochman, H.M., and J.D. Rodgers, "Pareto Optimal Redistribution," *American Economic Review*, Sept. 1969.

Itsumi, Y., "Distributional Effects of Linear Income Tax Schedules," *Review of Economic Studies*, June 1974.

Kolm, S., "The Optimal Production of Social Justice," in J. Margolis and H. Guitton (eds.), *Public Economics* London: Macmillan 1969.

Ng, Y.K., "Income Distribution as a Peculiar Public Good: The Paradox of Redistribution and the Paradox of Universal Externality," *Public Finance*, 28 (1973):1.

Scott, R.H., "Avarice, Altruism, and Second Party Preferences," *Quarterly Journal of Economics*, Feb. 1972.

Thurow, L.C., "The Income Distribution as a Pure Public Good," *Quarterly Journal of Economics*, May 1971.

Tobin, J., "On Limiting the Domain of Inequality," *Journal of Law and Economics*, Oct. 1970.

---

[g]For a somewhat similar approach—examining changes in the welfare level of each individual with a change in an income tax schedule—see Itsumi (1974). Note that the present formulation can be widened, to allow for $\partial c/\partial \sigma \neq 0$, so that national income varies with inequality; or for $\partial \lambda/\partial \sigma \neq 0$, the case where individuals' orderings in the income array—or, at least, their ex ante expectations of them—vary with inequality.

9 Optimal Tax Theory: A Synthesis

James A. Mirrlees

9.1. Introduction

The main purposes of this chapter are to unify some uncoordinated parts of the theory of optimal taxation, and to develop methods of analysis that can be quickly and easily applied to all kinds of optimal tax problems. The analysis is presented without attention to minor points of rigor (which I intend to treat elsewhere). As a result, the basic mathematical manipulations are relatively brief once the best ways of setting up the problems have been found. At the same time, a number of important details are treated in depth.

Theory can contribute to discussions about the levels of tax rates in a number of ways. It makes possible the calculation of optimal tax rates, to gain knowledge of how tax rates vary with objectives and possibilities. It shows how tax rates depend on certain indices (elasticities of various kinds, for example), thus indicating what form of evidence would be most useful and what influence that information would have on tax rates. It can formulate rules for optimal taxation which, though not expressed in terms of tax rates, may serve to attract attention to better measurements of the effects of economic policy. It can explore the consequences, for optimal tax rates or optimal taxation rules, of introducing considerations that have previously been absent or imperfectly present in models and policy discussions.

A number of papers have presented calculations of optimal tax rates under a variety of assumptions: Atkinson (1973), Mirrlees (1971) and Stern (1976) for income taxation; Atkinson and Stiglitz (1972) and Deaton (1975) for commodity taxation. I contribute nothing to that topic in the present chapter, which is concerned with formulae for optimal tax rates, and optimal taxation rules. Rules for commodity taxation have been discussed in many papers, including Diamond and Mirrlees (1971), Mirrlees (1975), Ramsey (1927) and Stiglitz and Dasgupta (1971). Formulae involving optimal tax rates have been derived by Atkinson and Stiglitz (1972) for commodity taxes, and Mirrlees (1971) for a nonlinear income tax.

There is a striking contrast in this literature between the analysis and

Reprinted, with permission of North-Holland Publishing Company, from the *Journal of Public Economics*, vol. 6, November 1976, pp. 327-358. Financial support by the National Science Foundation during the preparation of this paper is gratefully acknowledged. Parts of section 3 are based on a paper 'Optimal Incentive Schemes' presented at the Berlin Conference on Incentives, September 1973. Valuable comments have been received from P.A. Diamond, Y-K Ng, Jesus Seade, and referees.

interpretation of first-order conditions which is usually emphasized in work on commodity taxation, and the development (and numerical implementation) of formulae for marginal tax rates that is characteristic of theories of optimal income taxation. This contrast seems to be quite basic to the theory of optimal taxation, as I shall argue in section 9.2. Sections 9.2 and 9.3 are devoted to a relatively quick, and therefore nonrigorous, derivation of the main formal results in optimal tax theory, and a discussion of their interpretation. Section 9.4 outlines the conditions for a more general nonlinear theory.

The discussion of section 9.3 raises the question of the interrelations between optimal commodity taxes and an optimal nonlinear tax on (say) labor incomes. In section 9.5, first-order conditions for this case are derived, and discussed. This is the central part of the present chapter. The analysis provides a unification of previous theories of optimal taxation, in that it covers linear (commodity) or fully nonlinear taxation, or any mixture of the two. This approach also enables one to derive a general 'Paretian' tax rule, corresponding to a result previously obtained [Mirrlees (1975)] for the two-class case. The rule is a necessary condition that must hold independently of the welfare function used. Naturally this rule is far from enough to determine the optimal tax system. Using the whole set of first-order conditions, I discuss the implications of optimizing the labor-income tax for optimal commodity taxes, and *vice versa*. In particular, one would like to be able to gain some impression how the presence of commodity taxes bears upon the overall progression of the tax system, and on the progressivity of the labor-income tax. As yet, these implications are not entirely clear to me.

It is striking how easily the rules for the optimal provision of public goods can be obtained in the general setting introduced in section 9.5; and how simple the rules are. They are derived in section 9.6.

Finally in section 9.7 it is shown how the various optimality conditions derived in the paper are particular instances of a general principle which is quite simple to formulate. This principle shows clearly how both efficiency and distributional considerations operate in the rules for optimal economic policy.

Apart from this 'fundamental principle,' and the general 'duality' method used throughout, the most important particular new results of the chapter are the following:

(1) The general conditions for optimal nonlinear taxes derived in sections 9.3 and 9.4.
(2) A set of conditions in simple form, depending only on production prices and consumer preference orderings, which must necessarily hold for any tax equilibrium which is Pareto-efficient among the set of all tax equilibria. These conditions are stated at their simplest in equation (9.39).
(3) The conditions for optimal linear taxes in the presence of optimal nonlinear taxes—derived in section 9.5. These provide a strikingly simple criterion for

assessing the optimal impact of commodity taxation when there is an income tax.

(4) The form of the condition for optimal income taxation in the presence of commodity taxes (optimal or not), also presented in section 9.5.

(5) The conditions for optimal provision of public goods in the presence of an optimal income tax are given a neat and illuminating form, which has an interesting connection with the commodity-tax conditions just mentioned.

9.2. Optimal Taxation in the Linear Case

In the theory of optimal commodity taxation, it has been usual to consider a finite population of households, whose net demands will here be denoted by vectors:

$$x^1, x^2, x^3, \ldots, x^H .$$

These households face prices q for commodities, with

$$q = p + t,$$

where p are producer prices and t are tax rates. Thus each household has the *same* budget constraint $q \cdot x \leqslant 0$. In the present paper, I assume the following:

(i) Production available to consumers is constrained by a production constraint

$$p \cdot \sum_h x^h = A , \tag{9.1}$$

with p and A constant. This is not a serious restriction. The linear constraint can be thought of as a linear approximation to production possibilities in the neighborhood of the optimum, in which case the producer prices p are to be regarded as marginal costs and marginal products. So long as first-order necessary conditions are at issue, it does not matter that p is constant. A fuller discussion of production is given in Diamond and Mirrlees (1971).

(ii) Pure profits, if any, are paid to the State. This excludes certain interesting issues that have been discussed in the literature, but allows us to concentrate on the main taxation issues without having to deal with producer taxation alongside consumer taxation.

(iii) An individualistic welfare function,

$$W = \sum_h u^h(x^h) , \tag{9.2}$$

is to be maximized. The representation (9.2) is implied by complete separability of consumption by individuals, but is not necessary for most of the results of this paper, since only local changes are considered. (9.2) simply represents a convenient choice of utility functions representing individual preferences so that the marginal weights attached to utility levels are all equal.

The first-order conditions for optimal choice of the tax rates t (or, equivalently q) will be derived by duality methods. Let

$$m^h(q, u) \tag{9.3}$$

be the expenditure function for household h, i.e. the minimum expenditure required to attain utility u when prices are q. Then the (Slutsky) compensated demand functions for household h are

$$x^{ch}(q, u) = m_q^h , \tag{9.4}$$

where the subscript here and subsequently denotes differentiation. The utility level of household h will be denoted by v^h.

Then the optimal taxation problem can be expressed as

$$\operatorname*{Max}_q \sum_h v^h : \begin{cases} p \cdot \sum_h x^{ch}(q, v^h) = A , \\ \\ m^h(q, v^h) = 0, \quad (\text{all } h). \end{cases} \tag{9.5}$$

The second set of constraints here reflects the assumption that households have no lump-sum income or expenditure.

It is of the first importance to realize why the optimal commodity tax problem is best set without explicit reference to tax rates. Suppose q^* is the solution to the problem. Then $t^* = q^* - p$ are optimal tax rates. But the real equilibrium of the economy is unaltered if instead we have tax rates

$$t_\rho^* = \rho q^* - p \tag{9.6}$$

for any positive constant ρ. It follows that (except when no taxation is optimal) there is no answer to the question: which commodities should be taxed and which subsidized? The 'answer' varies with the arbitrary choice of a number ρ. A specific answer can be given if it is stipulated that some particular commodity is to have a zero tax rate; but that is usually an uninteresting device because there is no naturally untaxed commodity.

For this reason, one should not seek formulae for optimal tax rates in the general problem. One can hope to find equations identifying commodities whose net demand is encouraged, or discouraged, by the tax system, since these are real properties of the tax system, which remain invariant under the trivial change in tax rates described by (9.6). Having set the problem up as in (9.5) we shall find that such conditions appear almost immediately. The other advantage of this new way of setting up the problem is that it is more easily related to the problem of nonlinear taxation.

To obtain necessary conditions for the optimum in (9.5), introduce Lagrange multipliers for the constraints, and set the derivatives of the following expression with respect to $\nu^1, \ldots, \nu^H$, q (holding p constant) equal to zero:

$$L = \sum_h \nu^h - \lambda p \cdot \sum_h x^{ch}(q, \nu^h) - \Sigma\, \mu_h m^h(q, \nu^h). \tag{9.7}$$

Differentiating L with respect to ν^h, we obtain

$$1 = \lambda p \cdot x_\nu^{ch} + \mu_h m_\nu^h. \tag{9.8}$$

Differentiation with respect to q, with p and the ν^h constant, yields

$$\lambda p \cdot \sum_h x_q^{ch} + \sum_h \mu_h m_q^h = 0. \tag{9.9}$$

Using (9.4), and the symmetry of the Slutsky derivatives, we obtain from (9.9),

$$-\lambda \sum_h x_q^{ch} \cdot p = \sum_h \mu_h x^{ch}. \tag{9.10}$$

Now $x_q^{ch} \cdot q = 0$, by homogeneity. Therefore

$$\begin{aligned} -x_q^{ch} \cdot p &= x_q^{ch} \cdot (q - p) = x_q^{ch} \cdot t \\ &= \frac{\partial}{\partial \theta} x^{ch}(p + \theta t) \mid_{\theta = 1}; \end{aligned} \tag{9.11}$$

and we can write (9.10) in the form

$$\sum_h x_q^{ch} \cdot t = \frac{\partial}{\partial \theta} \sum_h x^{ch}(p + \theta t) \mid_{\theta = 1} = \Sigma\, (\mu_h/\lambda) x^{ch} \tag{9.12}$$

In words, the total substitution effects of a proportional change in all tax and subsidy rates should be proportional to a weighted sum of demands. We shall see that μ_h can be negative for some h. The weights in (9.12) are obtained from (9.8):

$$\frac{\mu_h}{\lambda} = (\lambda^{-1} - p \cdot x_v^{ch})/m_v^h = 1/(\lambda m_v^h) - p \cdot x_m^h(q,0)$$

$$= \frac{1}{\lambda m_v^h} + t \cdot x_m^h(q,0) - 1\ , \tag{9.13}$$

x^h is the uncompensated demand function, and x_m^h its derivative with respect to income. In words, the weight is the difference of a term proportional to the marginal utility of income, and the income-derivative of the household's income net of taxes.

The above conditions were derived on the assumption that there is no lump-sum taxation. It is always possible to have lump-sum taxation (or subsidization) at a uniform rate. If this is done, the constraints $m^h = 0$ should be replaced by the constraint $m^h = b$, with the subsidy b free to be chosen. The analysis is then unchanged, except that differentiation of the Lagrangean with respect to b yields a further condition

$$\Sigma\, \mu_h = 0. \tag{9.14}$$

λ and μ_h were introduced as multipliers dual to the government's revenue constraint (which is equivalent to (9.1) for given household incomes) and the constraints on household income. Thus λ is the social marginal utility of income transferred to household h, the production constraint being unchanged. Since the production constraint is $\Sigma\, m^h$ – taxes = A, the increase in income involves a tax change. The social marginal utility of income, ignoring this tax change, is $\lambda + \mu_h$. Diamond (1975) calls this the social marginal utility of income. μ_h can be termed the *social marginal utility of transfer.*

The form of the first-order conditions (9.12) differs from those derived in Diamond and Mirrlees (1971). The other form is readily derived from (9.8) and (9.9) by eliminating μ_h: after some manipulation one has

$$\lambda \frac{\partial}{\partial t} \sum_h t \cdot x^h(p + t, m) = \sum_h x^h/m_v^h\ . \tag{9.15}$$

In words, the revenue effects of tax changes should be proportional to welfare-weighted demands.

Of the two forms, (9.12) and (9.15), for the first-order conditions, we shall see that (9.12) corresponds best to the conditions for optimal nonlinear taxation.

Equation (9.12) is appealing chiefly because the left-hand side, $\Sigma\, x_q^{ch} \cdot t$, is a measure of the extent to which the tax system discourages a commodity. If the tax system is intensified, in the sense that all taxes and subsidies are changed proportionately, demands for commodities are subject to both income and substitution effects. The income effects, $-x^h_m x^h \cdot t$, are simply the income-derivatives of demand times taxes paid. The total substitution effect is $\Sigma x^{ch}_q \cdot t$ (as can be seen from (9.12)). Since the income effect has nothing to do with the way the tax system bears on commodities individually, it should be ignored in assessing the effects of optimal taxes. Thus, we can reasonably introduce the following definition.

Under a tax system, the *index of discouragement* of commodity i is

$$d_i = \sum_h \sum_j \frac{\partial x_i^{ch}}{\partial q_j} t_j \Big/ \sum_h x_i^h . \tag{9.16}$$

The first-order conditions for optimal commodity taxation can then be expressed as

$$d_i = \frac{\sum_h (\mu_h/\lambda) x_i^h}{\sum_h x_i^h} , \tag{9.17}$$

where μ_h/λ is given by (9.13), and satisfies $\Sigma(\mu_h/\lambda) = 0$.

9.3. Optimal Nonlinear Taxation

Linearity of the tax system plays an essential role in the previous section, because linearity defines control variables (q) for the optimization problem. With nonlinear taxation, the government can, in effect, impose any budget constraint it wishes on the members of population, the only restriction being that the constraint is the same for everyone. When policy options are extended in this way, it is best to consider a continuum population of households. Then one may avoid having as optimum policy an awkwardly shaped budget set with many corners. It is very restrictive, despite appearances, to describe the population by a single parameter n. Nevertheless we must usually do so to get neat results. The analysis will be carried out for the one-parameter case, n being distributed with density function $f(n)$. The many-parameter case is outlined in section 9.4.

For the nonlinear case, it is useful to identify a numéraire commodity. The notation is now that household n, with utility function $u(x, z, n)$, chooses a vector $x(n)$ of net demands for nonnuméraire goods and a net demand $z(n)$ for numéraire. u is a nondecreasing function of all variables. We have to consider allocations in which

$$x(n), z(n) \text{ maximizes } u(x, z, n) \text{ subject to } (x, z) \in B, \tag{9.18}$$

where B is the budget set, describing the effect of taxes and subsidies in combination with producer prices. It should be noted that the consumption set, of net demands feasible for the consumer, may vary with n. This will be ignored in the following, where the set of definition of u is supposed the same for all n.

To reduce (9.18) to a more manageable form, the method of Mirrlees (1971) is generalized. The idea is that, if we define

$$v(n) = u(x(n), z(n), n), \tag{9.19}$$

(9.18) implies that

$$v(n) - u(x(n), z(n), n) = 0 \leqslant v(m) - u(x(n), z(n), m), \tag{9.20}$$

i.e. $m = n$ minimizes $v(m) - u(x(n), z(n), m)$. Consequently,

$$v'(n) = u_n(x(n), z(n), n). \tag{9.21}$$

When x and z are differentiable with respect to n, differentiation of (9.19) shows that (9.21) is equivalent to

$$u_x \cdot x'(n) + u_z z'(n) = 0,$$

which we can write more neatly if we introduce the marginal rate of substitution,

$$s(x, z, n) = u_x/u_z, \tag{9.22}$$

as

$$z'(n) + s(x(n), z(n), n) \cdot x'(n) = 0. \tag{9.23}$$

We also have a second-order condition from the minimization of $v - u$:

$$v''(n) \geqslant u_{nn}(x(n), z(n), n). \tag{9.24}$$

This is equivalent (when x and z are differentiable) to

$$s_n(x(n), z(n), n) \cdot x'(n) \geqslant 0. \tag{9.25}$$

To deduce (9.25) from (9.24), differentiate (9.21) with respect to n:

$$v''(n) = u_{nx} \cdot x'(n) + u_{nz} z'(n) + u_{nn}.$$

Applying (9.22), we have

$$u_{nx} \cdot x'(n) + u_{nz} z'(n) \geqslant 0. \tag{9.26}$$

(9.23) allows us to replace $z'(n)$ in this inequality:

$$u_{nx} - u_{nz} \frac{u_x}{u_z} \cdot x'(n) \geqslant 0. \tag{9.27}$$

Since

$$\frac{\partial s}{\partial n} = \frac{u_{nx}}{u_z} - \frac{u_{nz} u_x}{u_z^2},$$

(9.27) is in turn equivalent to (9.25) (since $u_z > 0$ by assumption).

In an appendix to this chapter, it is shown that (9.21) in conjunction with a condition a little stronger than (9.25),

$$s_m(x(n), z(n), m) \cdot x'(n) \geqslant 0, \qquad \text{all } m, n, \tag{9.28}$$

together imply that (9.18) holds for some budget set B. When there are only two commodities, this is a very satisfactory situation. Then $s_n \geqslant 0$ is a sufficient assumption to ensure that (9.18) is equivalent to (9.21) and $z'(n) \geqslant 0$. It is this circumstance that makes the income-tax problem studied in Mirrlees (1971) manageable.

In the many-commodity case, we can replace the consumer constraint (9.18) by the weaker condition (9.21). If the solution of that problem satisfies (9.28), then it is a solution of the basic problem. This gives us an easy check on a computed solution, but it is perfectly possible that $s_n \cdot x'(n)$ will vanish for certain ranges of n in the optimum. In that case a more detailed analysis than the one below would be required.

We shall now obtain necessary conditions for the problem

$$\text{Max} \int v(n) f(n) \mathrm{d}n : \begin{cases} \int [p \cdot x(n) + z(n)] f(n) \mathrm{d}n = A, \\ \\ v'(n) = u_n(x(n), z(n), n). \end{cases} \tag{9.29}$$

Notice that production prices are based on z as numéraire. If labor is numéraire, $z(n)$ should be a negative number, being supplied by households, not demanded. Recollect that

$$v(n) = u(x(n), z(n), n), \tag{9.30}$$

and f is the density function describing the composition of the population. n is assumed distributed between 0 and ∞. In what follows, subscripts denote partial derivatives.

Having formulated the problem in this way, it will obviously pay to invert the utility function, writing

$$z(n) = \zeta(x(n), v(n), n). \tag{9.31}$$

In effect this transformation is a 'duality trick,' as we shall see in section 5. Since (9.31) is derived from (9.30), we can calculate the derivatives,

$$\zeta_x = -u_x/u_z = -s$$

$$\zeta_v = 1/u_z. \tag{9.32}$$

Converting (9.29) into Lagrangean form we set equal to zero the derivatives of

$$L = \int [(v - \lambda p \cdot x - \lambda\zeta)f + \mu v'(n) - \mu u_n(x, \zeta, n)] \, dn.$$

Differentiating in turn with respect to $v(\cdot)$ and $x(\cdot)$, we obtain (noting that $u_{nx} + u_{nz} \cdot (-s) = u_z s_n$),

$$\left(1 - \frac{\lambda}{u_z}\right)f - \mu\frac{u_{nz}}{u_z} - \mu'(n) = 0, \tag{9.33}$$

$$\lambda(s - p)f = \mu u_z s_n. \tag{9.34}$$

The last term in (9.33) is obtained by first integrating by parts the term $\mu v'$ in L. This leaves an integrated part $\lim_{n\to\infty}\mu(n)v(n) - \mu(0)v(0)$. Differentiation with respect to $v(0)$ and $v(\infty)$ (this can be checked by a more careful analysis), yields the further conditions

$$\mu(0) = 0, \qquad \mu(\infty) = 0. \tag{9.35}$$

Equation (9.34) holds only when $(x(n), z(n)$ is not up against the consumer's supply constraint. For example the possibility of a zero labor supply is not allowed. Though this point must be considered for numerical calculations, it will be ignored here as not being of great importance.

The first, simplest and most exciting, feature of these first-order conditions is the set of equations (9.34), which are statements about marginal tax rates. If the numéraire is untaxed, and τ_i is the *marginal* tax rate on commodity *i*, the marginal price facing the consumer is $p_i + \tau_i$, which he will equate to s_i, the marginal rate of substitution between that commodity and numéraire. (9.34) says that

$$\tau_i = \frac{\nu}{f} \frac{\partial s_i}{\partial n}, \qquad \nu = \mu u_z / \lambda. \tag{9.36}$$

To fix ideas for the moment, let *n* describe ability or willingness to work. Mathematically, this says that as *n* increases, individuals find it easier to do additional work of the same productive value, so that, for most goods, s_i should be an increasing function of *n*. The exceptional goods are those whose marginal utility falls faster than the marginal disutility of labor. (Remember that labor is measured not in units of time but in units of equal marginal productivity.) Normally it is thought right that the tax system should bear more heavily on the more able. Thus marginal tax rates are expected to be positive on most commodities. This being so, the numerical factor in (9.36) ought normally to be positive. In that case, our condition says that marginal taxes should be greater on commodities the more able would tend to prefer.

More explicitly, (9.36) implies that

$$\frac{\tau_i}{s_i} - \frac{\tau_j}{s_j} = \frac{\nu}{f} \frac{\partial}{\partial n}(s_i/s_j), \qquad \nu = \mu u_z / \lambda, \tag{9.37}$$

so that the question which commodity should be taxed more highly is answered by reference to the effect of an increase in *n* upon the slope of the individual's indifference curves.

This prescription is most agreeable to common sense; but it should be remembered that it is not true when only linear taxation is allowed. In that case, as we saw, more awkward statements about the effect of general tax changes on aggregate compensated demands must be made. It is the extra scope for policy allowed by nonlinearity that restores the 'common-sense' result.

Perhaps the most surprising feature of (9.34) is the strong implications that are independent of the welfare function assumed, or even the population distribution, namely (dividing the equations for different commodities).

$$\frac{s_i - p_i}{s_j - p_j} = \frac{s_{in}}{s_{jn}}. \tag{9.38}$$

Whether these equations hold can be tested by reference to indifference curves alone (and the way they vary with *n*). Therefore these equations must hold (for all *i* and *j*) *as a condition of Pareto-efficiency*. If they do not hold, there exists a tax system which would make everyone better off.

Since $(\partial/\partial n)\tau_i = (\partial/\partial n)(s_i - p_i) = s_{in}$, (9.38) takes an even neater form:

$$\frac{\partial}{\partial n}\frac{\tau_i}{\tau_j} = 0 . \tag{9.39}$$

Thus *it is necessary for Pareto-efficiency (relative to the set of tax equilibria) that the ratios of marginal tax rates are locally independent of n.* (9.39) is simple but mysterious. The τ_i are to be regarded as functions of x, z and n. We ask what τ' would make an n-man choose the demands of an $(n + dn)$-man. The ratios of these τ' have to be the same as the ratios of the marginal tax rates the $(n + dn)$-man actually faces. This is a strong requirement. No intuitive explanation of the result has occurred to me.

Returning to equation (9.37), we see that the marginal tax rates on commodities i and j should be the same for all individuals if s_i/s_j is independent of n. This means that x_i and x_j enter the utility function through a subutility function which is the same for everyone. More generally, if a subset of commodities, represented by a vector x^1, enters the utility function in the following way,

$$u = U(a_1(x^1), x^2, z, n), \tag{9.40}$$

all the commodities in x^1 should be taxed at the same rate. In particular, when utility has this form with no commodities in the second group, it is optimal to have a tax schedule for the numéraire alone, with no taxes on other commodities. This notable result generalizes that obtained by Atkinson and Stiglitz (1976) for the additively separable case. It is true also when n is multidimensional.

The remaining task, in interpreting the optimality conditions, is to use equation (9.33) to get more precise information about the sign and magnitude of the multipliers $\mu(n)$. Let us first, to encourage intuition, assign a special symbol to the marginal utility of numéraire (e.g. the marginal disutility of labor-value) which plays in the model much the role of the marginal utility of income in one- and two-good models:

$$\beta = u_z . \tag{9.41}$$

β is to be regarded as a function of x, z and n; and β_n, for example, means the partial derivative of β with respect to n; but $\beta(n)$ and $\beta_n(n)$ mean $\beta(x(n), z(n), n)$ and $\beta_n(x(n), z(n), n)$ respectively.

There are two convenient ways of integrating (9.33) for μ. Integrating as it stands, and using the boundary condition $\mu(0) = 0$, we get

$$\mu(n) = \int_0^n \left[1 - \frac{\lambda}{\beta(m)}\right] \exp\left[\int_n^m \beta_n(m')/\beta(m') \cdot \mathrm{d}m'\right] f(m)\,\mathrm{d}m. \tag{9.42}$$

The alternative equation for μ is obtained by rewriting (9.33) in the form

$$\frac{\mathrm{d}}{\mathrm{d}n}(\beta\mu) - s_z \cdot x'(n) \cdot \beta\mu - (\beta - \lambda)f = 0. \tag{9.43}$$

The derivation of (9.43) is based on the calculation

$$\begin{aligned} \frac{\mathrm{d}}{\mathrm{d}n}\beta &= \beta_n + \beta_x \cdot x'(n) + \beta_z z'(n) \\ &= \beta_n + u_{zx} \cdot x' + u_{zz}(-u_x \cdot x') \\ &= \beta_n + \mu_z \frac{\partial}{\partial z}(u_x/u_z) \cdot x' \\ &= \beta_n + \beta s_z \cdot x'. \end{aligned} \tag{9.44}$$

Integration of (9.43) yields the formula

$$\beta\mu = \int_0^n [\beta(m) - \lambda] \exp\left[\int_m^n s_z \cdot x'(m')\,\mathrm{d}m'\right] f(m)\,\mathrm{d}m. \tag{9.45}$$

(9.42) and (9.45) suggest two special cases that should be easy to handle, namely $\beta_n \equiv 0$ (which simplifies (9.42)) and $s_z \equiv 0$ (which simplifies (9.45)). Take the latter case. s is independent of z if and only if utility can be expressed in the form

$$u = U(a(x, n) + z, n). \tag{9.46}$$

This is the case where income effects vanish in ordinary consumer theory. If utility were to take this form, we should have

$$\beta\mu = \int_0^n [\beta(m) - \lambda] f(m)\,\mathrm{d}m \tag{9.47}$$

and, from (9.44), $(\mathrm{d}/\mathrm{d}n)\beta = \beta_n$. Consequently $\beta_n \leqslant 0$ implies that $\beta(m)$ is nondecreasing. Let $\beta(n_1) = \lambda$. Then (9.47) implies that $\mu \geqslant 0$ when $n \leqslant n_1$. But

$\mu = 0$ when $n = \infty$. Therefore $\beta\mu$ is equal to $-\int_n^\infty [\beta(m) - \lambda] f(m)\,dm$; and it follows that $\mu \geqslant 0$ for $n \geqslant n_1$ also.

What we have found is this: *in the no-income-effects case,*

$$\beta_n \leqslant 0 \tag{9.48}$$

is a sufficient condition for

$$\mu(n) \geqslant 0. \tag{9.49}$$

It will be recollected that the tax rules (9.34) then have their natural interpretation, for λ, f, and $u_z = \beta$ are all nonnegative.

Condition (9.48), stating that the marginal utility of numéraire is a decreasing function of n, for fixed x and z, expresses the assumption that consumers with larger n are less deserving. We have now shown (cf. the discussion of equation (9.36) above) that in the no-income-effect case, it is indeed implied that the tax system should bear more heavily on those with greater ability. But in general, it seems that one cannot establish the result; for the last term in equation (9.44), $\beta s_z \cdot x'$, is quite likely to be positive. There are other special cases, notably the two-commodity case with normality, for which a theorem can be established [cf. Mirrlees (1971)]. Also, cases where μ is negative for some n are odd in other respects. Consider (9.34) again,

$$\lambda(s - p) f = \mu u_z s_n,$$

and multiply by x':

$$(s - p) \cdot x' = \frac{\mu u_z}{\lambda f} s_n \cdot x'. \tag{9.50}$$

We know that $s_n \cdot x' \geqslant 0$ (equation (9.25)); and that $s \cdot x' = -z'$ (equation (9.23)). Therefore

$$\mu < 0 \text{ implies } p \cdot x' + z' \geqslant 0. \tag{9.51}$$

If the numéraire is not taxed, $-z$ is the consumer's expenditure, and the total tax paid by an n-man is

$$T(n) = -z(n) - p \cdot x(n). \tag{9.52}$$

It follows that

$$\mu < 0 \text{ implies } T'(n) \leqslant 0. \tag{9.53}$$

In words, μ is negative only if the tax system does not bear more heavily on consumers with greater n.

A number of economists have examined, usually for special cases, the implications for marginal tax rates of the boundary conditions that $\mu = 0$ at the ends of the skill distribution. Equation (9.34) suggests that marginal tax rates should be zero when $n = 0$ or ∞, provided that f does not tend to zero too rapidly. Phelps (1974) and Sadka (1974) have followed this idea for $n = \infty$, and more recently Seade (1975) has noticed a similar result for the lower end of the distribution. When the result holds at both ends, the tax system is neither progressive for all n, nor regressive. Calculations suggest to me that these end results are of little practical value. When the conditions for their validity hold, it is usually true that zero is a bad approximation to the marginal tax rate even within most of the top and bottom percentiles.

9.4. Multiple Characteristics

In the previous section, the population was described by a single parameter. The power of this assumption is shown in the conclusion that marginal tax rates are proportional to $\partial s_i/\partial n$. Matters are not quite so simple when the population is described by a *vector* n. Let us suppose there are $I + 1$ commodities, and J parameters describing the population.

It will be recollected that, in the one-parameter case, consumer utility-maximization implies that

$$v'(n) = u_n(x(n), z(n), n). \tag{9.54}$$

The argument leading to this conclusion is valid also for many parameters, and we therefore have

$$\frac{\partial v}{\partial n_j} = u_{nj}(x(n), z(n), n) \tag{9.55}$$

for each parameter. Thus we can read (9.54) as a vector equation. Similarly we obtain from second-order conditions the implication that the matrix

$$\left[\frac{\partial x}{\partial n_j} \cdot s_{nk}(x(n), z(n), n)\right] \tag{9.56}$$

is nonnegative definite. (This matrix is in fact symmetric, as one can deduce by differentiating (9.54) with respect to n.) The question then arises whether, as in the one-parameter case of (9.54), in conjunction with a condition similar to (9.56), implies utility maximization subject to some budget constraint. Fortunately it does so, as I shall establish elsewhere. This allows an argument that in a large class of cases the constraint (9.56), or rather a stronger form analogous to (9.28) can be neglected in deriving the first-order conditions for constrained maximization.

In that case, we have to consider a Lagrangean,

$$L = \int [\,\{v(n) - \lambda p \cdot x(n) - \lambda s\}\, f + \{v'(n) - u_n(x, \zeta, n)\} \cdot \mu(n)]\ \mathrm{d}n, \quad (9.57)$$

where integration is over the whole nonnegative orthant in the space of parameter vectors n, and $\mu(n)$ is, for each n, a vector of multipliers commensurate with n. As before, ζ is the function of x, v and n defined by $v = u(x, \zeta, n)$. Before differentiating L, we want to replace the term

$$\int v'(n) \cdot \mu(n)\, \mathrm{d}n = \int \ldots \int \sum_j \frac{\partial v}{\partial n_j} \mu_j(n)\, \mathrm{d}n_1 \ldots \mathrm{d}n_J$$

by something more convenient. This can be done by using a standard theorem in multidimensional calculus, which states that, for nice functions v, $\mu_1, \ldots, \mu_J$ defined in a closed region D,

$$\int_D \Sigma_j \frac{\partial v}{\partial n_j} \mu_j\, \mathrm{d}n + \int_D v\, \Sigma \frac{\partial \mu_j}{\partial n_j}\, \mathrm{d}n = \int_{\partial D} v\mu \cdot \mathrm{d}s, \quad (9.58)$$

where ∂D is the boundary of D, and $\mathrm{d}s$ is outward normal to this surface. This theorem allows us to write

$$L = \int [\,\{v - \lambda p \cdot x - \lambda \zeta\}\, f - v\, \nabla \cdot \mu - u_n \cdot \mu]\ \mathrm{d}n + \int_{\partial D} v\mu \cdot \mathrm{d}s, \quad (9.59)$$

with ∂D the boundary of the nonnegative orthant, and $\nabla \cdot \mu$ a standard notation for the divergence $\Sigma_j \partial\mu_j/\partial n_j$.

Setting the derivatives of L with respect to $x(n)$ and $v(n)$ equal to zero as in the one-dimensional case, we get

$$(s - p)f = \frac{u_z}{\lambda}\, s_n \cdot \mu\,, \quad (9.60)$$

$$\nabla \cdot \mu + \frac{u_{zn}}{u_z} \cdot \mu = \left(1 - \frac{\lambda}{u_z}\right) f\,. \quad (9.61)$$

(Note that $s_n \cdot \mu$ is a vector with components $\Sigma_j(\partial s_i/\partial n_j)\mu_j$, and $u_{zn} \cdot \mu$ is defined similarly.) These equations are supplemented by boundary conditions on μ obtained by considering variations of v on the boundary of the orthant:

$$\mu_j = 0 \text{ when } n_j = 0, \infty. \tag{9.62}$$

No doubt a thorough analysis of these conditions would be quite complicated. The basic ideas are tolerably clear when $I \geqslant J$. First one should consider the system of equations:

$$\begin{aligned} v &= u(x, z, n), \\ v' &= u_n(x, z, n), \\ (s - p) f &= \frac{u_z}{\lambda} s_n \cdot \mu . \end{aligned} \tag{9.63}$$

There are $I + J + 1$ of these equations. Consequently one can hope to solve for J variables μ_j/λ, the I variables x_i, and z, as functions of v, $v' = (\partial v/\partial n_1, \ldots, \partial f/\partial n_J)$, and n. Substituting in (9.61), one has

$$\Sigma \frac{\partial}{\partial n_j} \mu_j(v, v', n) + \Sigma \frac{u_{zn_j}(x(v, v', n), z(v, v', n), n)}{u_z} \mu_j(v, v', n)$$

$$= \left(1 - \frac{\lambda}{u_z}\right) f. \tag{9.64}$$

This is a second-order partial differential equation in v. It is to be associated with boundary conditions upon v and v' on the boundary of the nonnegative orthants which are defined by (9.62). For this to make sense, (9.64) should be an elliptic equation. Methods for computing the solution of such partial differential equations with given boundary conditions are available. Once (9.64) has been solved for v, $x(n)$ and $z(n)$ can be obtained from (9.63), thus defining the desired budget set. (Seade has shown me the method does not work when $I < J$.)

It is interesting to note that the budget set so obtained will in general be of dimension Min(I, J). So long as $J \leqslant I$, there is no reason why consumers of different types should not be choosing different consumption plans in the optimal equilibrium. Then the budget set defined as

$$B = \left\{(x(n), z(n)) \colon n \geqslant 0\right\} , \tag{9.65}$$

is of dimension J.

But if $J > I$, this set has dimension I. This has to be true because, for any given vector x, any consumer would choose the largest z with (x, z) in B. Therefore B may be restricted to vectors (x, z) with a unique z for each x, and that is a set of dimension I. It can be confirmed that (9.54) implies $(x(m), z(m)) = (x(n), z(n))$ for all m such that

$$s(x(n), z(n), m) = s(x(n), z(n), n), \tag{9.66}$$

so that a $(J - I)$-dimensional set of consumers chooses each point of B. To prove this, one uses the symmetry of the matrix $v'' - u_{nn}$, which is equal to

$$v'' - u_{nn} = u_z \sum_i \frac{\partial s_i}{\partial n_j} \frac{\partial x_i}{\partial n_k} . \tag{9.67}$$

The details are left to the reader.

When $J < I$, the budget set B can be extended to an I-dimensional set without introducing new consumption vectors that any consumer would wish to choose. Then it can be expressed in the form

$$z = c(x). \tag{9.68}$$

In the case $J = 1$, where B is 1-dimensional, it is often possible to describe the optimal budget set in the 1-dimensional form

$$x_i = a_i(z), \qquad i = 1, \ldots, I, \tag{9.69}$$

which may be preferable administratively. This requires, of course, that x_i and z are monotonically related in the optimum. It is only when $J > 1$ that some cross-dependence of tax rates is generally necessary for optimality.

The most important aspect of the conditions developed in this section, from the point of view of the previous section, is that the attractive simplicity of the marginal-tax-rate equation (9.36) has to some extent been lost in its generalized form (9.60). The signs of marginal tax rates can no longer be determined without prior knowledge of the multipliers μ_j. Correspondingly, the conditions for Pareto-efficiency come from

$$\Sigma \mu_j \frac{\partial}{\partial n_j} (\tau_{i1}/\tau_{i2}) = 0 , \tag{9.70}$$

and say that the $J \times (I - 1)$ matrix $[(\partial/\partial n_j)/(\tau_i/\tau_1)]$ has rank no greater than $J - 1$. This condition is empty when $J \geqslant I$. A principal purpose of this section has been to warn that the results of the previous section depend for their relative simplicity on the one-parameter assumption. At the same time, it should be remembered that only models with a small number of parameters are likely to be of any use for the practical implementation of optimal tax theory.

9.5. Optimal Mixed Taxation

The results of the nonlinear approach to the theory of optimal taxation are interesting and promising. What should be emphasized is the contrast with the linear results, that the nonlinear conditions say some rather clear things about tax rates, whereas the linear conditions say something about demand changes. It is hard to resist the appeal of conditions where tax rates appear explicitly. But this is achieved at considerable cost. The form of budget constraint the government is supposed to be able to impose is extremely general, allowing progression or regression in the taxation of all commodities. That is to say, the satisfaction of the first-order conditions must be expected to be inconsistent with a simple tax system, with constant tax rates, or even tax rates dependent upon the consumption of the commodity taxed alone. What worries me about this is not the difficulty of persuading government to adopt complicated tax systems, but the serious neglect of tax avoidance possibilities (by trade among consumers) which the comparison of these very general tax systems commits us to. In this section, I derive conditions for an optimal tax system in which some commodities (i.e. one at least) are subjected to nonlinear taxation, while the others are subject to constant tax rates. Thus, in particular, nonlinear taxation can be restricted to commodities in which retrading is impossible or perfectly observed.

The notation to be used in this section is:

x = vector of net demands for commodities subject to proportional taxation,
p = producer prices for these commodities,
q = consumer prices for these commodities,
z = vector of net demands for commodities subject to nonlinear taxation,
r = producer prices for these commodities.

The population is described by a single parameter n.

Define an expenditure function

$$m(q, z, v, n) = \mathrm{Min}\,[q \cdot x : u(x, z, n) = v]. \tag{9.71}$$

Then we can define a compensated demand function, in this case for the goods subject to proportional taxation only, with demand for the other goods given:

$$x^c(q, z, v, n) = m_q(q, z, v, n). \tag{9.72}$$

We are contemplating allocations in which, for each n,

$$x(n), z(n) \text{ maximize } u(x, z, n) \text{ subject to } (q \cdot x, z) \in B, \tag{9.73}$$

where B expresses the nonlinear taxation. For example, in the case where one good only is subject to nonlinear taxation, B would be described by $q \cdot x \leqslant wz - t(z)$, w being the price of that good.

As in the case of completely nonlinear taxation, we want to express (9.73) in a more readily manipulated form. To this end, define a partially indirect utility function,

$$u^*(q, y, z, n) = \text{Max}\left\{u(x, z, n) : q \cdot x \leqslant y\right\}. \tag{9.74}$$

(9.73) is equivalent to:

$$y(n) = q \cdot x(n), z(n) \text{ maximizes } u^*(q, y, z, n) \text{ subject to } (y, z) \in B, \tag{9.75}$$

$$x(n) \text{ maximizes } u(x, z(n), n) \text{ subject to } q \cdot xy(n). \tag{9.76}$$

We know already from section 9.3, and the appendix to the chapter, that (9.75) is equivalent to

$$v'(n) = u_n^*(q, y(n), z(n), n), \tag{9.77}$$

where

$$v(n) = u^*(q, y(n), z(n), n), \tag{9.78}$$

along with inequality constraints which can be neglected in a large class of cases. (9.76) is equivalent to

$$x(n) = x^c(q, z(n), v(n), n),$$

$$y(n) = m(q, z(n), v(n), n). \tag{9.79}$$

As a result of these transformations, we address ourselves to the following problem:

$$\text{Max} \int v(n) f(n) \, \mathrm{d}n,$$

subject to

$$\int [p \cdot x^c(q, z, v, n) + r \cdot z] f \, \mathrm{d}n = A,$$

$$v'(n) = u_n^*(q, m(q, z, v, n), z, n). \tag{9.80}$$

From this simple form, the first-order conditions for optimal mixed taxation are readily derived. The Lagrangean is

$$\begin{aligned} L &= \int \left\{[v - \lambda(p \cdot x^c + r \cdot z)]f + \mu v' - \mu u_n^*(q, m, z, n)\right\} \mathrm{d}n \\ &= \int \left\{[v - \lambda(p \cdot x^c + r \cdot z)]f - \mu' v - \mu u_n^*\right\} \mathrm{d}n - \mu(0)v(0) + \mu(\infty)v(\infty). \end{aligned} \tag{9.81}$$

The derivatives of L with respect to q, $\nu(\cdot)$, and $z(\cdot)$ are to be set equal to zero.

Optimizing first with respect to q, we obtain conditions for optimal commodity taxation:

$$\lambda \int p \cdot x_q^c f \, dn + \int \mu(u_{nq}^* + u_{ny}^* m_q) \, dn = 0. \tag{9.82}$$

As usual, Slutsky symmetry implies that

$$p \cdot x_q^c = (q - t) \cdot x_q^c = -t \cdot x_q^c = -x_q^c \cdot t. \tag{9.83}$$

To evaluate $u_{nq}^* + u_{ny}^* m_q$, we use the fact (Roy's theorem for the situation) that

$$u_q^* + u_y^* x(q, y, z, n) = 0, \tag{9.84}$$

where $x(q, y, z, n)$ is defined as the x that maximizes $u(x, z, n)$ subject to $q \cdot x \leqslant y$. (9.84) is an identity. Differentiating partially with respect to n, we get

$$u_{nq}^* + u_{ny}^* x + u_y^* x_n = 0. \tag{9.85}$$

Substitution of (9.83) and (9.85) into (9.82) yields

$$\left(\int x_q^c f \, dn\right) \cdot t = -\int \nu(n) x_n(q, y(n), z(n), n) \, dn \tag{9.86}$$

where

$$\nu(n) = u_y^* \mu / \lambda. \tag{9.87}$$

In section 9.2, it was argued that $-\left(\int x_q^c f \, dn\right) \cdot t$ is a satisfactory measure of the extent to which commodity taxes discourage consumption of the different commodities. (9.86) says that discouragement should be zero when $x_n = 0$. We shall see that ν is normally nonnegative in such cases as the model with n interpreted as ability. Then $x_{in} > 0$ implies that commodity i should be discouraged, while $x_{in} < 0$ implies that it should be encouraged.

This surprisingly simple criterion says that commodity taxes should bear more heavily on the commodities *high-n* individuals have relatively strongest tastes for. Notice that the criterion looks at the way in which demand change *for given income and labor supply* when n changes. The spirit of the criterion is more akin to the two-class criterion [Mirrlees (1975)] than to that of Ramsey (1927). But it is surprising, and satisfactory, that it is expressed as an integral of $\partial x / \partial n$ rather than an integral of x.

Turning to the conditions for nonlinear taxation, we differentiate L (9.81) with respect to $z(n)$ and $\nu(n)$:

$$-(p \cdot x_z^c + r)\lambda f = \mu(u_{ny}^* m_z + u_{nz}^*) \tag{9.88}$$

$$\mu' + u^*_{ny} m_v \mu = (1 - \lambda p \cdot x^c_v) f, \tag{9.89}$$

$$\mu(0) = 0, \qquad \mu(\infty) = 0. \tag{9.90}$$

These equations correspond in a general way to (9.34), (9.33) and (9.35) above. The correspondence can be brought out more clearly if we define the marginal rate of substitution between y and z:

$$s = u^*_z / u^*_y = - m_x. \tag{9.91}$$

Then

$$s_n = u^*_{nz}/u^*_y - s u^*_{ny}/u^*_y = (u^*_{nz} + u^*_{ny} m_z)/u^*_y, \tag{9.92}$$

and

$$\begin{aligned} p \cdot x^c_z &= q \cdot x^c_z - t \cdot x^c_z = m_z - t \cdot x_z - t \cdot x_y m_z \\ &= - (1 - t \cdot x_y) x - t \cdot x_z. \end{aligned} \tag{9.93}$$

Note also that

$$m_v u^*_y = 1 \tag{9.94}$$

and

$$\begin{aligned} p \cdot x^c_v &= q \cdot x^c_v - t \cdot x^c_v = m_v - t \cdot x_y m_v \\ &= (1 - t \cdot x_y)/u^*_y. \end{aligned} \tag{9.95}$$

Introducing the results of these calculations into (9.88) and (9.89), and using definition (9.87), we obtain

$$[(1 - t \cdot x_y)s + t \cdot x_z - r] f = v s_n, \tag{9.96}$$

$$\mu' + \frac{u^*_{ny}}{u^*_y} \mu = [1 - (\lambda / u^*_y)(1 - t \cdot x_y)] f. \tag{9.97}$$

In order better to appreciate these equations, it should be recognized that $(1 - t \cdot x_y)s + t \cdot x_z - r$ is the total marginal tax rates on the z commodities, including both linear and nonlinear taxes.

When applying the theory of optimal income taxation to an economy with many commodities, one would use a utility function for disposable income and labor which assumes given prices for commodities. Both in actual economies and optimized ones, these prices are not proportional to the social marginal costs of commodities. (9.96) and (9.97) show how one should allow for the differences. Calculations of optimal tax rates that have been done [e.g. Mirrlees (1971) and Stern (1975)] do not allow for this, so it is interesting to consider in which direction the results have been biased, and whether these calculated optimal rates are closer to the optimal income tax or the optimal total tax rate (including commodity tax effects).

The interrelations of the various equations are so complicated that no general answer to these questions seems possible. But it is instructive to consider the special case

$$u = U(a(x, n) + b(z, n)). \tag{9.98}$$

It will be recollected that, when $a_n \equiv 0$, it is optimal to have no commodity taxes (linear or nonlinear), so long as it is possible to tax the z-goods nonlinearly (section 9.3 above). That case is therefore of no interest for our present purpose. Instead take the case where

$$a \text{ is homogeneous of degree one in } x. \tag{9.99}$$

It is then easily seen that the functions $s(q, y, z, n)$ and $x(q, y, z, n)$ used in the theory above have the following properties:

$$s_y = 0, \tag{9.100}$$

$$x_y = x/y, \tag{9.101}$$

$$x_z = 0. \tag{9.102}$$

Also, in indirect form, $a = ya^*(q, n)$.

We need to know how $t \cdot x_y$ varies with n:

$$\frac{\mathrm{d}}{\mathrm{d}n} t \cdot x_y = \frac{\mathrm{d}}{\mathrm{d}n} \frac{t \cdot x}{y} = \frac{t \cdot x_n + t \cdot x_y y' + t \cdot x_z \cdot z'}{y} - \frac{t \cdot x}{y^2} y'$$

$$= \frac{t \cdot x_n}{y} + \frac{t \cdot x}{y^2} y' - \frac{t \cdot x}{y^2} y'$$

$$= \frac{t \cdot x_n}{y}. \tag{9.103}$$

Now, from (9.86), we have

$$\int vt \cdot x_n \, dn = -\int t \cdot x_q^c \cdot tf \, dn \geqslant 0, \tag{9.104}$$

by Slutsky. This suggests that, normally,

$$v \frac{d}{dn} t \cdot x_y \geqslant 0. \tag{9.105}$$

Trying to confirm that v is nonnegative, we use the computation (following the argument that led to (9.49))

$$\frac{d}{dn} u_y^* = u_{ny}^* + U''(ya^* + b)(y'a^* + b_z z')a^* = u_{ny}^*, \tag{9.106}$$

since $y' = -s \cdot z' = -(b_z/a^*) \cdot z'$. Also, note that

$$u_{ny}^* = U'' \cdot (ya_n^* + b_n)a^* + U' \cdot a_n^*. \tag{9.107}$$

A variety of assumptions would make the left-hand side of (9.107) nonpositive: for example, it is sufficient that

$$\frac{zU''(z)}{U'(z)} \leqslant -1, \quad \frac{\partial}{\partial n}(a^*/b) \leqslant 0. \tag{9.108}$$

Under these assumptions

$$\frac{d}{dn} u_y^* \leqslant 0. \tag{9.109}$$

We also have (from (9.106), and the definition of v, (9.87))

$$\frac{d}{dn} v = \left(\frac{u_y^*}{\lambda} - 1 + t \cdot x_y \right) f. \tag{9.110}$$

I shall show that, if (9.105) holds, $v \geqslant 0$ for all n. Suppose that on the contrary, $v(n_1) < 0$. Since $v(0) = 0$, there exists n_2 that $v(n_2) < 0$ and $v'(n_2) < 0$. Then, by (9.110), (9.105) and (9.109),

$$\frac{d}{dn}\left(\frac{1}{f} \frac{dv}{dn} \right) \leqslant 0 \text{ in a neighborhood of } n_2.$$

Consequently, ν' is nonincreasing in the neighborhood of n_2, and ν decreases. This must hold, then, for all $n \geqslant n_2$, and we conclude that

$$\nu(n) < \nu(n_2) < 0, \qquad \text{for all } n > n_2. \tag{9.111}$$

This contradicts the condition that $\nu \to 0$ as $n \to \infty$.

Collecting arguments, we have shown that, on the reasonable postulate that (9.105) holds,

$$\nu \geqslant 0, \qquad (\text{all } n) \tag{9.112}$$

$$\frac{\mathrm{d}}{\mathrm{d}n}(t \cdot x_y) \geqslant 0 \qquad (\text{all } n). \tag{9.113}$$

Thus the introduction of commodity taxes introduces an increasing term into the right-hand side of equation (9.110). Since ν begins and ends at zero, this seems to mean that ν should increase more slowly and then decrease more slowly than in the absence of commodity taxes: that is, ν should be smaller.

The consequences of this for tax rates may be understood most clearly for the case of a simple income tax, where labor is the only commodity subject to nonlinear taxation. Taking labor as numéraire, $r = 1$ and $-z$ is labor supplied (z being a negative number). Let the income tax be $\theta(-z)$. Then the budget constraint is $y = -z - \theta(-z)$, and the consumer equates $s = u_z/u_y$ to $1 - \theta'(-z)$. Thus the right-hand side of (9.96)

$$(1 - t \cdot x_y)s + t \cdot x_z - r = (1 - t \cdot x_y)(1 - \theta') + t \cdot x_z - 1$$

$$= -\frac{\partial}{\partial(-z)}[t \cdot x(q, -z - \theta, z, n) + \theta(-z)]$$

$$= -\text{ marginal total tax on labor earnings.}$$

$$= -\tau, \text{ say.}$$

(9.96) says that

$$\tau = -\nu s_n, \tag{9.114}$$

and, if n represents ability, $s_n = (\partial/\partial n)(u_z^*/u_y^*)$ should be negative, since n-men find it easier to supply labor.

We find, then, that lower ν implies lower τ: the tax system as a whole should it seems, bear less heavily upon labor on the margin than one would suppose if commodity taxes were not allowed for. From the calculations above (noting that $x_z = 0$ in the special case we are dealing with) we have

$$\theta'(-z) = \frac{\tau}{1 - t \cdot x_y} - \frac{t \cdot x_y}{1 - t \cdot x_y}, \tag{9.115}$$

so that θ' should be yet smaller than τ, if commodity taxes are predominantly positive.

In the above argument it was, first, assumed that individuals had a special form of utility function; and, second, an unproved (but reasonable) conjecture was made at (9.105). It would be even harder to push through a corresponding argument for the general case. Yet the argument provides some reason for believing that the usual calculations of income tax rates are too high, not only because the commodity tax system does and should do some of the work of the income tax; but also because the varying pattern of demand with ability normally requires a lower marginal total tax on labor income. It would be interesting to know whether calculations for plausible cases would support this conjecture. Though strongly suggested by the equations, it is hard to understand intuitively.

It is worth noting one further feature of the first-order conditions, namely that they contain within them some necessary conditions for Pareto-efficiency, which we can obtain by eliminating ν from equations (9.86) and (9.96):

$$-(\int x_q^c \, f \, \mathrm{d}n) \cdot t = \int \left\{(1 - t \cdot x_y)s + t \cdot x_z - r\right\} s_n^{-1} x_n \, f \, \mathrm{d}n. \tag{9.116}$$

These relations are not easy to interpret as they stand. The main point is that the weighting function $\nu(n)$ appearing in the conditions for commodity taxation and for income taxation must be the same. (9.116) could allow one to calculate optimal commodity tax systems once the optimal income tax was known, without further reference to the welfare function. It might be more interesting to use them as a means of identifying commodities which are affected in a grossly nonoptimal way by the tax system. But in this form, the efficiency conditions seem not much more than a theoretical curiosity.

This completes the discussion of mixed taxation. It is interesting to note that the optimality conditions (9.86), (9.96) and (9.97) contain within them *both* the conditions for optimality where full nonlinearity is possible *and* the conditions where only linearity is possible. The theory of linear taxation is obtained simply by omitting z and ignoring (9.96). In this case, $x_n = (\mathrm{d}/\mathrm{d}n)x$, and the right-hand side of (9.86) can be integrated by parts. The details will be left to the reader. The conditions for nonlinear taxation are obtained by letting x be one-dimensional. No control is then lost by setting $q = p$. Then (9.86) is irrelevant, and the remaining equations reduce to the theory of section 9.3.

9.6. Public Goods in an Optimal Mixed System

The point to be made in this section is a simple one. Let g be a public good, entering all utility functions (possibly trivially in some cases) and with production price π. In the Lagrangean (9.81), x^c, u_n^*, and m are now all functions of g as well as the other variables; and πg appears as an additional term in the production constraint, so that one subtracts $\lambda\pi g$ from the Lagrangean. Then differentiation with respect to g yields

$$\lambda \int p \cdot x_q^c f \, dn + \lambda\pi + \int \mu(u_{ng}^* + u_{ny}^* m_g) \, dn = 0. \tag{9.117}$$

By means of the usual manipulation in tax theory, we have

$$\begin{aligned} p \cdot x_g^c &= (q - t) \cdot x_g^c \\ &= m_g - t \cdot (x_g + x_y m_g) \\ &= - t \cdot x_g + (1 - t \cdot x_y) m_g. \end{aligned} \tag{9.118}$$

Furthermore, $m_g = - u_g^*/u_y^*$, and we want to define

$$\sigma = u_g^*/u_y^* = - m_g \tag{9.119}$$

as the marginal rate of substitution between income and the public good. Partial differentiation of (9.119) with respect to n gives

$$\begin{aligned} \sigma_n &= (u_{ng}^* - u_g^* u_{ny}^*/u_y^*)/u_y^* \\ &= (u_{ng}^* + u_{ny}^* m_g)/u_y^*. \end{aligned} \tag{9.120}$$

Using (9.118) and (9.120) we can write (9.117) in the form

$$\pi = \int (1 - t \cdot x_y) \sigma f \, dn + \int t \cdot x_g f \, dn - \int \nu \sigma_n \, dn. \tag{9.121}$$

This says that the supply of public goods should be at such a level that their marginal costs are equal to a sum of:

(1) individual marginal rates of substitution for the public goods, reduced by a proportion equal to the derivative of commodity taxes with respect to income spent on them (for that individual),
(2) the derivatives of total commodity tax revenue with respect to the provision of the public goods, less
(3) a weighted sum of terms expressing how the personal value of the public good varies with n.

The first two parts of this expression give a direct estimate of the social value of the good, adding marginal rates of substitution in the usual way, and making allowance for direct revenue effects. The last part of the expression corrects this estimate for distributional considerations. It uses the fundamental weighting factors $\nu(n)$ which played such an important part in the conditions for optimal taxation, and applies them to the quantities σ_n, which show how much preference for the public good varies with n. This is analogous to the way in which ν multiplied s_n and x_n in the optimal tax conditions. In the normal case with $\nu \geqslant 0$, the correcting term is negative if the more able have a stronger preference for the public good, positive if the less able have. Thus the rule encourages provision of public goods valued by the poor and discourages those valued by the rich. The existence of optimal taxes does not eliminate distributional considerations in the provision of public goods; but it does allow the distributional considerations to be analyzed out and expressed as a separate contribution to (or deduction from) the marginal social value of the good.

It will be recognized that, in the one-parameter case, ν can be deduced from the optimal taxes themselves through (9.96), and substituted in (9.121). Thus we obtain a further set of welfare-independent conditions which are necessary for Pareto efficiency. In the case of zero commodity taxes (or fully nonlinear taxation) these conditions take a rather neat form:

$$\pi = \int \left(\sigma - \tau_i \frac{\sigma_n}{s_{in}} \right) f \, dn, \tag{9.122}$$

where τ, the marginal tax on commodity i, is $s_i - p_i$. An alternative form is

$$\pi = \int \sigma \left(1 - \frac{\sigma_n / \sigma}{\tau_{in} / \tau_i} \right) f \, dn . \tag{9.123}$$

In this form it is plain that the social value of the public good is enhanced when its value for some individual responds more sensitively to n than do his marginal tax rates.

9.7. The Fundamental Principle of Optimal Tax Theory

We have derived necessary conditions for the optimality of various economic policy variables. These conditions have an essentially simple common structure, which it is the purpose of this section to emphasize.

If an economic policy is optimal, there is no change in it which will leave total welfare unchanged and at the same time generate a net addition to government revenue. Consider a small change in some policy, δP, and associate with it income transfers to and from individuals which are designed to keep total welfare constant. These transfers may be analyzed into two parts. First an income transfer δy_1 made that would, if behavior did not change, leave each individual's utility unchanged: this transfer is pure compensation for the initial policy change. Since it is not in general possible to make these δy_1 transfers in a lump-sum manner, individuals would want to change their behavior to benefit from the structure of these transfers. We therefore institute a second set of income transfers δy_2 whose effect is to leave *total* utility unchanged, while removing the incentive to change behavior arising from the first round of transfers. Specifically, we know that individuals always adjust their behavior in such a way that $v' = u_n$. Having chosen δy_1 so that $\delta v = 0$, δy_2 is now chosen so that $\delta v' = \delta u_n$.

These income transfers create changes $\delta y_1 + \delta y_2$ in government expenditures, which are partly offset by changes in tax revenue, δt_1 arising from the policy change δP, utility being kept constant, and δt_2 arising from the second-round income transfers δy_2.

If the policy were originally optimal, the net increase in government revenue does not increase whether the policy change is positive or negative. Thus

$$\int (\delta y_1 - \delta t_1 + \delta y_2 - \delta t_2) f \, \mathrm{d}n = 0. \tag{9.124}$$

δy_1 and δt_1 are easily computed from elementary considerations. Writing

$m(v, P, n)$ = income yielding utility v for n-man when policy is P, (9.125)

$t(v, P, N)$ = tax revenue from n-man when he has utility v and policy is P, (9.126)

we have

$$\delta y_1 = \frac{\partial m}{\partial P} \delta P = m_p \delta P, \tag{9.127}$$

$$\delta t_1 = \frac{\partial t}{\partial P} \delta P = t_p \delta P. \tag{9.128}$$

It remains to estimate $\delta y_2 - \delta t_2$. Remarkably, we find that

$$\int (\delta y_2 - \delta t_2) f \, \mathrm{d}n = - \int \nu(n) \left(\frac{\partial}{\partial n} m_p \right)_{m,P} \mathrm{d}n, \tag{9.129}$$

where m_P is differentiated with m,P held constant; and the multipliers ν (normally nonnegative) *are independent of the particular policy considered.* This is what we have been discovering in the previous sections of this chapter. There we also found that ν is the solution of the differential equation (rewriting (9.89))

$$u_y^* \frac{\mathrm{d}}{\mathrm{d}n}(\nu/u_y^*) + u_{ny}^*(\nu/u_y^*) = (1 - \lambda p \cdot x_\nu^c)f$$

$$= (1 - \lambda m_\nu + \lambda t_\nu)\, f, \tag{9.130}$$

with $\nu = 0$ at $n = 0, \infty$. The function $u^*(y, P, n)$ is related to the compensation function m by

$$\nu = u^*(m, P, n). \tag{9.131}$$

Thus the fundamental principle is that we can assess the value of a policy by associating with an n-man three numbers:

(1) m_p = pure compensation for the policy,

(2) $-t_P$ = reduction in taxes, at constant utility,

(3) $-(\nu/f)\,((\partial/\partial n)m_P)_{m,P}$ = distributional and incentive effects.

The total effect of the policy is measured by adding these numbers for everyone affected. For the three major policy tools examined in this chapter we have table 9-1. To appreciate the last row of the table, it should be understood that the instruments in the case of nonlinear taxes are best taken to be the demands $z(n)$ for the taxed commodities (marginal tax rates lead to very complicated equations which can only with considerable labor be reduced to the simple form).

The form in which commodity tax rules appear is also worth attention. For this case the cost of an increase in a commodity tax rate is

$$\int \left[x - (x_q^c \cdot t + x) - \frac{\nu}{f} x_n \right] f\, \mathrm{d}n. \tag{9.132}$$

If there are no nonuniform policies (such as nonlinear taxes), $x_n = (\mathrm{d}/\mathrm{d}n)x$, and the last term can be integrated by parts, so that we have the form

$$\int x_q^c \cdot t\, f\, \mathrm{d}n = \int \nu'(n) x\, \mathrm{d}n, \tag{9.133}$$

which is essentially equation (9.12) of section 9.2. In this case $\nu'(n)$ is the social marginal utility of income transfer.

In the general case, since ν is the multiplier dual to the constraint

$$0 = (\nu' - u_n)/u_y$$

$$= m_\nu \nu' + m_n$$

$$= \left(\frac{\partial}{\partial n} m(\nu(n), P, n) \right)_P, \tag{9.134}$$

Table 9-1
The Three Major Policy Tools

Policy Instrument	m_P	t_P
Proportional taxes	x	$\frac{\partial}{\partial t}(t \cdot x_q^c) = x_q^c \cdot t + x$
Public goods	$\sigma = u_g^*/u_y^*$	$\frac{\partial}{\partial g}(t \cdot x^c) = t \cdot x_g^c$
Nonlinear taxes	$s = u_z^*/u_y^*$	$\frac{\partial}{\partial x}(t \cdot x^c + p \cdot z)$

it is appropriate to call ν the *social marginal utility of income-difference.*

The striking feature of this analysis is that the distributional aspects of policy choice can be incorporated in a weighting function ν; which then defines a simple differential operator to be applied to m_P. m_P is the old measure of social value, which ignores revenue effects and the desirable 'distortions' arising from distributional considerations. It is easy to see how to supplement it with an estimate of revenue effects; and we now have a simple general principle showing how the remaining adjustment should be made. The method can be applied without difficulty to other types of economic policy, such as quantity rationing, wherever the simple equilibrium model of this chapter is thought to be appropriate.

References

Atkinson, A.B., "How Progressive Should Income Tax Be?" in *Essays in Modern Economics* J.M. Parkin and A. Nobay (eds.), New York: Macmillan, 1973.

Atkinson, A.B., and J.E. Stiglitz, "The Structure of Indirect Taxation and Economic Efficiency," *Journal of Public Economics* 1 (1972):97-119.

Atkinson, A.B., and J.E. Stiglitz, "The Design of Tax Structure: Direct versus Indirect Taxation," *Journal of Public Economics* 6 (1976):55-75.

Deaton, A.S., "Equity, Efficiency and the Structure of Indirect Taxation," Cambridge, mimeo, 1975.

Diamond, P.A., "A Many-Person Ramsey Tax Rule," *Journal of Public Economics* 4 (1975):335-342.

Diamond, P.A., and J.A. Mirrlees, "Optimal Taxation and Public Production," *American Economic Review* 61 (1971):8-27 and 261-278.

Mirrlees, J.A., "An Exploration in the Theory of Optimal Income Taxation," *Review of Economic Studies* 38 (1971):175-208.

Mirrlees, J.A., "On Producer Taxation," *Review of Economic Studies* 39 (1972):105-111.

Mirrlees, J.A., "Optimal Commodity Taxation in a Two-Class Economy," *Journal of Public Economics* 4 (1975):27-33.

Phelps, E.S., "Taxation of Wage Income for Economic Justice," *Quarterly Journal of Economics* 87 (1973):331-354.

Ramsey, F.P., "A Contribution to the Theory of Taxation," *Economic Journal* 37 (1927):47-61.

Sadka, E., "On Income Distribution, Incentive Effects and Optimal Income Taxation," *Review of Economic Studies*, 43 (1976):261-267.

Seade, J., "Progressivity of Income Taxation," Oxford, mimeo, 1975.

Stern, N.H., "On the Specification of Models of Optimum Income Taxation," *Journal of Public Economics* 6 (1976):123-162.

Stiglitz, J.E., and P.S. Dasgupta, "Differential Taxation, Public Goods and Economic Efficiency," *Review of Economics Studies* 38 (1971):151-174.

Appendix 9A

The following lemma will be proved, on the assumption that $u(x, z, n)$ is a twice differentiable function, increasing in z; and x, z are differentiable functions of n:

Lemma. If

$$v(n) = u(x(n), z(n), n), \qquad v'(n) = u_n(x(n), z(n), n), \tag{9A.1}$$

and for all m, n,

$$s_m(x(n), z(n), m) \cdot x'(n) \geqslant 0, \tag{9A.2}$$

then there exists B such that, for all n,

$$x(n), z(n) \text{ maximizes } u(x, z, n) \text{ for } (x, z) \in B. \tag{9A.3}$$

If (9.A.3) holds, and (9A.1) holds and for all n

$$s_n(x(n), z(n), n) \cdot x'(n) \geqslant 0. \tag{9A.4}$$

Recollect that $s = u_x/u_z$.

Proof. The second part of the theorem was proved in section 9.3 following equation (9.19).

For the first part, suppose on the contrary that there exist n_1, n_2 such that

$$u(x(n_1), z(n_1), n_2) > u(x(n_2), z(n_2), n_2). \tag{9A.5}$$

If $n_1 < n_2$ (a similar argument works if $n_1 > n_2$), (9A.5) implies the existence of n_3, $n_1 < n_3 < n_2$ such that

$$\frac{\partial}{\partial n} u(x(n), z(n), n_2) < 0 \quad \text{at } n = n_3. \tag{9A.6}$$

This derivative is equal to

$$u_x(x(n_3), z(n_3), n_2) \cdot x'(n_3) + u_z z'(n_3)$$
$$= u_z\,[s(x(n_3), z(n_3), n_2) \cdot x'(n_3) + z'(n_3)].$$

Therefore

$$s(x(n_3), z(n_3), n_2) \cdot x'(n_3) + z'(n_3) < 0. \tag{9A.7}$$

But (9A.1) implies that

$$s(x(n_3), z(n_3), n_3) \cdot x'(n_3) + z'(n_3) = 0. \tag{9A.8}$$

Since $n_3 < n_2$, (9A.7) and (9A.8) imply the existence of n_4, $n_3 < n_4 < n_2$, such that

$$s_n(x(n_3), z(n_3), n_4) \cdot x'(n_3) < 0, \tag{9A.9}$$

contradicting (9A.2).

This proves that (9A.3) holds with B defined as the set of $(x(n), z(n))$ as n runs through all values. Thus the lemma is proved.

10 Direct versus Indirect Pigovian Taxation

Agnar Sandmo

10.1. Introduction

The theory of externalities has gained new life recently both as an area for further theoretical developments and as a source of prescriptions for economic policies. No doubt this is due both to the inherent theoretical interest of the subject and to the increased possibilities for application which have emerged from the concern with policies designed to protect the physical environment.

One policy prescription which is solidly grounded in economic theory is the Pigovian tax solution: In the presence of negative external effects, and given the appropriate convexity conditions, an efficient allocation of resources can be achieved by levying taxes on the commodities generating external effects. Partly no doubt as the result of economists' advice the use of taxes and charges to control the environment is becoming of increasing interest both to politicians and administrators.

It may be natural to ask how the Pigovian tax solution stands up to the presence of related goods. In particular, one may ask the following question: Does implementation of the Pigovian principle require that a tax on an externality-creating commodity be accompanied by, e.g., taxes on complementary commodities or by subsidies on substitutes? In an otherwise perfect environment, i.e., an economy in which there are no other distortions and no constraints on government tax policy, the answer is no; with an optimal Pigovian tax, no other taxes or subsidies are needed to achieve efficiency.

If there are other distortions in the economy or limitations on tax policy, it is easy to see that the answer may be yes. A simple example is the case where, for some reason, the externality-creating commodity cannot be taxed; subsidising a substitute or taxing a complement may then obviously be better than doing nothing at all. However, this case may not be very interesting either from a theoretical or a practical point of view.

In an earlier paper (1975b), I discussed the case where the government has to raise a positive net revenue by means of indirect taxation, and where Pigovian taxes must be combined with other, distortionary, taxes. In that case the

Reprinted, with permission of North-Holland Publishing Company, from the *European Economic Review*, vol. 7, May 1976, pp. 337-349. Previous versions of this paper have been presented to seminars in Namur, Mannheim, Paris, Cambridge and Warwick. Helpful comments were received on all these occasions; I am particularly grateful to Peter Diamond, who pointed out a serious mistake in my original analysis, and to Shmuel Amir, Louis Gevers and Victor D. Norman.

Pigovian principle continues to hold in the sense that the marginal social damage is only reflected in the tax on the externality-creating commodity; all other taxes are determined according to the principles of efficient taxation in the no externalities case. However, a problem which did not arise in that analysis is the question of the appropriate tax base; it was assumed that the external effect was created by the total consumption of the commodity in question, so that the Pigovian principle calls for an ordinary commodity tax. This type of externality is what Meade (1952) has called 'creation of atmosphere', and it may be a very relevant one in many environmental problems.

A modification of this analysis consists of replacing total consumption with some more general function of the individual quantities consumed. Analytically, this is a generalization, since the case where individual quantities consumed enter only as a sum is obviously a special case. In the more general case a first-best implementation of the Pigovian principle is to tax individuals at different rates. If the government lacks the resources or the information to do this, second-best rules of optimal taxation are called for; see Diamond (1973). In an interesting recent contribution Green and Sheshinski (1976) have shown that in this case the superiority of indirect policies (e.g., subsidization of substitutes) cannot be ruled out.

The present chapter leads to conclusions which are analogous to those of Green and Sheshinski, but the assumptions behind the argument are different. When analyzing externalities it may be helpful to think in terms of a Lancaster-Muth model of consumption.[a] The arguments of consumers' utility functions are final goods which are produced in the households, using ordinary consumer goods as inputs in the production processes. Any one consumer good may be used as inputs into several such processes, and each process may require several kinds of consumer goods as inputs. The basic idea which we wish to explore is that externalities originate in the processes, not in the consumption of goods as such. Thus, it is the use of commodities in specific situations or for specific purposes which generate external effects, not their use as such. It is not difficult to think of suggestive examples. Cars used for transportation in congested urban areas generate serious externalities in the form of smoke, noise, time delays, etc., while cars used for long-distance travelling on highways hardly have any such effects. A few years ago the Norwegian government introduced a tax on plastic bags, the main argument being that their use contributed to a littering of the environment. However, after some time many people, including the garbage collectors, complained of the foul smell arising from the garbage cans because people no longer used plastic bags to wrap up their garbage. The tax has now been repealed. Taxes on alcohol and tobacco, to the extent that they can be justified by externality arguments, are subject to similar shortcomings. General commodity taxes have their obvious weaknesses in such cases.

[a]See Lancaster (1966) and Muth (1966). For the application of these ideas to the theory of public goods see Sandmo (1973, 1975a).

True, we would expect them to do some good, since they do raise the prices of some inputs into externality-creating processes. But they also raise the prices of inputs to processes which have no such effects, and thus introduce new distortions.[b]

The implication for optimal tax policy is clear: One should tax processes, not goods. But since, at least in a large number of cases, goods are the only feasible objects of taxation, the implication is that general commodity taxes are often not good enough; what we need are taxes on the use of certain commodities in certain processes. But the government normally has quite inadequate information and resources to manage such a tax system; it is therefore of interest to see what can be done when it is restricted to using commodity taxes in the ordinary sense of the word. In this paper we shall study a simple model of efficient taxation designed to throw some light on this problem. Section 10.2 sets out the basic assumptions of that model and solutions for optimal tax rates are derived and discussed in section 10.3. A problem related to the stability of the resulting equilibrium is discussed in more detail in section 10.4, while section 10.5 contains some concluding remarks. Throughout the chapter we are concerned with negative external effects; however, the results apply, with obvious modifications, to the case of positive external effects as well.

10.2 A Three-Commodity Model

Assume a competitive economy where labour is the numéraire commodity. Labor is the only factor of production and is used to produce two consumer goods with constant production coefficients; this obviously implies that producer prices are given. All consumers, of whom there is a large number n, are identical both as regards tastes and productivities. Let per capita consumption of leisure (or one minus the supply of labor) and the first consumer good be denoted x and y, respectively. The second consumer good is used for two different purposes (or in two different processes) in amounts z_1 and z_2, respectively. The second of these processes creates an external effect which is a function of the total amount of the second consumer good used in the process, $Z_2 (= nz_2)$. The utility function of the typical consumer can therefore be written as

[b]Although this chapter is concerned with externalities in consumption, it may well be that it is on the production side that the most important examples are to be found. Thus, the quality of factory smoke may be traced to specific inputs, but the effects of those inputs depend on which other inputs they are combined with, and this varies from one process to another. In discussing these problems with engineers, I have found that they tend to believe that commodity taxes cannot in practice be sufficiently fine-tuned to capture the technological complexities of environmental control.

$$u = u(x, y, z_1, z_2, Z_2). \tag{10.1}$$

The utility function is increasing in its first four arguments and decreasing in its fifth. It is assumed to be continuous, differentiable and strictly quasi-concave in its first four arguments.

In a competitive equilibrium a uniform price rules for uses of the second consumer good in the two processes, since they are perfect substitutes in production. Thus, each consumer maximizes his utility function (10.1) subject to his budget constraint

$$-(1 - x) + Py + Q(z_1 + z_2) = a. \tag{10.2}$$

Here P and Q are the consumer prices of the two consumer goods, and a is any lump-sum transfer received from the government. In maximizing (10.1) subject to (10.2) each individual consumer considers Z_2 to be given independently of his own decisions; this reflects the assumption that the individual considers himself to be small compared to the market, and that he is unaware of the fact that all others are exactly like himself.

Assuming that an interior solution exists, the first-order optimum conditions for the consumer are

$$\partial u/\partial x - \lambda = 0,$$

$$\partial u/\partial y - \lambda P = 0,$$

$$\partial u/\partial z_1 - \lambda Q = 0,$$

$$\partial u/\partial z_2 - \lambda Q = 0, \tag{10.3}$$

where the Lagrange multiplier λ is the marginal utility of income. This implies that the demand functions of the consumer can be written as

$$x = x(P, Q, a, Z_2),$$

$$y = y(P, Q, a, Z_2),$$

$$z_1 = z_1(P, Q, a, Z_2),$$

$$z_2 = z_2(P, Q, a, Z_2). \tag{10.4}$$

Note the presence of Z_2 as an argument of the demand functions. Z_2 is an argument in the utility function and will therefore affect the structure of demand; e.g., the existence of exhaust emission will in itself affect the consumer's demand for gasoline and other commodities.

As usual, we can write down Slutsky equations for the demand functions (10.4), e.g.,

$$\partial y/\partial P + y(\partial y/\partial a) = (\partial y/\partial P)_u, \tag{10.5}$$

and similar for the other price derivatives. The right-hand side of (10.5) is the substitution effect which we shall write more conveniently as S_{yP}; similarly, we shall write $(\partial z_1/\partial Q)_u$ as S_{1Q}, $(\partial z_2/\partial P)_u$ as S_{2P}, etc. The model implies of course that the direct substitution effects are neative, i.e.,

$$S_{yP} < 0, \quad S_{1Q} + S_{2Q} < 0. \tag{10.6}$$

Note that the model implies that it is the compensated effect of a change in Q on the *sum* $(z_1 + z_2)$ which is negative. In addition to the negativity condition on the own substitution effects we also have the so-called higher-order condition on substitution effects, which in this case can be written as

$$\begin{vmatrix} S_{yP} & S_{1P} + S_{2P} \\ S_{yQ} & S_{1Q} + S_{2Q} \end{vmatrix} > 0. \tag{10.7}$$

It does not detract much from the interest of the following discussion to strengthen slightly these conditions on substitution effects. The strengthening essentially amounts to assuming that if it were possible to differentiate the prices of z_1 and z_2 by a small amount at the optimum, then the resulting substitution effects would have all the regularity properties. It follows immediately that this would imply the conditions

$$S_{yP} < 0, \quad S_{1Q} < 0, \quad S_{2Q} < 0. \tag{10.8}$$

$$\begin{vmatrix} S_{yP} & S_{1P} \\ S_{yQ} & S_{1Q} \end{vmatrix} > 0, \quad \begin{vmatrix} S_{yP} & S_{2P} \\ S_{yQ} & S_{2Q} \end{vmatrix} > 0. \tag{10.9}$$

We shall refer to (10.6)-(10.7) and to (10.8)-(10.9) as the weak and strong regularity conditions, respectively. In our discussion of the optimal tax structure in the next section we shall assume that the strong regularity conditions hold. There seems to be good reasons for making this assumption. First, the numbering of the commodities Z_1 and Z_2 is arbitrary. Second, it seems to be extremely difficult to think of examples where additional possibilities admitted by the weak regularity conditions would be of any economic interest.

Finally, it will be useful to define the consumer's indirect utility function as $v(P, Q, a, Z_2)$. In the usual way it can be shown that

$$\partial v/\partial P = -\lambda y, \quad \partial v/\partial Q = -\lambda(z_1 + z_2), \quad \partial v/\partial a = \lambda. \tag{10.10}$$

These properties of utility and demand functions will be utilized in the analysis of optimal taxes, to which we now turn.

10.3. Tax Optimization

Since there are no public goods and no distributional problems in this economy, the role of government is limited to that of creating an efficient allocation of resources. If the government adopts a policy of laissez-faire, an equilibrium will be attained with consumer prices equal to producer prices and no government transfers. It is easy to show that this equilibrium is inefficient, and that efficiency calls for the government to raise the price of the second good when used in the second process by an amount reflecting the marginal social damage, $m = n\partial v/\partial Z_2$. This is the first-best Pigovian tax rule.

The difficulty about this proposal is of course that it involves pricing physically the same good differently according to the use that consumers make of it. Our assumption is that the information and control costs involved in this proposal are prohibitively high, and that the government is constrained to the use of ordinary commodity taxes. Let the amount of commodity taxes be s per unit of the first consumer good and t per unit of the second; labor is untaxed. The net revenue from the commodity taxes is redistributed to consumers in the form of a lump-sum subsidy of a per capita. Expressed in per capita terms, the government's budget constraint becomes

$$sy + t(z_1 + z_2) = a. \tag{10.11}$$

The government's objective is to maximize the utility of the representative consumer, as given by the indirect utility function v, subject to the constraint (10.11). The Lagrangean function becomes

$$L = v(P, Q, a, Z_2) - \mu\,[sy + t(z_1 + z_2) - a], \tag{10.12}$$

and the necessary optimum conditions can be found by setting the derivatives of L with respect to P, Q, and a equal to zero. Note that with the assumption of given producer prices, determining P and Q is equivalent to determining s and t. Utilizing (10.10), we can write the optimum conditions as

$$-\lambda y + m\frac{\partial z_2}{\partial P} - \mu\left[s\frac{\partial y}{\partial P} + y + t\left(\frac{\partial z_1}{\partial P} + \frac{\partial z_2}{\partial P}\right)\right.$$

$$\left. + \left(s\frac{\partial y}{\partial Z_2} + t\left(\frac{\partial z_1}{\partial Z_2} + \frac{\partial z_2}{\partial Z_2}\right)\right) n\frac{\partial z_2}{\partial P}\right] = 0, \tag{10.13}$$

$$-\lambda(z_1+z_2)+m\frac{\partial z_2}{\partial Q}-\mu\left[s\frac{\partial y}{\partial Q}+t\left(\frac{\partial z_1}{\partial Q}+\frac{\partial z_2}{\partial Q}\right)+(z_1+z_2)\right.$$

$$\left.+\left(s\frac{\partial y}{\partial Z_2}+t\left(\frac{\partial z_1}{\partial Z_2}+\frac{\partial z_2}{\partial Z_2}\right)\right)n\frac{\partial z_2}{\partial Q}\right]=0, \tag{10.14}$$

$$\lambda+m\frac{\partial z_2}{\partial a}-\mu\left[s\frac{\partial y}{\partial a}+t\left(\frac{\partial z_1}{\partial a}+\frac{\partial z_2}{\partial a}\right)-1\right.$$

$$\left.+\left(s\frac{\partial y}{\partial Z_2}+t\left(\frac{\partial z_1}{\partial Z_2}+\frac{\partial z_2}{\partial Z_2}\right)\right)n\frac{\partial z_2}{\partial a}\right]=0. \tag{10.15}$$

We now multiply (10.15) by y and add it to (10.13); similarly we multiply (10.15) by (z_1+z_2) and add it to (10.14). Using the Slutsky equations exemplified by (10.5), and the notation introduced previously we can write the resulting equations as

$$mS_{2P}-\mu\left[s\left(S_{yP}+n\frac{\partial y}{\partial Z_2}S_{2P}\right)\right.$$

$$\left.+t\left(S_{1P}+n\frac{\partial z_1}{\partial Z_2}S_{2P}\right)+t\left(S_{2P}+n\frac{\partial z_2}{\partial Z_2}S_{2P}\right)\right]=0, \tag{10.16}$$

$$mS_{2Q}-\mu\left[s\left(S_{yQ}+n\frac{\partial y}{\partial Z_2}S_{2Q}\right)\right.$$

$$\left.+t\left(S_{1Q}+n\frac{\partial z_1}{\partial Z_2}S_{2Q}\right)+t\left(S_{2Q}+n\frac{\partial z_2}{\partial Z_2}S_{2Q}\right)\right]=0. \tag{10.17}$$

Assuming the solution matrix to be non-singular, we can solve these equations for s and t to obtain[c]

$$s=\frac{m}{\mu}\frac{1}{D}(S_{2P}S_{1Q}-S_{2Q}S_{1P}), \tag{10.18}$$

$$t=\frac{m}{\mu}\frac{1}{D}(S_{2Q}S_{yP}-S_{2P}S_{yQ}). \tag{10.19}$$

Here the determinant of the solution matrix is

[c]These are of course not explicit solutions; the derivatives of the demand functions are themselves functions of the prices and therefore of the tax rates. But the solutions are still useful in characterizing the tax structure in terms of properties of the demand functions.

$$D = \begin{vmatrix} S_{yP} + \dfrac{\partial y}{\partial Z_2} nS_{2P} & S_{1P} + S_{2P} + \left(\dfrac{\partial z_1}{\partial Z_2} + \dfrac{\partial z_2}{\partial Z_2}\right) nS_{2P} \\ \\ S_{yQ} + \dfrac{\partial y}{\partial Z_2} nS_{2Q} & S_{1Q} + S_{2Q} + \left(\dfrac{\partial z_1}{\partial Z_2} + \dfrac{\partial z_2}{\partial Z_2}\right) nS_{2Q} \end{vmatrix} \tag{10.20}$$

We note first that μ can be interpreted as the marginal social value of an increase (from zero, in this case) of the government's net tax requirement. Since the introduction of such a requirement would simply mean a withdrawal of resources from the system, μ must be negative. We have already assumed $m < 0$, so that m/μ can be interpreted as the positive value, in terms of the numéraire, of the marginal social damage caused by the external effect. Both tax rates are proportional to the marginal social damage with factors of proportionality depending on properties of the demand functions.

To interpret the solution it is necessary to know something about the properties of D. This is the determinant of the Jacobian of the demand functions, excluding the income effects, and its sign can be discussed in terms of stability considerations. Specifically, static (Hicksian) stability requires that

$$S_{yP} + \frac{\partial y}{\partial Z_2} nS_{2P} < 0,$$

$$S_{1Q} + S_{2Q} + \left(\frac{\partial z_1}{\partial Z_2} + \frac{\partial z_2}{\partial Z_2}\right) nS_{2Q} < 0, \tag{10.21}$$

$$D > 0.$$

The economic meaning of these conditions may be seen from looking, e.g., at the first inequality in (10.21). From demand theory we know that $S_{yP} < 0$, which is a favourable condition for stability in that market. Assume now that $S_{2P} > 0$ and that $\partial y/\partial Z_2 > 0$. This means that the indirect effect of an increase in P, through increasing the level of the externality, is to increase the demand for y. If the latter effect is sufficiently strong it may actually lead to the demand for y being increased as its price goes up; it is this result which is ruled out by the assumption of stability.[d] The second inequality in (10.21) may of course be interpreted in a similar way, and so may the third, which takes care of the

[d]As an example, suppose that y represents the demand for bicycles, z_1 the demand for car use in long-distance transport, and z_2 the demand for car use in urban areas. An increase in P decreases y through the direct substitution effect, and it also increases z_2 and car congestion, the latter leading to an increase in y. By the stability assumption, the second effect does not outweigh the first, so that the net effect is a decrease of y.

interaction between markets. It should be observed that if the derivatives of the demand functions with respect to Z_2 were to vanish, stability would be guaranteed by the higher-order conditions on substitution effects, and there would thus be no need to make specific assumptions about stability.

Going back to the tax formulae (10.18) and (10.19), the following proposition is immediate:

Proposition 1. Under the strong regularity conditions (10.8)-(10.9) and the stability conditions (10.21), some tax on the externality-creating commodity ($t > 0$) *is always optimal.*

This result is hardly surprising. In particular, given the stability conditions (10.21) we have already ensured that the imposition of some positive tax on the externality-creating commodity will reduce the demand for it, which is what we wish to achieve.

The sign of the tax on the related good is somewhat more complicated to determine. Perhaps one's intuition would lead one to think that the crucial issue is whether z_2 and y are Hicksian complements or substitutes. However, this is not the whole truth. From (10.18) we have that whether s is positive, zero or negative is determined by the condition

$$S_{2P}S_{1Q} - S_{2Q}S_{1P} \gtreqless 0,$$

which, in view of (10.8), can be rewritten as

$$S_{2P}/S_{2Q} - S_{1P}/S_{1Q} \gtreqless 0. \tag{10.22}$$

Each of the fractions on the left measures the degree of complementarity of the commodity in question (z_1 or z_2) with commodity y, relative to their own price effects. Thus, each fraction measures the degree to which an increase in P is effective in decreasing the demand for z_i ($i = 1, 2$) relative to the decrease obtained by raising Q.[e] We thus have the following:

Proposition 2. Under the strong regularity conditions (10.8)-(10.9) and the stability conditions (10.21), the tax on the related good is positive, zero or negative as the relative degree of complementarity between y and z_2 *is greater than, equal to, or less than that between y and* z_1.

This result also makes economic sense. If z_2 and y are complements, it might

[e]Naturally, the definition of relative degree of complementarity does not presuppose that the commodities in question are Hicksian complements. If S_{1P} and S_{2P} are both positive the condition says (roughly) that y should be a stronger substitute for Z_1 than for Z_2 in order for $s > 0$ to be optimal.

indeed seem like a good idea to have a tax on y. But we have to take account of the fact that if z_1 and y are also complements, then a tax on y will further divert demand away from z_1, which is undesirable from an efficiency point of view. Clearly the most favorable conditions for a tax on the related good are that z_1 and y are substitutes and that z_2 and y are complements, with the reverse conditions indicating that a subsidy will be optimal. It may be of interest to look briefly at some special (limiting) cases which provide further insights into the working of the model.

(a) Assume that z_1 and z_2 are consumed in the fixed positive proportion $k_{12}; z_1 = k_{12} z_2$. The substitution effects for z_1 and z_2 are then proportional to each other, and we obtain $s = 0$ and $t > 0$ as properties of the optimal solution. Of course, this is closely related to the traditional case.

(b) If there are fixed positive proportions between y and z_2, so that $y = k_{y2} z_2$, the optimal policy involves $t = 0$ and $s > 0$. The externality process is taxed most efficiently through a tax on y, which is perfectly complementary with z_2.

(c) Finally assume that y and z_1 are perfectly complementary; $y = k_{y1} z_1$. Then it is easy to see from (10.18) and (10.19) that $t = -k_{y1} s$; s and t are of opposite sign. Given that it is optimal to have $t > 0$, the desirability of having $s < 0$ is explained by the fact that this works to restore the distortionary effect of an increase in Q on the demand for z_1 and y.

10.4. Further Remarks on the Stability Problem

The rules for optimal taxation that we have arrived at so far seem to accord rather well with economic common sense; indeed so well that there may be cause for some uneasiness on this point. For we know from the work of Buchanan and Kafoglis (1963) that one cannot rule out very counter-intuitive cases in the theory of externalities; they presented an example in which there are no income effects of any kind and where it still turned out that unregulated competition might result in an oversupply of a commodity creating positive external effects or an undersupply of a commodity with negative external effects. The latter case would seem to indicate that a subsidy, rather than a tax on the externality-creating good might be the appropriate policy, yet this is ruled out by our results, in particular by Proposition 1 above. It would seem to be the case, therefore, that we have made an assumption which is sufficient to rule out the Buchanan-Kafoglis possibility. It is of some interest to try to locate this assumption and to relate it to the work of Diamond and Mirrlees (1973), in which they seek to establish conditions sufficient to rule out the 'anomalous' case.

It is not difficult to see that it is the stability conditions (10.21) which are responsible for ruling out this case. In the Buchanan-Kafoglis argument it is the effect of the externality itself on the demand for the externality-creating commodity which gives rise to the anomaly, and in the present analysis it is precisely the same effect which presents problems for stability.

Diamond and Mirrlees (1973) derive their sufficient conditions mainly in terms of restrictions on the second-order derivatives of the utility functions. It would obviously take us too far afield to carry out a detailed comparison with that paper, particularly since it is really a side issue in the present context. However, it seems to be the case that all their conditions have the effect of restricting the signs and magnitudes of effects corresponding to our derivatives with respect to Z_2, and that the approach to the problem in terms of stability conditions may simply be an alternative to the one they take.

Whether the possibility of instability should be taken seriously or not is a difficult question. It seems hard to believe that it could be anything but a curiosity and that it is therefore legitimate to rule it out by the stability assumption or something equivalent to that. However, there may be aspects of the distinction between the short and the long run which is not done justice in a static model and which it might be worth pursuing in a dynamic context.

10.5. Further Comments and Conclusions

It is appropriate to conclude by discussing some further theoretical issues raised by the analysis as well as its policy implications.

A weakness of the analysis is clearly that it does not contain any discussion of the conditions for existence and uniqueness of the second best optimum. The existence and uniqueness of the consumer's optimum are guaranteed by the assumption of strict quasi-concavity; however, this does not in itself ensure the existence of a social optimum. From the existence proof of Diamond and Mirrlees (1971) we know that a crucial condition is the quasi-concavity of the utility function, and in the case of externalities this condition must be taken to apply to all arguments of the utility function. In the case of (1), we must require it to be strictly quasi-concave in all five arguments, not only in the first four. This is a rather strong requirement, but it has some appeal to economic intuition; the interpretation being that the consumer's willingness to pay (in terms of private goods) for a reduction in the level of the external effect, is an increasing function of that level for any constant value of the utility function.

It would be possible to generalize the model in various directions; of these, the most natural would seem to be to the case where consumers are not identical. As long as lump-sum transfers are unrestricted, so that conditions for the existence of a social utility function are satisfied, this extension does not seem to present any particular problems. In fact, our optimal tax formulae could then simply be reinterpreted as expressing the conditions for second-best Pareto optimal taxation.

The analysis of the previous sections suggests that the implementation of the Pigovian tax principle may call for more subtlety than seems to be recognized in much of the current literature. The main emphasis there has been on the difficulties associated with estimating the marginal social damage, and these have not concerned us in the present chapter. In addition, once one admits that externalities originate in processes and not in the consumption of certain commodities as such, the whole question of what constitutes an optimal price structure becomes much more complicated, and the complications arise because the uses made of a particular commodity in different processes are not priced separately in the market and are not separately taxable. The model discussed above illustrates this point. In stressing the distinction between the observable characteristics of consumers, on which tax policy has to be based, and the underlying characteristics that we are finally interested in, the model also affords an illustration of the fact that tax policy must be seen as an example of decision-making under imperfect information; this is discussed in more detail by Atkinson and Stiglitz (1976).

In this connection it may be worth pointing out that the model contains what may seem like a contradiction between its basic assumptions and its conclusions. For the basic assumption is that the tax authorities are unable to distinguish between z_1 and z_2; yet the reasons for the optimal tax structure depend crucially on assumptions about the substitution effects on each of these. So it seems that the tax authorities, in order to implement a second-best policy, must be assumed to know the very facts that they were assumed to be ignorant about in the first place.

Whether this should be considered a paradox depends on the view that one takes of models of optimal taxation, as well as one's view of the kind of situation to which the analysis in this paper is applicable. First, my own view of optimal tax models is basically that they are 'insight models'; they may tell planners something about the considerations to take into account when formulating actual tax policy and the tradeoffs between various objectives. They are not models which provide cookbook formulae for estimation and implementation. In that view the apparent paradox loses much of its significance. Second, as far as the interpretation of the model is concerned, it is certainly meaningful to assume that tax administrators could have rather good information about the signs and magnitudes of the various substitution effects although lacking the possibilities of implementing a first-best policy. E.g., it may well be possible to assess the effect of increased parking fees on traffic in a city on the aggregate level without having the information about individual drivers which would be necessary for the implementation of a tax on gasoline differentiated according to use.

Quite apart from costs of tax administration associated with problems of imperfect information, it seems reasonable to assume that each new tax involves some kind of fixed set-up costs. If this is the case, one might want to limit the number of taxes in the system even if it were to involve some sacrifice of fine-tuning in the control of externalities. But this would not necessarily imply a return to the principle of taxing only the externality-creating commodity; a tax or a subsidy on a related good might turn out to be the best single policy instrument, given both the nature of demand functions and the costs of administration.

References

Atkinson, A.B., and J.E. Stiglitz, "The Design of Tax Structure: Direct Versus Indirect Taxation," *Journal of Public Economics*, 6 (1976):55-75.

Buchanan, J.M., and M. Kafoglis, "A Note on Public Goods Supply," *American Economic Review* 53 (1964):403-414.

Diamond, P.A., "Consumption Externalities and Imperfect Corrective Pricing," *Bell Journal of Economics and Management Science*, (1973):526-538.

Diamond, P.A., and J.A. Mirrlees, "Optimal Taxation and Public Production–I," *American Economic Review* 61 (1971):8-27.

Diamond, P.A., and J.A. Mirrlees, "Aggregate Production with Consumption Externalities," *Quarterly Journal of Economics* 87 (1973):1-24.

Green J., and E. Sheshinski, "Direct versus Indirect Remedies for Externalities," *Journal of Political Economy* 84 (1976):797-808.

Lancaster, K.J., "A New Approach to Consumer Theory," *Journal of Political Economy* 74 (1966):132-157.

Meade, J.E., "External Economies and Diseconomies in a Competitive Situation," *Economic Journal* 62 (1952):54-67.

Muth, R.F., "Household Production and Consumer Demand Functions," *Econometrica* 34 (1966):699-708.

Sandmo, A., "Public Goods and the Technology of Consumption," *Review of Economic Studies* 40 (1973):517-528.

Sandmo, A., "Public Goods and the Technology of Consumption: A Correction," *Review of Economic Studies* 42 (1975a):167-168.

Sandmo, A., "Optimal Taxation in the Presence of Externalities," *Swedish Journal of Economics* 77 (1956):86-98.

11 Optimal Payroll Taxes and Social Security Funding—Some Transitional Problems for a Closed Economy

John S. Flemming

This chapter takes as its starting point the discussion of optimal taxation by Mirrlees [1971] swho used a model in which labor is the only productive factor and enjoys constant returns. My purpose is to extend his analysis in a number of directions using a two factor model in which capital is generated as the provision for retirement by overlapping generations who live for two periods. It is shown in section 11.1 that under certain assumptions the steady-state wage in such an economy is independent of any redistributive tax arrangements restricted to wage income. It is also shown that under the relevant conditions such a restriction involves no loss of welfare so that the optimality conditions are very similar to those derived by Mirrlees; they differ only to the extent that the utility function is necessarily different—being defined over two periods. An example of the optimal linear tax is given in appendix 11A.

In such a two-period model a linear redistributive wage tax (such as that considered in the appendix), is equivalent—in steady-state—to a social security system paying identical (poll) pensions to all retired people out of a fund financed by a proportional tax on the same generation's wage earnings. The equivalent social security system pays a pension with present value equal to the poll subsidy element in the redistributive wage tax scheme. For this equivalence the pension scheme must be fully funded in that the authorities hold investments equal to the present value of the pension rights of those who have contributed.

A serious problem with this analysis is that the introduction of any such redistributive wage tax will damage the interests of people who have already retired. This is because the return on their capital will be reduced as a result of the reduction of their successor's labor supply in response to the redistribution. This has two implications: if we restrict ourselves to intergenerationally Paretian improvements it may not be possible to implement the optimal tax system starting from a no-tax situation. A Paretian improvement might be made feasible by transfers from the first taxed generation to the previous generation; this would be equivalent to setting up a social security system which was not initially fully funded. In section 11.2 we prove the impossibility, under the conditions of

Reprinted, with permission of North-Holland Publishing Company, from the *Journal of Public Economics,* vol. 7, June 1977, pp. 329-349. This chapter draws on discussions with Peter Diamond, Martin Feldstein, and Jim Mirrlees to whom I am very grateful. The work was partly supported by the National Science Foundation. I have also benefited from the comments of two anonymous referees of the *Journal of Public Economics.*

section 11.1, of making the transition from one steady state to another in one generation if the *individual* members of the older generation in the transitional period are fully compensated. It may seem odd to use the Pareto criterion intergenerationally in the utilitarian optimal redistribution context. The main reason is to sidestep the optimal growth aspects of the problems which would otherwise intrude as in Feldstein [1974]. Note also that if our intragenerational redistribution were based on a Rawlsian Maximin criterion the problem discussed here would be particularly acute if one were to extend that criterion (as Rawls does not) to intergenerational comparisons. If the initial equilibrium were stationary with no redistribution, redistribution would make the poorest members of the last uncovered generation the worst off for all time. Thus, they at least must be compensated.

In section 11.3 we consider two alternative approaches to this problem, the first is to maintain the *social* welfare of the preceding generation by an unanticipated redistribution between its members which offsets the effect on their aggregated welfare of the fall in their total income. This redistribution has to be *unanticipated* because it would otherwise affect their labor supply and thus the welfare of the generation before that. If the condition that the effects of the scheme on the overlap generation of retirees be unanticipated, can be met, it is shown that the transition from the no-tax level of *social* welfare to the steady-state optimum in one generation, i.e., a step change in social welfare, *is feasible* under certain conditions on labor's share in income which are exemplified in appendix 11B.

The second approach, which is probably more relevant, is to compensate *individual* members of the preceding generation out of the revenue collected from the first taxed generation. If skill inequality is sufficiently great, and the effects of redistribution on labor supply is sufficiently small, some improvement along those lines will be feasible—however, it will not generally be possible to attain the full steady state optimum. Specific conditions are derived for the example of appendix 11A in appendix 11C.

The utility function in this example is very special even within the class of appropriately separable and homogeneous functions necessary for the independence result of section 11.1.

These exercises suggest two conclusions—neither of which has been proved. From the two examples of section 11.4 taken together it appears that an intergenerationally Paretian transition to the full steady-state optimum would require an element of unanticipated redistribution. The second example, together with the results of section 11.1, suggests that, even without unanticipated redistribution, steadily rising social welfare is possible; since this requires initial intergenerational transfers it can be regarded as an initially less than fully funded social security scheme; however, as funding is complete at the optimum, the degree of "fundedness" should probably rise over time. The trend in both the United States and the United Kingdom has been in the opposite direction; this might possibly reflect appreciation of an argument applicable to growing economies which is due to Samuelson and is considered briefly below.

11.1. Independence of the Steady-State Wage

The analysis of this chapter is based on a model (due to Samuelson [1958]) of overlapping generations, each generation lives two periods, in the first its members both work—for hours of their choice—and consume; in the second (retirement) period they only consume. (See also Diamond [1965].) Production involves the cooperation of one generation's labor with the previous generation's savings (capital). The population is heterogeneous in the effectiveness of its labor.

Our first result is a very simple lemma for an economy not subject either to population growth or technical change; the lemma relates to a purely redistributive tax/subsidy scheme. That is, all revenue is paid out in cash grants to consumers.

Lemma I: If every individual has the *same* utility function $U = U(C_1, H_1, C_2)$ which is *separable* as between consumption and work (so that $U(C_1, H_1, C_2) = U(f(C_1, C_2), H_1))$ *and if* the (sub-) utility function $f(C_1, C_2)$ is *homothetic* (so that $f_1/f_2 = \phi(C_1/C_2)$), *and if* there are constant returns in a well-behaved production function *then* the steady-state capital/labor ratio and wage and interest rates are all independent of any purely redistributive tax/subsidy scheme applied to first period labor income.

Proof:

$$MRS(C_1, C_2) = -(1 + r) = -\phi(C_1/C_2) \tag{i}$$

whence

$$C_1 = C_2\psi(r)$$

where

$$\psi(r) \equiv \phi^{-1}(1 + r)$$

Capital stock K is equal to the present value of aggregate second period consumption,

$$\Sigma C_2 = (1 + r)K = \Sigma C_1/\psi(r) \tag{ii}$$

From the summation of post-tax budget constraints given the redistribution of all tax revenue,

$$K + \Sigma C_1 = wL \tag{iii}$$

where L is aggregate effective labor supply.

From (ii) and (iii)

$$K(1 + (1 + r)\psi(r)) \equiv K \cdot \theta(r) = wL \tag{iv}$$

that is,

$$k \equiv K/L = w/\theta(r)$$

But from the constant returns production function

$$w = w(k) \qquad \text{and} \qquad r = r(k) \tag{v}$$

k is therefore determined independently of the wage tax schedule. From which it follows that w and r are also independent.

Remarks

(1) This result can easily be extended to cover exogenous population growth and labor augmenting technical progress.

(2) If equilibrium factor prices are independent of redistributive wage taxation the latter can be optimized in a partial equilibrium manner, which is essentially what Mirrlees [1971] and others have done by considering one factor models. Although the multiperiod nature of the utility function means that the optimal tax function is different in our present case it is independent of the parameter of the production function.

(3) Under the conditions on the utility function required for this result it has been shown by Atkinson and Stiglitz [1976] that a wage (or expenditure) tax is not inferior to an income tax that includes the return on capital in the tax base. The point is simply that the intertemporal distortion consequent on interest taxation could only be justified either by its tending to offset the distortion of the work/leisure choice arising from the wage tax, which is precluded in our case by the separability assumption; or by a difference in elasticity of demand in the two periods, which is precluded by the homotheticity assumption. (See also Diamond [1970].)

(4) This result is true although the restrictions imposed on the utility function do not imply any restriction on the sign of $\partial H_1/\partial r$ which Ordover and Phelps [1975] have found to be generally a crucial determinant of the relative weight of optimal taxation of wages and interest.

11.2. Transition from Steady State to Steady State

Typically, redistributive wage taxes will reduce the aggregate labor supply, and this is specifically true of the example of the appendix. Thus a scheme, whereby a tax, at the rate t, on wages, whose proceeds were distributed as a poll subsidy to those working at that time, was introduced "overnight," would reduce the labor supply relative to the available capital stock which would reflect the savings decisions of the previous generation.

If the economy is closed the reduced labor supply would raise the real wage above its steady-state value $\overline{w}$ while the interest rate would be depressed below $\overline{r}$. Thus if the tax is imposed on the second generation, r_2, which is the interest earned by the first generation, falls, preventing them from realizing their consumption plans and reducing their welfare relative to the no-tax situation. On the other hand Lemma 1 implies that the increase in the real wage is only transitory so that the welfare of successive generations is as in figure 11-1, where the excess of $\overline{S}(t)$ over $\overline{S}(o)$ reflects assumed redistributive benefits of the tax t.

Thus the introduction of a scheme designed to improve *intra*generational equity raises questions relating to *inter*generational equity and no treatment of the former is complete without some discussion of the latter. However, we must

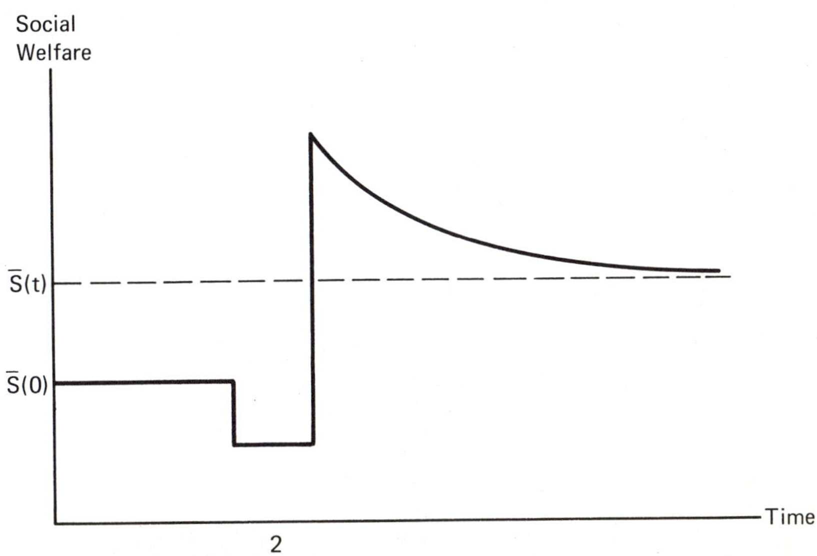

Figure 11-1. Transition in a Closed Economy.

proceed with caution; our life cycle model has a stationary solution even with no individual pure time preference. Thus if there is inequality in skills the no-tax equilibrium deviates from the full utilitarian optimum in two respects: (i) distribution is not optimal and (ii) the capital/labor ratio is too low.[a]

As this chapter is focused on the redistribution issue it is important to abstract from the optimal growth question. This is achieved, as mentioned above, by the adoption of an intergenerational Pareto criterion applied to a utilitarian index of the social welfare of each generation. An acceptable reform may reduce the welfare of an individual but not the social welfare of any generation.

Samuelson [1958, 1975] has shown that even this Paretian criterion requires intergenerational transfers, such as those effected by unfunded social security pensions, if the rate of growth of the effective labor supply exceeds the rate of interest. Hamada [1972] has considered Mirrlees-type taxes in a model similar to ours with optimal growth but only in steady states, ignoring the transitional issue which is our central concern.

Thus the question we shall examine (in a less than complete way) is what might be done to reap the benefits of redistribution without imposing any social welfare loss on any preceding generation. One possibility would be not to introduce the scheme "overnight" but to announce its impending introduction some periods earlier. By reducing labor supplied by the first covered generation the scheme tends to reduce the interest earned on the saving of the last uncovered generation. This is the end of the story if, as under the utility function of the appendix, the labor supply is unresponsive to the interest rate. In this case even under prior announcement only the last uncovered generation would lose.

The assumption that labor supply is unresponsive to the interest rate is not very important (once one has made the restriction required by Lemma 1) in the steady state, since the steady-state interest rate is independent of the tax structure. However, the same is not true of the transitional process.

The actual response of the system to prior announcement of redistribution thus generally depends on the effect of prospective interest rates on labor supply and also on the process by which expectations of such rates are formed. Considered as a class the previous generations must lose since their opportunity set has contracted: what is at stake is the distribution of this loss over the generations. If either labor supply or saving is interest responsive then the effect will ripple back to the date of the announcement if expectations are fully rational—however, the ripples may be heavily damped and may or may not oscillate over generations.

The prior announcement either has no effect or, more generally, leads to the losses being shared by several even earlier generations who will die before they

[a]This proposition is safe although, in the absence of pure time preference, no equilibrium capital/labor ratio exists unless capital satiation is possible.

could be compensated out of the scheme's own revenues. This is the second possible remedy. The fact that the initial effect of imposing the optimal tax/subsidy scheme is to raise w_2 above $\overline{w}$ implies that there might well be revenue available for such compensation. However, most forms of compensation to the last covered generation–notably a poll subsidy–would, if anticipated, reduce their labor supply with consequential losses to their predecessors.

To avoid this problem of anticipation the compensation must take the form of the interest subsidy necessary to restore them exactly to their no-tax situation. Under the assumption of Lemma 1 savings, and interest, are proportional to earnings so that compensation although conditional on saving is in fact proportional to earnings.

In this section we prove that full compensation by interest subsidy is not compatible with a step increase in social welfare, if no further intergenerational transfer are made.

Theorem: Under the conditions of Lemma 1, and the further condition that a redistributive wage tax reduces the steady-state aggregate labor supply, no step increase in social welfare can be achieved from the zero-tax situation if only one intergenerational transfer is made and that is an interest subsidy.

Proof: We proceed by *reductio ad absurdum.*

Suppose that full compensation by way of interest subsidy is possible so that the first generation expects and receives the steady-state equilibrium return $\overline{r}$ on their savings $K(0)$ where $K(0)$ is the steady-state supply of capital as a function of the redistributive tax regime, which is indexed by t ($t = 0$ is the no-tax case). The members of the second generation will enjoy $U(t)$ if they face the steady-state budget constraint appropriate to tax regime t, in which case they will supply labor $L(t)$. Total consumption at time 2 is then the consumption of the retired members of the first generation, which is $(1 + \overline{r})K(0)$, plus the consumption of the workers $F(t) - (1 + \overline{r})K(t)$ where $F(t)$ is steady-state output under regime t $[F(t) = F(K(t), L(t)) = L(t)f(\overline{k})]$. To meet this consumption demand we have output at time 2, $F_2 = F(K(0), L(t))$, *plus* the reduction in the capital stock $K(0) - K(t)$. Thus the feasibility of full compensation requires

$$(1 + \overline{r})(K(0) - K(t)) + F(t) \leqslant F_2 + (K(0) - K(t))$$

or

$$F(K(0), L(t)) \geqslant F(K(t), L(t)) + \overline{r}(K(0) - K(t)) = \overline{r}K(0) - \overline{w}L(t)$$

Since taxation reduces the labor supply, to which in the steady state, capital is proportional, $K(t) < K(0)$ while $\overline{r} = F_K(K(t), L(t))$; together with $F_{KK} < 0$ this suffices to show that the condition does not hold–the last part of the argument is illustrated in figure 11-2.

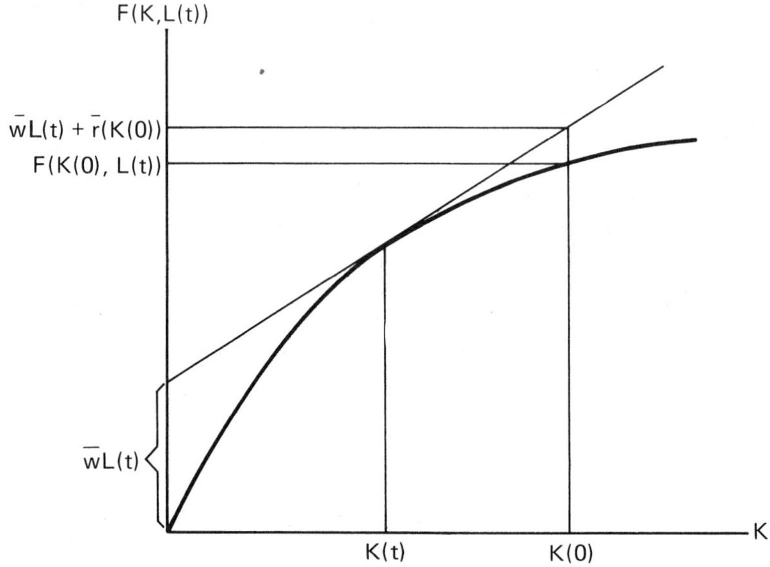

Figure 11-2. Impossibility of Transition During One Generation.

11.3. Alternative Approaches

In this section we consider two other possible ways of compensating the last untaxed generation. First we consider the feasibility of "compensating" by unanticipated redistribution. The second possibility is that the welfare of the second generation might rise (though not to $S(t^*)$) even if the cost of interest compensation for the retired generation were a prior charge on tax revenue.

Suppose that the first taxed generation is offered the budget constraint associated with the steady-state equilibrium with the optimal wage-tax schedule t^*. This will involve applying to them a tax schedule other than t^* but its specification does not concern us. In this case the first covered generation moves immediately to supplying labor $L(t^*)$ and they and their successors will enjoy $S(t^*)$.

This scheme if applied overnight will lead to the emergence of excess revenue $X(t^*)$:

$$X(t^*) = L(t^*)[F_L(K(0), L(t^*)) - F_L(K(t^*), L(t^*))]$$

$$= L(t^*)[F_L(K(0), L(t^*)) - F_L(t^*)]$$

$$= L(t^*)(w(K(0) \cdot L(t^*)) - \overline{w})$$

The condition for it to be possible to compensate the last uncovered generation for the loss they would otherwise suffer from the unanticipated introduction of a redistributive scheme is that the equal distribution of their diminished total resources, including the excess revenue, generate more utility than the unequal distribution of their original resources.

Assuming individual utilities to be additively separable over time this condition can be written as

$$NU_2\left(\frac{1}{N}[K(0)(1 + F_K(K(0), L(t^*))) + L(t^*)(F_L(0, t^*) - F_L(0))]\right.$$

$$\geqslant \sum_i U_2(S_i K(0)(1 + F_K\ 0))$$

where $U_2(\cdot)$ is the utility of second period consumption, N is the size of the population and S_i is the share of the ith individual in the no-tax capital stock.

If the production function $F(.,.)$ is Cobb Douglas with capital coefficient η_K while $U_2(\cdot)$ is isoelastic $(U_2(C_2) = (1/\gamma)C_2^\gamma)$ this condition can be written as

$$1 - \frac{\eta_K \cdot (F(0) - F(t^*)) - [F(K(0), L(t^*)) - F(t^*)]}{K(0) + \eta_K \cdot F(0)}$$

$$> \left(\frac{\sum_i S_i^\gamma}{N^{1-\gamma}}\right)^{1/\gamma}$$

Since t^* depends on S_i, γ and the labor "supply function" $L(\cdot)$ we cannot easily examine the general effects of changing these parameters on the probability of this condition holding. However under the conditions of Lemma 1 t^* is independent of η_K (as noted in remark 2). It is clear that if the share of capital (η_K) is small enough the condition will hold for any strictly positive degree of inequality.

An example is presented in appendix 11B for the case in which $\gamma = 0$ $(U_2(C_2) = \log C_2)$. In this case a sufficient condition is that $\eta_K < 1/3$.

The intuitive argument behind these results is that if capital's share is small enough the retirees were primarily relying on the capital to finance their consumption rather than the return on it; while only the latter is affected by the redistribution-induced reduction in labor supply.

Although this last result is much more encouraging than the impossibility theorem of section 11.2 it does depend on the redistribution between the retired members of the last untaxed generation being unanticipated. This is not very satisfactory even though it is "one off." In particular generations do, of course, overlap not only in the sense that children are born before their parents die, but also in the sense that children in different dynasties are born out of phase with one another. Our second approach is less vulnerable to these objections although the assumption that generation changes in different dynasties are "in phase" is retained.

The question we want to consider is as follows. Suppose that the arbitrary tax schedule t is imposed on all generations beyond some point. The compensation of the previous generation by the appropriate interest subsidy is financed by an additional poll tax on the first taxed generation. Under what conditions will this package raise the welfare of the first taxed generation? Clearly the restriction of the finance of the compensation to a poll tax diminishes the generality of the package. Unfortunately further losses of generality are involved in what follows.

If we restrict ourselves to linear taxes we can simplify the problem. It now becomes this: Suppose that the arbitrary marginal tax rate t is imposed on earnings of one generation and all its successors. Each generation after the first taxed generation has all the proceeds of its wage tax redistributed to its members as a poll subsidy. In the case of the first taxed generation compensation of their predecessors by the appropriate interest subsidy is a first charge on revenue and reduces the lump sum subsidy they receive. Under what conditions does their welfare rise?

The welfare of the first taxed generation depends among other things on the labor supply of the second taxed generation and so on and on. . . . Thus tractability is enormously increased if we can break the chain by making the labor supply independent of the interest rate as in the case considered in the appendixes. In appendix 11C we derive a condition for the welfare of the first taxed generation to be an increasing function of the tax rate where the tax rate is zero.

This condition requires that inequality exceed some strictly positive function of the parameter of the Cobb Douglas production function. Only when capital's share is zero is $(dS_i/dt)\,|_{t=0} > 0$ for ϵ inequality.

This result is not very surprising. In a steady-state context we could argue that any strictly positive inequality called for a positive tax because the marginal redistribution benefit is positive while, at $t = 0$, the marginal deadweight cost is zero. This argument breaks down in the present context because the first taxed generation suffers two deadweight burdens, the usual cost of distorted prices *plus* the transfer they have to pay to their predecessors if capital's share in income is positive and redistribution reduces the labor supply.

The result implies that the optimal steady state described in appendix 11A is not in general attainable. The optimal feasible steady state will either involve a lower tax rate and more inequality or permanent transfers from one generation to its predecessor or both. The effect of such transfers would be to reduce the capital/labor ratio, raising the rate of interest and reducing the steady state wage. Since the growth rate is zero while the interest rate is positive these transfers must imply a lower welfare level than that of the steady state, which would be optimal in the absence of transitional problems.

Whether or not transfers are a feature of the optimal feasible steady state it seems almost certain that the scale of such transfers diminishes along the optimal trajectory—that is, the "fundedness" of the equivalent social security scheme would rise over time. It would certainly not be 100 percent initially and might remain less than 100 percent even at the end.

References

Atkinson, A.B., and J.E. Stiglitz, "The Design of Tax Structure: Direct Versus Indirect Taxation," *Journal of Public Economics*, July 1976.

Diamond, P.A., "National Debt in a Neoclassical Growth Model," *American Economic Review*, Dec. 1965.

Diamond, P.A., "The Incidence of the Interest Income Tax," *Journal of Economic Theory*, Sept. 1970.

Feldstein, M.S., "The Optimal Financing of Social Security," Harvard mimeo (HIER 388), Cambridge, Mass., 1974.

Hamada, K., "Lifetime Equity and Dynamic Efficiency on the Balanced Growth Path," *Journal of Public Economics*, Nov. 1972.

Mirrlees, J.A., "An Exploration of the Theory of Optimal Income Taxation," *Review of Economic Studies*, Apr. 1971.

Ordover, J.A., and E.S. Phelps, "Linear Taxation of Wealth and Wages for Intragenerational Lifetime Justice: Some Steady State Cases," *American Economic Review*, Sept. 1975.

Samuelson, P.A., "An Exact Consumption Loan Model of Interest with or without the Social Contrivance of Money," *Journal of Political Economy*, Dec. 1958.

Samuelson, P.A., "Optimal Social Security," *International Economic Review*, Oct. 1975.

Appendix 11A

One utility function meeting the conditions of Lemma 1 is the natural extension of Mirrlees's semilog function

$$U = \log C + \log (1 - H)$$

namely

$$U = \log C_1 + \log (1 - H_1) + \log C_2 \tag{11A.1}$$

Solving for the optimal linear wage tax, for this special case, is not difficult: the budget constraint for a man of skill level n is

$$C_2(n) = \left\{(1 - t)\overline{w}nH_1 + A - C_1(n)\right\} (1 + \overline{r}) \tag{11A.2}$$

where A is the poll subsidy and $\overline{w}$ and $\overline{r}$ the invariant wage and interest rates. Under the log utility function

$$C_2^* = (1 + \overline{r})C_1^* \tag{11A.3}$$

whence

$$C_1(n) = \left\{(1 - t)wnH_1 + A\right\} /2 \tag{11A.4}$$

while

$$1 - H_1(n) = \frac{C_1}{(1 - t)\overline{w}n} \tag{11A.5}$$

so that

$$C_1(n) = \frac{(1 - t)\overline{w}n + A}{3} \tag{11A.6}$$

$$1 - H_1(n) = \frac{(1 - t)\overline{w}n + A}{3(1 - t)\overline{w}n} \tag{11A.7}$$

and

$$H_1(n) = \frac{2(1 - t)\overline{w}n - A}{3(1 - t)\overline{w}n} \tag{11A.8}$$

An n-man's effective labor supply is

$$nH_1(n) = \frac{2(1-t)\overline{w}n - A}{3(1-t)\overline{w}}$$

thus if the mean skill level is unity and the size of each generation is also one, the total effective labor supply is

$$L = \frac{2(1-t)\overline{w} - A}{3(1-t)\overline{w}} \tag{11A.9}$$

By the assumption that the tax is purely redistributive, i.e., that there is no net revenue

$$A = t\overline{w}L = \frac{t}{1-t} \cdot \frac{1}{3}(2(1-t)\overline{w} - A)$$

$$A = \frac{2\overline{w}t(1-t)}{3-2t} \quad \text{and} \quad L = \frac{2(1-t)}{3-2t} \tag{11A.10a,b}$$

Total capital supply is the same as total first period consumption which is one half of total earnings. Thus from (11A.10b)

$$K = \frac{\overline{w}L}{2} = \frac{\overline{w}(1-t)}{3-2t} \tag{11A.10c}$$

Results (11.10a,b,c) will be used in appendixes 11B and 11C, together with a Cobb Douglas function, to derive values of $\overline{w}$ and $\overline{r}$.

Substituting from (11A.3), (11A.4) and (11A.7) into (11A.1)

$$U(n) = \log\left\{\left(\frac{(1-t)\overline{w}n + A}{3}\right)^3 \frac{1+\overline{r}}{(1-t)\overline{w}n}\right\}$$

whence, using (11A.10a)

$$U(n) = \log\left\{\frac{1+\overline{r}}{n} \cdot \frac{\overline{w}^2(1-t)^2}{3^3}\left(n + \frac{2\iota}{3-2t}\right)^3\right\} \tag{11A.11}$$

To derive specific results on an optimal tax schedule both an instantaneous social welfare function, $S(U(n))$, and the distribution of skills, as measured by n, must be specified. Here, and again in appendixes 11B and 11C we use the simple additive *SWF*, $S(U(n)) = \int U(n)f(n)\,dn$. We also consider a very simple distribution–that there are two equally large classes of people will skill levels $1 \pm d$ respectively. Under these assumptions, and with $U(n)$ as in (11A.11), social welfare is maximized by solving the following problem.

$$\underset{t}{\text{Max}}\left\{\frac{(1-t)^4}{1-d^2}\left[1-d+\frac{2t}{3-2t}\right]^3\left[1+d+\frac{2t}{3-2t}\right]^3\right\}$$

$$=\underset{t}{\text{Max}}\left\{\frac{(1-t)^4}{1-d^2}\left[\frac{9}{(3-2t)^2}-d^2\right]^3\right\}$$

for which the first order condition is

$$d^2(3-2t)^3 - 9t = 0 \tag{11A.12}$$

The preceding argument assumed that every individual's optimum was internal although it follows from (11A.8) that for low enough n relative to $A/(1-t)\overline{w}$ hours of work become negative. For this reason the result (11A.12) must be restricted to an admissable range of inequality as represented by the value of d. In fact from (11A.6) and (11A.10a) the condition $H_1(1-d) \geqslant 0$ is

$$(1-d) \geqslant t/(3-2t)$$

$$d \leqslant 3(1-t)/(3-2t) \tag{11A.13}$$

in the limiting case where (11A.13) holds as an equality it follows from (11A.12) and (11A.13) that

$$d^2 = \frac{9t}{(3-2t)^3} = \frac{9(1-t)^2}{(3-2t)^2}$$

whence

$$t = (1-t)^2(3-2t)$$

which implies $t = 1/2$, $d = 3/4$, $A = \overline{w}/4$. Thus the analysis of this appendix is valid for $d \leqslant 3/4$, that is, in our two class society, if the more able are not more than seven times as able as the less able.

Appendix 11B

Suppose that the first taxed generation (generation 2) is offered the budget constraint associated with the steady-state equilibrium under the optimal tax schedule t^* so that their welfare and that of succeeding generations will be $S(t^*)$. We know from the previous section that consumption available for the retired generation (generation 1) ($C_{2,1}$) is given by

$$C_{2,1}(t^*) = (1 + \bar{r})K(0) + F[K(0), L(t^*)] - F[K(t^*), L(t^*)] - r(K(0) - K(t^*))$$

while

$$(1 + \bar{r})K(0) > C_{2,1}(t^*) > (1 + r)K(0) \tag{11B.1}$$

The second inequality 11B.1 reflects the transfer to the "first" generation of the excess revenue collected from the second generation whose gross wage w exceeds the equilibrium value $\bar{w}$ because

$$K_2 = K(0) > K(t^*)$$

which in turn reflects the fact that

$$L_2 = L(t^*) < L(0)$$

The question is whether this quantity of consumption, divided equally among the retired generation, could raise their aggregate welfare above its level in the absence of any tax scheme. Since the population is taken as unity, the utility of consumption equally divided between two people is log $[C_2^2(t)]$ while in the absence of taxation an "n man's" consumption in retirement is $(1 + \bar{r})$ $\bar{w}n/3$ so that, if $n = 1 \pm d$,

$$\log U_2(0) = \log ((1 + r)^2 (\frac{\bar{w}}{3})^2 (1 - d^2)$$

Thus the scheme of unanticipated equal distribution among them will "compensate" the first generation fully for its loss of aggregate consumption if

$$C_{2,1}(t) \geqslant (1 + r)\frac{\bar{w}}{3}\sqrt{1 - d^2} \tag{11B.2}$$

for which, from (11B.1), a sufficient condition is that

$$(1 + r)K(0) \geqslant (1 + \bar{r})\frac{\bar{w}}{3}\sqrt{1 - d^2} \tag{11B.3}$$

We have seen (equations (11A.10)) that $K(0) = \overline{w}L(0)/2 = \overline{w}/3$. Therefore (11B.3) is equivalent to

$$\frac{(1+r)}{(1+\overline{r})} \geqslant \sqrt{1-d^2} \tag{11B.4}$$

Conditions (11B.3) and (11B.4) are, of course, the conditions for redistribution to compensate the retired generation even if no fiscal transfer from the working generation were made.

Let the production function be Cobb-Douglas:

$$X = L^{\alpha} K^{1-\alpha} \tag{11B.5}$$

Then

$$r = (1-\alpha)\left(\frac{L(t)}{K(0)}\right)^{\alpha} = \overline{r}\lambda^{\alpha}(t) \tag{11B.6}$$

where, from (11A.9),

$$\lambda(t) \equiv \frac{L(t)}{L(0)} = \frac{3(1-t)}{3-2t} \tag{11B.7}$$

Thus 11B.4 can be written

$$\frac{1+\overline{r}\lambda^{\alpha}(t)}{1+\overline{r}} \geqslant \sqrt{(1-d^2)} \tag{11B.8}$$

We know from Lemma 1 that $\overline{r}$ depends only on the technology, that is. in our case $\overline{r}$ is a function of α. This relationship can be derived from (11A.10) which implies, for all t,

$$\left(\frac{L(t)}{K(t)}\right) = \frac{2}{\overline{w}}$$

whence, differentiating (11B.5) with respect to K

$$\overline{r} = X_K = (1-\alpha)\left(\frac{2}{\overline{w}}\right)^{\alpha}$$

while

$$\bar{w} = X_L = \alpha \left(\frac{2}{\bar{w}} \right)^{-(1-\alpha)}$$

so that

$$\bar{w}^{\alpha} = \alpha\, 2^{-(1-\alpha)}$$

and

$$\bar{r} = 2(1-\alpha)/\alpha \tag{11B.9}$$

Since $0 \leqslant \alpha$ and $\lambda \leqslant 1$ $\lambda^{\alpha} \geqslant \lambda$. Therefore (11B.8), which is sufficient for (11B.2), is implied by

$$\left(\frac{1+\bar{r}\lambda(t)}{1+\bar{r}} \right)^2 \geqslant 1 - d^2 \tag{11B.10}$$

$$d^2 \geqslant 1 - \left(\frac{1+\bar{r}\lambda(t)}{1+\bar{r}} \right)^2$$

$$\geqslant \frac{\bar{r}}{(1+\bar{r})^2} (1-\lambda(t))\,(2+\bar{r}(1+\lambda(t)))$$

From (11A.12) and (11B.7), provided $0 \leqslant d \leqslant 3/4$,

$$d^2 = (1-\lambda(t^*))(3-2\lambda(t^*))^2$$

at the optimum t. Thus, for $t = t^*(d)$, (11B.10) becomes

$$(3-2\lambda(t^*))^2 \geqslant \frac{\bar{r}}{(1+\bar{r})^2} (2+\bar{r}(1+\lambda(t^*))) \tag{11B.11}$$

Since

$$0 \leqslant \lambda(t^*) \leqslant 1$$

the LHS of (11B.11) is greater than one while the RHS is less than $2\bar{r}/(1+\bar{r})$, thus

$$1 \geqslant \frac{2\bar{r}}{1+\bar{r}} \qquad \text{i.e.,} \qquad 1 > \bar{r}$$

is sufficient for (11B.11), while, from (11B.9), this in turn implies

$$\alpha \geqslant 2/3 \tag{11B.12}$$

This condition is stated in the text as a capital share (η_K) less than 1/3 being sufficient for redistribution to compensate the retired generation.

Appendix 11C

Suppose that the arbitrary tax rate t is imposed at time 2 and the interest subsidy $(\bar{r} - r_2)$ is paid to those then retired with the balance of the revenue being distributed as a poll subsidy among the workers of the second generation—under what conditions will their welfare thereby be raised?

The poll subsidy for the second generation is given by

$$A_2 = tw_2L_2 - (\bar{r} - r_2)K(0) \tag{11C.1}$$

where from (11A.9)

$$L_2 = \frac{2(1-t)w_2 - A_2}{3(1-t)w_2} = \frac{1}{3}(2 - Z_2) = \lambda_2 L(0) = 2\lambda_2/3 \tag{11C.2}$$

where

$$Z_2 = \frac{A_2}{(1-t)w_2} \tag{11C.3}$$

and

$$\lambda_2 = \frac{L_2}{L(0)}$$

Note that

$$Z_2 = 2(1 - \lambda_2) \tag{11C.4}$$

and

$$\lambda_2 = \frac{2 - Z_2}{2}$$

while

$$w_2 = \bar{w}\lambda_2^{-(1-\alpha)} \qquad r_2 = \bar{r}\lambda_2 \tag{11C.5}$$

whence (11C.1) can be written as

$$(1-t)Z_2w_2 = tw_2\lambda_2L(0) - r(1 - \lambda_2^{\alpha})K(0)$$

or dropping the subscript 2,

$$2(1-t)\cdot(1-\lambda)=2t\lambda/3-\overline{r}(1-\lambda^{\alpha})\lambda^{1-\alpha}/3$$

that is,

$$\overline{r}\lambda^{1-\alpha}=\lambda(6-4t+\overline{r})-6(1-t) \tag{11C.6}$$

For the argument to follow we need to know the value of $d\lambda/dt=\lambda'(t)$ which, from (11C.6), is given by

$$(1-\alpha)\overline{r}\lambda^{-\alpha}(t)\lambda'(t)=\lambda'(t)\,(6-4t+\overline{r})-4\lambda(t)+6$$

whence at $t=0$

$$\lambda'(0)=\frac{-2}{6+\alpha\overline{r}}$$

and from (11B.9)

$$\lambda'(0)=\frac{-2}{6+2(1-\alpha)}=\frac{-1}{4-\alpha} \tag{11C.7}$$

The welfare of the second generation is S_2; if $S_2=\ln\hat{S}_2$

$$\hat{S}_2=\exp S_2=\frac{(1+r_3)^2(1-t)^4w_2^4}{3^6(1-d^2)}((1+Z_2)^2-d^2)^3 \tag{11C.8}$$

while

$$r_3=(1-\alpha)\left(\frac{L_3}{K_3}\right)^{\alpha} \tag{11C.9}$$

In the absence of further intergenerational transfers L_3 is given by (11A.10) as

$$L_3=\frac{2(1-t)}{3-2t}$$

while

$$K_3=\frac{(1-t)w_2L_2+A_2}{2}=\frac{(1-t)w_2}{2}\,(L_2+Z_2)$$

$$= \frac{(1-t)w_2}{3}(1+Z_2) \tag{11C.10}$$

If *any* improvement in social welfare along this route is to be possible we need

$$\left.\frac{d\hat{S}_2}{dt}\right|_{t=o} > 0$$

From (11C.8)

$$\frac{d\hat{S}_2}{dt} = \frac{2\hat{S}_2}{1+r_3}\frac{dr_3}{dt} - \frac{4\hat{S}_2}{(1-t)} + \frac{4\hat{S}_2}{w_2}\frac{dw_2}{dt}$$

$$+ \frac{3\hat{S}_2 2(1+Z_2)}{(1+Z_2)^2 - d^2}\frac{dZ_2}{dt} \tag{11C.11}$$

From (11C.9)

$$\frac{dr_3}{dt} = \alpha r_3\left(\frac{1}{L_3}\frac{dL_3}{dt} - \frac{1}{K_3}\frac{dK_3}{dt}\right) \tag{11C.12}$$

while from (11A.10)

$$\frac{1}{L_3}\frac{dL_3}{dt} = \frac{-1}{(3-2t)(1-t)} \tag{11C.13}$$

and from (11C.10)

$$\frac{1}{K_3}\frac{dK_3}{dt} = \frac{-1}{1-t} + \frac{1}{w_2}\frac{dw_2}{dt} + \frac{1}{1+Z_2}\frac{dZ_2}{dt} \tag{11C.14}$$

From (11C.3) and (11C.4)

$$\frac{dw_2}{dt} = -(1-\alpha)\overline{w}\lambda_2^{-(2-\alpha)}\lambda_2'(t) \tag{11C.15}$$

$$\frac{dZ_2}{dt} = -2\lambda_2'(t)$$

Thus from (11C.12)-(11C.15)

$$\left.\frac{dr_3}{dt}\right|_{t=o} = \alpha\bar{r}\,(\frac{-1}{3} - (-1 - (1-\alpha)\lambda'(0) - 2\lambda'(0)))$$

while from (11C.7) this can be written as

$$\left.\frac{dr_3}{dt}\right|_{t=o} = 2(1-\alpha)\frac{2}{3}\frac{3-\alpha}{4-\alpha} = -\frac{2(1-\alpha)^2}{3(4-\alpha)}$$

Thus from (11C.11), (11C.15) and (11C.16)

$$\left.\frac{1}{\hat{S}_2}\frac{d\hat{S}_2}{dt}\right|_{t=o} = \frac{-4(1-\alpha)^2}{(1+\bar{r})3(4-\alpha)} - 4 + \frac{4(1-\alpha)}{4-\alpha} + \frac{12}{1-d^2}\frac{1}{4-\alpha} \tag{11C.17}$$

and this is positive if and only if

$$(1-\alpha) + \frac{3}{1-d^2} > (4-\alpha) + \frac{\alpha(1-\alpha)^2}{3(2-\alpha)}$$

that is, if

$$\frac{3}{1-d^2} > 3 + \frac{\alpha(1-\alpha)^2}{3(2-\alpha)}$$

or

$$d^2 > \frac{\alpha(1-\alpha)^2}{18 - 8\alpha - 2\alpha^2 + \alpha^3}\;. \tag{11C.18}$$

Condition (11C.18) is not very restrictive, as the RHS has a maximum of about 0.01 that is $d > 0.1$, n max/n min $> 11/9$ would always suffice. However, it is clear that if only one intergenerational transfer takes place, as in this case, a situation could exist in which there was a little inequality which would ideally warrant a redistributive tax which could not be implemented for the reasons given here. It is also probable that a similar argument would show that complete convergence on the optimum could not be achieved although that would be in the context of a sequence of intergenerational transfers along which the transfers would almost certainly decline as a proportion of revenue, that is, the fundedness of the scheme, viewed as a social security arrangement, would rise over time.

12 Power and Taxes

Robert J. Aumann and
Mordecai Kurz

12.1. Introduction

Perhaps the most fundamental element in the theory of the public sector is the view that the government is an exogenous, benevolent economic agent. The benevolence of the government is often expressed by assuming it to maximize a "social welfare" function of the form $\int u_t(x(t))\mu(dt)$, where the u_t are utility functions, x is an allocation of consumption bundles and μ is a distribution of agent types; in other words, simply the sum of individual utilities. With such a social welfare function Arrow and Kurz [2] were able to derive optimal investment and taxation programs while Mirrlees [12], Sheshinski [19] and others were able to derive optimal tax policies for a population with heterogeneous endowment.

We do not think that this view is without merit. There are perhaps some public issues with regard to which a consensus may be reached, and then such an approach may suffice to explain the behavior of the government. But more often, redistributive effects are a central issue; and then the actions of the government, and in particular its tax policies, can be understood only as an endogenous consequence of the political forces that enable it to maintain power. For this reason one should investigate the connection between tax policies and the political forces that shaped those policies to begin with.

We propose to regard income distribution, taxation, the production of public goods and other actions of the public sector as determined by a political process simultaneously with the economic process of exchange and production. This means that we propose to study an economic-political equilibrium where the power of each individual is reflected both in the political and the economic sphere.

The present chapter is our first paper on this subject, where we formulate the basic structure and motivate it. All of our work in this chapter deals with a world in which there is only one commodity ("money"), to be thought of as an aggregate of all real commodities. This enables us to focus on the purely

Reprinted, with permission of the Econometric Society, from *Econometrica* vol. 45, July 1977, pp. 1137-1161. This research was supported by U.S. National Science Foundation Grant GS-40104 at the Institute for Mathematical Studies in the Social Sciences at Stanford University, and by a grant from the Israel National Council for Research and Development at the Hebrew University of Jerusalem. We are greatly indebted to Kenneth Arrow for an extremely helpful conversation on the subject of this paper; the interpretation of δ_t in terms of "fear of ruin" (section 12.6) is an outcome of that conversation.

redistributive aspect of government policy. In another paper [4] we treat a more complex and realistic multicommodity model in which we discuss such matters as the relations between taxes and prices for various goods.

The basic tool that deals with the conflict part of our theory comes from game theory; it is the "Harsanyi-Shapley-Nash Value for Non-Transferable Utility Games" (Shapley [18]). The highlights of our results are as follows:

a. If a democratic power structure (majority vote) is assumed, then an income tax emerges which can be progressive, regressive or neutral.
b. The size of the tax depends upon attitudes toward risking large losses. We shall introduce a new measure for the attitude toward such risks, which we shall call "the fear of ruin." This may be contrasted with the Arrow-Pratt [1, 16] measures of risk aversion, which measure attitudes towards small risks only. The connection with risk is somewhat startling, since there is no overt element of risk in the model; however, a closer examination of the situation, which will be undertaken below, shows that considerations of risk do enter naturally.
c. The tax structure involves a personal support level and negative taxation for low income people. (The "support" is what the individual receives from the government in the absence of any income.)
d. The marginal tax rate is always between 50 percent and 100 percent.

The treatment in this paper will be on the conceptual level, and will not be entirely rigorous from the mathematical viewpoint. A rigorous treatment, with complete proofs, may be found in [4]. The "heaviest" parts of this paper from the mathematical viewpoint are sections 12.4 and 12.9; readers who are willing to forego the precise definition of the Shapley value, and of the corresponding concept of value allocation, may skip these sections.

12.2. The Income Redistribution Game

In the model of this chapter there is only one commodity, to be thought of as an aggregate of all "real" commodities; for convenience we shall call it "money."[a] There is a set T of agents ("society"), each one of whom has an initial endowment of money ("gross income"). It is assumed that there are many agents, and that each individual one is "small"; that is, removing him would not appreciably affect society. By a political procedure to be specified below, the agents in T will be taxed, and the resulting revenue will be distributed among

[a]We use the term "money" where often economists use the term "income." We wish to keep the ideas behind these terms distinct: in our terminology, the commodity "money" provides the units in which wealth or income are measured. Thus we can talk of "income," "gross income," and "net income" as specific quantities of money received by individuals (or groups) in various circumstances.

them; what is left to an agent after that is called his "net income" (it may exceed gross income). We shall be interested only in the relation between gross and net income–i.e., in the total effect of both taxation and redistribution–and not in the two processes separately.

The political procedure is majority rule. This means that any coalition containing more than half the agents can impose taxes and then redistribute them in any way it pleases. In particular, it may divide among its own members the taxes collected from the minority.

It might be objected that in a democracy, one aims at "uniform" tax laws, i.e., laws under which people with the same income are taxed in the same way; this would preclude taxing two people differently just because one is in the ruling coalition while the other is not. But in fact, tax laws are not uniform, as witness the myriads of different rules for different kinds of taxpayers and different kinds of income–rules that are often deliberately slanted to favor various pressure groups.[b] Moreover, it must be recalled that what we are discussing here is not just taxation, but rather the total effect of government activity on incomes. Though theoretically one might require uniform taxation, there can be no such requirement on government spending; and spending can easily be determined by the majority to wipe out any undesired effects of uniform taxation requirements. Finally, we are even willing to concede that total income redistribution may in fact exhibit certain aspects of uniformity, if the concept is interpreted broadly. But we would argue that this is the *result* of democratic forces at work–a compromise between clashing pressure groups–rather than a precondition for democracy. In formal terms, we would expect such uniformity as an *outcome* of the theory; a conclusion, not a hypothesis.

Since the majority can, in principle, tax the minority at 100 percent and return nothing to it, it would seem at first sight that the total endowment of society becomes available to whomever is in the majority. Thus individual endowments would lose their significance, and we would be led to a completely egalitarian analysis. While this kind of analysis is not without interest, it appears too extreme to be considered relevant to the problem of income distribution in a democracy.

We now appear to be caught in a dilemma. On the one hand, majority rule appears to lead immediately to the extreme of total egalitarianism. On the other hand, if one ignores politics and does not allow the majority to redistribute income, one is simply left with the initial income distribution. How, then, can one account politically for the type of taxation scheme that is observed, in which some redistribution takes place but net income still remains related to gross income?

To answer this question, we make an assumption that we consider a basic ingredient of a democratic society, namely that

[b]No adverse value judgment is intended. Pressure groups are what democracy is all about–they are as essential to healthy politics as competition is to a healthy economy.

every agent can, if he wishes,
destroy part or all of his endowment.

It goes without saying that the part that is destroyed cannot be taxed. If one thinks of one's endowment as labor, then the above means that there is *no forced labor*: an individual may, if he wishes, "destroy" his labor, by simply working less (or not at all).[c]

It may not be immediately clear why this assumption changes anything—after all, who would want to destroy his endowment—what good would it do to anybody? The answer is that it gives the minority very considerable *threat power*—power that is vital in determining taxes. There are numerous cases in history where farmers' revolts against the tax collector were associated with the destruction of crops; this was recently demonstrated by the French farmers of Normandy who destroyed their crops on the roads against President De Gaulle. Also, a strike involves the destruction of endowment (in the form of labor services) in the face of what are considered unfavorable terms of trade or excessive taxation. Though the minority certainly cannot guarantee to itself any part of its endowment, nevertheless it can say to the majority "it will be neither mine nor thine."[d] This is a powerful threat, which can force the majority to compromise. And it is this compromise that underlies the delicate balance between individual rights and society's needs inherent in all tax schemes.

There is another element that enters the description of our model. Every agent is assumed to have a von Neumann-Morgenstern (N-M) utility [20] for money. The reader may ask, of what possible relevance can N-M utility functions—which really measure attitudes toward risk—be in a situation that contains no overt elements of risk? The answer is that on the contrary, we are dealing with a situation that is replete with risky elements. The bargaining associated with entry into (or exclusion from) a ruling coalition is a risky business, as are the threats of the minority and of the majority once coalitions have been formed. One's attitude toward these risks is a decisive factor in how well one can do in the bargaining, even though in the end no random mechanism is used to determine the payoff, i.e., no risks are taken by anyone.

To sum up, the *Income Redistribution Game* is played as follows: each agent starts out with an endowment and a utility function. Redistribution decisions are made by majority vote, but each agent has the right to destroy some or all of his endowment.

Our results turn out to be insensitive to the exact strategic description of the game (e.g., whether destruction decisions are made before, after, or simultaneously with announcement of tax laws) and therefore we will leave these matters unspecified.

---

[c]In this interpretation no positive utility is assigned to leisure. See the discussion in section 12.10, subsection b.

[d]I Kings 3, 26.

12.3. The Formal Description of Society

Society—the set of "agents" or "players"—will be denoted T. We will model our assumption that society consists of many individually small agents by taking T to be a *continum*[e] (like a line or a region) rather than a finite set. In such a model it is best to think of an agent as an infinitesimal subset dt of T; however, we will usually still find it convenient to label agents by points t in T, where the label t is to be thought of as a "typical" point in the infinitesimal set[f] dt.

Next, we require some formal way of measuring the size of coalitions (i.e., sets of agents), in order to be able to say when they are in the majority. If T were finite one could do this simply by counting. Since T is a continuum, counting will not do, and one must specify the measure of size exogenously. We therefore assume given a nonnegative measure[g] μ on the coalitions, with $\mu(T) = 1$ (the *population measure*). Intuitively, one should think of $\mu(S)$ as the proportion of traders in S; thus S is in the majority if and only if $\mu(S) > 1/2$. Note that the measure $\mu(dt)$ of a single agent can be thought of as the reciprocal of the number of people in society.

Finally, for each t in T, there is given a nonnegative number $e(t)$ (t's *endowment*) and a function u_t on the nonnegative numbers (t's *utility*). The endowment function e is to be thought of as a density function, like the density functions that occur in probability theory; the actual endowment of an agent t is $e(t)\mu(dt)$, and the total endowment of a coalition S is $\int_S e(t)\mu(dt)$. If x is a function on T denote $\int_S x(t)\mu(dt)$ simply by $\int_S x$, and $\int_T x(t)\mu(dt)$ by $\int x$. Thus the total endowment of a coalition S is $\int_S e$.

We shall require some assumptions. The first is:

(12.3.1) *The population measure μ is nonatomic.*

Nonatomicity means that T can be cut up into coalitions all of which have μ-measure as small as we like; intuitively, it means that the agents are individually negligible. We shall also assume:

(12.3.2) *The u_t are increasing, concave, continuously differentiable at positive values of the argument, and continuous at 0.*

(12.3.3) $\infty > \int e > 0$.

[e] Compare Aumann and Shapley [5], especially Section 29, or Hildenbrand [10]. Technically T is taken as a measurable space, isomorphic to the unit interval with the Borel subsets. Only measurable sets are to be thought of as coalitions.

[f] One may think of T as an interval that is cut up into a large number of small subintervals dt, each of which is labelled by a point t in it.

[g] A *measure* is a function μ on the coalitions such that $\mu(S \cup W) = \mu(S) + \mu(W)$ when S and W are disjoint, and more generally,

$$\mu(\cup_{i=1}^{\infty} S_i) = \Sigma_{i=1}^{\infty} \mu(S_i)$$

when the S_i are disjoint.

(12.3.4) *The u_t are uniformly bounded,*[h] *and $u_t(1)$ is uniformly positive.*[i]

(12.3.5) $u_t(0) = 0$.

Assumptions (12.3.1) and (12.3.2) are substantive, and without them we could not prove our result. The first half of (12.3.3)–that $\infty > \int e$–merely says that e is integrable, i.e., that the total wealth of society is finite, whereas the second half–that $\int e > 0$–merely says that some significant set of agents has a positive endowment, without which the whole situation becomes trivial. Assumption (12.3.4) is also of a technical nature, and it might be possible to dispense with it or at least weaken it. Assumption (12.3.5) is, of course, merely a normalization.

There are also some very technical measurability assumptions, which we will not spell out here. The interested reader is referred to [4].

As usual, an *allocation* is a nonnegative function x on T such that $\int x = \int e$; here, too, we must view x as a density function. If x is a nonnegative function on T, we shall abuse our notation slightly by writing $u(x)$ for the function on T whose value at t is $u_t(x(t))$; the notation $u'(x)$ is to be interpreted analogously, u_t' being the first derivative of u_t. Since all individual quantities are scaled down to infinitesimal size, it is useful to think even of the utilities as densities; i.e., to think of t's utility for an allocation x as $u_t(x(t))\mu(dt)$.

12.4. The Solution Concept

The game described in section 12.2 is "played" on two levels. First, there is maneuvering to determine which players will be in the majority and minority coalitions respectively; and then, there is a conflict between the two coalitions that actually form, involving threats by both sides. Our aim is to find an outcome that avoids conflict and assigns to each player a payoff reflecting his opportunities on both levels of play; in short, a reasonable compromise. It is our view that the notion most suitable for this purpose is the concept of value introduced by Shapley [17], as adapted to variable threat games by Harsanyi [9], to nontransferable utility (NTU) games by Shapley [18], and to games with a continuum of players by Kannai [11] and Aumann and Shapley [5]. The underlying ideas date back to the Nash variable threat model [15]. This history explains why we will refer to the solution concept adopted here as the Harsanyi-Shapley-Nash NTU value.

To explain this solution concept, we start with finite games. Recall that a *finite coalitional game* (or simply *game*) consists of a finite set T (the "players")

[h] $\sup_{x,t} u_t(x) < \infty$.

[i] $\inf_t u_t(1) > 0$. This implies that $\inf_t u_t(x) > 0$ for all x.

together with a function v that associates with each subset S of T ("coalition") a real number $v(S)$ (the "worth" of S), such that $v(\emptyset) = 0$. A *payoff vector* is a measure ξ on the coalitions; intuitively, $\xi(S)$ represents the sum of the payoffs to all members of S. Since T is finite, ξ is determined by its values $\xi(\{t\})$ on one-player sets, so that it may be thought of as the vector of payoffs to the individual players.

A *value* [17] is an operator that associates with each game v a payoff vector ϕv satisfying certain plausible axioms. Here we will quote only the *efficiency* axiom, according to which

$$(\phi v)(T) = v(T) \tag{12.1}$$

and the *additivity* axiom, according to which

$$\phi(v + w) = \phi v + \phi w \tag{12.2}$$

Shapley [17] also showed that the value is given by the formula

$$(\phi v)(\{t\}) = E(v(S_t^R \cup \{t\}) - v(S_t^R)) \tag{12.3}$$

where S_t^R is the set of players preceding t in a random order R on the set of all players, and E is the expectation operator when all orders on T are assigned equal probability. Formula (12.3) means that the value of a player is the expectation of his contribution to the worth of the players preceding him in a random order of all players.

The concepts of coalitional game and value discussed above have been extended from a finite player set to a continuum of players; see [5,11]. As in the finite case, the value associates to a coalitional game v a payoff vector ϕv, where by "payoff vector" we mean a measure on coalitions.

We turn now to the problem of defining a coalitional game corresponding to the income redistribution game described in section 2. This means that we need to specify the "worth" $v(S)$ of each coalition S. In attempting to do that we are faced with two basic difficulties: First, the utilities of the players are not "comparable," so that it is meaningless to speak of one player getting, say, twice as much utility as another; on the other hand, any measure of the worth of a coalition must obviously involve some kind of aggregation of the utilities of the individuals, and it is difficult to see how such an aggregation can be carried out in the absence of comparability. The second difficulty is that even if we could somehow aggregate utilities to determine how much each outcome is worth to each coalition, we still would not know how to determine the worth of a coalition. This is because even after coalitional lines are drawn, the majority and the minority are faced with a fairly complex strategic situation in which threats, counterthreats, and compromises play a crucial role. It is not at all clear a priori how these strategic considerations would interact and to what outcome they would lead.

Recall that since u_t is an N-M utility for t, it follows that for any positive constant λ, λu_t is also an N-M utility. In formal terms, the problem of comparability is that the constants λ can be chosen entirely arbitrarily, with no restriction that they must be the same for different players. Solving this problem means finding a criterion of comparability—i.e., somehow fixing a "weight" $\lambda = \lambda(t)$ for each agent t. If that were done, then one could define the aggregate utility of a coalition S for an allocation $\boldsymbol{x}$ by the expression[j]

$$\int_S \lambda(t) u_t(x(t)) \mu(dt) = \int_S \lambda u(x)$$

Let us for the moment postpone discussing the choice of weights λ, and proceed at once to the second question, namely that of determining the worth of a coalition in view of the strategic possibilities open to it and its complement. Suppose, then, that the function λ is given; we wish to determine the worth $v_\lambda(S)$ of a coalition S. Consider first the case $S = T$. This is easier because the assumption that the coalition T of all agents has "formed" means that all agents are cooperating; hence it is only a question of maximizing total aggregate utility $\int \lambda u(x)$ subject to $\int x = \int e$, and there is no question of threats, counterthreats, and compromises. To achieve this maximum, the players will presumably reallocate the initial endowment between them in some way; the resulting distribution of net income will be an allocation, i.e., $\int x = \int e$, since total net income must equal total gross income (remember that we are only discussing redistribution of income). The aggregate utility of T will then be $\int \lambda u(x)$. Since the coalition T will act to maximize this aggregate utility, we may conclude that[k]

$$v_\lambda(T) = \max \left\{ \int \lambda u(x) : \int x = \int e \right\} \tag{12.4}$$

Suppose next that $S \neq T$. We will think of $v_\lambda(S)$ as being the aggregate utility of S if it "forms" and bargains as a unit with the agents outside of S. In analyzing this situation, we use a simplified version of the model of Nash [15]. Suppose both S and its complement $T \backslash S$ commit themselves to carrying out certain threats—let's call them σ and τ respectively—if an accommodation between them is not reached. Let's say that carrying out these threats will yield to S and $T \backslash S$ aggregate utilities of, say, $f = f_\lambda(\sigma, \tau)$ and $g = g_\lambda(\sigma, \tau)$ respectively. Thus after the threats are made, the surplus utility over which they are

[j]This notion of "aggregate utility" is of course not without conceptual difficulties, but its intuitive meaning in connection with the NTU value has been discussed by Shapley [18] and Aumann [3], and we will not repeat the discussion here.

[k]Fine points such as questions of existence of the maximum will be steadfastly ignored in this chapter.

bargaining (and that somehow has to be split between them) is $v_\lambda(T) - f - g$, where $v_\lambda(T)$ is given by (12.4). Under these circumstances, symmetry conditions (cf. Nash [14]) indicate a compromise in which this surplus will be evenly divided between them, so that the resulting aggregate utility to S should be

$$f + \frac{v_\lambda(T) - f - g}{2} = \frac{1}{2}[v_\lambda(T) + (f - g)] \tag{12.5}$$

and similarly, to $T \backslash S$ it should be

$$\frac{1}{2}[v_\lambda(T) - (f - g)] \tag{12.6}$$

Of course each of the sides will try to choose its threat in a way that is most advantageous to its final payoff. Hence, if we set

$$H = H_\lambda^S(\sigma, \tau) = f - g = f_\lambda(\sigma, \tau) - g_\lambda(\sigma, \tau)$$

then we may conclude from (12.5) and (12.6) that S will wish to maximize, and $T \backslash S$ to minimize, the expression H. By the minimax theorem[1] for 2-person 0-sum games, there is a number $w = w_\lambda(S)$ such that S can guarantee that H will be at least w, and $T \backslash S$ can guarantee that it will be at most w. Presumably S and $T \backslash S$, if formed, would act to "cash in" on these guarantees; so that one could then expect an outcome that yields to S and $T \backslash S$ aggregate utilities of $\frac{1}{2}(v_\lambda(T) + w_\lambda(S))$ and $\frac{1}{2}(v_\lambda(T) - w_\lambda(S))$ respectively. Thus given the function λ we may define the worth $v_\lambda(S)$ by

$$v_\lambda(S) = \frac{1}{2}(v_\lambda(T) + w_\lambda(S)) \tag{12.7}$$

We are interested in the value ϕv_λ of the game v_λ.

But there is a difficulty here. To see it note first that the value ϕv_λ calls for a "redistribution of utilities," since the worths $v_\lambda(s)$ defined in (12.4) are in units of "aggregate utility." In fact, we cannot redistribute utility, but only income; thus it is possible that the value ϕv_λ is not attainable–i.e., there is no redistribution of income (or allocation) that yields each agent the utility that he is assigned by the payoff vector ϕv_λ. In fact, we might remark parenthetically that in general there is not even any allocation that will yield S and $T \backslash S$ the amounts (12.5) and (12.6); that is because (12.5) and (12.6) involve an even split of surplus aggregate *utility*; and in our model, utility, though one may

[1]We remind the reader that we are ignoring "fine points" such as verifying that the conditions for the minimax theorem hold.

assume it interpersonally comparable, is certainly not transferable—only money can be transferred. Thus the compromises implicit in (12.5) and (12.6), as well as the larger compromise implicit in the value ϕv_λ, may simply be infeasible.

And as if that were not sufficiently worrisome, we must remind the reader that we have not yet resolved the problem of determining the weights λ.

Fortunately, these two difficulties cancel each other out. We will show that there is a unique[m] function λ such that ϕv_λ is feasible; thus the feasibility problem and the problem of determining λ solve each other. Formally, we define a *value allocation* to be an allocation x such that there exists a λ for which

$$(\phi v_\lambda)(dt) = \lambda(t)u_t(x(t))\mu(dt) \tag{12.8}$$

for all agents t (or equivalently, $(\phi v_\lambda)(S) = \int_S \lambda u(x)$ for all S). This means that the value assigns to each agent precisely the utility he receives under the allocation x. Thus the value is feasible without any "transfers of utility"; the only transfers are those of money.

The Harsanyi-Shapley-Nash value just defined, and the corresponding concept of value allocation, have been thoroughly discussed elsewhere [3, 15, 18], and we will not enter into another such discussion here. A few words about the concept may, however, be in place. Integrating (12.8) and using the efficiency axiom (12.1), we find

$$v_\lambda(T) = (\phi v_\lambda)(T) = \int \lambda u(x)$$

From this and (12.4) it follows that the maximum that defines $v_\lambda(T)$ is achieved at the value allocation x; hence the marginal utilities $\lambda(t)u'_t(x(t))$ must be equal for all agents t with positive income. This means that although utility itself is not transferable, if one scales the utilities u_t by multiplying them by $\lambda(t)$, then in the neighborhood of a value allocation, utility is "locally transferable"; i.e., small amounts of utility can effectively be transferred by transferring money.

Of course for any allocation x one can find λ's with this property—it is only necessary to choose $\lambda(t) = 1/u'_t(x(t))$. But when one then proceeds to calculate ϕv_λ, one will in general find that it is infeasible. Thus the value allocation is uniquely determined by requiring utility comparisons to be made in such a way so that utility is locally transferable, *and* that the allocation be a reasonable compromise, from the point of view of the Shapley value.

12.5. The Main Theorem: Statement and Preliminary Discussions

Main Theorem: The income redistribution game has a unique value allocation x. This allocation satisfies

[m]This is true only in the income redistribution game described here; in general one will not get uniqueness of the λ in an NTU game, though the set of appropriate λ may be expected to be in some sense "small."

$$\frac{u_t(x(t))}{u'_t(x(t))} + x(t) = c + e(t) \tag{12.9}$$

for all t, where c is a positive constant.

Note that

$$c = \int \frac{u(x)}{u'(x)} \tag{12.10}$$

this follows from integrating (12.9) and using $\int x = \int e$.

We will demonstrate the Main Theorem informally in section 12.9. A formal proof is given in [4].

Let us explore some implications of the main theorem. First, we have:

Implication 12.5.1: For agents with the same utility function, net income is an increasing function of gross income $e(t)$.

This follows from the fact that by Assumption (12.3.2), the left side of (12.9) is an increasing function of $x(t)$.

Next, note that

$$t\text{'s income tax}^{n} = e(t) - x(t) \tag{12.11}$$

Hence, the *marginal income tax rate* $M(t)$ is the derivative of $e - x$ with respect to e at $e = e(t)$, when x is implicitly defined as a function of e by the equation

$$\frac{u_t(x)}{u'_t(x)} + x = c + e$$

Implicit differentiation of this equation yields:

Implication 12.5.2: Assume that u_t *is twice continuously differentiable. Then*

$$M(t) = 1 - \frac{1}{2 + \dfrac{-u''_t u_t}{u'^2_t}} \tag{12.12}$$

where u_t *and its derivatives are calculated at* $x(t)$.

In particular,

---

[n] It should be recalled that we are really discussing the net effect of taxation *and* redistribution; use of the word "tax" to describe the combination of both processes is merely a matter of convenience. Note also that the decrement in t's income is actually $(e(t) - x(t))\, \mu(dt)$; thus $e(t) - x(t)$ is really "tax density" rather than "tax."

$$\frac{1}{2} \leqslant M(t) < 1 \tag{12.13}$$

that is, the marginal rate is always at least 50 percent! In section 12.10 we return to this matter of the surprisingly high marginal rate.

Let us now interpret the main theorem in terms of the total rather than the marginal tax. From (12.9) and (12.11) we obtain

$$t\text{'s income tax} = \frac{u_t(x(t))}{u_t'(x(t))} - c \tag{12.14}$$

Since $x(t)$ is the allocation of income to agent t and since $u_t'(x(t))$ is his marginal utility of income, $\lambda(t) = 1/u_t'(x(t))$ is the *money price* of a unit of t's utility. Thus in the final compromise, agent t receives utility with money valuation $V(t)$ defined by

$$V(t) = \lambda(t)u_t(x(t)) = \frac{u_t(x(t))}{u_t'(x(t))} \tag{12.15}$$

Combining (12.9), (12.10), and (12.15), we find

Implication 12.5.3: t's income tax = $V(t) - \bar{V}$, where $\bar{V}$ is the average[o] *of the $V(t)$.*

This means that a person's tax is the surplus of the dollar value of his utility over the average of the dollar values of everybody's utilities. Thus we get a tax structure which is negative on the lower part of the scale, i.e., provides for positive public transfer to low income agents. In fact if we denote the elasticity of utility by

$$\eta(t) = \frac{u_t'(x(t))}{u_t(x(t))} x(t)$$

then (12.9) can be solved to read

$$x(t) = \frac{\eta(t)}{1 + \eta(t)} (c + e(t))$$

If agent t has no income, that is, $e(t) = 0$, then this yields a social "support" (or negative tax) to agent t of size $[\eta(t)/(1 + \eta(t)]c$. As his income increases the agent pays a positive marginal income tax $M(t)$ until the support is exhausted at which time the agent begins to pay a positive amount of total taxes.

---

[o] $\bar{V}$ is of course the same as the constant c of (12.9) and (12.10); we use the notation $\bar{V}$ only to emphasize the interpretation of this constant as a mean of the $V(t)$.

12.6. The Fear of Ruin

In the discussion above (at (12.14)), we saw that

$$t\text{'s income tax} = \frac{u_t(x(t))}{u_t'(x(t))} - c$$

where c may be viewed as a constant tax credit. Let us now interpret the term $u_t(x(t))/u_t'(x(t))$, in terms of behavior under uncertainty.

For simplicity, set $x = x(t)$, $u = u_t(x)$, $u' = u_t'(x)$. The expression u/u' will be called t's *fear of ruin* at x. To understand why, let us consider its reciprocal u'/u, which will be called t's *boldness* at x. Suppose that t is considering a bet in which he risks his entire fortune x against a possible gain of a small amount h. The probability q of ruin would have to be very small in order for him to be indifferent between such a bet and retaining his current fortune. Moreover, the more unwilling he is to risk ruin, the smaller q will be. Thus q is an *inverse* measure of t's aversion to risking ruin, and a direct measure of boldness; obviously q tends to 0 as the potential winnings h shrink. We assert that the boldness is the *probability of ruin per dollar of potential winnings* for small potential winnings, i.e., it is the limit of q/h as $h \to 0$. To see this, note that for indifference we must have

$$u(x) = (1 - q)u(x + h) + qu(0) = (1 - q)u(x + h)$$

Hence

$$\frac{q}{h} = \frac{(u(x + h) - u(x))/h}{u(x + h)}$$

and as $h \to 0$, this tends to u'/u.

We conclude that *the tax equals the fear of ruin at the net income, less a constant tax credit.* Thus the more fearful a person, the higher he may expect his tax to be.

Next, set $u'' = u_t''(x)$, and let us examine the term

$$\delta_t = -uu''/u'^2 \tag{12.16}$$

appearing in the expression (12.12) for the marginal tax rate. We have

$$\delta_t = \frac{-u''/u'}{u'/u}$$

The denominator of the right side is the boldness; its numerator is the measure of *absolute risk aversion* (of t at x), as defined by Arrow [1] and Pratt [16]. To interpret this concept, let us suppose that t considers an even-money bet in a small amount. Since he is risk averse (i.e., $u'' < 0$), the probability p for success would have to be greater than 1/2 in order for him to be indifferent between this bet and simply retaining his current fortune x. The probability premium $p - 1/2$ is a measure of his aversion to risk at x; because u is differentiable, it tends to 0 as the size of the bet shrinks. The measure of absolute risk aversion is the probability premium per dollar of bet size for small bets, i.e., it is the limit of $(p - (1/2))/h$ as $h \to 0$, where h is the size of the bet.

Conceptually, there are two components that enter into the boldness coefficient. One is t's attitude toward risking his fortune; the other is his attitude toward small winnings. We know that he is risk averse, i.e., that even at even money he requires a probability premium for entering into a risk. Obviously this aversion is a factor in determining the probability q that entered into the calculation of boldness. If we wish to measure his attitude "purely" toward risking his fortune, we must somehow cancel out the component that measures his aversion to small risks. This motivates us to define the *pure boldness* as the ratio between boldness and absolute risk aversion, i.e., as $-(u'/u)/(u''/u')$. The *pure fear of ruin* is defined as the reciprocal of the pure boldness, i.e., the δ_t in formula (12.16).

The absolute boldness has the same dimensions as the absolute risk aversion, namely 1/dollar. Therefore the pure boldness and pure fear of ruin are both dimensionless, that is, invariant under changes in the unit of utility or the unit of money.

Returning now to the taxation picture, we see from (12.12) that *the marginal tax rate depends only on the pure fear of ruin* δ_t *and is directly related to it*: the higher the pure fear of ruin, the higher is the marginal tax rate.

The concept of fear of ruin introduced here is of interest also in an entirely different context, namely that of the Nash Bargaining Problem [14]. Consider a case in which two players are bargaining over the division of a fixed amount R of money, and suppose that their utility functions are u_1 and u_2 respectively, where $u_i(x)$ represents the utility of i for receiving the amount x out of this bargaining process. Assume that the u_i are concave and differentiable and $u_i(0) = 0$. Then the Nash solution calls for maximizing $u_1(x_1)u_2(x_2)$ subject to $x_1 + x_2 = R$. This maximum is attained at the unique point (x_1^*, x_2^*) for which $x_1^* + x_2^* = R$ and

$$\frac{u_1'(x_1^*)}{u_1(x_1^*)} = \frac{u_2'(x_2^*)}{u_2(x_2^*)} \tag{12.17}$$

We thus find that the Nash solution calls for that compromise which makes the two players *equally fearful of ruin*, where ruin is here taken to mean disagreement. This provides an alternative interpretation of the Nash solution, which has sometimes been ignored by economists because of its strongly cardinal nature. (For another interpretation, see Harsanyi [8].)

12.7. Illustrations

In this section we will assume that the endowment function $e(t)$ is bounded. From (12.9) it follows that $x(t) \leqslant c + e(t)$. Since e is bounded, it follows that in any particular example net income of all individuals must lie in a fixed finite interval, which we shall call the "relevant range." The behavior of the utility functions outside of this interval is irrelevant–the results do not change if we change the utility functions outside of the relevant range. In the illustrations of this section, we will describe the utilities only in the relevant range; outside of that, they can be chosen arbitrarily as long as they remain bounded and sufficiently differentiable. For example, when we refer to "linear utilities," we mean "utilities that are linear in the relevant range;" the utilities cannot, of course, be linear on the entire real line, since that would violate the boundedness condition.

Example 12.7.1: Linear Utilities

One's first impression is that the threat possibilities make the rich (i.e., high endowment) players extremely powerful: not only do they have a higher endowment, but also more to threaten with. It might even be thought that they would end up richer than before. But this is not the case. From the linearity of the u_t one obtains $(u_t(x)/u_t'(x)) + x = 2x$, and hence $x = (1/2)(c + e)$. Integrating, one obtains $c = e(T)$; thus

$$x(t)\mu(dt) = \frac{1}{2}(\textstyle\int e)\mu(dt) + \frac{1}{2}e(t)\mu(dt) \qquad (12.18)$$

The expression $(\int e)\mu(dt)$ represents t's "equal share" of society's endowment, i.e., what he would get if society's endowment $(\int e)$ were divided equally among all agents. Of course, $e(t)\mu(dt)$ and $x(t)\mu(dt)$ are t's gross and net income respectively. Thus (12.18) says that the net income distribution is a 50-50 compromise between the gross income distribution and an entirely egalitarian distribution–a far cry from our above guess that the rich will get richer! What is happening is that by compromising after a threat to destroy its endowment, the minority can hold on to half of its endowment, while the other half goes to the majority. Thus the term $(1/2)e(t)\mu(dt)$ represents that part of one's income that is not taxed; whereas the term $(1/2)(\int e)\mu(dt)$ represents that part that results from the fact that one has a priori a 50-50 chance of being in the ruling coalition.

In tax terms, we have a tax rate of 50 percent, with an exemption in the amount of the equal share; this results in a support in the amount of half the equal share, since the exemption can lead to negative taxable income. Alternatively, one could say that everybody gets taxed at a straight 50 percent (with no support), and that the resulting revenue is redistributed *equally* among the entire population.

Example 12.7.2: $u_t(x) = x^{\alpha}$, $\quad 0 < \alpha < 1$

Let us try again to guess the result beforehand. Here we have decreasing marginal utility; the less a person has, the greater his marginal utility of income. This kind of situation usually favors the rich, since they are less prone to threats. For example, suppose two people with utility function $\sqrt{x}$ who are worth \$0 and \$10,000 respectively must agree on how to share an additional \$10,000, or else lose the additional amount entirely. Then the Harsanyi-Shapley-Nash value (which in this case boils down to the bargaining solution of Nash [14]) dictates that the richer man will receive approximately \$6,404, while the poorer one will receive only \$3,596 (see (12.17)). Thus, it seems safe to guess that in Example 12.7.2 the rich will be relatively better off than in Example 12.7.1.

Unfortunately, we are wrong again. Here

$$\frac{u_t(x)}{u_t'(x)} + x = \frac{\alpha + 1}{\alpha} x$$

and we find

$$x(t) = \frac{1}{\alpha + 1} (\textstyle\int e) + \frac{\alpha}{\alpha + 1} e(t)$$

Again, we get a compromise between the endowment and the equal share, but in a more egalitarian ratio (when $\alpha = 1/2$ it is 2/3 to 1/3). The smaller α–i.e., the more intensely the poor suffer–the more egalitarian the outcome: an effect exactly the opposite of what we had thought!

The explanation is simple. A rich man who finds himself in the minority is subject to ruin (i.e., 0 utility) just as much as a poor man; and therefore in the minority, he is as prone to threats as the poor man. Thus the increased fear of ruin (x/α as compared with x in the linear case) works to the advantage not of the rich man, but of the majority. Since everybody has an equal chance of being in the majority, this tips the scale away from the initial endowment and towards the egalitarian outcome.

In tax terms, we get a tax rate of $1/(\alpha + 1)$ (which may be anywhere between 1/2 and 1), an exemption in the amount of the equal share, and a possibility of negative tax. Alternatively, one could say that everybody gets taxed at the rate $1/(\alpha + 1)$, with no exemption, and that the resulting revenue is distributed equally among the entire population.

Example 12.7.3: $u_t(x) = x^{\alpha(t)}, \qquad 0 < \alpha(t) \leqslant 1$

Here the fear of ruin varies from agent to agent. One would expect that the more fearful agent—the one with lower $\alpha(t)$—is penalized in the tax structure, since he is more prone to threats. This is indeed the case. We have

$$\frac{u_t(x)}{u_t'(x)} + x = \frac{\alpha(t)+1}{\alpha(t)}\,x$$

and hence

$$x(t) = \frac{\alpha(t)}{\alpha(t)+1}\left[\left(\int \frac{e}{\alpha+1} \Big/ \int \frac{\alpha}{\alpha+1}\right) + e(t)\right]$$

The tax is given by

$$e(t) - x(t) = \frac{1}{\alpha(t)+1}\left[e(t) - \alpha(t)\left(\int \frac{e}{\alpha+1} \Big/ \int \frac{\alpha}{\alpha+1}\right)\right]$$

This means that the agent who is more fearful of ruin has both a higher tax rate and a lower support.

Example 12.7.4: $u_t(x) = \log(1 + x)$

From (12.12) we get a marginal tax rate of $1 - 1/(2 + \log(1 + x(t)))$, which rises with $x(t)$, and hence also with $e(t)$. Thus in the case of this very classical utility function, the tax is progressive.

Example 12.7.5: $u_t(x) = x + \sqrt{x}$

We have

$$\frac{-u_t''u_t}{(u_t')^2} = \frac{1}{2(1+2\sqrt{x})} + \frac{1}{2(1+2\sqrt{x})^2}$$

which decreases as x increases. Hence by (12.12) the marginal tax rate decreases as $x(t)$ increases, and hence also when $e(t)$ does. The tax is thus regressive; the rate goes from near 2/3 when $x(t)$ is small, to near 1/2 when it is large. What is happening is that when x is close to 0, u_t behaves very much like $\sqrt{x}$, and as it moves up, it behaves more and more like x. The results then follow the pattern of Examples 7.1 and 7.2.

In the next section we will see that there are examples in which the tax is progressive, neutral, and regressive at different points in the range of income.

12.8. Further Discussion of the Marginal Tax Rate

We have seen (12.13) that the marginal rate is always between 1/2 and 1. In section 12.7 we saw that the tax may be progressive, regressive, or neutral, i.e., that the marginal rate may be increasing, decreasing or constant as a function of wealth. This section is devoted to the question of just what we can say about the behavior of the marginal rate, i.e., to characterizing those functions of wealth that can appear as marginal tax rates.

Call a function u *admissible* if it is bounded, concave, increasing, twice continuously differentiable at positive values of the argument, continuous at 0 and satisfies $u(0) = 0$. Let u be admissible, and for $x > 0$, let

$$m(x) = 1 - \frac{1}{2 + (-u''(x)u(x)/u'(x)^2)} \tag{12.19}$$

the marginal tax rate of an individual with utility function u and net income x is precisely $m(x)$. Clearly

$$1/2 \leqslant m(x) < 1 \tag{12.20}$$

We can also say something about the marginal tax rates of the very rich; we have

$$\limsup_{x\to\infty} m(x) = 1 \tag{12.21}$$

Indeed, because of the concavity of u,

$$(x/2)u'(x) \leqslant u(x) - u(x/2)$$

Because u is bounded, the right side approaches 0, and hence $\lim_{x\to\infty} xu' = 0$. Arrow [1] has proved that when utility is bounded, $\liminf_{x\to\infty}(xu''/u') \geqslant 1$. Hence

$$\liminf\,(u''u/u'^2) = \liminf \frac{xu''/u'}{xu'/u} = \frac{\liminf\,(xu''/u')}{\lim xu'/\lim u} = \infty$$

Hence $\limsup m(x) = 1$, as claimed.

Equation (12.21) says that for arbitrarily large net incomes, the marginal tax rate comes close to 1. On the other hand, it cannot come *too* close too often; letting R^+ be the nonnegative part of the real axis, we have

$$1/(1-m) \textit{ is integrable over any interval in } R^+ \tag{12.22}$$

Indeed, when the interval has positive end points, this follows from

$$\frac{1}{1-m} = 2 - (u''u/u'^2) = (x + (u/u'))'$$

when the left end point is 0, it follows from a limiting argument using $u/u' \to 0$ as $x \to 0$.

The question now arises whether anything can be said about m other than (12.20), (12.21), and (12.22), that is, whether any function m satisfying these three conditions is the marginal tax rate associated with some admissible utility function. The answer is no; $u = \log(1+x)$ is not admissible, but the corresponding m (see Example 12.7.4) satisfies all three conditions. However, we have:

Remark 12.8.1: Let m_0 be any continuous function on the positive real numbers satisfying (12.20) *and* (12.22)*. Then for each $K > 0$ there is an admissible u whose m coincides with m_0 for $x \leqslant K$.*

This says that (12.20) and (12.22) are enough to characterize marginal tax rates if we restrict ourselves to bounded net incomes. Of course, (12.21) is irrelevant when one is looking only at a bounded set of x.

To prove Remark 12.8.1, we can simply set

$$u(x) = \exp\left(\int_0^x (1 - y + \int_0^y (1 - m_0(z))^{-1} dz)^{-1} dy\right) - 1$$

when $x \leqslant K$; when $x > K$, we adjust u smoothly so that it is bounded. Such a u satisfies all the requirements.

Remark 12.8.1, together with equations (12.20) and (12.22), provides a characterization of those functions that can appear as marginal tax rates when one restricts oneself to a bounded set of net incomes.

12.9. An Informal Demonstration of the Main Theorem

Though the proof of the main theorem is somewhat technical, it is possible, by using the calculus of infinitesimals, to outline the underlying ideas rather quickly. This we will now do. A completely rigorous proof will be presented in [4].

Write

$$r_\lambda(S) = \sup \left\{ \int_S \lambda u(x) : \int_S x = \int_S e \right\} \tag{12.23}$$

$$q_\lambda(S) = \begin{cases} r_\lambda(S) & \text{if } \mu(S) \geqslant 1/2 \\ 0 & \text{if } \mu(S) < 1/2 \end{cases} \tag{12.24}$$

Intuitively, $r_\lambda(S)$ is the maximum total utility (when weighted by the $\lambda(t)$) that S can get for itself by reallocating precisely its own endowment among its members, i.e., neither taking anything from other people nor having anything taken away from it nor destroying anything. On the other hand, $q_\lambda(S)$ is the maximum aggregate utility that S can *assure* itself.

In this demonstration we assume that $r_\lambda(S)$ is finite and that the sup is actually attained. These assumptions can be removed.

Step 1: We have

$$w_\lambda(S) = q_\lambda(S) - q_\lambda(T \backslash S) \tag{12.25}$$

An optimal pair of strategies in the threat game H_λ^S *is for the majority to take from the minority everything that the minority does not destroy (i.e., to tax at* 100 *percent), and for the minority to destroy its entire endowment.*[p]

Demonstration: First let S be in the majority. By taxing at 100 percent and reallocating its own endowment, S can assure that its own payoff will be at least $r_\lambda(S)$, and that of its complement 0. Therefore it assures itself a payoff of $r_\lambda(S)$ in the game H_λ^S. On the other hand, by destroying its endowment, the minority can assure that the majority's payoff in H_λ^S will not be more than $r_\lambda(S)$. Hence the strategies described are indeed optimal, and when $\mu(S) > 1/2$, (12.25) is proved. The argument when S is in the minority is similar, using the fact that $T \backslash S$ is then in the majority.[q]

Step 2:

$$\phi v_\lambda = \phi q_\lambda$$

Demonstration: Define the game $q_\lambda^{\#}$ dual[r] to q_λ by $q_\lambda^{\#}(S) = q_\lambda(T) - q_\lambda(T \backslash S)$. By reversing orderings in assumption (12.3.3), one can easily show that $\phi q_\lambda^{\#} = \phi q_\lambda$. On the other hand, from equations (12.7) and (12.25) it follows that $v_\lambda = (1/2)q_\lambda + (1/2)q_\lambda^{\#}$. The result then follows from the additivity axiom for the value (12.2).

[p]Of course these threats are not carried out in the compromise that is finally reached.

[q]In this heuristic treatment we ignore the case in which $\mu(S)$ is exactly 1/2. In the rigorous treatment of Aumann-Kurz [4] it is of course taken into account.

[r]Compare Aumann and Shapley [5], p. 140, or Milnor and Shapley [13].

Step 3: Suppose $v_\lambda(T)$ is attained at $\mathbf{x}$*. Let p be the shadow price associated with this maximization, i.e.,* $p = \lambda(t)u'_t(x(t))$ *when* $x(t) > 0$*. Then*

$$(\phi q_\lambda)(dt) = \frac{1}{2}r_\lambda(T)\mu(dt) + \frac{1}{2}(\lambda(t)u_t(x(t)) - p(x(t) - e(t)))\mu(dt)$$

Demonstration: Let us fix attention on a particular agent; in this demonstration it will be convenient to refer to him directly as dt, rather than by the label t. Denote by S the set of all agents up to and including dt in a random order on all the agents; the value $(\phi q_\lambda)(dt)$ is the expectation of the contribution $q_\lambda(S) - q_\lambda(S \backslash dt)$ of dt to S (see (12.3)). The probability is 1/2 that S is in the minority, in which case dt contributes nothing. With probability $\mu(dt)$ (i.e., the reciprocal of the number of players), S is in the majority with dt and in the minority without him, i.e., dt is "pivotal." Because the ordering is random and there are many agents, S is almost surely an almost perfect sample of all the agents (insofar as utilities, endowments and the $\lambda(t)$ are concerned). That is, S is just like T, but is operating at half the scale (because $\mu(S) = 1/2$). In this case, therefore, dt's contribution is $r_\lambda(S) = (1/2)r_\lambda(T)$.

Finally, with probability 1/2, S is in the majority with and without dt. Again because of the random order, S is almost surely an almost perfect sample of the population T of all agents, and dt's contribution $r_\lambda(S) - r_\lambda(S \backslash dt)$ is the same as if he were the last agent, i.e., the same as $r_\lambda(T) - r_\lambda(T \backslash dt)$. But now a simple computation (see for example, Aumann [3], Section 8, Step 5) shows that the latter contribution is just

$$(\lambda(t)u_t(x(t)) - p(x(t) - e(t)))\mu(dt) \tag{12.26}$$

Summing up, dt contributes nothing with probability 1/2, $(1/2)r_\lambda(T)$ with probability $\mu(dt)$, and (12.26) with probability 1/2. So his expected contribution $(\phi q_\lambda)(dt)$ is precisely as asserted.

Step 4: If $\mathbf{x}$ *is a value allocation, then there is a constant c satisfying* (12.9).

Demonstration: That $\mathbf{x}$ is a value allocation means that $u(\mathbf{x})$ is a value, i.e.,

$$\lambda(t)u_t(x(t))\mu(dt) = (\phi v_\lambda)(dt)$$

(see (12.8)). Combining this with Steps 3 and 4, we get

$$\lambda(t)u_t(x(t)) = \frac{1}{2}r_\lambda(T) + \frac{1}{2}(\lambda(t)u_t(x(t)) - p(x(t) - e(t)))$$

whence

$$\frac{1}{p}\lambda(t)u_t(x(t)) + x(t) = \frac{1}{p}r_\lambda(T) + e(t) \tag{12.27}$$

From this it follows that $x(t) > 0$, and hence $p = \lambda(t)u_t'(x(t))$. Inserting this into (12.27) and setting $c = r_\lambda(T)/p$, we deduce (12.9).

Step 5: If $\boldsymbol{x}$ *is an allocation satisfying* (12.9), *then it is a value allocation.*

Demonstration: First note that $x(t) > 0$, since $c > 0$. Hence $u_t'(x(t))$ is defined and is positive. Set $\lambda(t) = 1/u_t'(x(t))$, and set $p = 1$; then (12.9) may be written in the form

$$\lambda(t)u_t(x(t)) = c + p(e(t) - x(t)) \tag{12.28}$$

Integrating and recalling that $\boldsymbol{x}$ is an allocation, we obtain

$$\int \lambda u(x) = c$$

Because $\lambda(t)u_t'(x(t)) = 1$, the integral on the left actually achieves the maximum defining $r_\lambda(T)$, i.e., $c = r_\lambda(T)$. Inserting this in (12.28) and rearranging, we find

$$\lambda(t)u_t(x(t)) = \frac{1}{2}r_\lambda(T) + \frac{1}{2}(\lambda(t)u_t(x(t)) - p(x(t) - e(t)))$$

Hence by Steps 3 and 2,

$$\lambda(t)u_t(x(t))\mu(dt) = (\phi v_\lambda)(dt) \tag{12.29}$$

Since $\boldsymbol{x}$ is an allocation, it follows from (12.29) and (12.8) that it is a value allocation, as was to be shown.

Step 6: There are precisely one allocation $\boldsymbol{x}$ *and one real constant* c *satisfying* (12.9), *and this constant is necessarily positive.*

Demonstration: Define

$$g_t(x) = \frac{u_t(x)}{u_t'(x)} + x$$

g_t is increasing and continuous, is defined for all nonnegative numbers, vanishes at 0, and tends to infinity as $x \to \infty$. Hence its inverse g_t^{-1} is defined and has the same properties. Moreover, $g_t(x) \geqslant x$, and so

$$g_t^{-1}(y) \leqslant y \tag{12.30}$$

with strict inequality holding when $y > 0$.

For each nonnegative number γ, define

$$f(\gamma) = \int_T g_t^{-1}(\gamma + e(t))\mu(dt) \tag{12.31}$$

by (12.30) and Assumption (12.3.3) the integral is finite. Again using (12.30) we get

$$f(0) < \int e$$

Next, if we go to the limit under the integration sign[s] in (12.31) and use the fact that $g_t^{-1}(x) \to \infty$ as $x \to \infty$, then we deduce that for sufficiently large γ,

$$f(\gamma) > \int e$$

Moreover f is strictly increasing (since the g_t^{-1} are) and continuous.[t] Hence there is one and only one γ with $f(\gamma) = \int e$; denote this γ by c and set

$$x(t) = g_t^{-1}(c + e(t)) \tag{12.32}$$

By construction $\boldsymbol{x}$ is an allocation, and together with c satisfies (12.9). Conversely, if $\boldsymbol{x}$ and c satisfy (12.9), then integrating (12.9) yields $c = \int u(x)/u'(x) > 0$, and then inverting (12.9) yields (12.32). Integrating (12.32) yields $\int e = \int_T g_t^{-1}(c + e(t))\mu(dt)$, and hence c and $\boldsymbol{x}$ can only be those already found. This completes Step 6.

Demonstration of the Main Theorem: We have shown in Steps 4 and 5 that an allocation $\boldsymbol{x}$ is a value allocation if and only if there is a constant c satisfying (12.9). By Step 6, there are precisely one $\boldsymbol{x}$ and c satisfying (12.9); and $c > 0$. Hence there is precisely one value allocation, and it satisfies (12.9); which is what the Main Theorem asserts.

12.10. Additional Discussion of the Results

In the development above we passed over issues that are important but perhaps somewhat controversial. This we did for the sake of continuity; we now wish to address ourselves to some of these issues.

Aggregation

Our purpose in this paper is to try to expose the effect of political power on income redistribution. Taxation has other important aspects, such as its effect on relative prices in a multicommodity economy and aspects relating to the

[s]This may be justified by a standard theorem like Fatou's lemma or the monotone convergence theorem.

[t]This follows from the fact that $|g_t^{-1}(y_2) - g_t^{-1}(y_1)| < |y_2 - y_1|$, which in turn follows from the definition of g_t.

production of private and public goods. The reader will agree, however, that an important element of taxation is the redistributive one, even in the case in which there is no overt cash redistribution, but all revenue is used for the provision of public goods. The relatively simple model of this chapter deals with the redistributive element only; other, more complex issues are left for subsequent studies.

Pareto Optimality, Second Best and the Problem of Leisure

An argument may be made in connection with the fact that one of the axioms underlying the Shapley value is Pareto optimality. This means that the value allocation $\boldsymbol{x}$ is Pareto optimal, in spite of the fact that we are introducing an explicit income tax into the system. It is known that the introduction of income taxation may in theory lead individuals to take more leisure than they would take in the absence of taxation, and so may lead to outcomes that are not Pareto optimal.

Certain aspects of the nonoptimality of taxation are implicit in the fact that any agent may destroy his endowment. If we think of one component of the endowment as "labor services," then within the context of the threat game, coalitions may threaten to withhold their labor services from the market. The problem arises with regard to the final compromise embodied in the value allocation $\boldsymbol{x}$. What we are saying is that as part of the compromise, each individual promises to offer the same amount of labor services as before the bargaining process. Thus if $\boldsymbol{e}(t)$ was the endowment of agent t, this same endowment will be offered to the market at the end. The difficulty with this is that in a decentralized, democratic society an individual may choose to work as much as he wishes. He thus may accept the compromise tax function but then work less and end up with a new $\boldsymbol{e}^{\tau}(t)$ which is the taxable income arising from a tax schedule τ. The usual argument is that $\boldsymbol{e}^{\tau}(t)$ and $\boldsymbol{e}(t)$ may not be the same and the allocation based on $\boldsymbol{e}^{\tau}(t)$ may not be Pareto optimal.

Although we think there may be possibilities of reformulating our model so as to take into account these "incentive effects" of taxation, we hesitate to do so because of the rather mild empirical evidence in support of "incentive effects." Both historical and cross-section analysis indicate a negligible wage elasticity of labor supply for males and a slightly higher elasticity for females (see for example, Hall [7] and Boskin [6]). Thus our assumption appears to be supported by the empirical evidence.

Individualized Tax Schedules

Our Main Theorem indicates that the tax rate depends upon the agent's utility function as well as on his gross income; thus the solution calls for individualized tax rates. The same phenomenon arises in all welfare theoretic treatments that seek optimal income distribution. For example, the criterion of "equal marginal utility of income" entails individualized taxation. Naturally we are aware of the fact that taxes ought to be "uniform"; this question was discussed already in section 12.2, in a somewhat different context (that of majority power in the threat game). As we said there, the extremely complex tax laws that one observes are in fact designed to provide some degree of individualization. Moreover, it must be remembered that we are discussing redistribution as well as taxation; though taxation may be required to be "uniform," certainly there is no way to prevent individualized redistribution.

Cardinality

The cardinal nature of the results may disturb some economists, who prefer the ordinal concepts that are familiar from general equilibrium theory. The point is that in the context of a power struggle, where threats are involved, it is to be expected that intensity of preference will play a determining role. Even on a purely intuitive level, it seems clear that in a bargaining situation, the more fearful side, or the side that is more "intense"—more interested in the outcome—is also the weaker one. "Fear" and "intensity" are cardinal concepts, and it would seem that they must be explicitly taken into account in any situation involving bargaining. For this reason we would expect value theories to be necessarily cardinal; on the contrary, it is surprising that such results can be obtained without interpersonal comparisons. For a more detailed analysis, see Shapley [18].

Our cardinal results should be contrasted with those of Aumann [3], who investigated value allocations in societies using the economic mechanism of exchange only, without any political voting mechanism. One of the surprising conclusions of that study was that though cardinal utilities enter in an essential manner into the description of the model, the outcomes are independent of the choice of cardinal utilities, and depend on ordinal preferences only. The reason for this phenomenon is that in a nonatomic market situation, the marginal contribution of an agent is essentially the same almost whatever coalition he joins, so that the result of the coalitional maneuvering is a foregone conclusion and there is little or no risk. But here that is far from being the case, as there is an enormous difference between being in the majority and being in the minority. The willingness to risk being in the minority—and to have the minority make threats—is therefore of vital importance. This explains in particular why the fear of ruin is decisive, since the optimal threat of the minority is precisely to ruin its members, and only in that way can it get a fair deal from the majority.

The High Tax Rates

An eyebrow-raising result of this study is that the marginal tax rate must be at least 50 percent. This result is due to our assumption of absolute majority rule. It can be shown that if the voting rules are altered to give some weight to wealth, the tax rates tend to be smaller.[u]

In fact, the power structure of existing societies does generally give weight to wealth; that is, wealthier individuals have more say in decision making. In a representative democracy, the extra weight given to wealth arises from the fact that in their votes, the representatives are more responsive to the stronger pressure groups: in addition to the fact that the elected representatives come from the wealthier classes, the need to use resources in running for office enables the owners of wealth to form more effective pressure groups. The result is a lower marginal tax than is indicated in this study, which might be considered the extreme case of "pure democracy."

Concavity and Boundedness of the Utility Functions

Concavity is merely an assertion of general risk averseness. Boundedness is a natural assumption in the context of von Neumann-Morgenstern utilities, since unbounded utilities lead to the St. Petersburg Paradox.

Interpretation of the Weights λ

The weight $\lambda(t)$ should be considered a measure of the importance of t's utility, arising endogenously out of the given power structure; indirectly, it is an index of t's power. Society behaves as if it were maximizing the expression $\int \lambda u(x)$, i.e., the sum of individual utilities weighted by their relative importance. This expression resembles the social welfare function mentioned in the introduction; but the underlying idea is quite different, since the equilibrium values of λ change if we change the initial distribution of wealth or if we change the utilities. But apart from that we eschew all the paternalistic, ethical connotations of the phrase "social welfare," and so prefer here to call $\int \lambda u(x)$ a *social power function.* Society maximizes total weighted utility, where the more powerful individuals are considered more important–i.e., are given more weight. Of course we are not advocating this (or any other) procedure; but most observers will agree that in fact, society takes much less account of "equity" or "fairness" than of power.

This may at first sound cynical; but when one examines its implications more carefully it turns out to be quite the opposite: a reaffirmation of the importance of democracy. Since social decision making is a function of power, it follows that to achieve equity in the outcome, one must build equity into the political institutions. A system that concentrates power in the hands of the few,

[u]In the extreme case in which decisions are reached by a majority vote of the wealth rather than of the population (i.e., "money votes") there are no taxes at all; i.e., the tax rate is 0.

even with the most idealistic intentions, must in the end benefit the few. It has long been known that income distributions in countries with rightist totalitarian regimes are more skewed than in the western democracies; but as Wiles [21] has shown,[v] this is to some extent true also for leftist totalitarian regimes (once one removes the cosmetic layers under which official figures are buried). So it is not the ideology that is decisive, but the power structure; and if we want a more equitable society, we must develop institutions that spread the political power as thinly and evenly as possible.

References

1. Arrow, K.J., *Aspects of the Theory of Risk-Bearing* Helsinki: Yrjö Jahnssonin Säätiö, 1965.

2. Arrow, K.J., and M. Kurz, *Public Investment, the Rate of Return, and Optimal Fiscal Policy*, Baltimore: Johns Hopkins Press, 1970.

3. Aumann, R.J., "Values of Markets with a Continuum of Traders," *Econometrica*, 43 (1975):611-646.

4. Aumann, R.J., and M. Kurz, "Power and Taxes in a Multi-Commodity Economy," *Israel Journal of Mathematics*, to appear.

5. Aumann, R.J., and L.S. Shapley, *Values of Non-Atomic Games* Princeton: Princeton University Press, 1974.

6. Boskin, M.J., "The Economics of Labor Supply" in *Income Maintenance and Labor Supply*, G.G. Cain and H.W. Watts (eds.), New York: Academic Press, 1973, pp. 163-181.

7. Hall, R.E., "Wages, Income, and Hours of Work in the U.S. Labor Force," in *Income Maintenance and Labor Supply*, G.G. Cain and H.W. Watts (eds.), New York: Academic Press, 1973, pp. 102-162.

8. Harsanyi, J.C., "Approaches to the Bargaining Problem Before and After the Theory of Games: A Critical Discussion of Zeuthen's, Hicks's and Nash's Theories," *Econometrica*, 24 (1956):144-157.

9. _______: "A Bargaining Model for the Cooperative n-Person Game," in *Contributions to the Theory of Games IV*, R.D. Luce and A.W. Tucker (eds.), Princeton: Princeton University Press, 1959, pp. 325-355.

10. Hildenbrand, W., *Core and Equilibria of a Large Economy*, Princeton: Princeton University Press, 1974.

11. Kannai, Y., "Values of Games with a Continuum of Players," *Israel Journal of Mathematics*, 4 (1966):54-58.

12. Mirrlees, J.A., "An Exploration in the Theory of Optimum Income Taxation," *Review of Economic Studies*, 38:114 (1971):175-208.

13. Milnor, J.W., and L.S. Shapley, *Values of Large Games II: Oceanic Games*, RM-2649, the RAND Corporation, Santa Monica, 1961.

[v]We are indebted to E. Sheshinski for this reference.

14. Nash, J.F., "The Bargaining Problem," *Econometrica*, 18 (1950):155-162.

15. ______, "Two Person Cooperative Games," *Econometrica*, 21 (1953):128-140.

16. Pratt, J.W., "Risk Aversion in the Small and in the Large," *Econometrica*, 32 (1964):122-136.

17. Shapley, L.S., "A Value for n-Person Games," in *Contributions to the Theory of Games II*, H.W. Kuhn and A.W. Tucker (eds.), Princeton: Princeton University Press, 1953, pp. 307-317.

18. ______, "Utility Comparisons and the Theory of Games," in *La Décision*, Paris: Editions du Centre National de la Recherche Scientifique, 1969, pp. 251-263.

19. Sheshinski, E., "The Optimal Linear Income-tax," *Review of Economic Studies*, 39:119 (1972):297-302.

20. von Neumann, J., and O. Morgenstern, *Theory of Games and Economic Behavior*, Princeton: Princeton University Press, 1944.

21. Wiles, P., *Distribution of Income: East and West*, Amsterdam: North Holland Publishing Company, 1974.

13 Political Limits of Traditional Stabilization Policy

Carl Christian von Weiszäcker

The disappointment of the public with traditional monetarist, Keynesian, and post-Keynesian policy proposals to stabilize price level and employment is almost a world wide phenomenon. Academic economists in their large majority still adhere to one of the different traditional schools of thought and so do the experts in the government and central bank bureaucracies as well as in economic journalism, who in their youth have been trained by those economists. What is the reason for this great contrast of opinion between the economists and the rest of the world? I do not claim to have a complete answer to this question. But the conflict of opinion between politicians and economists—apart from the weaknesses of the political side—may partly be due to certain preferences and aversions of economic model builders who thereby may get a biased view of the economic and political process.

To support my view of the economists' bias, I should like to quote two British economists whose fame rests very much on unorthodox views. One of them is Keynes, who made the well-known remark: "In the long run we are all dead." I don't know of any other insight of economists into the true nature of things which has a better chance to be appreciated by those who have the responsibility to make decisions *now*, that is the politicians. But economists appear to have a special preference for the long run. The other British economist whose criticism of orthodoxy I want to mention is Professor Kaldor. In his lecture on "The Irrelevance of Equilibrium Economics" [1] he criticizes the orthodox traditionalists for their insufficient understanding and analysis of the Smithian principle of division of labor. I do not agree with the consequences drawn by Kaldor, but I do agree with his criticism. Have we really sufficiently well understood the consequences of the division of labor?

Let me point out some obvious consequences of the division of labor which are perhaps of relevance for the problem of stability.

The division of labor means that people and firms specialize in the services and commodities they sell, but they do not specialize in the commodities they buy and consume. For many markets this implies: there are many more buyers than sellers in any given market. This has consequences for the structure of market transactions: The seller benefits from economies of scale in performing certain functions related to the transaction, such as storage, informational activities (e.g., advertising, know how). In particular, every seller meets many buyers who have different need for the commodity in question. It follows that it is mainly the buyer whose wishes are relevant for the quantity to be transacted. It is then a time-saving device, if the seller standardizes the bargaining process in such a way that he offers to sell any quantity of the commodity—within certain limits—for a price fixed by the seller and equal for all buyers. This description is adequate for the transaction of consumption goods. Markets for intermediate products may deviate from it and labor markets function in a markedly different way. From the macroeconomic point of view, it is important to draw the following conclusion. A change in aggregate demand will have its immediate impact on quantities transacted. Only later will price revisions take place.

Rigidity of wages cannot quite be explained in the same way, although, I believe, it is also related to producer specialization. The cooperative nature of production leads to the result that the number of sellers on the labor markets is much larger than the number of buyers. But it is still true, that the sellers are specialized. They sell all or most of their labor on the same market, and labor is for most of them the main article they sell. So the price for their labor is the most important of all market prices. In addition, labor is a peculiar commodity. Its productivity in the cooperative process of production depends to a large degree on the willingness of the seller to cooperate, even after he has sold that commodity. If this remuneration is considered unjust by himself (as he compares it with the remuneration of others) his productivity will drop. Standards and social norms of just remuneration only change slowly through time. The bad psychological effects (and their bad effects on productivity) of wage changes that are not in line with these norms are an important factor to explain sticky wages. In addition, the same producer specialization explains why coalitions and collective bargaining are an important element in wage determination. But these bargaining processes are complicated and time-consuming. After a contract has been reached, it must have a certain duration to pay off the investments in time and nerves that went into the bargaining process preceding the contract.

It would be interesting to elaborate on the following thought experiment: what would be the consequences of specialization not in production but in consumption? By analogy to the description of specialization in production, we should conclude that here prices are set by purchasers and quantities by sellers. As a sideline of my main argument I should like to make an observation on the theoretical foundations of modern and traditional monetarism. If there is producer specialization, a rise in the quantity of money will raise the propensity of purchasers to spend, thereby raise the volume of transactions until at last this volume has adapted to the higher quantity of money. If there were consumer specialization, a rise in the quantity of money will reduce the propensity to sell (and thereby acquire liquidity). Transactions will then decline, the disequilibrium between the quantity of money and the volume of transactions becomes larger. The process seems to be less stable. This suggests that the theoretical foundations of monetary theory should contain explicit reference to the division of labor, as was already suggested by Adam Smith.

I should also like to mention that Leijonhuvud's [2] interpretation of Keynes's work could be related to what we have discussed here. Leijonhuvud considers the theory of Keynes to be a theory of economic systems in which quantities react faster than prices on changing market conditions. Producer specialization may provide the reason for such market behavior.

A further implication of the division of labor lies in the structure of coalitions and interest groups. The high cost of forming, maintaining, and controlling coalitions puts a heavy premium on such coalitions from which its members can expect high returns. But then specialization of production and diffuseness of consumption imply the prevalence of producer coalitions rather than consumer coalitions. Thus, the important problems of political economy are those of relative income shares of producers rather than relative prices of consumer goods. If pressure of producer coalitions prevails, inflation may for a while be an expedient device to make inconsistent demands consistent. In an analogous way we would expect that deflation is the problem of a society with consumer specialization.

Let me now approach the problem of the long run. Economists are specialists for the analysis of the interaction of many elements in a complex system. Thus, their comparative advantage lies in the prediction of the final outcome of a complicated process of interaction, and this means their comparative advantage is the long run. The general public on the other hand has difficulties in distinguishing between long run and short run effects of policy measures. This means that the electorate imputes present day economic conditions to the ability and willingness of the present government to solve the economic problems. Hence governments which want to stay in power are forced to have a very high rate of time preference with respect to benefits and costs of policy measures. This time preference may vary depending on the amount of time available until the next general election takes place. But on the whole, it is rather high. If we combine the high rate of time preference of governments with the observation that quantities tend to react faster on changed market conditions than prices do, we conclude that politicians have a strong bias towards expansionary measures of economic policy. Monetary and fiscal restraint, if they endanger full employment and full utilization of capacities, will be used with much greater care than measures designed to stimulate demand. Expansionary policies first harvest the benefits of higher employment and production and only later pay the cost of higher rates of inflation. Restrictive measures first pay the cost of reduced production and employment and only later result in more stable prices.

The long run result of this high time preference of government is what has come to be called stagflation: high rates of inflation and high rates of unemployment at the same time. I skip the detailed description leading to this result. It has been discussed extensively by economists.

In recent years, many governments have tried to solve their problems by using the instrument of price and wage controls. By and large, one can say that these experiments have failed. Economists have a good explanation for this. Using the analytical framework developed so far in this paper, we may formulate the reason as follows: if price rigidity is the cause of the policy bias leading towards inflation and stagflation, then price controls will only aggravate this bias. They are an additional artificial element of price rigidity and thus are apt to be used mainly to postpone the detrimental effects of expansionary monetary and fiscal policies.

If it is true that the problem of economic stabilization is mainly a political one, due to the electorate's false imputation of the causes of the general economic condition, then the solution, if there is any solution, must be one which takes the behavior of politicians and their high rate of time preference into account. The proposal which I want to make is specifically designed for that purpose. For expository simplicity let me adopt the monetarist doctrine which says that in the long run there exists proportionality between the quantity of money in the economy and the nominal value of national product. An additional assumption is that in the long run the volume of real national product is not greatly influenced by the quantity of money available. I shall later discuss modifications which may become necessary, if the monetarist model is not so useful. From it follows the conclusion that in the long run the price level will be proportional to the supply of money. My proposal is to transform the long run effects of changes in the money supply into short run effects by means of price controls. This can be done as follows.

The government imposes by decree a certain price level on the economy. This price level cannot be chosen arbitrarily by the government, rather it must change in proportion to the money supply available in the economy. This restriction by law in the choice of the price level is the important point of the proposal. It implies an immediate effect of a change in monetary policy on the rate of inflation, and thus enables politicians to pursue a policy of price stabilization with immediate effects. The essence of the proposal is to use price controls for the purpose of reducing price rigidity or enhancing price flexibility. The formula which ties the percentage rate of change of the imposed price level (π) to the percentage rate of change of money supply (μ) is as follows. Let ξ be the trend rate of growth of real national product. We then propose

$$\pi_t = \mu_{t-1} - \xi_{t-1}$$

where the index t refers to, say, quarters. The time lag of monetary policy on the price level thus would be approximately a quarter of a year. I shall modify this formula later, after having discussed additional details of the proposal.

What we here are interested in, is the price level in the economy as a whole, not so much any particular price. It is therefore not necessary to fix all prices in the economy. Only the average has to be fixed. How can one fix an average without having to fix each individual item? The answer is known to the trained economist from the theory of rationing. There, one simply has to introduce transferable rationing coupons. If we really insist that the average level of consumption be a predetermined number, then we must be aware that the market price of the rationing coupons may become negative. This is an unusual thought, because, probably for good reasons, the instrument of rationing at the demand side has never been used in situations of surplus production. Such situations were dealt with by rationing the opportunities to produce and supply. But these good reasons do not apply here. Hence every firm starts out every quarter with the obligation to change its prices by the percentage rate of the above formula. By trading with other firms it can deviate from this formula. If the natural tendency to raise prices is stronger than corresponds to the formula, everybody who raises his price has to pay for it. At least he has to pay the opportunity cost of not being able to sell his price changing coupons. If the natural tendency to raise prices is weaker than corresponds to the formula, then everybody who raises prices will get rewarded, because now the coupon implying the license and obligation to raise prices has a negative market price. The more coupons he uses up by raising his prices the more he benefits from the market of transferable coupons.

It may seem paradoxical to try to fight inflation by a scheme which in certain circumstances may even encourage people to raise prices. But let us remember that the guinea pigs in our thought experiment are not the people who set prices in the market economy. Our guinea pigs are the government and the central bank. And the purpose is to reward and punish these guinea pigs very soon for any actions they take with respect to the money supply. Since no government likes the political repercussions of inflation, the punishment of a policy that would be inflationary in the long run consists of an encouragement of price rises in the short run.

It is reasonable that each firm receives "coupons" to raise prices in proportion to its value added from the government. The total number of coupons corresponds to the formula above. The "coupons" can be traded freely, but the transactions are recorded in an official book, so as to avoid the disappearance of coupons in case they should have a negative price. Each firm is allowed and obliged to pass on price changes of its inputs unless these inputs contribute to value added. In this way the administrative intervention in the process of price formation reduces its degrees of freedom only by one. Market forces are much less restricted in their functioning than under a complete system of price controls.

Is such a system viable and reasonable? There are two interrelated main aspects of this question. One is the black market problem, the other is the problem of distortions of incentives in the economic process. The black market aspect can be reduced to the problem of distortions. Of course, the higher the distortions, the greater is the danger of black markets, just as tax evasion and smuggling are problems growing with the square of the tax rates or the tariff rates. Similarly here: the black market problem is only important if the free market price for coupons to change prices is considerable. The technical aspects of the control are not too severe: of course, in principle, every price has to be under some kind of control. But firms selling different commodities can be allowed to use a price index. Sales between firms are not such a problem if the buying firm is interested in having the price change recorded in order to pass it on to its customers without having to have a coupon. Black markets are mainly a problem if the seller has no interest in selling his commodity at the official price. If the buyer knows that the seller would rather sell his commodity at the official price than not sell it at all, it is difficult for the seller to sell the good at a higher black market price. Now, in a largely oligopolistic world this is the situation as long as the official price is not completely unrealistic. At the consumer level consumer information services may also perform this function of checking on the actual prices paid.

Let me now approach the problem of distortion. The degree of distortion can as a first approximation be measured by the price of the coupon to change prices. Thus, we can concentrate on the question what this price will be.

Let us now remember that under our monetarist assumptions the price level change imposed by the government is the total or long run result of the change in money supply. Given that these monetarist assumptions are correct, the average price of the licenses will be zero. There will be about as many situations in which past expansionary monetary measures have not had their full price effect as situations in which contractionary monetary measures have not yet worked themselves out fully. After a period of relative monetary contraction the price of the coupons will be positive, after a period of monetary expansion the coupons are obligations to raise prices and they have a negative price.

Let us now introduce speculation and forward markets for these licenses. The business cycle as well as the period until most of the price effect of a change in money supply has become reality, is a period of about three to five years. Thus, the cycle of the price for licenses will have about the same length. A firm can therefore expect that within a period of one or at most two years the price of the license will change signs. But this will be an effective check on too high market prices for the licenses. The basic reason for this optimism concerning the size of distortions implied by the scheme is clear: the scheme does not work against market forces, it only removes a certain inertia of the price system.

There is, of course, the problem that the income velocity of money does not remain constant in the long run or that indeed it may be influenced by the effects of the proposed scheme. Also it will not be easy to find the correct initial price level to be decreed, as we are not completely sure about future effects of past monetary policies at the start of the scheme. There is therefore no guarantee that the average price of these coupons will really be zero. But this problem can be solved by making our formula slightly more sophisticated. Let λ_t

be the price of the coupon in period t, let $\hat{\lambda}_t$ be an exponentially weighted average of license prices in the periods preceding t, let α be a positive constant. We then impose the following rate of change of the price level

$$\pi_t = -\xi_{t-1} + \mu_{t-1} + \alpha\hat{\lambda}_{t-1}$$

The correction term $\hat{\lambda}_{t-1}$ operates like a safety valve so as to avoid too large distortions caused by the system. If prices for licenses in the past have had a bias to the positive side, then more price rises are allowed in the present. This will have a depressing effect on the price of licenses. The appropriate choice of the weighting system in the construction of $\hat{\lambda}_t$ is a matter of further investigation. The system must have a sufficiently long memory to avoid its instability, on the other hand, too long a memory implies inefficiencies in the adaption process. Similarly there exists a problem in the choice of α. If α is chosen too high, the safety valve is too big: no pressure whatsoever can be accumulated and the system has no effect. If α is chosen too small, the system may explode, the prices of the licenses may deviate too much from zero to keep the system viable.

Another way to explain the philosophy of the proposed system is to draw a diagram, in which the price of the product of a firm is on the horizontal axis and its profits are on the vertical axis. Take first the firm close to a situation of pure competition, say, a farmer growing wheat. His price-profit curve looks like that shown in figure 13-1. Now take the oligopolist or monopolist. His price profit curve looks like that shown in figure 13-2.

It can easily be established that the Kalecki-Lerner degree of monopoly is inversely porportional to the second derivative of the price profit curve at its peak. The higher the "degree of monopoly," the flatter is the price profit curve. What does this mean? It means that a firm in a pure competition situation knows

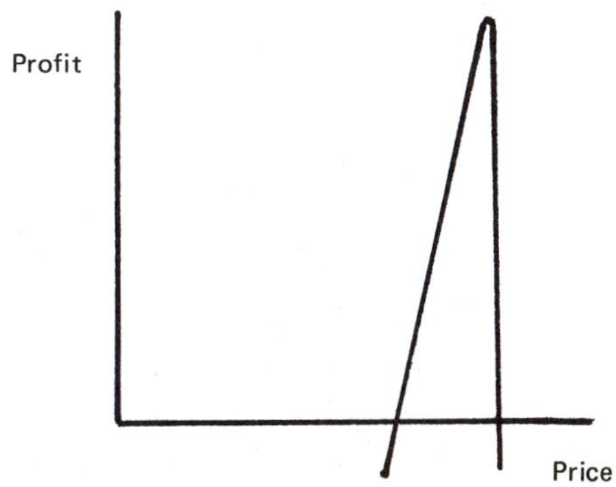

Figure 13-1. Price-Profit Curve for Pure Competition.

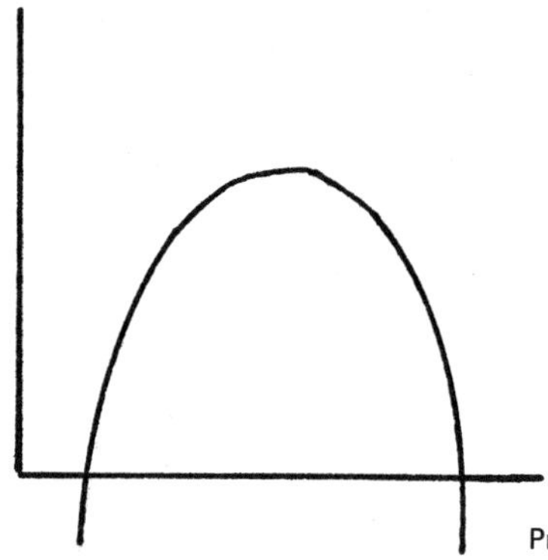

Figure 13-2. Monopolist's Price-Profit Curve.

which price to ask and it immediately changes the price, as demand or cost conditions change. On the other hand, it will be difficult and expensive to induce it to choose a price different from the one at which the profit curve obtains its maximum. This is the basis of economists' aversion to price controls and their argument that black markets will ensue. The oligopolist is much less certain about his optimal price. When demand conditions change, he first will wait and see before he changes his price. The flat profit curve, on the other hand, will make it easier to induce firms to deviate from their profit maximum.

I believe that oligopolistic market structure is typical for our economies. This appears to be particularly true for markets close to the consumer. Thus the consumer price index is the slowest to react on changes in monetary policy. It appears that in our economies the conditions are fulfilled which make our proposed scheme a reasonable one.

It is perhaps worthwhile to compare the proposal with the proposal of indexation, which has become quite popular among economists in recent times. Indexation, of course, has two aspects. One aspect is that it may be a device to protect people against the implications of inflation and the uncertainty about the future development of the purchasing power of money. Nobody will deny the advantages of indexation in this respect. Another, and more difficult, aspect is the question of whether indexation helps or hinders the fight against inflation. Friedman in the United States, Giersch in Germany, and many others claim that indexation helps to fight inflation. One of their arguments is that whenever monetary and fiscal policy start being successful in bringing the rate of inflation below the commonly expected level, indexation of wages and interest payments shifts the price effect of anti-inflationary policy on towards costs and thereby reduces the production and employment effects of restrictive policies. On the other hand, there is the traditional argument, that indexation will only accelerate the wage-price spiral and hence make anti-inflationary policies even more difficult. There are economists who believe that indexation definitely would and, where applied, did have strongly inflationary effects in a situation of unexpected changes in terms of trade between industrial products and raw materials as occurred recently. If we accept the idea that in the short run other than monetary forces have an influence on prices and if we also accept the idea, that in particular costs are an important short run factor to explain prices, then much can be said for the argument that indexation in many instances has a destabilizing effect on the system. For then any random nonmonetary influence on prices will by indexation automatically be shifted to wages and costs in general and this then will again be shifted forward to prices and thus will amplify the primary "random" price effect.

I believe it is somewhat risky to make a variable that is difficult to control directly (consumer prices) even more important by introducing consumer price escalator clauses. Things are, of course, quite different, if one would combine indexation with the scheme proposed here. For under this scheme the national price level is under a particularly good control. Then indexation helps to keep costs in line with prices in the short run, and this, given the strong short run influence of costs on prices, helps to draw the natural price level nearer towards the imposed price level. Thus the idea of indexation helps to make the proposed system work.

The proposal so far rests on the assumption of the monetarist doctrine which says two things: in the long run nominal income is proportional to the money supply, and real income is unaffected by the money supply. In a sense, this doctrine is almost trivially true. One only has to accept two propositions:

(1) The choice of the numeraire is irrelevant for the location of an equilibrium of real variables.
(2) Any interference into the real money supply will only have transitory effects, because there exists only one quantity of real money compatible with equilibrium.

The second assumption is implied by the assumption that the basic economic process has a natural tendency towards a unique, moving, but essentially stable equilibrium. I would go along with these assumptions, but, of course, the really interesting question to ask is whether this tendency towards an equilibrium is strong or tenuous. It is known that the sun in our planetary system will in the long run be in an equilibrium where it will no longer emanate any heat or light. But this is not very useful in the context of forecasting the climate on the earth in the coming centuries or the weather of next week. In a system exposed to constant external shocks an equilibrium is only of interest if the system will have a strong tendency towards this equilibrium. For the monetarist doctrine this means that there must be a sufficiently strong force to keep the income velocity of money close to its (perhaps moving) equilibrium value. Empirical evidence of recent years seems to indicate that the velocity was rather stable.[a]

But this need not be true for all times or even now for all countries. Perhaps the statistical stability of the income velocity of money is only the result of a policy of the central bank not to resist changes in the money supply if the pressure put on the bank is large enough.

The proposal does not rest completely on the monetarist doctrine. A highly flexible velocity of money would make the specific proposal so far discussed unsustainable. For wide differences between the natural and the imposed price level would mean too strong an interference with market forces and this would lead to a breakdown of the proposed system. But it is possible to conceive of modifications that would keep the central idea and rid the scheme of its reliance on the monetarist doctrine. Other disadvantages have to be settled for instead. Because of those I prefer at the moment the monetarist version of the scheme discussed so far. One alternative would be the following: The government makes a forecast of the development of GNP in nominal terms for twelve months ahead. This forecast is made every three months. There exists a trend rate of growth of real GNP. The Government then imposes a rate of inflation which is the difference between the forecasted rate of growth of nominal GNP and the trend rate of growth of real GNP. The allocation of price changes subject to the global government constraint again can be left to market forces by means of the system of transferable coupons. Forecasting errors of the government will have to be taken into account in the following way: if GNP turns out to be higher than forecasted, the government has to issue correspondingly more coupons, if GNP falls short of the forecast the government has to issue fewer coupons. Since these coupons will be issued every quarter, we obtain the following formula for the imposed rate of inflation in quarter t:

imposed rate of inflation in quarter t = 1/4

× [forecasted rate of growth of GNP for the twelve months ahead

compared to last twelve months – trend rate of growth of annual real GNP]

+ [percentage underestimate of GNP of 12 months before t

– percentage underestimate of GNP of 12 months before $t-1$]

Some other but trivial refinements are probably necessary because of the time lag of statistical data gathering about the GNP.

This modified scheme has the advantage of not relying on any theory about the determinants of nominal GNP. But this is also its disadvantage. Political manipulation of GNP forecasts by the government are easier than manipulations

[a]Sachverständigenrat zur Begutachtung der gesamtwirtschaftlichen Entwicklung, *Vollbeschäftigung für Morgen*, Stuttgart and Mainz, 1975, chapter 5.

with the statistics relating to the supply of money. If the money supply really is as important as the monetarists believe, then the original scheme is much to be preferred.

The question arises, why should any government or ruling political party be inclined to accept such a proposal, since it is so obvious that distrust of governments is the plan's basic philosophy? Why should any government bind itself by such a scheme? The answer to this question must be by analogy. The same question could be asked with respect to any constitutional check on the powers of government. Why should politicians ever agree to limit the power of government, since after all, the government is run by politicians. The answer is quite obvious: in a democratic and free society we have to assume that politicians are willing to check the power of government as long as these checks are binding not only for themselves but also in the case that their opponents come to power. In other words: a player of the political game may not be willing to agree to change the rules, if only his influence or power would be reduced. But he may agree to a change in the rules of the game, if the rules are sufficiently abstract so that they apply to anyone performing a certain role, be it he himself or be it his opponent. If he considers the change in the rules to be intrinsically reasonable, and if it is binding on everyone who wins the next general election, he may agree to it.

To the politician applies what applies to the large majority of people: I may, at a specific instance, regret the fact that a speed limit on all roads prevents me from driving faster; but this does not yet make me into a principal opponent to this general rule. I am prepared to accept abstract rules limiting everybody's freedom (if I consider them to be reasonable), even though my own freedom will also be limited by this rule. Distrust of governments, as it is expressed in this paper, is not the same as the belief that politicians are morally incapable to change the general rules of the political game, if they consider this change to be reasonable in principle.

References

1. Kaldor, N., "The Irrelevance of Equilibrium Economics," *Economic Journal* 82 (1972):1237-1255.

2. Leijonhufvud, A., *On Keynesian Economics and the Economics of Keynes*, Oxford University Press, London, 1968.

Appendix 13A
Mechanics of the Price Control Coupon System

This appendix outlines in somewhat more detail what these coupons are and how they are allocated among firms.

One coupon of unit size allows and obliges its holder to raise the price of a commodity by one percent within the current quarter, if that commodity had a sales volume of $100 in the last quarter. The same unit coupon can be used to raise the price of a commodity by x percent, if the sales volume of the coupon was $1/x$ times $100 in the last quarter. If a firm sells more than one commodity, it is of course free to allocate its price increases among the different commodities as it likes. Thus, if a firm had a sales volume of $100,000 in commodity A and a sales volume of $200,000 in commodity B, and if the firm holds 3000 coupons, it has the choice for example between (1) raising both prices by one percent or (2) raising price A by three percent and keeping price B the same or (3) raising price B by one and a half percent and keeping price A the same or (4) lowering price A by 10 percent and raising price B by 6½ percent or any other combination of price changes that amounts to an average price rise of one percent.

Price increases of inputs purchased from other firms have to be transformed into corresponding price increases of the firm's outputs within a quarter. Assume that these purchases amount to $200,000 in our example. If, in the present quarter, the firm's inputs purchased from other firms are raised in price by an average of one percent, then within the same or the next quarter the firm has to raise its average price by two-thirds of one percent. Again it is free to choose the structure of price increases as long as the composite effect is two-thirds of one percent. If the price of inputs purchased from other firms rises, this, so to speak, generates coupons in the firm. They can be used to raise the firm's price or they can be transferred to other firms at the going (positive or negative) coupon price. If the firm lowers a price, it generates coupons just in the same way. The coupons distributed by the government at the beginning of the quarter are allocated in proportion to last quarter's value added of the different firms.

Since coupons sometimes are assets and sometimes are liabilities, they would have to be registered at some official office. Each firm has a coupon account with this office which records all activities that generate or use up coupons. This bookkeeping is fairly straightforward and thus will not use up substantial real resources.

It is probably necessary to apply the price control to the average of prices ruling within a quarter. Consider for simplicity of exposition a single commodity supplier. The average price of the quarter t is

$$p_t = \frac{1}{n} \sum_{i=1}^{n} p_{ti}$$

where p_{ti} is the price ruling on the ith day of quarter t. If the firm holds coupons in the amount corresponding to a one percent price rise in the current quarter, then it would have to take care that p_t is one percent higher than p_{t-1}. There exists, of course, the problem, whether the firm's administration is able to keep the records of price changes (sometimes forced on the firm by market forces at very short notice) sufficiently up to date so that it can comply with the rules of the game, even if it honestly tries it. Therefore, one should allow an administrative lag of the following kind. Assuming that each firm should be able to know its prices of day i on day $i + 7$, the administrative lag should be made two weeks. The administrative lag would allow the firm to add up to two weeks to the averaging period which normally is the quarter, so that it would be able to correct the average price by implementing price changes. In addition, each firm would be allowed to transfer a certain small (positive or negative) fraction of coupons from one quarter to the next. This transfer allowance must be kept small, for it would otherwise be used to avoid or substantially postpone compliance with the rules of the scheme.

Sanctions against violations of the scheme would consist of fines proportional to net balances of coupons at the end of quarters after subtraction of the interquarter shifting allowance. The fines would have to be sufficiently substantial to make violation unattractive.

As was indicated in the text, the scheme only makes sense, if my conjecture is right, that coupon prices will be relatively low in absolute value, and thus will not be too great a burden to firms. If this conjecture is wrong, and if indeed coupon prices are high, then the scheme has failed and should be abandoned. This being so, the administrative burden of policing compliance with the system can be kept low. The incentive to cheat rises with the price of the coupons (in absolute value). The administrative effort to secure compliance is, as a first approximation, proportional to the incentive to cheat. Hence either the incentive to cheat is low and therefore the price control administration can be small, or the incentive to cheat is high, but then we are not interested in preventing cheating and hence again we don't need a substantial price control bureaucracy.

A forward market of coupons probably will arise and it certainly serves a useful function in stabilizing coupon prices. Any large difference of coupon prices corresponding to adjacent quarters on the forward market would be eliminated by arbitrage in a broad sense of the word: if, for example, today's coupons are expensive and next quarter's coupons have a low (perhaps even negative) forward price, then any firm can generate today's coupons by lowering product prices and buy next quarter's coupons on the forward market, which will allow it to return to its present product prices. Considering the rule of thumb discussed in the text—that the average price of the coupons will be zero—a speculator should be able to make some money by selling coupons forward whenever coupon prices on most forward markets for the nearest ten to twenty quarters are positive. This being the case, speculation and arbitrage will keep coupon prices close to zero.

Price controls always encounter difficulties with new products. These difficulties do not arise with the present scheme. Products that are only modified versions of existing products can be treated as if they were the product they replace. The existence of the coupons may have some impact on the firms' policy with respect to these modifications. But this impact will be slight given the low prices of coupons. Since the direction of this impact will change through time, its net result in the long run will be even less important. Moreover, the impact itself may even be beneficial in the short run: in a period of relatively restrictive monetary policy a positive coupon price will encourage firms to offer cheaper versions of existing products with, say, fewer accessories etc. But this is just what perhaps is appropriate for the consumer in a time of declining (or declining rates of growth of) disposable incomes. Considering the structure of modern competition, I don't believe that there is a danger of secret quality deterioration of products due to the coupon system. If somebody wants to make money by cheating the consumer, there is no reason why he should not already have done this without the coupon system. Should positive coupon prices induce firms to reduce product quality more than zero coupon prices do, then, by the same argument, negative coupon prices will induce firms to reduce product quality less than zero coupon prices do.

Really new products do not cause a problem either. Their initial price can be chosen by the firm without any interference from the authorities. After the introduction, the product can be treated like any other product. There seems to be little danger that the coupon system will have a distorting effect on the initial price of the new product. This price reflects the firm's evaluation of the market conditions for the product, and this is what counts for the commercial success of the product. To choose a "wrong" initial price for the product for the purpose of gaining on the coupon-market will in most cases not pay off as long as these coupon prices are not too high in absolute value. In those cases in which low coupon prices do have a distorting effect it can be shown that this distorting effect implies only a small loss of social welfare. Moreover, in such cases, the coupon system provides an indirect subsidy for the development of new products, something which may not be bad at all from the social welfare point of view.

The treatment of fundamentally new products also applies to products which by their nature are only produced once such as paintings and other works of art or science. Here it would of course be nonsensical to try to find out price changes, and hence price control does not apply here.

The scheme only applies to domestic prices. Prices of exports and of imports are not under the control of the scheme. Just as in the case of the value added tax this means that exports are treated as functionally equivalent to final demand (except for the fact that the domestic government does not care about prices that have to be paid by foreigners) and imports are treated as if they were a part of value added. Changes in import prices do not "create" positive or negative coupons for importers. On the other hand, the government allocation of coupons is in proportion to value added plus imports. This set-up implies that changes in the level of import prices are supposed to be absorbed by the firms and not to be passed on to consumers. This is only realistic if these price changes are not very great. Under a system of floating exchange rates, rises in import prices (in foreign currencies) due to foreign inflation can be compensated by a sufficiently restrictive monetary policy which will drive down the exchange rates of foreign currencies. If import prices reflect a change in the terms of trade with other countries, then any noninflationary (or nondeflationary) policy will have to demand from the firms that they absorb these price changes by trying to reduce domestic costs, such as wages.

14 Inflation, Income Taxes and the Rate of Interest: A Theoretical Analysis

Martin S. Feldstein

Income taxes are a central feature of economic life but not of the growth models that we use to study the long-run effects of monetary and fiscal policies. The taxes in current monetary growth models are lump sum transfers that alter disposable income but do not directly affect factor rewards or the cost of capital. In contrast, the actual personal and corporate income taxes do influence the cost of capital to firms and the net rate of return to savers. The existence of such taxes also in general changes the effect of inflation on the rate of interest and on the process of capital accumulation.[1]

The current chapter presents a neoclassical monetary growth model in which the influence of such taxes can be studied. The model is then used in sections 14.2 and 14.3 to study the effect of inflation on the rate of interest and on the capital intensity of the economy. James Tobin's (1955, 1965) early result that inflation increases capital intensity appears as a possible special case. More generally, the tax rates and saving behavior determine whether an increase in the rate of inflation will increase or decrease steady-state capital intensity.

The analysis also shows that the net real rate of interest received by savers may be substantially altered by the rate of inflation. Section 14.3 discusses the desirability of adjusting the taxation of interest income to eliminate these arbitrary effects of inflation. The fourth section discusses the implications of this for the welfare effects of inflation and the optimal rate of growth of the money supply.

14.1. A Growing Economy with Inflation and Income Taxes

This section presents a one-sector neoclassical model of economic growth with inflation and income taxes. The model differs from that of Tobin (1965) in two fundamental ways: 1) the savings rate depends on the net real rate of return earned by savers; 2) there are personal and corporate interest income taxes as

Reprinted, with permission of the American Economic Association, from the *American Economic Review*, vol. 66, December 1976, pp. 809-820. I am grateful to the University of California at Berkeley for the opportunity to prepare this paper while I was Ford Research Professor. The National Science Foundation supported the project on the effects of fiscal programs on capital accumulation and income distribution of which the current study is a part. I am grateful for discussions with Stanley Fischer, Steven Goldman, and David Hartman.

well as a lump sum tax.[2] Because the analysis of the model in section 14.2 will focus on comparative steady-state dynamics, only these steady-state properties will be discussed here.

The steady-state economy will be characterized by an inflation rate $\pi = Dp/p$ and a nominal interest rate of i. The real rate of interest is, by definition, $r = i - \pi$. In order to consider the effects of adjusting the tax treatment for the rate of inflation, separate tax rates will be specified for the real and inflation components of the nominal rate of interest. The personal income tax will tax real interest payments at θ_1 and the inflation component at θ_2. The net nominal rate of return is thus $i_N = (1-\theta_1)r + (1-\theta_2)\pi$. In our current tax law $\theta_1 = \theta_2$ so that $i_N = (1-\theta)(r+\pi) = (1-\theta)i$. With complete inflation indexation, $\theta_2 = 0$ and $i_N = (1 - \theta_1)r + \pi$; the net real rate of interest received by households is thus $r_N = i_N - \pi = (1 - \theta_1)r$.

The economy is characterized by an exogenously growing population

$$N = N_0 e^{nt} \tag{14.1}$$

The labor force is a constant fraction of the population. Production can be described by an aggregate production function with constant returns to scale. The relation between aggregate output per capita (y) and aggregate capital stock per capita (k) is

$$y = f(k) \tag{14.2}$$

with $f' > 0$ and $f'' < 0$. For simplicity, both technical progress and depreciation are ignored.

14.1.1 The Demand for Capital

The investment and financing behavior of firms is influenced by the corporate income tax. An important feature of the corporation tax is that the interest paid on corporate debt may be deducted by firms in calculating taxable profits while dividends paid on corporate equity may not be deducted. Although the method of finance need not affect the analysis in models without a corporate income tax, it is necessary in the current model to identify the method of finance. Because the focus of the current chapter is on the effect of inflation on the rate of interest, I will assume that all corporate investment is financed by issuing debt.[3] The tax deduction of interest payments may also be adjusted for inflation: let τ_1 be the tax rate at which the real component of interest payments is deducted and let τ_2 be the tax rate at which the inflation component can be deducted. The net rate of interest paid by firms is then $(1-\tau_1)r+(1-\tau_2)\pi$.[a]

[a] In steady-state growth with fully anticipated inflation there is no need to distinguish between short-term debt and long-term debt.

In the absence of the corporation tax, the firm maximizes its profit by investing until the marginal product of capital is equal to the real rate of interest, $i-\pi$. Stated somewhat differently, the firm's capital stock is optimal when the marginal product of capital $[f'(k)]$ plus the nominal appreciation in the value of the capital stock per unit of capital (π) is equal to the nominal rate of interest:

$$f'(k) + \pi = i \tag{14.3}$$

The effect of the corporation tax on this optimality condition depends on the way that depreciation is treated by the law. Consider first the simple case in which capital lasts forever, i.e., in which there is no depreciation. The corporation tax then reduces the net-of-tax marginal product of capital to $(1-\tau_1)f'(k)$. There is no tax on the unrealized appreciation of the capital stock. The firm maximizes profits by increasing the capital stock until the net nominal return on capital $(1-\tau_1)f'(k)+\pi$ is equal to the net nominal rate of interest, $(1-\tau_1)r+(1-\tau_2)\pi$. The first-order optimum of equation (14.3) therefore becomes

$$f'(k) = r - \left(\frac{\tau_2}{1-\tau_1}\right)\pi \tag{14.4}$$

If the capital stock does depreciate, $f'(k)$ can be interpreted as the marginal product of capital net of the cost of replacing the capital that has been used up in production. If the corporation tax allows the deduction of the replacement cost of this depreciation, the net-of-tax marginal product of capital is again $(1-\tau_1)f'(k)$ and equation (14.4) continues to hold. I will use this condition to describe the demand for capital.[4]

14.1.2. Liquidity Preference

The real value of household assets is the sum of the real values of outside money (M/p) and corporate bonds (B/p):

$$A = \frac{M}{p} + \frac{B}{p} \tag{14.5}$$

Since outside money bears no interest, the ratio of money to bonds that households will hold is a decreasing function of the after-tax nominal rate of return on bonds, $i_N=(1-\theta_1)r+(1-\theta_2)\pi$. The real value of bonds (B/p) is also the real value of the capital stock (K). The liquidity preference relation can therefore be written in per capita terms as

$$\frac{m}{k} = L[(1-\theta_1)r + (1-\theta_2)\pi]\,,\ L' < 0 \tag{14.6}$$

where $m=M/pN$, the real money balances per capita. In steady state, m/k must remain constant. Equivalently, M/pK remains constant, i.e., the rate of growth of M is equal to the rate of growth of pK or $\pi+n$. Thus[5]

$$\pi = \frac{DM}{M} - n \tag{14.7}$$

14.1.3. The Supply of Savings

In steady-state growth, the supply of savings (S) is proportional to the households' real disposable income (H). The savings propensity may of course depend on the real net return that savers receive:

$$S = \sigma(r_N) \cdot H \tag{14.8}$$

Disposable income is equal to national income (Y) minus both the government's tax receipts (T) and the fall in the real value of the population's money balances ($\pi M/p$).[b] The total taxes are the sum of the corporate tax, the personal interest income tax, and a residual tax that may be regarded as a lump sum or payroll tax. The government uses these tax receipts plus the increase in the money supply (DM/p) to finance its purchases of public consumption (G). Disposable income is therefore

$$H = Y - T - \frac{\pi M}{p} = Y - G + \frac{DM}{p} - \frac{\pi M}{p} \tag{14.9}$$

Since $\pi = DM/M - n$,

$$H = Y - G + nM/p \tag{14.10}$$

If public consumption is a constant fraction of real national income ($G = \gamma Y$), per capita disposable income is

$$h = y(1 - \gamma) + nm \tag{14.11}$$

Per capita saving is therefore

$$s = \sigma(r_N) \cdot [y(1 - \gamma) + mn] \tag{14.12}$$

[b]The capital loss on corporate bonds is just offset by the difference between the real and nominal interest rates paid by firms. There are no corporate retained earnings.

14.1.4. Growth Equilibrium

All savings must be absorbed in either additional capital accumulation or additional real money balances:

$$S = DK + DM/p \tag{14.13}$$

The constant ratio of capital to labor in steady-state growth implies that $DK = nK$. Similarly, the constancy of $m = M/pN$ implies that the rate of growth of (M/p) is nM/p. The requirement of equilibrium growth is therefore, in per capita terms,

$$s = nk + nm \tag{14.14}$$

or

$$\sigma(r_N) \cdot [(1-\gamma)y + nm] = nk + nm \tag{14.15}$$

This completes the specification of the model. It is useful to collect now the six equations that jointly determine y, h, k, m, r, and π:

$$y = f(k) \tag{14.2}$$

$$h = y(1-\gamma) + mn \tag{14.11}$$

$$\sigma[(1-\theta_1)r - \theta_2\pi] \cdot h = nk + nm \tag{14.13'}$$

$$f'(k) = r - \left(\frac{\tau_2}{1-\tau_1}\right)\pi \tag{14.4}$$

$$m = L\,[(1-\theta_1)r + (1-\theta_2)\pi]\,k \tag{14.6}$$

$$\pi = \frac{DM}{M} - n \tag{14.7}$$

The exogenous variables are the rate of population growth n, and the government policy variables $\theta_1, \theta_2, \tau_1, \tau_2$, and DM/M.

14.2. The Effects of Changes in the Rate of Inflation

The model of section 14.1 will now be used to study the effects of inflation on capital accumulation and interest rates. Although the rate of inflation is endogenous, the model can be decomposed to obtain π as the difference between the two exogenous variables, DM/M and n. The analysis can then proceed to use the remaining five equations with π regarded as predetermined.

By appropriate substitution for y, h, m, and r in equation (14.13′), the growth equilibrium provides the basic relation between the equilibrium capital intensity and the steady-state rate of inflation:

$$\sigma[(1-\theta_1)(f' + \pi\tau_2/(1-\tau_1)) - \theta_2\pi] \cdot [(1-\gamma)f + nkL] = nk(1+L) \quad (14.16)$$

where the arguments of L in equation (14.6) are not explicitly specified. Total differentiation with respect to k and π yields equation (14.17).

$$\frac{dk}{d\pi} = \frac{(1-\sigma)nk[(1-\theta_1)\tau_2/(1-\tau_1)+(1-\theta_2)]L' - h[(1-\theta_1)\tau_2/(1-\tau_1)-\theta_2]\sigma'}{\sigma[(1-\gamma)f'+nL] - n(1+L) - (1-\sigma)nkL'(1-\theta_1)f'' + h'\sigma'(1-\theta_1)f''} \quad (14.17)$$

The denominator can be shown to be unambiguously negative if the savings rate is a nondecreasing function of the real rate of return, $\sigma' \geqslant 0$.[c] With this condition, the denominator is clearly negative if $\sigma[(1-\gamma)f'+nL]-n(1+L)<0$. To show that this inequality is true, multiply by k and substitute $m=kL$ to obtain the equivalent condition

$$\sigma[(1-\gamma)kf' + nm] - (nk + nm) < 0$$

From equation (14.15),

$$nk + nm = \sigma[(1-\gamma)f + nm]$$

The required condition is therefore

$$\sigma[(1-\gamma)kf' + nm] < \sigma[(1-\gamma)f + nm]$$

or $kf' < f$ which clearly holds. The sign of $dk/d\pi$ is therefore the opposite of the sign of the numerator.

The first term of the numerator,

$$(1-\sigma)nk[(1-\theta_1)\tau_2/(1-\tau_1) + (1-\theta_2)]L'$$

[c]This is equivalent to $\phi'(r_s) \geqslant 0$ in the asset demand equation (14.8). In a life cycle model, this occurs if an increase in the real net rate of interest causes a postponement in consumption. In the simple two-period model in which all income is earned in the first period, $\phi'(r_N) \geqslant 0$ is equivalent to an elasticity of substitution of the two-period utility function that is greater than or equal to one. Although I will only discuss the implications of $\sigma' \geqslant 0$, the opposite may be true and its implications deserve examination.

is unambiguously negative because the demand for money is inversely related to the nominal rate of interest, $L' < 0$. If the savings rate is an increasing function of the real net rate of interest ($\sigma' > 0$), the sign of the second term and therefore of the entire numerator depends on the nature of taxation. In two important special cases, the second term is zero and therefore the numerator is negative:

1. *Full Tax Indexing*: There is full indexing of the taxation of interest income, i.e., the personal income tax is on the real rate of interest only ($\theta_2 = 0$), and the corporation tax allows a deduction only for real interest payments ($\tau_2 = 0$).
2. *Equal Tax Rates*: There is no indexing of the taxation of interest income but the rate of corporation tax is the same as the rate of personal income tax, i.e., $\theta_1 = \theta_2 = \tau_1 = \tau_2$.

In both these cases, $(1-\theta_1)\tau_2/(1-\tau_1) - \theta_2 = 0$ so that the second term is zero, the numerator is negative and $dk/d\pi > 0$. In these cases the sensitivity of the savings rate to the net rate of interest (σ') influences the magnitude but not the direction of the impact of inflation on equilibrium capital intensity. The direction of the impact reflects the reduction in desired liquidity that results from the higher nominal rate of interest that accompanies inflation. A smaller ratio of real money balances to capital implies that a larger fraction of savings is channeled into real capital accumulation. The resulting increase in capital intensity lowers the real net rate of interest; if savings respond positively to this rate of interest, there is a reduction in the rate of savings that partly offsets the portfolio composition effect but that cannot reverse its sign. This dampening effect of the savings response appears as the term $h\sigma'(1-\theta_1)f''$ that increases the absolute size of the denominator.

Neither of the two cases considered above corresponds to the current situation in the United States. There is no indexing of the taxation of interest payments. The real and inflation components of the nominal interest rate are treated in the same way by both the personal and corporate income taxes: $\theta_2 = \theta_1$ and $\tau_2 = \tau_1$. Because of the progressivity of the personal income tax, a simple comparison of the corporate and personal income tax rates is not possible.[d]. I will therefore consider the implications of both $\theta < \tau$ and $\theta > \tau$ where the common rate of the income tax is denoted $\theta = \theta_1 = \theta_2$ and that of the corporate tax is denoted $\tau = \tau_1 = \tau_2$. The analysis will assume that the savings rate is an increasing function of the net rate of interest; the reader can easily discover the implications of reversing this assumption.

When the corporation tax rate exceeds the personal tax rate, inflation induces an increase in the savings rate that reinforces the reduction in liquidity. To understand the nature of this reinforcing effect, recall from equation (14.4) that

[d]The actual problem of comparison is even more complex because individuals as well as corporations are borrowers.

$$r = f'(k) + \left(\frac{\tau_2}{1 - \tau_1}\right)\pi \qquad (14.18)$$

With $\tau_2 = \tau_1$, the nominal rate of interest is

$$i = r + \pi = f'(k) + \frac{\pi}{1 - \tau} \qquad (14.19)$$

Since the personal income tax is levied at rate θ on this nominal rate of interest, the real net rate received by savers is

$$r_N = (1 - \theta)i - \pi = (1 - \theta)f'(k) + \left(\frac{\tau - \theta}{1 - \tau}\right)\pi \qquad (14.20)$$

At any given level of capital intensity, $f'(k)$ is a constant and the direct effect of an increase in π is to increase r_N whenever $\tau > \theta$. This increase in r_N induces a higher rate of saving and therefore greater capital accumulation. More formally, it is clear from equation (14.17) that increasing the value of τ causes an increase in $dk/d\pi$ whenever $\sigma' > 0$.

Equation (14.20) also shows that when the corporation tax rate is less than the personal tax rate, inflation induces a reduction in r_N and therefore in the savings rate. The net effect of inflation on capital intensity depends on the relative strength of the negative savings effect and the positive liquidity effect. There is no unambiguous a priori conclusion. Recall that inflation increases capital intensity if and only if the numerator of equation (14.17) is negative. With $\theta_1 = \theta_2 = \theta$ and $\tau_1 = \tau_2 = \tau$, this condition reduces to $dk/d\pi > 0$, if and only if,

$$h(\theta - \tau)\sigma' + (1 - \sigma)nk(1 - \theta)L' < 0 \qquad (14.21)$$

A series of substitutions and manipulations shows that this condition is equivalent to

$$\frac{\eta_L}{\eta_S} > \frac{a}{(1 - \sigma)m} \cdot \frac{\theta - \tau}{1 - \theta} \cdot \frac{i_N}{r_N} \qquad (14.22)$$

where $\eta_L = -i_N L'/L$, the elasticity of the demand for real money balances relative to capital with respect to the nominal net rate of interest, and $\eta_S = r_N \sigma'/\sigma$, the elasticity of the savings rate with respect to the real net rate of interest.[e] Recall

[e]If $r_N < 0$, η_s is not well defined. The inequality (14.7) can instead be written

$$\frac{L'/L}{\sigma'/\sigma} > \frac{a}{(1 - \sigma)\, m} \cdot \frac{\theta - \tau}{1 - \theta}$$

whenever $\sigma' > 0$ even if $r_N < 0$.

that $a=k+m$, total wealth per person, and that $r_N=i_N-\pi$. Note that (14.22) shows that $dk/d\pi>0$ is more likely when the demand for liquidity is interest sensitive (η_L is large) and when savings behavior is not sensitive to the net yield (η_S is small). The required inequality is clearly satisfied in the cases that were previously considered: $\theta\leqslant\tau$ (or $\eta_S=0$). But if $\theta>\tau$ and $\eta_S>0$, the inequality in (14.22) may not be satisfied. When inequality (14.22) is false, an increase in the rate of inflation reduces equilibrium capital intensity. Consider therefore some plausible values for the right-hand side. At the end of 1974, total private wealth was approximately \$4 trillion. A useful empirical measure of the stock of outside money is the monetary base, the sum of currency in circulation and member bank reserves at the Federal Reserve Banks. At the end of 1974, the monetary base was approximately \$100 billion. With an average saving rate of $\sigma=0.1$, the value of $a/(1-\sigma)m$ is approximately 40.[f] If $\tau=0.5$ and $\theta=0.6$ (14.22) is equivalent to

$$\frac{\eta_L}{\eta_S} > 10\frac{i_N}{r_N} \tag{14.23}$$

Starting from a situation in which there is no inflation (i.e., $i_N=r_N$), the introduction of positive inflation will increase capital intensity only if $\eta_L>10\eta_S$. With a substantial rate of inflation, the condition for $dk/d\pi>0$ is even more difficult to satisfy. From equations (14.19) and (14.20), we obtain

$$\frac{i_N}{r_N} = \frac{(1-\theta)f'(k) + \left(\frac{1-\theta}{1-\tau}\right)\pi}{(1-\theta)f'(k) + \left(\frac{\tau-\theta}{1-\tau}\right)\pi} \tag{14.24}$$

If, for example, $\pi = f'(k) = 0.12$, equation (14.24) implies that $i_N/r_N = 0.144/0.024 = 6$. The inequality in (14.23) now implies that $dk/d\pi > 0$ only if $\eta_L > 60\eta_S$.[g]

[f]Restricting attention to outside money ignores the role of private banks in creating liquidity. A broader measure of the money supply, defined as currency plus demand deposits, was \$285 billion at the end of 1974, implying $a/(1-\sigma)m = 16$. However, most of the money supply measured in this was "inside money" and not appropriate to the current model.

[g]There is substantial controversy about the magnitudes of η_L and η_S. In earlier econometric studies, I found $di/d \ln M$ was approximately 10, implying that η_L is approximately 0.01 (see the author and Gary Chamberlain, and the author and Otto Eckstein). The estimates of η_S range from negative to positive, but none of the estimates measures r_N correctly as the real net-of-tax rate of return. Obviously, even a very moderate positive value of η_S would exceed the η_L reported above.

The above examples are only illustrative. They nevertheless indicate that, in an economy with a relatively high rate of tax on interest income, an increase in the rate of inflation may decrease capital intensity. More generally, the presence of taxes may reduce or magnify a positive effect of inflation on capital intensity.

14.3. Effects of Inflation on Interest Rates

The relation of the interest rate to the rate of inflation is substantially influenced by the presence of the corporation and personal income tax. This is true even if inflation has no effect on the capital intensity of production. As a result, the real net rate of return earned by savers also generally depends on the rate of inflation.

The basic marginal productivity relation derived above,

$$r = f'(k) + \left(\frac{\tau_2}{1 - \tau_1}\right)\pi \tag{14.25}$$

implies that the nominal rate of interest is

$$i = f'(k) + \left(\frac{1 + \tau_2 - \tau_1}{1 - \tau_1}\right)\pi \tag{14.26}$$

and the real rate of return is

$$r_N = (1 - \theta_1)f'(k) + \left(\frac{(1 - \theta_1)\tau_2 - (1 - \tau_1)\theta_2}{1 - \tau_1}\right)\pi \tag{14.27}$$

Consider first the effect of inflation on the nominal rate of interest. Irving Fisher originally explained that the nominal interest rate would rise by the rate of inflation, thus leaving the real interest rate unchanged. The force of his argument rests on the equivalence of the real interest, the cost of capital to the firm, and the real return to savers. Although all three would be equal in the absence of taxation, the current analysis has shown that this is not true in an economy with corporate and personal income taxes. Tobin's analysis (1965) modified Fisher's conclusion: because inflation reduces the demand for money balances, it increases capital intensity, lowers the real rate of return and thus causes the nominal rate of interest to rise by less than the rate of inflation. Again this analysis ignores the effect of the personal and corporate income tax.[6]

In contrast, equation (14.26) implies that

$$\frac{di}{d\pi} = \frac{1 + \tau_2 - \tau_1}{1 - \tau_1} + \left(\frac{dk}{d\pi}\right) f'' \tag{14.28}$$

Fisher's conclusions that $di/d\pi = 1$ corresponds to the special case of no taxes and interest insensitive demand for real money balances.[h] In Tobin's analysis this is modified by the fall in the marginal product of capital, $df'/d\pi = (dk/d\pi)f'' < 0$, where $dk/d\pi$ reflects a portfolio composition effect but no savings effect. The magnitude of this portfolio composition effect is, however, very small. Even if the relevant money supply is defined to include inside money, the value of the money stock is less than 10 percent of the value of real assets. Thus, even if some rate of inflation would completely eliminate the demand for money, the equilibrium capital stock would rise by less than 10 percent. With a Cobb-Douglas technology, the marginal product of capital would fall by less than one-tenth of its previous value. It is difficult therefore to imagine that the absolute value of the portfolio effect, $(dk/d\pi)f''$, exceeds 0.01.

In the more general case in which taxes are recognized, the nominal rate of interest may rise by substantially more than the rate of inflation. With no tax indexing, $\tau_2 = \tau_1 = \tau$, and

$$\frac{di}{d\pi} = \frac{1}{1 - \tau} + \left(\frac{dk}{d\pi}\right) f'' \tag{14.29}$$

With no change in capital intensity, $di/d\pi = (1 - \tau)^{-1}$; a corporate tax rate of $\tau = 0.5$ implies that the nominal rate of interest rises by *twice* the rate of inflation. The analysis of Section 14.2 shows that $dk/d\pi$ may be greater or less than zero. The nominal rate of interest may therefore rise by either more or less than *twice* the rate of inflation.[7]

With tax indexing, $\tau_2 = 0$, and

$$\frac{di}{d\pi} = 1 + \left(\frac{dk}{d\pi}\right) f'' \tag{14.30}$$

Here with no change in capital intensity the original Fisherian conclusion that $di/d\pi = 1$ obtains. Section 14.2 also showed that with full tax indexing ($\theta_2 = \tau_2 = 0$), the sign of $dk/d\pi$ is determined by the portfolio composition effect and thus $(dk/d\pi)f'' < 0$. With full tax indexing of interest payments, the nominal interest rate will rise by slightly less than the rate of inflation.

Consider now the effect of inflation on the real net rate of interest received by savers. Equation (14.27) implies

---

[h]Equation (14.17) shows that $\tau_1 = \tau_2 = \theta_1 = \theta_2 = 0$ and $L' = 0$ imply $dk/d\pi = 0$.

$$\frac{dr_N}{d\pi} = \left[\frac{(1-\theta_1)\tau_2 - (1-\tau_1)\theta_2}{1-\tau_1}\right] + (1-\theta_1)\left(\frac{dk}{d\pi}\right) f'' \qquad (14.31)$$

If there are no taxes and the demand for real balances is not sensitive to the rate of interest, equation (14.31) yields the Fisherian conclusion that the real return to savers is unaffected by inflation, $dr_N/d\pi = 0$. In two further special cases, the effect of inflation on the real net interest rate is limited to the relatively small portfolio composition effect: $(1-\theta)(dk/d\pi)f'' < 0$. If there is a full tax indexing ($\theta_2 = \tau_2 = 0$) or equal tax rates for corporations and households ($\theta_1 = \tau_1$ and $\theta_2 = \tau_2$), the first term of equation (14.31) is zero and the sign of $dk/d\pi$ depends only on the portfolio composition effect.[i]

More generally, however, inflation can have a substantial effect on the savers' real net rate of return. If there is no indexing, equation (14.31) reduces to

$$\frac{dr_N}{d\pi} = \left(\frac{\tau - \theta}{1-\tau}\right) + (1-\theta)\left(\frac{dk}{d\pi}\right) f'' \qquad (14.32)$$

If the corporate tax rate exceeds the personal tax rate, the first term is positive and the second term is negative.[j] The real net rate of return may either rise or fall. If the personal tax rate is higher than the corporate tax rate, the first term is negative. Section 14.2 showed that in this case $dk/d\pi$ can be either positive or negative. If $dk/d\pi < 0$, an increase in the rate of inflation reduces the saver's real net return. If $dk/d\pi > 0$, the change in r_N depends on the balancing of the two effects.

The case in which $dk/d\pi = 0$ illustrates the potential magnitude of the effect of inflation on r_N when $\theta > \tau$. If the marginal product of capital is $f'(k) = 0.12$ and the personal tax rate is $\theta = 0.6$, the net rate of return in the absence of inflation is $r_N = (1-\theta)f' = 0.048$. If the corporate tax rate is $\tau = 0.5$, a 12 percent rate of inflation reduces r_N by 0.024 to half of its previous value, $r_N = 0.024$.

This substantial sensitivity of r_N to inflation is a result of our tax system. Equations (14.32) and (14.17) show that without taxes ($\theta = \tau = 0$), r_N is unaffected by inflation except for the small liquidity effect on capital intensity.[k] A tax system in which the effective tax rate on capital income changes with the rate of inflation is arbitrary and inequitable.[l] If the definition of taxable interest

---

[i]Recall that equation (14.17) and the discussion in Section 14.2 established that either of these conditions makes $dk/d\pi > 0$.

[j]Section 14.2 showed that $\tau > 0$ implies $dk/d\pi > 0$.

[k]With $L' = 0$, r_N is constant.

[l]A number of recent discussions have emphasized that real tax liabilities should be independent of inflation. This has prompted proposals to adjust the income tax by the consumer price index so that the progressivity of the rate schedule does not cause inflation to increase real tax burdens. These have also been proposals to change the taxation of capital gains by adjusting the "cost" basis for changes in the consumer price index.

income is altered to tax only the real interest ($\theta_1 > 0$, $\theta_2 = 0$) and to allow companies to deduct only the real component of interest payments ($\tau_1 > 0$, $\tau_2 = 0$), the return to savers will remain constant except for the liquidity effect; this is seen for $\tau_2 = \theta_2 = 0$ in equations (14.31) and (14.17). Complete indexing in this way also keeps unchanged the ratio of the tax paid to the net return. The magnitude of the possible changes in effective tax rates and net yields under our current tax system indicates the importance of revising the definition of taxable income and expenses to neutralize the effects of inflation.

14.4. The Welfare Effects of Inflation

Studies of the welfare effects of anticipated inflation have focused on the distortion in the demand for money that results from inflation.[8] More recently, Edmund Phelps has pointed out that the revenue from inflation permits a reduction in other distorting taxes so that some inflation is part of an optimal set of taxes when lump sum taxation is not possible. These studies have been done with a basic model in which there are no interest income taxes. The current analysis suggests an additional important effect of inflation on economic welfare: inflation changes the distortion in saving that is due to the tax on interest income.

The corporation tax and the personal interest income tax introduce a differential between the marginal productivity of capital [$f'(k)$] and the real net rate of return received by savers (r_N). Equation (14.27) implies that with no indexing this relation is

$$r_N = (1 - \theta)f'(k) + \left(\frac{\tau - \theta}{1 - \tau}\right)\pi \tag{14.33}$$

The differential between r_N and $f'(k)$ depends on the tax rates and the rate of inflation. If $\tau > \theta$, a positive rate of inflation can reduce the distorting effect of taxation. With $\pi = [\theta(1-\tau)/(\tau-\theta)]f'(k)$, the net rate of return to savers is equal to the marginal product of capital. If, however, $\tau < \theta$, a positive rate of inflation increases the differential between $f'(k)$ and r_N.

Phelps stressed that the increase in money that causes inflation is also a source of government revenue that permits a reduction in distortionary tax rates.[m] With a corporation tax and a personal interest income tax, the effect of inflation on government revenue is more complex. With no indexing of interest

[m]Phelps used a model in which the tax is levied on wage income and distorts the labor-leisure choice. The current model could easily be extended to include such a tax. Tax induced changes in labor supply are equivalent to changes in the labor force participation rate and would not alter the effects of inflation on the capital intensity of production or the rate of interest. See the author (1974b).

income, a rise in nominal interest payments increases revenues from the personal income tax but decreases revenues from the corporation tax. Total tax payments will rise with an increase in nominal interest payments if $\theta > \tau$ and will fall if $\theta < \tau$.

Since nominal interest payments per capita are ik, the net tax revenue on these payments is $(\theta - \tau)ik$. The change in net revenue from this source when inflation increases is therefore

$$\frac{d[(\theta - \tau)ik]}{d\pi} = \frac{\theta - \tau}{1 - \tau}\left\{k + [\pi + (1 - \tau) \cdot (f' + kf'')]\left(\frac{dk}{d\pi}\right)\right\} \tag{14.34}$$

Since the sign of $f' + kf''$ depends on the form of the production function, the sign of the right-hand side of (14.34) cannot be unambiguously determined without further restrictions. In the most plausible case,[n] $[\pi + (1 - \tau)(f' + kf'')] > 0$ so that the change in net revenue is negative if $\tau > \theta$ and $dk/d\pi > 0$. Section 14.2 showed that $\tau > \theta$ does imply $dk/d\pi > 0$ and therefore that inflation reduces tax revenue. In the opposite case of $\theta > \tau$, and increase in inflation may increase revenue.[o]

The relation between the effect on revenue and the effect on the differential between $f'(k)$ and r_N should be noted. When $\tau > \theta$, a small positive rate of inflation reduces the differential between $f'(k)$ and r_N but also causes a reduction in tax revenue from this source. Although the distortion in the supply and demand for capital is reduced, the fall in net revenue requires an increase in tax rates that increase distortion elsewhere. Conversely, when $\tau < \theta$, a positive rate of inflation exacerbates the distortionary differential between $f'(k)$ and r_N but may yield an increase in tax revenue that permits a reduction in other distortionary taxes.

Of course, if the corporation tax and the personal income tax are fully adjusted so that they recognize only real interest payments, there is no effect of inflation on either the differential between $f'(k)$ and r_N or on the net tax revenue.[p] A more complete adjustment by the government would also provide interest bearing money that would eliminate both the liquidity and revenue effects of inflation. But until such changes are made, determining the optimal steady-state rate of inflation requires balancing at least three effects of inflation on economic welfare: 1) the welfare loss that results from reduced liquidity; 2) the change in welfare that results from the increase or decrease in the

---

[n]Note that kf''/f' is the elasticity of the marginal productivity of capital with respect to the capital intensity. With Cobb-Douglas technology, this is $\alpha - 1$ and $[\pi + (1-\tau)(f' + kf'')]$ is unambiguously positive. Unless the elasticity of substitution is very great, the sign of $[\pi + (1-\tau)(f' + kf'')]$ will be positive.

[o]If $\theta > \tau$, net revenue will increase with inflation if $dk/d\pi > 0$. Section 14.2 showed that $\theta > \tau$ leaves the sign of $dk/d\pi$ uncertain. If the portfolio composition effect dominates the savings effect, $\theta > \tau$ does imply $dk/d\pi > 0$. In this case, an increase in inflation causes an increase in tax receipts.

[p]There will be a small effect on tax revenue because of the increase in capital intensity that results from the change in portfolio composition.

differential between the marginal product of capital and individuals' marginal rate of substitution; and 3) the change in other distorting taxes that results from the increase or decrease in the net tax revenue in response to inflation. With this broader model of economic effects, it is no longer possible to conclude as Friedman (1969) did that the optimal rate of inflation is negative or as Phelps did that the optimal finance of government expenditures should include a heavy tax on liquidity through a high rate of inflation. A full evaluation of the optimal rate of inflation with our current tax rules is a subject for another study.

14.5. Conclusion

This paper has explored the impact of inflation in a growing economy. The presence of the corporate and personal income taxes substantially alters the effect of inflation on the capital intensity of production, the market rate of interest, and the real net return to savers. The existing theories of the optimal rate of anticipated inflation must be revised in light of these effects. The analysis also suggests that recent proposals to adjust the tax rules for inflation should be modified to include a specific adjustment for the inflation premium in the rate of interest.

There are several directions in which this research might usefully be extended. First, the model of financial behavior was highly simplified. It might be enriched to include corporate equity finance, household borrowing, and the use of inside money.[9] Second, the current paper focuses only on the steady-state effects of fully anticipated inflation. An analysis of the transition path would be valuable. Third, a model with two sectors would allow an analysis of the problems considered by Duncan Foley and Miguel Sidrauski as well as the issues raised by a tax that is limited to the corporate sector.

With a richer analytic structure, it would be both possible and necessary to introduce evidence with which to quantify the effects that have been discussed. The problem of inflation is likely to remain with us for a long time to come. It is important to improve our analytic understanding of its effects and to adjust our institutions accordingly.

Notes

1. Income taxes have been studied in *nonmonetary* growth models by Peter Diamond, the author (1974a, b), and Kazuo Sato. Of course, the effects of inflation cannot be examined in such models.

2. In the more general model of David Levhari and Don Patinkin, the savings rate does depend on the rate of return but there are no corporate or personal income taxes.

3. It would of course be desirable to have a more general model in which corporate debt and equity co-exist. The exclusion of equity in the current analysis and the full deductibility of corporate interest payments imply that the present value of corporation taxes is zero. The present model might therefore be regarded as an approximation to a model in which equity profits are intra-marginal and all marginal investments are financed by debt (see Joseph Stiglitz). Dale Henderson and Thomas Sargent studied the effect of inflation in an economy in which firms finance all investment by issuing equity. Because they use a short-run analysis with no accumulation of capital, their conclusions cannot be compared to those of the current analysis. After this paper was accepted for publication, Jerry Green, Eytan Sheshinski, and I developed a more general extension of the current analysis in which firms use an optimal mix of equity and debt finance.

4. The *U.S.* corporation tax does not allow replacement cost depreciation but partly offsets historic cost depreciation with accelerated depreciation schedules. An analysis of the effect of historic cost depreciation is presented in the paper by the author, Green, and Sheshinski.

5. Jerome Stein examined a more general Keynes-Wicksell model in which the adjustment of price to the excess demand for cash balances is not immediate. Stanley Fischer explained that in the long run a steady rate of increase of the money supply will come to be anticipated, causing the Keynes-Wicksell behavior to converge to the familiar neoclassical behavior of equation (14.7). All of the results of the current paper will therefore continue to hold in a Keynes-Wicksell version of the current model.

6. Martin Bailey provides a similar analysis of the effect of inflation on the rate of interest through the change in money balances. His analysis is static and also ignores taxation.

7. Recent empirical studies suggest that during the past decade the long-term corporate bond rate has increased by approximately the increase in the rate of inflation (see the author and Chamberlain, the author and Eckstein, and Robert Gordon). This is smaller than the steady-state increase suggested by the analyses above, especially since there was unlikely to have been any substantial induced change in capital intensity during so short a period. The difference reflects the failure of the above analysis to allow for equity financing, historic cost depreciation, and personal capital gains taxation. In addition, the estimated $di/d\pi$ in the studies noted above may differ from the value of $di/d\pi$ in a sustained inflation.

8. The analysis of this issue began with Milton Friedman (1942) and Bailey. Subsequent contributions are discussed in Robert Clower, Harry Johnson, and Edmund Phelps.

9. A model with equity finance is presented in Feldstein et al. forthcoming.

References

Bailey, M.J., "Welfare Cost of Inflationary Finance," *Journal of Political Economy*, 64, Apr. 1956:93-110.

Clower, R.W., "Is There an Optimal Money Supply?–II," in M. Intriligator, ed., *Frontiers of Quantitative Economics,* Amsterdam: North-Holland Publishing Company, 1971, 289-99.

Diamond, P.A., "Incidence of an Interest Income Tax," *Journal of Economic Theory* 2 (Sept. 1970):211-24.

Feldstein, M.S., (1974a) "Incidence of a Capital Income Tax in a Growing Economy with Variable Savings Rates," *Review of Economic Studies*, 41 (Oct. 1974):505-13.

_______, (1974b) "Tax Incidence in a Growing Economy with Variable Factor Supply," *Quarterly Journal of Economics*, 88 (Nov. 1974):551-73.

_______, and G. Chamberlain, "Multimarket Expectations and the Rate of Interest," *Journal of Money, Credit, Banking*, 5 (Nov. 1973):873-902.

_______, and O. Eckstein, "The Fundamental Determinants of the Interest Rate," *Review of Economics and Statistics*, 52 (Nov. 1970):363-75.

_______, J. Green, and E. Sheshinski, "Inflation and Taxes in a Growing Economy with Equity and Debt Finance," *Journal of Political Economy*, forthcoming.

Fischer, S., "Keynes-Wicksell and Neoclassical Models of Money and Growth," *American Economic Review*, 62 (Dec. 1972):880-90.

Fisher, I., *The Theory of Interest*, New York: Macmillan 1930.

Foley, D., and M. Sidrauski, *Monetary and Fiscal Policy in a Growing Economy*, New York: Macmillan 1971.

Friedman, M., "Discussion of the Inflationary Gap," *American Economic Review*, 32 (June 1942): 308-14; reprinted in his *Essays in Positive Economics*, Chicago: University of Chicago Press 1953, 251-62.

_______, "The Optimum Supply of Money," in his *The Optimum Supply of Money and Other Essays*, Chicago: Aldine Publishing Co. 1969.

Gordon, R.J., "Inflation in Recession and Recovery," in A. Okun and G. Perry (eds.), *Brookings Papers*, Washington: Brookings Institution 1971, 1, 105-58.

Henderson, D.W., and T.J. Sargent, "Monetary and Fiscal Policy in a Two-Sector Aggregative Model," *American Economic Review*, 63 (June 1973):345-65.

Johnson, H.G., "Is There an Optimal Money Supply?–I," in M. Intriligator (ed.), *Frontiers of Quantitative Economics,* Amsterdam: North-Holland Publishing Company 1971, 279-88.

Levhari, D., and D. Patinkin, "The Role of Money in a Simple Growth Model," *American Economic Review*, 58 (Sept. 1968):713-53.

Phelps, E.S., "Inflation in the Theory of Public Finance," *Swedish Journal of Economics*, 75 (Mar. 1973):67-82.

Sato, K., "Taxation and Neoclassical Growth," *Public Finance*, no. 3, 22 (1967):346-67.

Stein, J., "Monetary Growth Theory in Perspective," *American Economic Review*, 60 (Mar. 1970):85-106.

Stiglitz, J., "Taxation, Corporate Financial Policy, and the Cost of Capital," *Journal of Public Economics*, 2 (Feb. 1973):1-34.

Tobin, J., "A Dynamic Aggregative Model," *Journal of Political Economy*, 63 (Apr. 1955):103-15.

_______, "Money and Economic Growth," *Econometrica*, 33 (Oct. 1975):671-84.

15 Taxation, Inflation and Monetary Policy

Eytan Sheshinski

15.1. Introduction

The concept of taxable income which is widely accepted by economists is that of total accretion (see for example Simons (1938, p. 49)) and Musgrave (1965, p. 165)). According to this concept, all accretions to wealth are included, in whatever form or from whatever source they are received. As a matter of principle it is obvious that accretion as an index of equality should be measured in real terms. The value of net worth at the end of the period must be deflated in order to determine the change in net worth. The application of this principle calls for the exclusion from taxable income of capital gains that reflect an increase in the price level, and for allowance for losses suffered from the holding of claims (such as money).

In favor of disregarding capital gains that do not reflect real income increases, it has sometimes been argued that wage increases in inflationary times also reflect gains that are not real and that, accordingly, comprehensive money income is an appropriate tax base (Groves (1959)). In reply, it has been convincingly demonstrated by Diamond (1975) that a comprehensive tax base would discriminate against taxpayers whose income has a sizeable profit component. The reason is that inflation affects capital and labor incomes differently, resulting in a greater percentage increase in income from capital than in income from labor. He has further shown that a deduction of the inflation rate times the value of assets will preserve the relative contributions to the tax base of the two sources of income. Thus, equity consideration calls for such an *inflation exclusion*, to be available to all types of investment. But there are obvious difficulties in providing exclusion to all assets, an example being money holdings (cash). Since cash earns zero money income, the application of an inflation deduction with full loss offset would call for tax credits for holders of cash. The accounting and bookkeeping that would be involved seem prohibitive. Diamond has therefore suggested to provide an exclusion only, allowing no tax credits. However, the provision of an inflation exclusion to some assets only, introduces efficiency considerations into this issue. Thus, partial allowance for inflation may lead to a waste of resources used to convert assets from those without to those with such an exclusion. Given that application of the principle with full loss offset to all assets is impracticable, we may therefore wish to consider provision of only a partial inflation exclusion to assets for which it is feasible. The problem is examined in this chapter by means of a simple model of anticipated inflation, in which individuals may invest either in assets for which full or partial inflation exclusion is provided, or in cash, for which no loss offset is allowed.

Among other issues, we shall examine the short and long run effects of taxation and of the provision of an inflation deduction on the rate of inflation and on the level of savings.

We do not discuss the long run optimum tax and deduction rates, because it turns out that for a given tax revenue, these instruments are perfect substitutes, that is, their relative size does not affect the equilibrium configuration.

Our analysis leads us, however, to discuss the optimality of monetary policy in the long run. There seems to be a remarkable agreement among most writers (for example, Phelps (1965), Samuelson (1968) and (1969), Friedman (1969)) that the laissez faire system does not lead automatically to optimality of the quantity of real balances. The argument is that the cost of holding money for the individual is necessarily different from the cost to society. While the cost to the individual is measured by the (money) rate of interest, the cost to society is ordinarily assumed to be (practically) zero. The suggested recipe for optimality is therefore to satiate the economy with money, that is, to increase the quantity of real balances to a point where their marginal utility (or product) is zero. In an optimum the cost of holding money should be driven down to zero. Following Phelps we call this situation "full liquidity."

It seems, however, that the foregoing reasoning has overlooked an important point. Specifically, although there is no direct cost of providing nominal money bills there may be an economic cost of providing the economy with *real* money balances. This cost results from the fact that an increased quantity of real money can be absorbed in the economy only through the market mechanism, and this may lead to changes in the real part of the system. Thus, for example, if the quantity of real balances increases, consumers may feel better off and increase their consumption expenditures which will reduce the accumulation of physical capital. It is then possible that the cost involved in the expansion of real money may outweigh the gains before full liquidity is reached.

The model considered here is one of *imperfect control*, where the government operates a relatively small number of basic instruments which are not capable of eliminating the social cost of money. In analyzing this problem we shall assume that the utility functions of the private and government sectors are identical and that the difference between the two sectors (in off-steady-state situations) arises from better foresight on the part of the government. In particular, the private sector will be assumed to behave according to (changing) "static-expectations," even under dynamic conditions, while the government will be assumed to have a full evaluation of the future.

In the foregoing model money cannot be made neutral in the short run because of inadequacy of the instruments. We cannot, therefore, expect to have full liquidity in the short run if the economy is off-steady-state. However, even under steady-state conditions, money is not neutral except in the absence of imperfections created by, say, taxes. In principle, there may be a stationary optimum (or optima) where the optimum quantity of money is short of full liquidity because of the real social cost of increasing real balances. We shall illustrate this by an example which is in itself not very realistic but is indicative of similar situations that may arise under realistic conditions. In the example we shall assume that the rate of monetary expansion is the only instrument available to the government, and that the utility function is of the additive logarithmic form.

The upshot of the foregoing statements is that a policy of full liquidity is not necessarily optimal in the short run or in the long run if there is imperfect foresight and imperfect control in off-steady-state situations.

15.2. The Model

15.2.1. The Individual's Optimum Conditions

We assume that the individuals in the economy can be represented by one family. This family lives forever and the number of its members L increases by n percent per unit of time so that $L_t = L_0 e^{nt}$. The utility function of the representative unit is given by

$$U = \int_0^\infty e^{-\delta t} u(c_t, m_t) dt \tag{15.1}$$

where c_t is physical consumption *per capita* planned for time t and m_t is the amount of *real* balances per capita at time t. The latter are related to nominal balances M by

$$m_t = \frac{M_t}{P_t L_t} \tag{15.2}$$

where P_t is the expected price level of the physical good in terms of nominal money. The instantaneous utility function, $u(.)$, is assumed to have the usual concavity properties of neoclassical production functions. In addition we have a positive subjective discount rate δ.

Let w_t and r_t be the expected real wage rate and real rate of interest at time t. The money rate of interest i is related to the real rate of interest by $i_t = r_t + p_t$, where $p_t = \dot{P}_t / P_t$ is the expected rate of change of the price level.

The stock of capital per capita k owned by the individuals is rented to firms and yields the *money* rate of interest i.

The material wealth of the individuals is given by $a = k + m$. To this we must add their human wealth h which consists of the present value of the wage stream. The latter is given by

$$h_u = \int_u^\infty w_s e^{n(s-u)} e^{-\int_u^s r_x d_x} = \int_u^\infty w_s e^{-\int_u^s \rho_x dx} \tag{15.3}$$

where u denotes the individual's planning time and where $\rho_x = r_x - n$. If w_s converges and ρ_x converges to a positive constant (as along steady states) then h_u is well-defined.

Finally, we add the present value of real government transfers g which is given by the same expression as (15.3) with transfers at time s, v_s, substituted for w_s. Again if v_s converges to a constant, then g is well-defined.

Denote the total wealth of the individual by y_u, so that $y_u = a_u + h_u + g_u$. Then feasibility of his consumption plan can be taken to mean that $y_u \geqslant 0$ for all u along the plan horizon. Since $\dot{a}_u = \rho_u a_u - i_u m_u - c_u + w_u + v_u$, $\dot{h}_u = \rho_u h_u - w_u$ and $\dot{g}_u = \rho_u g_u - v_u$, we have

$$\dot{y}_u = \rho_u y_u - (c_u + i_u m_u) = \rho_u y_u - \overline{c}_u \tag{15.4}$$

where we use the fact that money does not earn any interest and it is subject to a "depreciation" rate p. The value of *total* consumption, $\overline{c} = c + im$, includes both ordinary consumption and consumption of services of liquid assets. Solving (15.4) we obtain

$$y_u = e^{\int_0^u \rho_x \rho_s} \left(y_0 - \int_0^u \overline{c}_s e^{-\int_0^s \rho_x dx} ds\right) \tag{15.5}$$

for some initial date $t = 0$. It follows that feasibility implies

$$y_0 \geqslant \int_0^u \overline{c}_s e^{-\int_0^u \rho_x dx} ds \qquad \text{for all} \qquad u \geqslant 0 \tag{15.6}$$

meaning that the present value of consumption for any u cannot exceed initial wealth.

Denote the present value of consumption in (15.6) by z_u. We may assume that $i \geqslant 0$. Since both c and m are nonnegative we have $\overline{c} \geqslant 0$. It follows that $\dot{z}_u \geqslant 0$. Noting that z_u is bounded from above and nondecreasing we know that there exists $\lim_{u \to \infty} z_u = z$ (say). From (15.6), $z \leqslant y_0$. However, if $z < y_0$, then it is obviously possible to construct an alternative feasible consumption path which has more consumption than the original one over some finite interval, and no less consumption elsewhere. Since $u_c = \partial u / \partial c > 0$, the original path cannot be a candidate for an optimal one. We may thus define an *efficient program* as one which satisfies $z = y_0$, that is, a program which satisfies the budget constraint with equality. By (15.5), then, an efficient program satisfies

$$\lim_{u\to\infty} y_u e^{-\int_0^u \rho_s ds} = 0 \tag{15.7}$$

meaning that the present value of "terminal" net worth is zero.

The consumer's optimum problem is to maximize (15.1) subject to (15.4) and the nonnegativity conditions on y, c and m. Assuming an interior solution, the *Euler Conditions* for the optimal paths c_u, m_u and y_u are given by

$$\frac{u_m(c_u, m_u)}{u_c(c_u, m_u)} = i_u \tag{15.8}$$

$$\frac{\dot{u}_c(c_u, m_u)}{u_c(c_u, m_u)} = \rho_u - \delta \tag{15.9}$$

We may solve the differential equation (15.9) to obtain

$$\hat{u}_{c,u} = \hat{u}_{c,0} e^{-\int_0^u (\rho_s - \delta) ds} \tag{15.10}$$

where $\hat{u}_{c,u}$ is the value of u_c corresponding to the *Euler path* at time u. Combining (15.7) and (15.10) we obtain the transversality condition

$$\lim_{u\to\infty} e^{-\delta u} \hat{u}_{c,u} y_u = 0 \tag{15.11}$$

which holds for any efficient path of y_u. It can be shown by standard methods that a feasible path which satisfies (15.4), (15.8), (15.9) and (15.11) is optimal, that is, it maximizes (15.1).

15.2.2. Static Expectations: Explicit Solutions

An explicit solution of the optimal path can be found with the additional assumption that the consumer expects all the exogeneous variables to remain constant, that is, static expectations,

$$\rho_u = \rho, \quad p_u = p \quad w_u = w, \quad v_u = v \qquad (\rho = r - n > 0, \quad i = r + p > 0) \tag{15.12}$$

The budget relation (15.6), which we have shown to hold with equality, is now given by

$$a_0 + \frac{w + v}{\rho} = \int_0^\infty (c_u + im_u) e^{-\rho u} dn \tag{15.13}$$

where $a_0 = k_0 + m_0$ is the initial real value of assets per capita.

Assume further that the utility function $u(.)$ is of the additive-log form

$$u(c, m) = \log c + \beta \log m \tag{15.19}$$

Under these assumptions (15.8) and (15.9) become

$$\frac{\beta c_u}{m_u} = i \tag{15.8'}$$

$$\frac{\dot{c}_u}{c_u} = \rho - \delta \tag{15.9'}$$

(15.9′) can be solved to yield

$$c_u = c_0 e^{(\rho - \delta)u}$$

Substituting this solution in (15.13), using (15.8′), we may solve for the demand for c_0 and m_0

$$c_0 = \frac{\delta}{1 + \beta}(a_0 + \frac{w + r}{\rho}) \tag{15.15}$$

$$m_0 = \frac{\delta\beta}{(1 + \beta)i}(a_0 + \frac{w + r}{\rho}) \tag{15.16}$$

Note that the money rate of interest i, must be positive if m_0 is to be positive and finite. As expected, the demand functions (15.15) and (15.16) are seen to have negative price and positive wealth derivatives.

15.2.3. Macro Relations

The foregoing maximization takes place at an actual time $t = 0$ (to distinguish from the individual's planning time denoted by u). By relating the consumer's expectations to prevailing values of the exogeneous variables, and the latter to the macro variables by means of an aggregate production function and market equilibrium conditions, the dynamic path of the economy can be traced.

The production function in the economy is of the neoclassical type and is given by

$$\dot{k}_t + \lambda k_t + c_t = f(k_t), \qquad \lambda = n + \mu \tag{15.17}$$

where λ is the sum of the rate of population growth and physical depreciation μ.

Transfer payments to individuals are equal to the government's deficit, which is covered by an increase in the money supply, $v_t = \dot{M}_t/P_tL_t$, or $v_t = \theta_t m_t$ where $\theta_t = \dot{M}_t/M_t$. By definition, the time rate of change in m_t is given by

$$\dot{m}_t = (\theta_t - p_t - n)m_t \tag{15.18}$$

where p_t is now the *actual* rate of price change, which implies instantaneous adjustment of expectations or "warranted price expectations."[a] Competitive equilibrium in labor and capital markets implies

$$\rho_t = f'(k_t) - \lambda, \qquad w_t = f(k_t) - k_t f'(k_t) \tag{15.19}$$

We assume that ρ_t is positive for all t (which entails $r = f' - \mu > f' - \lambda = \rho > 0$). This assumption is justified, as will be seen below, along any equilibrium path.

Using the relations $a = k + m$, $v = \theta m$, (15.15) and (15.19), we may express the demand for consumption at time t as

$$c_t = \frac{\delta}{1+\beta}\left(k_t + m_t + \frac{f(k_t) - k_t f'(k_t) + \theta_t m_t}{f'(k_t) - \lambda}\right) \tag{15.20}$$

Interpreting (15.16) in macro terms, and assuming that at each moment of time the expectations about the instantaneous rate of price increase p are determined so as to be consistent with momentary equilibrium, the condition for instantaneous equilibrium in the money market is

$$m_t = \frac{\delta\beta}{(1+\beta)(f'(k_t) - \mu + p_t)}\left(k_t + m_t + \frac{f(k_t) - k_t f'(k_t) + \theta_t m_t}{f'(k_t) - \lambda}\right) \tag{15.21}$$

We may solve (15.21) for p_t, and by substitution of this solution and (15.20) into equations (15.17) and (15.18) obtain the dynamic path of the economy for given initial conditions (k_0, m_0) at $t = 0$, and for any given function θ_t, $t \in [0, \infty]$.

The simplest case is to take θ_t as constant,[b] say, θ. It turns out that for *any* such policy, there exists a unique steady state of the system, with $\dot{k} = \dot{m} = 0$. Obviously, by (15.18), in steady state $p = \theta - n$. It is interesting to note that the

[a]Note that static expectations imply, generally, unfulfilled expectations. However, in steady states ($p_t = p$) the consumer will have perfect foresight.

[b]The more ambitious target of choosing the function θ_t so as to maximize the utility integral, has been examined by Liviatan and Sheshinski (1971).

system can be shown to be unstable for deviations from steady state. A similar result has been obtained by Uzawa (1966) under somewhat different assumptions, but also with instantaneous adjustment of expectations, which seems to be the crucial assumption for this result.[c]

We shall now introduce into the system an income tax and examine its implications on individual behavior and on the equilibrium configuration.

15.3. Income Taxation

15.3.1. Equity and Efficiency

Since we assume that labor is supplied inelastically, we can concentrate on the effects of taxation on the income from capital.

In the presence of a positive inflation rate, the shortcoming of a comprehensive tax base applied to money income is that it results in a greater percentage increase in taxable income from capital than from labor income. This inequity provides an argument for an adjustment for inflation of the return to capital. Specifically, we shall consider an inflation exclusion, allowing a deduction from taxable income that depends on the inflation rate times the value of capital assets.

Equity and efficiency both call for the inflation exclusion to be available for any type of investment. This is necessary in order to have the net relative rates of return from various investments independent of the inflation rate. There are, however, some obvious difficulties in applying the inflation exclusion to all assets. The asset that raises the most obvious difficulties is cash. Since cash yields zero monetary gains (although it provides monetary benefits in the form of liquidity), the application of an inflation deduction on cash holdings would call for tax credits for individuals holding cash. The nontaxation of liquidity benefits could be removed, in principle, by including these imputed benefits, equal (in equilibrium) to the rate of return on other assets times the amount of cash, in taxable income. But the accounting and record keeping that would be involved seem prohibitive.

It is thus reasonable to consider an adjustment for inflation by means of an exclusion only, allowing no tax credit for the failure of cash to yield at least the inflation rate. Allowing an inflation adjustment only for some assets and none for others clearly involves an efficiency loss, generated by resources used to convert assets from those without to those with the inflation exclusion. It may therefore be appropriate to provide only for partial adjustment of those assets for which exclusion is available. We attempt here to evaluate these considera-

[c]Under the more general assumption of adaptive expectations, it can be shown that for a sufficiently slow speed of adjustment, the system is stable (instantaneous adjustment means, of course, an infinite speed of adjustment).

tions relating to the provision of an inflation adjustment, from the point of view of the individual and from the point of view of society.

15.3.2. Equilibrium Conditions

Suppose that taxable income is defined as the money return on the value of capital minus a fraction ϵ $(1 \geqslant \epsilon \geqslant 0)$ of the rate of inflation times the value of capital. Taxable income per unit of capital is thus $i - \epsilon p = r + (1 - \epsilon)p$. A *full* inflation exclusion $(\epsilon = 1)$ means that only real income is taxable, while *no* exclusion $(\epsilon = 0)$ means that all nominal returns are taxable. Let the tax rate be $\tau \geqslant 0$. For the individual, real after-tax return of a unit of capital per capita is now given by

$$\bar{\rho} = \rho - \gamma \qquad \text{where } \gamma = \tau(i - \epsilon p) \tag{15.22}$$

Accordingly, the opportunity cost of cash holdings is now $\bar{i} = i - \gamma$.[d] The individual's optimum conditions are given by (15.8′) and (15.9′) with $\bar{\rho}$ and $\bar{i}$ replacing ρ and i, respectively. Assuming that tax receipts are returned to the individual by *lump-sum transfers*, the budget constraint, (15.4), remains unchanged. Under the assumption of static expectations, the solutions for c_0 and m_0 are found to be:

$$c_0 = \frac{(\rho - \bar{\rho} + \delta)\bar{i}}{\bar{i} + i\beta}(a_0 + \frac{w + v}{\rho}) = \frac{(\gamma + \delta)\bar{i}}{\bar{i} + i\beta}(a_0 + \frac{w + v}{\rho}) \tag{15.15′}$$

$$m_0 = \frac{(\rho - \bar{\rho} + \delta)}{\bar{i} + i\beta}(a_0 + \frac{w + v}{\rho}) = \frac{(\gamma + \delta)}{\bar{i} + i\beta}(a_0 + \frac{w + v}{\rho}) \tag{15.16′}$$

The previous solutions (15.15) and (15.16) are seen to be special cases of (15.15′) and (15.16′) when $\gamma = 0$.

Using the relations $a = k + m$ and $v = \theta m$, and assuming that the demand and supply of money at any time t are equal, (15.21) becomes

$$m = \frac{(\gamma + \delta)\beta}{\bar{i} + i\beta}(k + m + \frac{f - kf' + \theta m}{f' - \lambda}) \tag{15.21′}$$

[d] These calculations can be deduced directly from the budget equation, which (in real terms) is now given by

$$c_u + \dot{k}_u + (n + p_u)k_u + \dot{m}_u + (n + p_u)m_u = (i_u - \gamma_u)k_u + w_u + v_u$$

or

$$\dot{y}_u = \bar{\rho}_u y_u - (c_u + \bar{i}_u m_u)$$

The net return on assets being $\bar{\rho}_u$, while the implied consumption value (liquidity) of a unit of real balances is i_u.

Again, the previous solution, (15.21), is seen to be a special case of (15.21′) when $\gamma = 0$. Equation (15.21′), the condition for momentary equilibrium in the money market, can be solved for the rate of price change,[e]

$$p = \frac{\delta\beta x - (1+\beta-(1+\beta x)\tau)(f' - \mu)}{1+\beta-(1-\epsilon)(1+\beta x)\tau} \equiv \pi(k, m, \theta, \tau, \epsilon) \tag{15.23}$$

where

$$x = 1 + \frac{k}{m} + \frac{\frac{1}{m}(f - kf') + \theta}{f' - \lambda}$$

Using (15.23) and (15.15′), consumption at any time t can be expressed by

$$c = \frac{(\gamma+\delta)\bar{i}}{\bar{i}+i\beta}\left(k + m + \frac{f - kf' + \theta m}{f' - \lambda}\right) \equiv \hat{c}(k, m, \theta, \tau, \epsilon) \tag{15.20'}$$

15.3.3. Short Run Effects of Monetary Expansion

In the short run k and m are constant, and equilibrium is attained by adjustment of the rate of inflation and consumption. Thus, given k and m, the effect on π of an increase in θ can be directly calculated from (15.23):

$$\pi_\theta = \frac{\beta(\gamma+\delta)}{(1+\beta-(1-\epsilon)(1+\beta x)\tau)(f' - \lambda)} > 0 \tag{15.24}$$

where a subscript denotes partial derivative with respect to this variable.

The short run change in consumption due to an increase in θ is found from (15.20′):

$$\hat{c}_\theta = \frac{m}{\beta}(1 - \tau(1-\epsilon))\pi_\theta = \frac{m(1-(1-\epsilon))(\gamma+\delta)}{(1+\beta-(1-\epsilon)(1+\beta x)\tau)(f' - \lambda)} > 0 \tag{15.25}$$

These results are stated in the following:

Proposition 1. In the short run, an increase in the rate of change of money supply increases the rate of inflation and the level of consumption.

[e]The necessary and sufficient condition for existence of a solution to (15.21′) is that $(\gamma+\delta)\beta/(\bar{i}+i\beta) < 1$. This condition guarantees that the denominator in (15.23) is positive.

15.3.4. Short Run Effects of Taxation

Given k and m, the effects on π of an increase in τ or ϵ can also be calculated from (15.23):

$$\pi_\tau = \frac{(1+\beta x)(f' - \mu + p(1-\epsilon))}{1+\beta-(1-\epsilon)(1+\beta x)} > 0 \tag{15.26}$$

and

$$\pi_\epsilon = \frac{p(1+\beta x)}{1+\beta-(1-\epsilon)(1+\beta x)} < 0 \tag{15.27}$$

An increase in the tax rate creates a substitution effect in favor of the demand for real balances, (15.16′). In order to bring demand into equilibrium with the given supply of money, this increase generates an increase in the (actual and expected) rate of inflation. An increase in the inflation exclusion rate has exactly the opposite effect:

Proposition 2. In the short run, an increase in the income tax rate increases, and an increase in the inflation exclusion rate decreases, the rate of inflation.

Short run changes in consumption due to an increase in τ or ϵ are found by differentiating (15.20′), using (15.21′), and using (15.27)

$$\hat{c}_\tau = \frac{m}{\beta}[(1-\tau(1-\epsilon))\pi_\tau - r - p(1-\epsilon)]$$

$$= \frac{(f' - \mu + p(1-\epsilon))(x-1)m}{1+\beta-(1-\epsilon)(1+\beta x)} > 0 \tag{15.28}$$

since $x > 1$. Similarly, using (15.27)

$$\hat{c}_\epsilon = \frac{m}{\beta}[\tau p + (1-\tau(1-\epsilon))\pi_\epsilon]$$

$$= -\frac{\tau p(x-1)m}{1+\beta-(1-\epsilon)(1+\beta x)} < 0 \tag{15.29}$$

We thus have:

Proposition 3. In the short run, an increase in the income tax rate increases, and an increase in the inflation exclusion rate decreases, the level of consumption.

Notice that the government's tax revenue is equal to $\gamma k = \tau(i - \epsilon p)k$, so that a constant k and a given revenue imply a constant γ. Since only γ appears in the equilibrium equations (15.20′) and (15.21′), we have:

Proposition 4. Changes in the tax rate and in the inflation exclusion rate that keep the government's tax revenue constant, do not affect the short run equilibrium values.

15.4. Long Run Effects

15.4.1. Steady State

Inserting (15.20′) and (15.21′) into (15.17) and (15.18), we obtain the dynamic equations for the economy

$$\dot{k} = f(k) - \lambda k - c = f(k) - \lambda k - \hat{c}(k, m, \theta, \tau, \epsilon) \equiv z(k, m, \theta, \tau, \epsilon) \qquad (15.30)$$

and

$$\dot{m} = (\theta - p - n)m = (\theta - \pi(k, m, \theta, \tau, \epsilon) - n)m \equiv s(k, m, \theta, \tau, \epsilon) \qquad (15.31)$$

Equations (15.28) and (15.29) determine the dynamic path of the economy for given initial conditions (k_0, m_0) at $t = 0$, and with any arbitrary policies (θ, τ, ϵ), for $t \in [0, \infty]$.

Let us examine the steady-state properties of the model for constant values of θ, γ, and ϵ, and for $\dot{k} = \dot{m} = 0$, that is,

$$z(k, m, \theta, \tau, \epsilon) = 0 \qquad \text{and} \qquad s(k, m, \theta, \tau, \epsilon) = 0 \qquad (15.32)$$

It can easily be shown that at $\tau = \epsilon = 0$, we have for *any* θ: $f' - \lambda - \delta = 0$, that is the "*Modified Golden Rule*" path.[f] Denote this path by (k^*, m^*). From the individual's equilibrium condition (15.8′), it is seen that on this path

$$m^* = \frac{\beta(f - \lambda k^*)}{\delta + \theta} \qquad (15.33)$$

By differentiating (15.32) at $\tau = \epsilon = 0$, using (15.20′) and (15.23), we obtain:

$$z_k = \delta - \hat{c}_k = \delta - \frac{\delta m}{1 + \beta} \frac{\partial x}{\partial x} = \frac{\beta\delta}{1 + \beta} + \frac{mf''}{1 + \beta} \left(\frac{f - \lambda k}{m} + \frac{\theta}{\delta}\right)$$

[f]Note that the steady-state level of capital per capita, k^*, is *independent of* θ. Thus, monetary policy does not affect, in the long run, the real part of the system. This dichotomy disappears once taxes are introduced, as seen below.

$$z_m = -\hat{c}_m = -\frac{\delta + \theta}{1 + \beta} < 0 \tag{15.34}$$

$$s_k = -\pi_k = -\frac{\delta\beta}{1+\beta}\frac{\partial x}{\partial x} + f'' = -\frac{\delta\beta}{1+\beta}\left[\frac{1}{m} - \frac{f''}{\delta}\left(\frac{f-k}{m} + \frac{\theta}{\delta}\right)\right] + f'' < 0$$

$$s_m = -\pi_m = -\frac{\delta\beta}{1+\beta}\frac{\partial x}{\partial m} = \frac{\beta(f - \lambda k)}{(1+\beta)m^2} > 0$$

In the (k, m) plane, the slope of the curve defined by $s(.) = 0$ is thus positive:

$$\left.\frac{dm}{dk}\right|_{s=0} = -\frac{s_k}{s_m} > 0 \tag{15.35}$$

The slope of the curve defined by $z(.) = 0$ depends on the sign of z_k. We assume that the first term in z_k, (15.34), is relatively small so that $z_k < 0$. Under this assumption

$$\left.\frac{dm}{dk}\right|_{z=0} = -\frac{z_k}{z_m} < 0 \tag{15.36}$$

By (15.35) and (15.36), at $\tau = \epsilon = 0$, if an equilibrium steady state exists then it is unique (figure 15-1).

Now, by (15.32) and (15.28) $z_\tau = -\hat{c}_\tau < 0$. Since $z_m < 0$ an increase in τ (around $\tau = 0$) requires, in order to keep $z = 0$, a decrease in m. By (15.32) and (15.26), $s_\tau = -\pi_\tau < 0$. Accordingly, since $s_m > 0$, an increase in τ requires an increase in m.

In figure 15-1, the equilibrium steady state with $\tau > 0$, is denoted by k^{**} and m^{**}. We may conclude that:

Proposition 5. In steady state, an income tax reduces the capital labor ratio but may increase or decrease the amount of real balances.

It is easy to see that an increase in the inflation exclusion rate has the opposite effect of an increase in the tax rate.

15.5. The Optimal Monetary Policy

The government has several instruments—monetary (θ) and fiscal (τ and ϵ)—which it can use to achieve certain goals. Let us assume first that there exists a fixed positive tax $\tau > 0$ with a full inflation exclusion $\epsilon = 1$ (for a *given* tax revenue, γk, we have seen that a substitution of τ for ϵ does not affect the

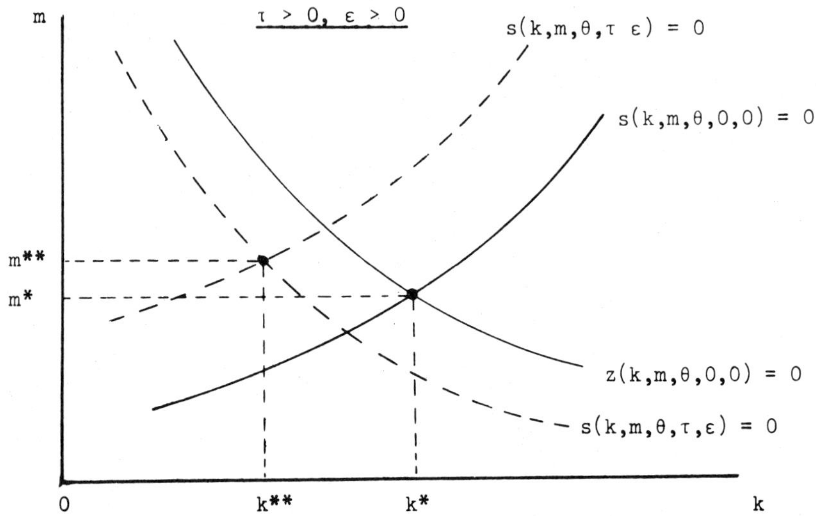

Figure 15-1. Equilibrium Steady State.

equilibrium values), and that the government wants to choose θ so as to maximize the welfare of the individuals.

We may derive from (15.8′), (15.20′) and (15.30) the modified *steady-state* relation (15.33) in the presence of a tax

$$m = \frac{\beta(f - \lambda k)}{(1 - \tau)(f' - \mu) + \theta - n} \tag{15.33′}$$

which reduces to (15.33) when $\tau = 0$ and $k = k^*$. The graph of (15.33′) for a given k ($< k^*$ as was shown above) is given in figure 15-2. The reason for the negative relation is that in steady states an increase in θ increases k, which reduces the rate of return and consequently the demand for money. It can also be seen that the economy may "produce" any amount of m provided θ is sufficiently close to $-(1 - \tau)(f' - \mu) + n$. The question is whether in these circumstances it is at all possible to have an *optimal* stationary state with a *finite* m.

Given the dynamic equations (15.30) and (15.31), the government wants to determine the time path of θ_t so as to maximize the value of the utility integral (15.1) given the initial values of k_0 and m_0.

The economic meaning of the optimality conditions for the government's program can be best explained by using the *Maximum Principle* formulation. The relevant imputed value of the "national income" at each t is given by

$$H = u(\hat{c}(k, m, \theta, \tau, \epsilon), m) + q_z z(k, m, \theta, \tau, \epsilon) + q_s s(k, m, \theta, \tau, \epsilon) \qquad (15.37)$$

where q_z and q_s are the undiscounted shadow prices of $\dot{k}$ and $\dot{m}$, which should be considered as continuous functions of time. The first order conditions for a maximum yield

$$u_c \hat{c}_k + \dot{q}_z + q_z(z_k - \delta) + q_s s_k = 0 \qquad (15.38)$$

$$u_c \hat{c}_m + u_m + q_z z_m + \dot{q}_s + q_s(s_m - \delta) = 0 \qquad (15.39)$$

$$u_c \hat{c}_\theta + q_z z_\theta + q_s s_\theta = 0 \qquad (15.40)$$

$$\lim_{t\to\infty} \bar{e}^{st} q_{z_t} k_t = 0; \qquad \lim_{t\to\infty} \bar{e}^{st} q_{s_t} m_t - 0 \qquad (15.41)$$

where subscripts denote partial derivatives. The first two equations are concerned with the effects of k and m on H along the optimal path. Along this path the gains and losses associated with a change in k or m must exactly offset each other as stated in these equations. As for (15.40), it is the condition that H should be maximized with respect to the control variable θ at each moment of

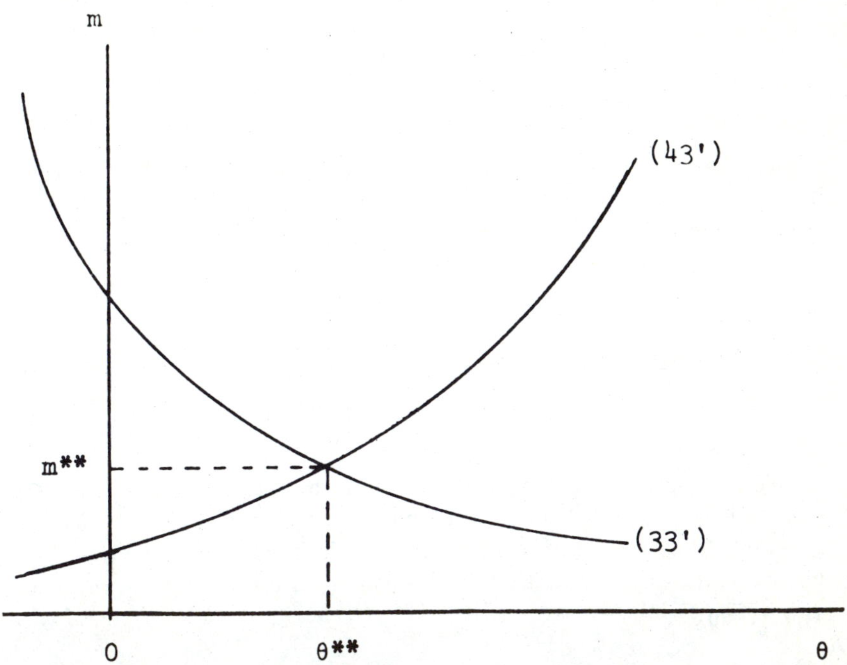

Figure 15-2. The Optimum Stationary State.

time. Indeed in our model we have $H_{\theta\theta} = c_\theta^2 u_{cc} < 0$ for all t. Suppose that s_θ and c_θ are positive (actually, c_θ is positive, and s_θ is positive around k^*, when $\tau = 0$). Then a positive shadow price for money implies $q_z > u_c$. This means that the same physical unit of our good has a higher value in investment than in consumption. This paradox is resolved if we remember that the shift from c to $\dot{k}$ cannot be accomplished directly but only through the instrument θ. Now, if we reduce c through θ it must involve additional loss via the reduction of $\dot{m}$.

Equations (15.38)-(15.40), together with the accumulation equations (15.30) and (15.31), the "end-conditions" (15.41) and the initial values k_0 and m_0 determine the optimal time path for the economy. Because of the complexity of the system we cannot analyze this time path by conventional graphical (or other) methods. The most one can hope to do is to analyze the steady-state solution of the system.

We are now interested in examining whether there exists a steady state, with $\dot{k} = \dot{m} = \dot{q}_z = \dot{q}_s = 0$, which satisfies the first order conditions for an optimal path. From (15.30) we have the relationships $z_\theta = -\hat{c}_\theta$, $z_m = -\hat{c}_m$, $z_k = f - \lambda - \hat{c}_k$. From (15.31) we have $s_\theta = m - \pi_\theta m$, $s_m = -\pi_m m$, $s_k = -\pi_k m$. Conditions (15.38)-(15.40) thus become

$$(u_c - q_z)\hat{c}_k + q_z(f' - \lambda - \delta) - q_s \pi_k m = 0 \tag{15.42}$$

$$(u_c - q_z)\hat{c}_m + u_m - q_s \pi_m m = 0 \tag{15.43}$$

$$(u_c - q_z)\hat{c} + q_s m - q_s \pi_\theta m = 0 \tag{15.44}$$

Assuming that $\epsilon = 1$ we have $\pi_k m = \beta\hat{c}_k - (1-\tau)f''m$, $\pi_m m = \beta\hat{c}_m - (1-\tau)(f' - \mu) - \theta + n$ and $\pi_\theta m = \beta\hat{c}_\theta$. Equations (15.42)-(15.44) can then be further simplified

$$(u_c - q_z - \beta q_s)\hat{c}_k + q_z(f' - \lambda - \delta) + q_s(1-\tau)f''m = 0 \tag{15.42'}$$

$$(u_c - q_z - \beta q_s)\hat{c}_m + u_m + q_s((1-\tau)f' - \mu) + \theta - n) = 0 \tag{15.43'}$$

$$(u_c - q_z - \beta q_s)\hat{c} + q_s m = 0 \tag{15.44'}$$

We have seen, (15.25), that $\hat{c}_\theta > 0$. Hence by (15.44') $u_c - q_z - \beta q_s < 0$. Substituting in (15.43') the expressions for $\hat{c}_m$, $u_c = 1/c = 1/(f - \lambda k)$ and $u_m = \beta/m$, it can be shown that for small τ and a given k, (15.43') is a strictly monotone, increasing relation between θ and m.[g] Thus, for given q_z, q_s and k,

---

[g]From (15.20),

$$\hat{c}_m = \frac{(\gamma + \delta)\bar{i}}{\bar{i} + i\beta}\left(1 + \frac{\theta}{f' - \lambda}\right) > 0$$

which is a function of θ only. Now,

equations (15.33′) and (15.43′) determine a unique pair (m^{**}, θ^{**}). It remains to show that the system as a whole is consistent, that is, that all variables can be determined simultaneously. This can be demonstrated by numerical calculations which we have performed with particular examples.[h]

The important thing to note about the solution displayed in figure 15-2, is that it is obtained for a finite m, which implies positive u_m and q_s, in spite of the fact that it is feasible to create any value of m. Thus, the optimum stationary state is short of *full liquidity.*

It should be noted that when $\tau = 0$, the present model *does* give full liquidity ($m = \infty$, with $\theta = -\delta$) as the unique optimum stationary solution. It seems therefore, that for the given expectations' structure, the imperfect control model in the absence of taxes, still tends to the "bliss" solution. It is only with the additional "imperfection" created by the presence of taxes, that a "non-bliss" solution becomes optimal. It would be interesting to examine whether other expectation structures could provide for such an optimum even in the absence of taxes. In any case, we have demonstrated that in an economy with "imperfections" of various kinds–due to individuals' erroneous expectations, taxes etc.–the optimum policy may drive the economy to a stationary state short of full liquidity.

References

Diamond, P.A., "Inflation and the Comprehensive Tax Base," *Journal of Public Economics*, 4 (Aug. 1975):227-244.

Friedman, M., *The Optimum Quantity of Money and Other Essays*, Chicago: Aldine Publishing Co., 1969, pp. 1-51.

Groves, H.M., "Taxation of Capital Gains," in *Tax Revision Compendium* vol. 2, Washington D.C.: Government Printing Office, 1959, p. 1199.

Liviatan, N., and Sheshinski, E., "Optimal Money, Expectations and

(footnote g continued)

$$\hat{c}_{m\theta} = \frac{(\gamma + \delta)\bar{i}}{(\bar{i} + i\beta)(f' - \lambda)} +$$

$$+ \left(1 + \frac{\theta}{f' - \lambda}\right) \frac{(\tau(f' - \mu) + \delta)}{((f' - \lambda + \theta)(1 + \beta) - \tau(f' - \mu))}$$

$$\times \left(1 - \frac{(f' - \lambda + \theta - \tau(f' - \mu))(1 + \beta)}{((f' - \lambda + \theta) - \tau(f' - \mu))(1 + \beta) + \tau\beta(f' - \mu)}\right) > 0$$

For $\gamma \sim 0$, $\hat{c}_{m\theta} \sim 1/(1 + \beta)$, and $\hat{c}_{m\theta}$ approaches $1/1 + \beta$ from above. Since, by $\hat{c}_\theta \sim m/1 + \beta$ and, by (44′) $u_c - q_z - \beta q_s \sim -(1 + \beta)q_s$, we can see from (15.43′) that the relation between θ and m is positive.

[h]Available upon request from the author.

Government Controls," *Technical Report No. 12, Project for the Evaluation and Optimization of Economic Growth,* University of California, Berkeley, 1970.

Musgrave, R.A., *The Theory of Public Finance*, New York: McGraw-Hill, 1959.

Phelps, E.S., *Fiscal Neutrality Toward Economic Growth*, New York: McGraw-Hill, 1965.

Samuelson, P.A., "What Classical and Neoclassical Monetary Theory Really Was," *Canadian Journal of Economics*, Feb. 1968:1-15.

Samuelson, P.A., "Non-Optimality of Money under Laissez Faire," *Canadian Journal of Economics*, May 1969:303-308.

Simons, H., *Personal Income Taxation*, Chicago: University of Chicago Press, 1938.

Uzawa, H., "On a Neoclassical Model of Economic Growth," *Economic Studies Quarterly*, 17 (1966).

16 Should Government Subsidize Risky Private Projects?

Joram Mayshar

With the growth of public involvement in economic life the subsidization of private projects has become a common practice. In many countries, government subsidization of new private ventures through easy loans, matching grants, tax rebates, protective tariffs and the like has become of far greater significance for industrial and agricultural growth than direct public investment. In this chapter we shall examine whether considerations of risk provide a justification for subsidies to private projects.

The theoretical literature dealing with this topic is very limited. Indeed only cursory remarks in the debate concerning the social rate of discount have been devoted to the practice of subsidization. The relevant issues in the debate on the social rate of discount can be represented by the viewpoints of Jack Hirshleifer on the one hand and Kenneth Arrow and Robert Lind on the other. Hirschleifer's general conclusion is that if capital markets are perfect, public projects should be evaluated using the risk-adjusted discount rate employed in the private sector for projects with a "comparable" type of risk. Arrow and Lind accept Hirshleifer's proposition but argue that it is generally inapplicable since capital markets are not perfect. Their own principal conclusion is that if a public project is independent of all other projects in the economy, then, whether or not the capital markets are perfect, the government should use a riskless rate of discount. Their underlying reasoning (which is quite separate from the often cited risk-pooling argument) is that the total cost of risk bearing of an independent public project is made negligible by the spreading of the risk over the entire population of taxpayers.

While on the issue of the social discount rate Hirshleifer and Arrow-Lind reach different conclusions due to different underlying assumptions, on the issue of subsidization they differ without an apparent difference in assumptions. Their conflicting conclusions on subsidization can best be illustrated by the example suggested by Arrow and Lind which compares the social desirability of two alternative investment schemes, both employing the same resources in an independent project. If the project were to be undertaken by a private firm its expected rate of (net) return would be 10 percent but the risk-adjusted rate

Reprinted, with permission of the American Economic Association, from the *American Economic Review*, vol. 67, March 1977, pp. 20-28. The author is very much indebted to Peter Diamond for his help and encouragement. A critical survey of the debate on the social rate of discount under uncertainty can be found in the article by Martin Bailey and Michael Jensen.

would be only 5 percent. On the other hand, if government undertook the project its expected rate of return would be 6 percent, which is also the market's riskless rate of return. As Arrow and Lind make clear, the fact that the private firm adjusts for risk even though the project is independent indicates that the capital markets are imperfect and do not facilitate the sufficient spreading of the private project's risk. Hirshleifer, considering a similar example parenthetically commented (p. 270) that the adoption of the public project can be justified only as a "second best"–"For, granted the premises, it would clearly be most efficient for the government to borrow in order to subsidize the higher-expected-yield private investment . . . rather than [to undertake the] lower-yield public investment."

Arrow and Lind have taken issue with this recommendation for subsidization. They argue that because of its independence, the costs of risk-bearing of the public project can be ignored whereas the risk-bearing costs of the private project are real costs to the economy. By the Kaldor-Hicks principle of potential compensation the public project is thus to be preferred. They reject the recommendation for subsidization on the grounds that (p. 375): ". . . a program of providing direct subsidies to encourage more private investment does not alter the costs of risk-bearing and, therefore, will encourage investments which are inefficient when the costs of risk are considered."

The major point of this chapter is that subsidization of private risky projects *is* a justified, even necessary, practice given two conditions: that the capital markets are incomplete and that income taxation exists. Indeed, if to the above example we introduce income taxation at a rate of 50 percent, then we find that it is the private project which ought to be undertaken in preference to the public project. In order that the private project be undertaken it must be subsidized by the government. By way of a guideline we find below that the required subsidy could take the form of a loan at a reduced rate of 3.5 percent, which would be low enough to encourage further expansion of the private project.

The intuitive reason for our general conclusion in favor of the subsidization of private projects rests on an observation made by Evsey Domar and Richard Musgrave: "By imposing an income tax on the investor, the treasury appoints itself as his partner." Therefore when taxes exist and when, due to capital market deficiencies, the government's attitude towards risk differs from that of the private investor, it is in the government's interest that the investment decision reflects its own concerns in the assumed partnership. In particular, if the government is more neutral towards risk than the private investor, then it ought to subsidize the project in order to further its level of investment.

In the controversy between Hirshleifer favoring subsidies, and Arrow and Lind arguing against subsidies, we thus end somewhere in the middle–favoring subsidies but for different reasons than those suggested by Hirshleifer. It should be emphasized however that our argument does not differ in its general approach from that of Arrow and Lind's. Rather, since a new consideration of taxation is introduced it should be regarded as complementary to theirs. However, whereas Arrow and Lind argue (p. 375) that "The program which produces the desired result is one to insure private investments [rather than to subsidize them]," we find here that it is income taxation, itself a form of insurance, which creates the very case for subsidization.

16.1. Sandmo's "Farm Model"

The preceding heuristic argument in favor of subsidization will be analyzed more rigorously by use of a very stylized model. The model is based on Agnar Sandmo's ingenious representation of an "unincorporated economy," itself an adaptation of Peter Diamond's contrasting "stock-market economy." The model represents a polar case of an economy without a system of capital markets; its results, however, are clearly not limited to that polar case only. We can think of Sandmo's model as representing a farm economy in which due to the lack of capital markets, the individual farmers have to bear the entire risks of production. The only financial market in the farm economy is a loan market run by the central bank. The loan market is assumed to operate costlessly and to involve no risks of default. We further assume that only a single good exists in that economy ("corn") and that consumption takes place in a single future period.[a] The source of the uncertainty with regard to the future state of nature is "technological," that is, it is like the weather, independent of actions in the economy.[b]

Let there be n individual farmers (or producers-consumers), each one operating a farm (henceforth–a firm) with a given technology such that for current inputs of y_j, the future's uncertain output is $f_j(y_j)\phi_j(\theta)$, where θ denotes the state of nature.[c]. The term $\phi_j(\theta)$ which represents a pattern of returns across the various states of nature can be considered as a "composite good."[d] This composite good consists of $\phi_j(\theta')$ units of the θ'-contingent commodity, for each state of nature θ'. (To recall, the Arrow-Debreu θ'-contingent commodity offers

[a]In Sandmo's original model present-period consumption is included. We exclude this extension so as not to confound the main argument with the possible (yet not necessary) intertemporal distortions caused by taxation.

[b]The assumption of technological uncertainty is significant in our analysis. We neglect here entirely the often made argument which justifies subsidization on the grounds that many of the "nontechnological" risks (such as the risk of temporary insolvency) facing private investors are not "social" risks.

[c]The multiplicative form of the production function is *not* essential for our argument. We could, for example, allow firm j to produce $\sum_{k=1}^{K} f_{jk}\phi_{jk}(\theta)$ future output for $h_j(f_{j1}, \ldots, f_{jK})$ present inputs. Such formulation, which when K equals the number of states of nature can be the most general, will overburden the exposition without significantly changing our results.

[d]If the probability assessments of all individuals were the same (which, unlike Sandmo, we do not assume), a natural normalization of the composite goods would be to set $E\phi_j(\theta) = 1$ for all j.

the delivery of a unit of future consumption if and only if the state θ' occurs.) We can thus think of firm j as producing $f_j(y_j)$ units of the composite good $\phi_j(\theta)$. The "production function" $f_j(y_j)$ is assumed to satisfy the standard assumptions (i.e., $f_j'(y_j) > 0, f_j''(y_j) < 0$ for all $y_j \geqslant 0$).

In addition to investment in production, each farmer can make, or receive, loans from the central bank at a given rate of safe return r. His budget constraint is thus:

$$y_j + b_j = w_j \qquad j = 1, \ldots, n \tag{16.1}$$

where b_j is the amount of bonds held (i.e., of loans made out), and w_j the initial wealth of farmer j. The farmer's future gross income will then be $f_j(y_j)\phi_j(\theta) + [1 + r]b_j$. We assume now that a uniform income tax of a rate t $(0 \leqslant t < 1)$ exists in the economy. As the basis for income taxation we take a measure of net income—the excess of gross future income over initial wealth.[e] We furthermore assume that all the government's revenue $G(\theta)$, derived from tax collection, from public production, and from profits of the central bank, is redistributed to the farmers according to preassigned fractions τ_j, $j = 1, \ldots, n$ $(\sum_{j=1}^{n} \tau_j = 1)$. The individual farmer's future consumption is thus:

$$c_j(\theta) = (1 - t)[f_j(y_j)\phi_j(\theta) + (1 + r)b_j] + tw_j + \tau_j G(\theta) \qquad j = 1, \ldots, n \tag{16.2}$$

Each farmer j is assumed to attempt to maximize the expected utility of his future consumption $E_j u_j(c_j(\theta))$ using his own subjective probability assessments. The utility function $u_j(c_j)$ is assumed to satisfy the standard assumptions (i.e., $u_j'(c_j) > 0, u_j''(c_j) \leqslant 0$ for any $c_j \geqslant 0$).[f]

We denote:

$$S_j^i = \frac{E_i u_i'(c_i(\theta))\phi_j(\theta)}{E_i u_i'(c_i(\theta))} \tag{16.3}$$

The function S_j^i will be termed here as the "subjective valuation" by individual i of a marginal unit of the composite good $\phi_j(\theta)$. This function, which is but the marginal rate of substitution between the composite good $\phi_j(\theta)$ and safe future consumption, can be alternatively interpreted as the subjective marginal-certainty-equivalent of the composite $\phi_j(\theta)$.[g]

The first order conditions for an individual j maximizing his expected

[e]The results of the paper are insensitive to the particular form of taxation assumed here. However it is significant that the tax is imposed at the same rate on income from production and from loans, so that no distortions are introduced.

[f]We will ignore throughout the paper the possibility of default, i.e., of $c_j(\theta) < 0$.

[g]If the certainty equivalent π_{ij} is defined by $E_i u_i(c_i(\theta) + s\phi_j(\theta)) \equiv E_i u_i(c_i(\theta) + \pi_{ij}(s))$, then it is simple to show that $S_j^i = \pi_{ij}'(0)$.

utility, constrained by (16.1) and (16.2) and taking $\tau_j G(\theta)$ as given, can now be written as:

$$f_j'(y_j)S_j^j = 1 + r \qquad j = 1, \ldots, n \tag{16.4}$$

The condition (16.4) is assumed to define implicitly the investment level that will be adopted by farmer-investor j. This condition has a standard interpretation requiring the equation of the (subjective) value of the marginal product of the investment resource to its price (in terms of the alternative future consumption foregone.)[h]

Following Sandmo, public production is introduced to the farm model in a stylized way by assuming that the government can produce in the same risk classes as the private sector. That is, public firm k for inputs z_k would yield a future output of $g_k(z_k)\phi_k(\theta)$, the functions $g_k(z_k)$ satisfying the standard assumptions, $k = 1, \ldots, n$. Public investment is assumed to be financed by debt, through the central bank. The equilibrium riskless rate of return will be determined then so as to just exhaust the available investment resources; that is:

$$\sum_{j=1}^{n} y_j + \sum_{j=1}^{n} z_j = \sum_{j=1}^{n} w_j \tag{16.5}$$

16.2. The Social Optimum

Following Diamond's concept of a "constrained Pareto-optimum" we define the "social optimum" as the allocation of resources that a social planner maximizing social welfare would select, given the existing market structure. The planner has thus to choose optimal levels for private and public investments (y_j, z_j for $j = 1, \ldots, n$) and to select the return r so as to maximize social welfare, assumed here to be given by the individualistic function $\sum_{j=1}^{n} \lambda_j E_j u_j\ (c_j(\theta))$. For technical reasons of easing the exposition we furthermore assume that the government can redistribute initial resources in a lump-sum fashion (or alternatively that initial wealth is already optimally distributed). The constraints on the social planner are the resource constraint (16.5), the definition of individuals' consumption (16.2) and the definition of the government combined revenues:

$$G(\theta) = \sum_{j=1}^{n} g_j(z_j)\phi_j(\theta) + t\sum_{j=1}^{n} f_j(y_j)\phi_j(\theta) - (1 + r)(1 - t)\sum_{j=1}^{n} b_j - t\sum_{j=1}^{n} w_j \tag{16.6}$$

The assumption of the possibility of lump-sum initial wealth redistribution yields the first order condition:

[h]Alternatively, one can use risk-adjusted rates of return to express (16.4) as $f_j(y_j) = (1 + r)(S_j^j)^{-1}$. Sandmo uses that approach and interprets $(S_j^j)^{-1}$ as a "risk margin."

$$\lambda_j E_j u_j'(c_j(\theta)) = \nu \qquad j = 1, \ldots, n \tag{16.7}$$

With that condition, the other first order conditions, in addition to (16.5) become:

$$f_j'(y_j)[(1-t)S_j^j + t \sum_{i=1}^{n} \tau_i S_j^i] = 1 + \rho \qquad j = 1, \ldots, n \tag{16.8}$$

and

$$g_j'(z_j) \sum_{i=1}^{n} \tau_i S_j^i = 1 + \rho \qquad j = 1, \ldots, n \tag{16.9}$$

We assume that these first order conditions do indeed define the social optimum.

The shadow price $1 + \rho$ in conditions (16.8) and (16.9) measures the social value of present resources in the economy in terms of safe future consumption. Thus ρ can be considered as the social rate of discount. It is interesting to note here that if foreign borrowing and lending at a uniform rate r^* were open to the government, then the social discount rate ρ would be replaced in the conditions (16.8) and (16.9) by the international rate r^*.[i]

Conditions (16.8) and (16.9) provide the socially optimal rules for private and public investment. We now briefly examine the public investment rule (16.9) and show that it can be considered as a generalization of both the investment criteria proposed by Hirshleifer and by Arrow and Lind.

In analogy to the interpretation of S_j^j for the individual producer, the term $\sum_{i=1}^{n} \tau_i S_j^i$ can be interpreted as the "social valuation" of the composite good $\phi_j(\theta)$. Condition (16.9) will then require the equalization of the social value of marginal investment in each public firm to the social price of investment resources—the gross social rate of return. The social valuation of any composite good $\phi_j(\theta)$ is a weighted average of consumers' subjective valuations of that composite, the weights being their (marginal) shares in that composite good as received from the government.

If a stock market existed in which all individuals could costlessly trade shares in the stock of firm j, then we would obtain $S_j^i = S_j^j$ for all i. This result can be explained by noting that the market trading in the stock of firm j can be regarded as tantamount to direct trading in the composite good $\phi_j(\theta)$. Such trading equates all individuals' subjective valuations of this composite good to its (implicit) market price. The social valuation of the composite $\phi_j(\theta)$ would then be equal to the private subjective valuation. Following Diamond and Sandmo we then obtain that if the market rate of return r were to equal the social rate of

[i] In this case the resource constraint (16.5) would drop and the government's combined revenue in (16.6) would increase by $[1 + r^*]\,[\sum_{j=1}^{n} w_j - \sum_{j=1}^{n} y_j - \sum_{j=1}^{n} z_j]$.

discount ρ, the optimal rule for investment by the public firm j would be to imitate the investment rule of the private firm in that same risk class. This is exactly the investment rule advanced by Hirshleifer.

On the other hand, rule (16.9) also implies the Arrow-Lind recommendation that in the case of independent projects the government should be neutral towards risk, provided the population is large enough.[j] When a public project j is statistically independent from all other projects in the economy (in particular there is then no private project j in the same risk class), and when only a small share in it accrues to each individual, (assuming $\tau_i = 1/n$ for all i), the subjective valuations can be shown to be approximated by:[k]

$$S_j^i \cong E_i\phi_j(\theta) - \frac{1}{n}A\,(c_i(\theta))g_j(z_j)\,\mathrm{Var}_i\,\phi_j(\theta) \qquad i = 1, \ldots, n, (i \neq j) \qquad (16.10)$$

where

$$A_i(c_i(\theta)) = -\frac{E_i u_i''(c_i(\theta))}{E_i u_i'(c_i(\theta))} \qquad (16.11)$$

is a measure of risk aversion comparable to the Arrow-Pratt measure of absolute risk aversion. If n is large enough and if all assessments $E_i\phi_j(\theta)$ are the same, then in computing the social valuation of $\phi_j(\theta)$, we would get

[j]The fact that the Arrow-Lind argument is just a subcase of (16.9) was somehow overlooked by Sandmo (see p. 300).

[k]From the definition of S_j^i in (16.3), to verify (16.10), (16.11) we have to show that

$$E_i u_i'(c_i(\theta))\psi_j(\theta) \cong sE_i u_i''(c_i(\theta))\,\mathrm{Var}_i\phi_j(\theta),$$

where we denote here

$$\psi_j(\theta) = \phi_j(\theta) - E_i\phi_j(\theta),\ s = 1/ng_j(z_j).$$

For each state of nature θ we can approximate $u_i'(c_i(\theta))$ by a Taylor series around $s = 0$, i.e., around

$$\hat{c}_i(\theta) = c_i(\theta) - s\phi_j(\theta)\colon u_i'(c_i(\theta)) \cong u_i'(\hat{c}_i(\theta))$$
$$+ u_i''(\hat{c}_i(\theta))s\phi_j(\theta) + u_i'''[\hat{c}_i(\theta)]\,(s^2/2)\phi_j^2(\theta).$$

Substituting from the similar Taylor series approximation of $u_i''(c_i(\theta))$ we then have for each θ:

$$u_i'(c_i(\theta))\psi_j(\theta) \cong u_i'(\hat{c}_i(\theta))\psi_j(\theta) + u_i''(c_i(\theta))s\phi_j(\theta)\psi_j(\theta)$$
$$- u_i'''[\hat{c}_i(\theta)]\,(s^2/2)\phi_j^2(\theta)\psi_j(\theta).$$

Under conditions which permit taking the expectation of the last expression (in particular, if $\psi_j(\theta)$ is bounded), we then obtain our desired result. Here we have to use the independence of $\hat{c}_i(\theta)$ (and thus also of any function of it) from $\phi_j(\theta)$, and to use the smallness of s in order to neglect the last term which involves s^2.

$$\sum_{i=1}^{n} \tau_i S_j^i \cong E\phi_j(\theta)$$

Thus condition (16.9) for optimal public investment indeed reduces to the Arrow-Lind condition of risk neutrality in the case of independent projects.

For our purposes, however, the major interest lies not with the rule for public investment, but rather with the socially optimal rule for private investment given by (16.8).

16.3. The Case for Subsidization

The striking feature in the optimal rule for private investment (16.8) is the term $[(1-t)S_j^j + t \sum_{i=1}^{n} \tau_i S_j^i]$. That term represents the valuation of the composite good $\phi_j(\theta)$ which is required from a social point of view for optimal production by the private firm j.[1] This valuation is a weighted average of the private and social valuations of the composite; the weights are the shares in the private output accorded to each of the respective "partners" by the tax structure. Condition (16.8) thus formalizes the argument given in the introduction that the government's attitude towards risk should be taken into account in the determination of the private level of investment.

Defining now the "excess social value" of $\phi_j(\theta)$ as:

$$\eta_j = \frac{\sum_{i=1}^{n} \tau_i S_j^i}{S_j^j} - 1 \qquad , j = 1, \ldots, n \tag{16.12}$$

condition (16.8) for the optimal private investment can then be rewritten as:

$$f_j'(y_j) S_j^j [1 + t\eta_j] = 1 + \rho \qquad j = 1, \ldots, n \tag{16.13}$$

From condition (16.13) it is clear that if no taxation existed, provided that the market rate of return is properly set (i.e., $r = \rho$), the private investment rule (16.4) will be socially optimal. Thus the social optimum could be decentralized. In particular, no form of subsidization will then be necessary. This conclusion reaffirms the Arrow-Lind argument in the dispute with Hirshleifer over the need for subsidization. Similarly, if there existed costlessly operating markets trading in the shares of all firms, then, due to the arguments given above, the excess social values η_j of each and every firm would be zero. In that case, too, private production would be socially optimal.

---

[1]Note that if the tax rate were 100 percent, the optimal rule for the now-nationalized private firms would be the same as the rule (16.9) applicable for public firms.

However, when the capital markets are deficient as assumed here in the farm model, the excess social values are not likely to vanish. In this case when taxation exists, it is clear by comparison of (16.13) and (16.4) that decentralized private investment would not be socially optimal. The reason that the market forces would fail to obtain the social optimum is that taxation introduces an element of externality. Through the distribution of the tax revenue the tax collected from each private investor provides otherwise unavailable hedging to all other individuals. It is quite clear that investors are not likely to take into account this effect on others when making their own investment decision. Thus, some form of government intervention in private investment decisions will have to be employed in order to reach the "first best" social optimum feasible in the given market structure.

Among the various government actions possible to induce socially optimal private investment, we will consider here only the setting of differential rates of return. Indeed it is quite obvious that if the central bank were to set a rate r_j for the transactions of firm j where:

$$1 + r_j = [1 + \rho]\,[1 + t\eta_j]^{-1} \qquad j = 1, \ldots, n \tag{16.14}$$

then decentralized private investment would be optimal. Since for riskless firms the rate that would be set is ρ, we can think of that rate as the proper market rate of return.

To illustrate the use of the formula (16.14), as well as the general argument for subsidization, we return now to the example examined in the introduction. To that example, of the statistically independent alternative private and public projects, we now introduce a 50 percent tax rate.[m] In accordance with rule (16.8) the private project should then be evaluated using an average of the returns to the private investors and to the public at large. Since, due to the project's independence the latter return equals the expected return, the social return of the private project will be 1.075, an average of the 1.05 private risk-adjusted rate and the 1.1 expected rate. The private project will then be clearly superior to the public project whose social return is only 1.06. However, since the private entrepreneurs consider only the share of the project's benefits which accrues to themselves, they are not likely to undertake the project whose 5 percent net return to them falls short of the 6 percent return prevailing in the market. Thus, the government should subsidize the private project. According to (16.12) we can compute $\eta_j = (1.1/1.05) - 1 \cong 0.048$, and by (16.14): $1 + r_j = 1.06(1 + (1/2)(0.048))^{-1} \cong 1.035$. Hence if we assume that for the project size considered, the average return of the private project equals its marginal return, then formula (16.14) suggests that the government should

[m]The data of that example can be interpreted as providing: $(1/y)\, f_k(\bar{y})E\phi_k(\theta) = 1.1$; $(1/(y)f_k(\bar{y})S_k^k = 1.05$; $(1/y)\, g_k(\bar{y}) \sum_{i=1}^{n} \tau_i S_k^i \cong (1/\bar{y})\, g_k(\bar{y})E\phi_k(\theta) = 1.06$; $r = \rho = 1.06$.

encourage the private firm towards further investment by offering it loans at a subsidized rate of 3.5 percent.

In general, whether firm j will indeed face a subsidized rate of return for its borrowing (i.e., $r_j < \rho$) will depend on whether the excess social value of its output is positive. To analyze under what conditions the excess social value is positive we resort now to the use of a specific form of the subjective valuations, the form which would hold in mean variance analysis:[n]

$$S_j^i = E_i \phi_j(\theta) - A_i \operatorname{cov}_i(\phi_j(\theta), c_i(\theta)) \qquad i,j = 1, \ldots, n \tag{16.15}$$

where $A_i = A_i(c_i(\theta))$ was defined above in (16.11). If we further assume that all probability assessments are the same and that $\tau_i = 1/n$, $A_i = A$ for all i, we would get in the farm economy that:

$$S_j^j \eta_j = (1-t)A\,[f_j(y_j)\sigma_{jj} - \frac{1}{n}\sum_{i=1}^{n} f_i(y_i)\sigma_{ij}] \tag{16.16}$$

where $\sigma_{ij} = \operatorname{cov}(\phi_i(\theta), \phi_j(\theta))$. Thus if $\sigma_{ij} \leqslant 0$ for all $i \neq j$ we would clearly have $\eta_j > 0$, that is, for a firm uncorrelated or negatively correlated to the rest of the economy, excess social value would be positive. Moreover, from (16.16) it can be easily shown that the social value of the total private output exceeds the private evaluation of that output, i.e.:[o]

$$\sum_{j=1}^{n} f_j(y_j)[\sum_{i=1}^{n} \tau_i S_j^i - S_j^j] = \sum_{j=1}^{n} f_j(y_j) S_j^j \eta_j \geqslant 0 \tag{16.17}$$

This result indicates that in some sense most η_j have to be positive. Negative social value should be regarded as the exception. For the excess social value of a firm j to be negative, according to (16.16) the firm would have to be highly

[n]It is shown by Mayshar that the subjective valuation S_j^i will take the form of (16.15) if $u_i(c_i)$ is quadratic, if $c_i(\theta)$ and $\phi_j(\theta)$ are joint-normally distributed, or, as in (16.10) above, if $\phi_j(\theta)$ is only a small share in $c_i(\theta)$ and is independent of that remainder share of $c_j(\theta)$.

[o]By use of (16.16),

$$\sum_{j=1}^{n} f_j(y_j) S_j^j \eta_j = (1-t)A\,[\sum_{j=1}^{n} f_j^2(y_j)\sigma_{jj}$$

$$- (1/n)\sum_{j=1}^{n}\sum_{i=1}^{n} f_j(y_j) f_i(y_i)\sigma_{ij}] = (1-t)A \sum_{j=1}^{n} \operatorname{Var}[f_j(y_j)\phi_j(\theta)$$

$$- (1/n)\sum_{i=1}^{n} f_i(y_i)\phi_i(\theta)] \geqslant 0.$$

Given the structure of the farm model this term will be zero only if all firms were identical (and in particular in the same risk class) or if there were no aversion to risk in the economy, or if the tax rate were 100 percent.

correlated with most other firms, relatively inefficient (so that its "output" $f_j(y_j)$ would be relatively low) and also of a relatively low risk (i.e., a low σ_{jj}). The last consideration is due to the fact that the excess social value measures the divergence between social and private valuations, a divergence which is higher for private firms that are more risky and which therefore take larger risk margins than necessary from a social point of view.

The preceding analysis suggests that we should expect the social valuations to exceed the private valuations for most firms. That result would mean that for attainment of the social optimum most firms would have to face subsidized rates of return that are lower than the riskless rate.

16.4. Second Best

The subsidization of the rates of return in the private sector was seen in the preceding section to facilitate the decentralization of the social optimum—the "first best" given the market structure. We now briefly consider the implication of possible government inability or unwillingness to charge different rates of return to different private firms. In that case the social planner seeking a "second best" would have to select levels of public investments z_j and a market rate of return r so as to maximize the social welfare function, given the overall resource constraint (16.5) and the fact that levels of private investments are set privately according to (16.4).

The intuitive results of this second best problem should be quite clear—the government ought to set the market rate of return below the shadow price of resources in order to encourage private investments. The technical solution of the second best becomes rather messy since now we also have to take into account the effects of changes in the policy variables on private investments. To facilitate an easier exposition we thus assume once more that condition (16.7), which requires the equalization of the social value of marginal safe future consumption for all individuals, holds.

The first order condition with regard to the optimal selection of the market interest rate can then be written as:

$$\rho - r = (1+r)t\Big(\sum_{i=1}^{n} \frac{\partial y_i}{\partial r}\Big)^{-1} \sum_{i=1}^{n} \eta_i \frac{\partial y_i}{\partial r} \equiv (1+r)t\,\overline{\eta} \qquad (16.18)$$

where $\overline{\eta}$ is an average of the various measures of excess social values η_i. If the presumption that most η_i are positive is correct, then $\overline{\eta}$ will probably be positive. Thus the market rate of return in the second best will have to be lower than the social rate of return.[p] Using (16.18), the rule for optimal public investment will be:

[p]Also here, if the government were able to borrow and lend in the international loan market at a uniform rate r^*, then ρ would be replaced by r^*.

$$g_j'(z_j)\sum_{i=1}^{n}\tau_i S_j^i = (1+r)(1+t\overline{\eta}) + (1+r)t\overline{\eta}\sum_{i=1}^{n}\left(1-\frac{\eta_i}{\overline{\eta}}\right)\frac{\partial y_i}{\partial z_j}\quad j = 1,\ldots,n \qquad (16.19)$$

If we were to ignore the direct effects of public investment on private investments, the second best rule for public investment would indicate, on the one hand, use of the social valuation of output (generally higher than the private subjective valuation) as in the first best, and on the other hand, use of a safe rate of return equal to the social rate of return but higher than the market rate of return. In order to evaluate the net result of the two effects on possible divergence of the public and private rules for investment, we can rewrite (16.19) (ignoring the effects $(\partial y_i/(\partial z_j))$ as:

$$g_j'(z_j)S_j^j = (1+r)\left(1+\frac{t\overline{\eta}-\eta_j}{1+\eta_j}\right) \qquad j = 1,\ldots,n \qquad (16.20)$$

Thus in all risk classes with excess social value higher than the average multiplied by the tax rate, the public rule for investment requires higher investment than would have been undertaken had the comparable private criteria for investment been adopted.

16.5. The Role of Taxation

The reader may wonder why the tax rate was not considered as one of the endogenous variables in the determination of the social optimum. If we indeed maximize social welfare with respect to the income tax rate t, the first order condition which results requires (assuming that (16.7) holds) the equalization of the social and private valuations of the total output of the private sector. Under the simplifying assumptions which led to equation (16.17) above, this condition will necessitate a 100 percent tax rate, that is, the nationalization of the entire private sector! Examination of this perplexing result will help to clarify the particular role of taxation in the farm model and the argument for subsidization.

The tax system in the farm economy does not provide any disincentives for efficient private investment and production. This characteristic of the model clarifies why a very high tax rate might be considered feasible; however, it does not explain why a high tax rate might be deemed desirable. To explain this result the exact nature of the income tax in the model must be examined. That tax system is basically a scheme of a negative income tax. It may alternatively be characterized as a form of mutual insurance[q] since every individual is required to pay a share of his risky profits into a common pool from which he then receives

[q]Unlike the standard forms of insurance, in the present case of income taxation "premiums" are paid only *after* the state of nature is revealed.

a share of the total sum collected. Since we assumed the absence of capital markets, this tax-insurance mechanism is the only means by which individuals in the farm model can obtain some hedge for their own risky enterprises. In the absence of any efficiency disincentives it is thus quite plausible that under some homogeneity conditions a full coverage, that is, a 100 percent tax rate, will be socially desirable.

When the capital markets are perfect, it is quite clear that the insurance element in the tax scheme provides no improvement of the market's allocative mechanism. Indeed, in this case it can be shown that if initial lump-sum redistribution of resources were possible, the social optimum could be reached without the use of the now superfluous system of income taxation. In fact, however, capital markets, even in the developed Western economies are not perfect. (In particular, insurance markets for future wage income are seriously deficient.) In this case our analysis indicated that the income tax structure can be thought of as providing some form of insurance. It is this aspect of insurance in the tax system which also creates the externality effect referred to above—one investor's taxed profits provide hedging for others.

Domar and Musgrave (and more recently Joseph Stiglitz and several others) have argued that income taxation is likely to lead by itself to increased private risk-taking.[r] Our analysis indicates that even where this result holds, when capital markets are imperfect, private risky investment should in general be further encouraged, because of its positive external insurance effects. It should be emphasized that the above general argument—that income taxation provides a form of insurance and introduces an externality—does not require many of the assumptions that were made in the analysis for expositional purposes. In particular, the assumptions that lump-sum initial redistribution is possible, that the whole tax revenue is returned to the public, or that it is returned according to preassigned shares, can be significantly relaxed.

16.6. Conclusion

In the preceding analysis we have presented a case for the subsidization of risky private projects. This case was based on two key assumptions which hold in most countries: the existence of an operative income tax system and the incompleteness of the capital market structure. It is common knowledge that in reality a general practice of subsidization may create serious distortions and lead to abuse of public funds. (For a detailed empirical analysis of the practice of subsidization and its distortionary effects on firms which adopt "subsidy maximizing"

[r]The above result on the equivalence of income taxation (with revenue redistribution) to initial lump-sum redistribution when capital markets are perfect indicates that one should not expect any general increase in risk-taking in this case. This conclusion points out a limitation of the partial equilibrium approach adopted by Domar and Musgrave (and Stiglitz) which ignores the use of the collected tax revenues.

policies, see N. Finger.) However, if considered as an alternative to direct public investment with its own known inefficiencies, subsidization of private projects may prove nevertheless to be the preferred practice.

References

Arrow, K.J., and R.C. Lind, "Uncertainty and the Evaluation of Public Investment Decisions," *American Economic Review*, 60 (June 1970):364-378.

Bailey, M.J., and M.C. Jensen, "Risk and the Discount Rate for Public Investment," in M.C. Jensen (ed.) *Studies in the Theory of Capital Markets*, New York: Praeger 1972.

Diamond, P.A., "The Role of a Stock Market in a General Equilibrium Model with Technological Uncertainty," *American Economic Review*, 56 (Sept. 1967):759-776.

Domar, E.D., and R.A. Musgrave, "Proportional Taxation and Risk Taking," *Quarterly Journal of Economics*, 58 (1944):387-422.

Finger, N., *The Impact of Government Subsidies on Industrial Management: The Israeli Experience*, New York: Praeger 1971.

Hirshleifer, J., "Investment Decision Under Uncertainty: Applications of the State-Preference Approach," *Quarterly Journal of Economics*, 60 (May 1966):252-277.

Mayshar, J., "Mean Variance Analysis: A Positive Approach," unpublished, Hebrew University, Jerusalem, 1975.

Sandmo, A., "Discount Rates for Public Investment Under Uncertainty," *International Economic Review*, 13 (June 1972):287-302.

Stiglitz, J.E., "The Effects of Income, Wealth and Capital Gains Taxation on Risk Taking," *Quarterly Journal of Economics*, 63 (May 1969):263-283.

17 Contracting for Optimal Delivery Time in Long-Term Projects

Alex Cukierman and
Zalman F. Shiffer

17.1. Introduction

A substantial part of investment activity consists of projects which are executed to order over prolonged periods of time. For the execution of such projects the buyer and the seller set up a contract which specifies among various other conditions the delivery date of the complete project (and sometimes its interim stages as well) and the amounts, timing, and conditions of payment. Such methods of contracting are quite common in long-term investments in public utilities (such as power plants), and the construction of ships, planes, roads, bridges, and other private and public goods whose production process is spread over long periods of time. Provided the producer's costs and the buyer's benefits from the project reflect, respectively, costs and benefits to society, there is a well-defined socially optimal delivery time which depends only on these costs and benefits and on the social rate of discount.

However, the "best" delivery time from the point of view of the producer depends on the relation between the stream of payments he receives and the stream of costs that he incurs. This can create a divergence between the socially optimal completion time and the one that is optimal from the contractor's point of view even under the assumption that the two parties' rates of discount equal the social one. Even in cases in which there are penalties for delayed delivery, the delivery dates preferred by the seller may be different from the socially optimal one. Moreover, when payments are tied to specific stages of production, as is the case in many long-term projects, the contractor does not necessarily choose a production plan that minimizes the present value of costs for any given delivery time, and thus creates an additional social waste.

Among the efforts to analyze the behavioral implications of the type of contracting between buyer and seller is Zarnovitz (1962), who determines the optimal price and delivery period when a single seller is faced by a demand that depends on both price and delivery period.[a] McCall (1970) discusses the effects

 Partial financial support from the Foerder Institute for Economic Research is gratefully acknowledged. We are indebted to the editor of the *Bell Journal of Economics*, to Tsvi Ophir, and to an anonymous referee for helpful comments. Thanks are also due to Ellie Kirschner and Uriel Procaccia for legal advice. Any remaining errors are, however, our sole responsibility.

[a]However, Zarnowitz does not deal with the incentive effect of the payment schedule on the contractor's preferred delivery time explicitly.

of various types of contracts with respect to the allocation of losses as a result of misestimation of costs. The problem of the length of production is also analyzed by Carlson (1973), who tries to measure it empirically and ascertain some of the factors influencing it. However, to the best of our knowledge, no attempt has been made to analyze the effects of payment structures on the length of the production process chosen by the contractor as well as on its relation to the socially optimal completion time.

Within the context of a bilateral monopoly, it is shown in section 17.2 that if the parties to a long-term contract maximize the sum of their benefits, they will agree on the socially optimal delivery time as the contract delivery time. The relative bargaining power will determine only the present value of payments from buyer to seller. Some evidence on the types of payment schedules which arise in actual contracts in various industries is presented and discussed.

Analysis of frequently used patterns of payment in section 17.3, however, suggests that payment schedules usually create an incentive for the contractor to stretch the period of completion beyond the socially optimal one and may lead him to a nonoptimal choice of cost structure, if payments are tied to work progress.

In section 17.4 some patterns of payments which do not create a divergence between the contractor's optimal delivery time and the socially optimal delivery time are proposed and their relative merits are discussed. This is done in a framework in which the possibility of a suboptimal choice of costs by the contractor does not manifest itself.

Section 17.5 addresses itself to this last problem, which arises when payments are tied to interim work progress. A method that eliminates incentives to produce at more than minimal discounted costs for any given delivery period, while preserving the tying of payments to the stages of production and resulting in an optimal delivery period, is suggested. The problem is analyzed under both the assumption that the buyer benefits only from the completed project and the alternative assumption that he may benefit from intermediate stages of production as well.

Finally, the effects of inflation on completion time are discussed in section 17.6. It is shown that the socially optimal delivery time is not affected by inflation and some modifications in the optimal structures of payments for inflationary conditions are suggested. As will be evident, the same type of analysis applies to a private buyer as well as to buyers who are public agencies—though in this last case there is a presumption that valuations reflect the social benefits of the project, in which event the suggested patterns of payments may be regarded as a regulation that assures a socially optimal time of delivery.

17.2. The Socially Optimal Completion Time and Commonly Used Payment Schedules

When contracting for the delivery of a long-term project, the benefits to the buyer often accrue from the delivery day and on, while the benefits to the contractor are usually dispersed over the project's execution period, depending on the agreed upon time-table of payments.[b] Often, at least, part of these payments are payable only on the completion of some specified stages of production. Such payment schedules are the common practice in many projects that are produced to order over a substantial period of time with outlays that are expanded gradually over that period.

There is ample evidence to the effect that distributed payment schedules are common practice, especially in construction contracts. Some of the factors that encourage the use of such schedules as well as empirical evidence that they occur are discussed at the end of this section. At this point we shall turn to the more formal discussion.

Formal Determination of the Optimal Delivery Time

The effects of distributed payment schedules will be analyzed within the context of a bilateral monopoly, since this market structure seems to be a good approximation of reality in specialized long-term investments in some public construction projects as well as in some branches of manufacturing.[c] As will become clear later (at the end of section 17.3) some aspects of the argument will generalize to situations of competitive bidding.

Let A stand for the given monetary value of the completed project to the buyer at completion date. The present value of this project at the time of contracting is:[d]

$$Z(T) = Ae^{-rT}, \tag{17.1}$$

where T is completion time and r the (continuous) rate of return that the buyer gets on his investments. For simplicity of exposition, assume that the buyer's and seller's marginal internal rates of return are equal and that their common value equals the social rate of return.

Let V be the present value of net payments from the buyer to the contractor. V depends on the rate of discount used and on the size and timing of

---

[b] There are, of course, cases in which some benefits to the buyer occur when some of the intermediary stages of production are completed. To keep the argument simple, we shall concentrate on the case in which all the project has to be completed if the buyer is to derive any benefit from it. The case in which benefits are derived when intermediary stages are completed is investigated as well in section 17.5.

[c] Elements of bilateral monopoly are present within the American manufacturing sector. See Fellner (1965, p. 20, footnote 1). The construction of highways and bridges in Israel displays bilateral monopoly features as well. This is also the case in some government contracts to producers of specialized armaments.

[d] We assume A to be constant for simplicity. However, the argument generalizes easily to the case in which $Z(T) = Ae^{(-r+g)T}$, where g represents the combined effect of growing valuations of project services and obsolescence. See also note aa.

net payments. Both the size and timing of payments may be predetermined or depend on work progress (for example, when there is a concluding payment on delivery or a penalty clause). We shall emphasize the dependence of V on the delivery date T by referring to the function as $V(T, \ldots)$, bearing in mind that it depends on other factors as well. The buyer's target is to maximize the present value of his net benefits which is represented by the expression:

$$\Pi_b = Z(T) - V(T, \ldots). \tag{17.2}$$

The contractor, on the other hand, wishes to maximize the difference between $V(T, \ldots)$ and the present value of his costs of production. We shall assume that it is possible to execute the project at various speeds. The discounted value of the contractor's costs depends on the rate of discount, the techniques, speed and work sequence chosen, and the termination date. Let $X(T)$ be the minimal discounted value of costs of a production plan with delivery date T. Then the contractor wishes to maximize[e]

$$\Pi_c = V(T, \ldots) - X(T). \tag{17.3}$$

While there is a natural conflict of interest between the parties regarding the distribution of the net gain, economic rationality should lead them to the adoption of a delivery date for which the sum of their profits ($\Pi_b + \Pi_c$) is maximized. In other words, they should agree on an optimal delivery date for which $Z(T) - X(T)$ is maximized. The conflict of interests will express itself only in the allocation of this sum between the parties.

The optimal solution is presented graphically as T_s in figure 17-1. It is easy to ascertain that when there is an internal solution[f] the following first-order condition will hold at T_s : $\frac{dZ}{dT}(T_s) = \frac{dX}{dT}(T_s)$. This result is not surprising. Indeed, we can look at it as an application of the standard result of bilateral monopoly (see, for example, Fellner (1965), pp. 245-247). The result of that analysis is that output will be uniquely determined at the joint profit maximization level and that price will merely serve to allocate profit between the parties. Inasmuch as "output" is given in our analysis, delivery *time* is set to maximize joint profits and the relative bargaining powers express themselves through the present value of payments, V.[1]

One can look at the same problem from a different angle. Suppose that the functions $Z(T)$ and $X(T)$ reflect, respectively, the project's true present value of benefits and costs to society. Then society wants to maximize

---

[e]There may be situations in which the contractor's profits are maximized if a production plan that does not minimize costs is chosen. This problem is taken up separately in Scheme C of section 17.3 and note s.

[f]Without limiting the generality we assume that all functions are twice differentiable. An internal solution means also that there is at least a range of T in which $\frac{dX}{dT} < 0$.

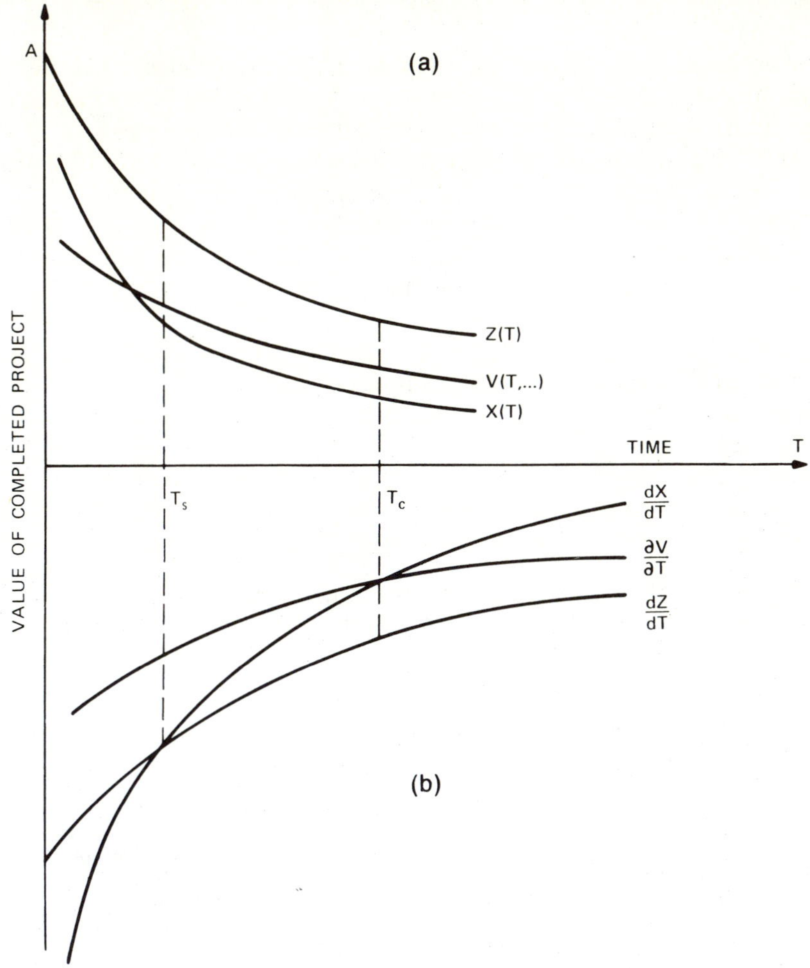

Figure 17-1. The Socially Optimal and the Contractor's Best Delivery Time.

$$G = Z(T) - X(T) = \text{II}_b + \text{II}_c, \tag{17.4}$$

which implies that the socially optimal completion time, T_s, will be determined by the first-order condition $\frac{dZ}{dT} = \frac{dX}{dT}$ independently of the V function. Moreover, it is the same completion time that rational economic agents will settle on. From the social point of view, the V function is not important; it is only a device for transferring income between the two sides, without affecting total social welfare as long as $T = T_s$. For the two parties, on the other hand, it is quite important, but if they act so as to maximize the sum of their gains, they will settle T at T_s

and let their conflict of interests determine only the allocation of benefits between themselves.

Note that the arguments do not depend on the interpretation of the interest rate as a market rate or as a marginal internal rate of return. In the first case *r* should be interpreted as the market rate of interest, which also equals the social rate of discount,[g] while in the second case it is the buyer's and seller's common marginal internal rate of return, which by assumption equals the social rate of discount.[h] To put it differently, the socially optimal delivery time depends only on the structure of costs and benefits of the project and the numerical value, but not the interpretation, of the discount rate *r*.

Commonly Used Payment Schedules–Discussion and Empirical Evidence

Evidence from various countries and industries suggests that distributed payment schedules are common practice. For example, Gill (1969, p. 233) summarizes the British experience in these words:

> The large expenditures which builders and contractors have to incur . . . render it usual to make provision in the contract for payments on account of the price during construction of the works. . . . Sometimes the several installments become due upon the attainment of particular stages of the work. . . . Sometimes there may be an implied stipulation on the part of the employer to pay from time to time reasonable installments of the whole cost to the contractor during the progress of work.

Similar arrangements are also common in the United States (including government contracts).[2] The American Jurisprudence volume on Building and Construction Contracts (1964, p. 18) states: "Building or construction contracts frequently provide for partial payments to be made to the contractor as the work progresses either periodically or upon the completion of specified stages of the work."

Distributed payment schedules may arise because of the risks each side to the contract takes when it "pays" today in money or kind to the other for

[g]This is based on the notion that the capital market is perfectly competitive and that there are no externalities. Under those circumstances economic rationality implies that both the buyer and the seller will undertake projects up to the point at which their internal rates of return equal the market rate, which in turn equals the social rate of discount in the absence of externalities. The presence of externalities will change this result; however, its investigation lies beyond the scope of our analysis.

[h]If the marginal internal rates of return differ from the social rate of discount in the presence of imperfect capital markets, a well-known diseconomy is imposed on society. The assumption in the text is made for analytical convenience, since we wish to focus the discussion on an additional diseconomy which is present even when the private and the social rates of return are equal.

something to be delivered in the future. The buyer, for instance, is uncertain prior to delivery about the ability and willingness of the seller to deliver the completed project with strict observance of all specifications.[3] In such cases the buyer obviously has a better protection if he still did not pay the total price of the project. Even with perfect capital markets, symmetric considerations on the part of the seller with respect to the buyer's solvency will motivate the seller to require the buyer to pay him at least for part of the project prior to delivery. This is particularly true when the project is tailor-made to the buyer. It could be argued that those risks could be shifted to professional risk-bearing agents. However, where the buyer and the seller are fairly specialized, they may be better equipped to evaluate the risks of contract nonfulfillment by either of them than professional risk-bearing agents. In such situations the cost of shifting these risks to professional risk-bearing agents could be prohibitive. Distributed payment structures which depend on the stages of production alleviate some of those risks for both sides to the contract. In many cases they may also save the parties the costly recourse to legal action.

A related factor contributing to distributed payment schemes is that a distributed payment schedule sometimes provides the needed financing to the seller. This factor is particularly important when the cost of the project is substantial. The existence of such distributed payment schemes creates a structure of incentives that has a substantial influence on the final delivery period chosen by the contractor. If such payment schedules are devised mainly with considerations different from the delivery period in mind, the final delivery period may be different from both the socially optimal delivery period and the delivery period specified in the contract.[i]

17.3. The Effects of Commonly Used Payment Schedules on the Contractor's Delivery Time

The Socially Optimal Delivery Time and the Contractor's Delivery Time

We have shown that there is no *a priori* ground for disagreement about the optimal delivery time. In practice, however, the actual delivery time often differs from the agreed one. This may, of course, result from unexpected changes in circumstances or from miscalculations. We shall assume out this kind of explanation and concentrate on the case in which the contractor may have an incentive to depart from the joint optimal delivery time once the contract is concluded.

---

[i]It is true that nonfulfillment penalties exist in many contracts and are addressed to this question. However, the incentive properties of such fines in combination with the distributed payment schemes will not, in general, achieve the desired period unless specifically designed to do so.

The problem is the following: any contract implies (even if implicitly) a structure of payments not only for the agreed upon production schedule, but also for different schedules.[j] In many cases the contractor may find that he can increase *his* discounted profits by not abiding to the contracted time schedule.[k] Moreover, he may also find it profitable to choose a production plan that does not involve least cost techniques (see Scheme C, below). Both kinds of behavior create social waste.

In this subsection we shall address ourselves only to the influence of $V(T)$ on delivery time under the assumption that, for every T, least cost techniques are employed. Under this assumption it can be shown that if the decrease of the present value of the finished project to the buyer, as a result of postponement of delivery, exceeds the decrease in the present value of the payments to the contractor, at every completion time, the contractor's optimal delivery time will be larger than the socially optimal one. Formally, if

$$\frac{\partial V}{\partial T} > \frac{dZ}{dT} \text{ at every } T, \tag{17.5}$$

the contractor will have an incentive to stretch completion beyond the agreed upon socially optimal time. This can be seen by reference to figure 17.1b, in which the marginal changes in Z, V and X, as a result of a marginal change in T, are plotted as functions of delivery time T.[l] The social optimum, T_s, occurs in the figure at the point at which $\frac{dX}{dT} = \frac{dZ}{dT}$. Since (17.5) holds for every T, the curve $\frac{\partial V}{\partial T}$ is above the curve $\frac{dZ}{dT}$ and consequently cuts the curve $\frac{dX}{dT}$ at a larger delivery period than T_s.

Thus, the contractor will necessarily prefer a delivery time, T_c, higher than the socially optimal one.[m]. The same result in terms of total conditions is shown in figure 17.1a.[n] If the slope of $V(T)$ exceeds that of $Z(T)$, $V(T) - X(T)$ will be maximized at T_c, which exceeds T_s.

---

[j]This property holds independently of the possibility of a contingent claims contract in which delivery may depend on what events transpire (a possibility that we rule out).

[k]We assume that the seller neglects the possible effects of such a strategy on his reputation and future earning power and believes that there is a range of deviations from the contracted delivery time for which the buyer will find it unprofitable to go to court. See also note t.

[l]Since all present values decrease when delivery time increases, their curves are plotted in the negative quadrant.

[m]Note that even if there is a multiplicity of global social optima, the contractor will necessarily delay delivery beyond all of them if condition (17.5) is fulfilled.

[n]The second-order conditions for a maximum of Π_c and G are $\frac{\partial^2 V}{\partial T^2} - \frac{d^2 X}{dT^2} < 0$ and $\frac{d^2 Z}{dT^2} - \frac{d^2 X}{dT^2} < 0$, respectively. They imply that the marginal curves $\frac{\partial V}{\partial T}$ and $\frac{dZ}{dT}$ cut the marginal curve $\frac{dX}{dT}$ from above as in figure 17.1b. Note that the textual argument does not depend on the well-behaved form of the X and V functions in figure 17.1 (while the form of the Z function follows necessarily from our assumptions).

The object of the penalty schemes discussed in section 17.4 will be to get $\frac{\partial V}{\partial T} = \frac{dZ}{dT}$.

Incentive Deficiencies of Commonly Used Payment Schedules

We turn now to the investigation of three commonly used payment schemes. It will be shown that under two of these schemes there is an obvious incentive for the contractor to delay delivery beyond T_s. This could also be the result of adopting the third scheme, which, in addition, may result in a suboptimal choice of cost structure.

Scheme A. Under this scheme all payments are executed at predetermined dates independently of the project's progress.[o] As the magnitude and timing of all payments is given, so is their present value. In other words $\frac{\partial V}{\partial T} = 0$ and obviously $\frac{\partial V}{\partial T} > \frac{dZ}{dT}$ for all T. As was shown above, this will result in a choice of T_c higher than T_s.[p]

Scheme B. Under this scheme the payment of at least a part of the agreed upon price is delayed until the project is delivered (the rest being payable at predetermined dates). We then have

$$\frac{\partial V}{\partial T} = -rP_T e^{-rT}, \tag{17.6}$$

where P_T is the payment executed upon delivery of the project.

Provided the project is viable from the point of view of the buyer, we certainly have $A > P_T$. Hence, $\frac{\partial V}{\partial T} > \frac{dZ}{dT} = -rAe^{-rT}$, and the contractor's delivery time again exceeds the socially optimal one.

Scheme C. Consider now an arrangement under which payments at any point of time depend on work progress up to that point (for example, the proportion of payments disbursed may be equal to the proportion of total outlays incurred by the contractor, or payments may be disbursed upon the accomplishment of definite stages).[q] In this case we shall also have $\frac{\partial V}{\partial T} > \frac{dZ}{dT}$ provided two assumptions hold:

[o]There may be one payment (for example, when the contract is signed) or several payments.

[p]As a variation of Scheme A (and also of B and C) there are sometimes penalty clauses for delaying delivery beyond agreed termination time. We do not wish to investigate at this stage such fine schemes, many of which are not optimal. However, we deal with this point in section 17.4.

[q]See section 17.2 for a discussion of contracts which are based on such schemes.

(a) When the delivery date is delayed by a certain length of time ΔT, the progress of no part of the project is delayed by more than ΔT.[r]
(b) $Z \geqslant V$, i.e., the project is viable.

Assumption (a) means that as a consequence of delaying delivery by ΔT the proportional decrease in V will be smaller than or equal to that of Z. Let the present value of payments when delivery time is T be $V(T)$. If each of the payments is delayed exactly by ΔT we shall have $V(T + \Delta T) = e^{-r\Delta T} V(T)$. As some of the payments may be delayed less than that,

$$\frac{V(T + \Delta T)}{V(T)} \geqslant e^{-r\Delta T}. \tag{17.7}$$

Now, when delaying delivery by ΔT, the proportional decrease of Z is exactly:

$$\frac{Z(T + \Delta T)}{Z(T)} = \frac{Ae^{-r(T+\Delta T)}}{Ae^{-rT}} = e^{-r\Delta T}. \tag{17.8}$$

From (17.7) and (17.8) it follows

$$\frac{V(T + \Delta T) - V(T)}{V(T)\Delta T} > \frac{Z(T + \Delta T) - Z(T)}{Z(T)\Delta T}. \tag{17.9}$$

Taking limits as $\Delta T \rightarrow 0$ and noting that $\frac{dZ}{dT}$ is negative, we get

$$\frac{\partial V}{\partial T} \bigg/ \frac{dZ}{dT} \leqslant \frac{V}{Z}. \tag{17.10}$$

It follows from (17.10) and assumption (b) that the present value of payments decreases more slowly than the present value of benefits to the buyer. Thus, a payment schedule that is tied to the stages of production will create an incentive for the contractor to delay delivery beyond the social optimum provided an increase in delivery time does not delay any payment by more than the delay in delivery time.

This scheme has an additional undesirable property which is absent in Schemes A and B. Under those schemes the V function does not depend on intermediate stages of production. Consequently, the contractor maximizes his

[r]We do not restrict ourselves to the condition that no physical part of the project is delayed by more than ΔT, but only to the condition that no proportion of "progress" as defined for the sake of payments is delayed by more than ΔT.

profits for any termination date he chooses by selecting production techniques that minimize the present value of his production costs. In Scheme C, however, the contractor can influence the V function by changing the dates of termination of specific production stages. Hence, he may be able to maximize his profits for certain ranges of delivery dates by a choice of techniques that do not minimize his discounted costs of production. As a result, both the producer's optimal delivery time will change and he will not necessarily deliver the finished product at the minimal discounted costs, for that delivery period, any longer.[s] Thus, an extra burden is imposed on society, since delivery is not necessarily made with the minimal possible costs.

To sum up, the cause for the divergence between the contractor's and the socially optimal delivery time in all three payment schedules is the fact that the cost incurred by the contractor when he changes the delivery date or the production plan differs from the social cost. Not all payment schedules will necessarily make the contractor's optimal delivery time larger than the socially optimal one. However, unless the payment schedule is devised in a way specifically designed to unify the social and the contractor's optimal delivery time, the two will usually diverge.

It should be emphasized that the adverse effects of a defective payment scheme do not depend on the bilateral monopoly assumption. Assume that the buyer solicits a significant number of proposals from qualified, competing contractors. Although the one who gets the contract will earn only competitive returns, this fact does not destroy his incentive to take advantage of the defective features of the payment scheme once the negotiations are completed.

[s]To illustrate such a situation, consider the case where there are two payments in the contract; one on completion of I percent of the project and the rest on final delivery. Let the first payment be a proportion α of the total undiscounted price P. Let total discounted costs, $\hat{X}$, for any final completion time T depend on the timing t_I of completion of the first I percent of the project. If total discounted costs are minimized for any given I, the intermediate completion time t_I will be determined from the conditions $\frac{\partial \hat{X}}{\partial t_I}(t_I,T) = 0$, $\frac{\partial^2 \hat{X}}{\partial t_I^2} > 0$. However, the contractor determines t_I for any given T with the aim of maximizing his discounted profits, namely

$$\max_{\{t_I\}} \Pi_c = P[\alpha e^{-rt_I} + (1-\alpha)e^{-rT}] - \hat{X}(t_I, T),$$

from which we get the first-order condition $-r\alpha Pe^{-rt_I} = \frac{\partial \hat{X}}{\partial t_I}(t_I,T)$, which implicitly determines t_I for a given T. Hence the necessary condition for cost minimization is not fulfilled and the producer does not deliver at T with the minimum value of discounted costs. Moreover, since $\frac{\partial \hat{X}}{\partial t_I}$ equals a negative number instead of being equal to 0, it follows from the second-order condition for cost minimization that he will complete the first I percent of the project too early. Note that this distortion does not exist when there are no payments which are tied to the stages of production since the partial derivative of V with respect to t_I is 0 in this case.

More generally, whatever the delivery date agreed upon in the contract (whether it is the bilateral monopoly delivery date or any other delivery date) the payment schedule will almost always create a divergence between the contractor's delivery time and both the contract and the socially optimal delivery time unless a suitable incentive structure is built into the contract.

17.4. Optimal Payments and Fines Schedules

The previous discussion brings forward the following question: Is it possible to construct practical payment arrangements which will eliminate the contractor's incentives to adopt a socially suboptimal production plan?[t] In what follows we shall address ourselves to this question under increasingly general conditions. (Throughout the present section we shall assume that least cost techniques obtain and deal only with the determination of the delivery period.)

Fines and Premiums

Assume first that the sole requirement of the payment schedule is to ensure that the contractor delivers at the socially optimal time T_s. A sufficient condition for getting this result is to have $\frac{\partial V}{\partial T}$ equal $\frac{dZ}{dT}$ for all T. This could be achieved by the following method.

Method 1. Payments are executed at predetermined dates independently of the progress of the project, but the contractor pays the buyer a fine equal to rA over all the life of the project for as long as he does not deliver.

Hence the present value of payments to the buyer in this case will be

$$V(T) = \overline{B} - rA \int_0^T e^{-rt}dt, \tag{17.11}$$

where $\overline{B}$ is the present value of the buyer's payments to the seller which is independent of delivery time. Differentiating (17.11) and (17.1) with respect to T and comparing, we obtain:

$$\frac{\partial V}{\partial T} = -rAe^{-rT} = \frac{dZ}{dT}. \tag{17.12}$$

[t]The buyer may, of course, have recourse to legal action in such a case, but he can hardly count on getting costlessly the "correct" compensation for such noncompliance. Besides, from the social point of view it is important to get the optimal delivery time (rather than have *ex post* the right compensation to the buyer). The best way to assure this result is to build into the contract the right incentives for the seller.

Thus, this structure of fines transfers the exact amount of the loss from waiting for both the buyer and society to the seller. In terms of figure 17-1a, $V(T, \ldots)$ is parallel to $Z(T)$. In marginal terms $\frac{\partial V}{\partial T}$ for Method 1 is identical to $\frac{dZ}{dT}$ in figure 17-1b. This method is simple and has the advantage that the contractor will deliver at the socially optimal time, even if for some reason it differs from the agreed upon delivery time. Also, when the buyer is looking for a contractor through a tender, he can save on his searching costs by demanding this fine schedule as a prerequisite and by letting the bidders compete on the level of $\bar{B}$.

Contractors may object to such a method on the grounds that they should not pay fines for nondelivery before the delivery date agreed upon in the contract. This should be easily solvable by an appropriate increase in the present value of payments from buyer to seller. An alternative way around this somewhat artificial difficulty is to let the buyer pay the seller a premium of rA per unit of time in case of early delivery for all the time period between the early delivery and the delivery date specified in the contract. This variant of the method also assures that the curves $\frac{\partial V}{\partial T}$ and $\frac{dZ}{dT}$ in figure 17-1b become identical, thus assuring $T_s = T_c$. However, rather than imposing fines, it gives premiums for early delivery and leaves the incentive properties unaltered.

This method (in its two variants) is also appropriate for regulatory agencies which would like to assure a socially optimal time of completion in long-term projects without having to determine what the costs are in each case. Again, all they need to introduce, either as a regulation or as a recommendation, is project-long fines or a combination of fines and premiums to the seller; other payments by the buyer will be independent of delivery time.

If the buyer wants to condition his final payment on delivery of the project, method 1 can be modified as follows.[u]

Method 2. All payments except the last are made at preagreed dates independently of the project's progress. The last payment is made only on delivery. The seller pays over the project's duration a fine equal to the rate of interest on the *difference* between the delivery value of the project to the buyer and the last payment to the seller. This method assures again full internalization of delays by the seller. The fine at every moment is $r(A - B)$, where B is the sum to be paid on delivery. As a result, the present value of payments to the contractor is

$$V = B_0 + Be^{-rT} - r(A - B) \int_0^T e^{-rt} dt, \qquad (17.13)$$

[u]The discussion of section 17.2 implies that in some cases the most efficient insurer of the hazards associated in dealing with the seller from the buyer's point of view is the buyer himself. A possible insurance from the buyer's point of view is in abstaining from paying the total price previous to actual delivery. Method 2 allows this while preserving the desirable features of Method 1.

where B_0 is the present value of the payments which are independent from delivery time. Differentiating (17.13) with respect to T, it is easily seen that $\frac{\partial V}{\partial T} = -rAe^{-rt} = \frac{dZ}{dT}$. In terms of figure 17-1b, the curves $\frac{\partial V}{\partial T}$ and $\frac{dZ}{dT}$ are again identical. This gives the contractor an incentive to deliver at the social optimum.[v]

In reality, contracts are sometimes made with penalties for delays and on occasions with premiums for early delivery. However, those fines and premiums are in many instances discontinuous functions of delivery time. For example, premiums for early delivery are sometimes lump sums which do not take into account how early the delivery is. Such discontinuities clearly create divergences between the contractor's and the socially optimal delivery time. However, even in those cases in which the penalty schedule is continuous and built to reflect actual losses of delays to the buyer, it will not necessarily give the right solution for the delivery time, if some of the payments depend on the delivery date, or, more generally, on work progress.[w] This point is often overlooked, even in those contracts which have the "right" fine schedule.

17.5. Optimal Payments Schedules When the Cost Structure Depends on the Timing of Payments and When Some Benefits Are Derived Before Final Completion

It has been assumed in section 17.4 that, given the planned completion period, the producer will always choose the pattern of production that will minimize total discounted costs for that completion period, independently of the pattern of payments. This assumption certainly holds if payments, except the final one, do not depend on the stages of production, because if the producer is a profit maximizer, he will try to minimize discounted costs for any given planned production period.[x] However, when payments are tied to the progress of the project, as in Scheme C of section 17.3, we see that the producer will not necessarily produce at minimal discounted costs. On the other hand, we know that the tying of payments to work progress fulfills the important social task of

[v]For $B = 0$ we get the fixed over time payment schedule as a particular case.

[w]Formally, if the change in the present value of gross payments from the buyer to the contractor when T increases is $\frac{\partial H}{\partial T}$ and the change in the present value of fines paid by the contractor is $\frac{dF}{dT}$, we have $\frac{\partial V}{\partial T} = \frac{\partial H}{\partial T} - \frac{dF}{dT}$, and unless $\frac{\partial H}{\partial T} = 0$, an equality of $\frac{dF}{dT}$ and $\frac{dZ}{dT}$ will result in a divergence between T_e and T_s. If, in addition, it depends on the work progress, we are still left with the possibility of a nonoptimal choice of cost structure.

[x]It may, of course, hold also because of technological or organizational constraints to which the contractor is subject.

minimizing certain risks (discussed in section 17.2). This stage of affairs begs the question whether it is possible to construct a method of payments which does depend on work in progress, but does not give the contractor incentives to produce inefficiently and to delay delivery beyond what is socially optimal. Such a method is suggested below.

Method 3. Payments are tied to the completion of definite stages of production and it is agreed in advance at what dates in time those stages should be completed. If a stage of production on which a payment is due is delayed, the undiscounted payment is *increased* so as to keep its present value constant.[y] Accordingly, the payments are denominated in constant present value units. In addition to that, the contractor pays the buyer a fixed charge equal to the rate of interest on the value of the finished product to the buyer for as long as the project is not delivered. As a result, the buyer pays the seller only as work progresses, thus reducing his risks. However, since his payments are denominated in constant present value terms, the present value of the producer's receipts is divorced from the points in time at which he reaches the stages of production on which payments are due. Hence, he no longer has any incentive to produce at more than minimal discounted costs.

The present value of the combined payments and fines of Method 3 is

$$V(T) = D - rA \int_0^T e^{-rt}dt, \tag{17.14}$$

where D is the *constant* present value of the payments.[z] Neither the size nor the timing of these payments is known in advance. However, since their present value is constant, the slope of V will be determined everywhere by the fines imposed on the contractor. Hence, as with Methods 1 and 2, $\frac{\partial V}{\partial T} = -rAe^{-rT}$. Thus, in figure 17-1a, $\frac{\partial V}{\partial T}$ and $\frac{dZ}{dT}$ are again identical, which also assures that the contractor's and the socially optimal delivery time will be equal.[aa]

---

[y]Conversely, if it is completed earlier than agreed, the undiscounted payment will be *decreased* so as to keep its present value constant.

[z]Let a payment of size P_i be due when stage i is completed and let its completion be due at time $\bar{T}_i$, $i = 1 \ldots n$, then $D \equiv \sum_{i=1}^{n} P_i e^{-r\bar{T}_i}$. If stage i is actually completed at time $\tilde{T}_i$, $i = 1 \ldots n$, then the present value of payments will be $\sum_{i=1}^{n} P_i e^{r(\tilde{T}_i - \bar{T}_i)} e^{-r\tilde{T}_i}$, which again equals D, irrespectively of the actual timing of payments.

[aa]If the benefits A to the buyer are a *known* function, $\psi(T)$, of delivery time, the change in benefits to the buyer as a result of a change in T is $\frac{dZ}{dT} = e^{-rT}\psi'(T) - re^{-rT}\psi(T)$. The method in the text can be adapted for this case by changing the structure of fines as follows. Require a fine that is equal to the rate of interest on the value of the finished product to the buyer at every moment plus a compensation for the decrease in the undiscounted value of

We turn now to the case in which the buyer may derive benefits when some intermediary stages of production are completed. For example, the lower floors of a skyscraper may be used before the higher ones are finished or it may be possible to operate independently certain segments of a vertically integrated industrial complex. In this case there will be socially optimal delivery times for each of those intermediary stages. Each of those will be characterized (as in the case of only one beneficial stage) by the equality of the marginal change in discounted costs as a result of a delay in delivery, for that stage, with the marginal change in the discounted buyer benefits caused by the delay of that stage. As before, the contractor's preferred completion time for that stage need not coincide with the social optimum. The optimal method can be adapted to take care of this case as follows.

Method 4. Payments as in Method 3 are specified in constant present value terms. However, the fine paid at each period by the contractor applies only to the difference between the value of the finished product to the buyer and its value to the buyer at that period's stage of completion. The fine, as before, is equal to the rate of interest on this difference. Let A_i be the increase in the value of benefits to the buyer as a result of completion of the ith stage of production. Let T_i be the completion time of the ith stage. Then if there are still m distinct uncompleted stages of production that affect the undiscounted benefits derived by the buyer, the present value of those benefits, evaluated in terms of the initial period, is given by

$$Z_m = \sum_{i=1}^{m} A_i e^{-rT_i}. \tag{17.15}$$

The present value of payments as evaluated in terms of the contracting date for the method proposed is

$$V = D - r\sum_{i=1}^{m} A_i \int_0^{T_i} e^{-rt_i} dt_i, \tag{17.16}$$

(footnote aa continued)
the project to the buyer as a result of postponement of delivery. Both fines are payable continuously. The present value of payments will then be

$$V(T) = D + \int_0^T (\psi'(t) - r\psi(t))e^{-rt} dt.$$

It is easily seen that again this will assure $\frac{\partial V}{\partial T} = \frac{dZ}{dT}$ for every T. However, the method is more complicated in that it requires the specification of the function $\psi(T)$ in the contract.

where D has the same meaning as in (17.14). By differentiating (17.15) and (17.16) with respect to T_i, $i = 1 \ldots m$, it is easily seen that

$$\frac{\partial V}{\partial T_i} = -rA_i e^{-rT_i} = \frac{dZ}{dT_i}, \quad i = 1 \ldots m. \tag{17.17}$$

Thus, the losses to the buyer as a result of a delay in the completion of stage i ($i = 1 \ldots m$) are completely passed over to the seller. This gives him an incentive to deliver each stage at the socially optimal delivery time for that stage. Note that the case in which there is an interdependence between the benefits derived by the buyer from each completed stage, on the one hand, and the identity of the other stages which are already completed, on the other, can also be handled by the method proposed. All that needs to be done is to replace all or some of the benefit parameters A_i for the uncompleted stages of production by others whenever a stage of production is completed.[bb]

17.6. Modifications as a Result of Inflation

The analysis up to now implicitly assumes a constant price level. However, when the price level changes over the execution time of the project, some changes may occur in behavior and in the optimal payment schedules. In what follows, we shall assume that inflation is neutral in the sense that it affects neither the relevant relative prices nor the real rate of interest r. Thus, the nontrivial additional problems which arise when a change in the general price level is accompanied by changes in relative prices and the real rate of interest, are neglected.[cc] The buyer is not directly affected by inflation, since he will get a real asset whose present value should be discounted at the unaffected real rate of interest. If the nominal rate of interest n is equal as in a Fisherian (1896) world to the real rate r plus the expected with certainty rate of inflation q, then the present value of costs does not change, since the expected increase in costs is cancelled by the increase in the nominal rate of inflation.[dd] Hence the social optimum T_s is not affected by inflation. It is a function of real costs and benefits only.[ee]

[bb]In this case the contract should specify what the value of each stage of production is to the buyer for each partition of the other stages between completed and uncompleted stages.

[cc]Changes in relative prices and the real rate of interest could also occur under a stable general price level. While they may be more pronounced under an unforeseen inflation, they are by no means a necessary result of changes in the price level *per se*.

[dd]This is equally true if the rate of inflation and, consequently, the nominal rate of interest are expected to vary through time.

However, the present value of payments function is affected. It is decreased since now the discount factor is larger. There is also a change in the slope of this function as a result of inflation and, thereby, a change in the producer's optimal delivery time.[ff] Since there is no change in the socially optimal delivery time as a result of inflation, the change in the contractor's optimal delivery time will obviously affect the divergence between those two times. Although it is not possible to say, in general, whether the contractor's optimal delivery time will increase, decrease towards the social optimum, or even decrease below it, a divergence between the social and the contractor's optimal delivery time will most probably develop. Hence, some modification of the optimal fines methods as embodied in equation (17.14) is called upon and is described in what follows.

Method 5. Payments may or may not be tied to the stages of production and are fully linked to the rate of inflation. If they are tied to the stages of production, they are as in Method 3 specified in constant present value units. Thus, if a stage

---

(footnote ee continued)

[ee]With no inflation let $f(t,T)$ be the optimal density of proportional costs incurred at period t when completion time is T. Then total minimal discounted costs for delivery period T may be written:

$$X(T) = C(T) \int_0^T f(t,T)e^{-rt}dt, \tag{i}$$

where $0 \leqslant f(t,T) \leqslant 1$, $C(T)$ are total undiscounted costs for delivery period T, and

$$\int_0^T f(t,T)dt = 1. \tag{ii}$$

With expected inflation at rate q, undiscounted costs are expected to increase at rate q and they are discounted at the nominal rate $n = r + q$. Hence, in the face of inflation total discounted costs are

$$C(T) \int_0^T f(t,T)e^{qt}e^{-nt}dt = C(T) \int_0^T f(t,T)e^{-rt}dt = X(T).$$

Similarly, the discounted buyer benefits are $Ae^{qt}e^{-nT} = Ae^{-rT} = Z(T)$. Hence, neither total discounted costs nor discounted benefits to the buyer change as a result of inflation. Consequently, the marginal conditions for a socially optimal delivery time are unchanged and are still represented by the curves $\frac{dX}{dT}$ and $\frac{dZ}{dT}$ in figure 17.1b.

[ff]Let P_i be the amount of the total price payable at period i, then without inflation $V = \sum_{i=0}^{n} P_i e^{-rt_i(T)}$, where the total price P is such that $P = \sum_{i=0}^{n} P_i$ and some or all of the partial derivatives of t_i with respect to T may be zero depending on whether the ith payment depends on the progress of the project or not. Without inflation the contractor's best delivery time, T_c, is determined from the condition: $\frac{\partial V}{\partial T} = -r \sum_{i=0}^{n} P_i e^{-rt_i(t)} \frac{\partial t_i}{\partial T} = \frac{dX}{dT}$. With inflation $V = \sum_{i=0}^{n} P_i e^{-nt_i(T)}$ where $n > r$. Hence, all the present value of payments curve in figure 17.1 is decreased. The marginal condition for the contractor's delivery time with inflation is

$$\frac{\partial V}{\partial T}_{INF} = -n \sum_{i=0}^{n} P_i e^{-nt_i(T)} \frac{\partial t_i}{\partial T} = \frac{dX}{dT}.$$

of production on which a payment is due is delayed, then in addition to the linkage additions to the payment, it is blown up by the *real* rate of interest and it is decreased, again using the real rate as a discount factor, if the stage of production is reached earlier than specified in the contract. As a result, the real present value of payments is independent of both the rate of inflation and the interim progress of the project. From commencement of the project to its completion, the seller pays the buyer at every moment the real rate of interest, *fully escalated*[4] on the value of the project at delivery time to the buyer evaluated at constant prices[gg]—namely, the fine at moment t in real terms is: rA. Since both payments and fines are specified in real terms, they should be discounted at the real rate of interest. Hence, the present value of payments and fines of Method 5 is

$$V = D - rA \int_0^T e^{-rt} dt, \tag{17.18}$$

which is identical to equation (17.14). Consequently $\frac{\partial V}{\partial T}$ and $\frac{dZ}{dT}$ will again be identical (see figure 17-1b), thus assuring that the social and the contractor's delivery times will be identical. This method, as in the no inflation case, does not depend on the knowledge of the cost function and is easily applicable. It also does not impose inflation risks on the seller or the buyer when there are uncertainties with respect to the rate of inflation and does not require knowledge of the inflation rate in advance.

17.7. Concluding Comments

A defective contractual relationship between economic agents is a potentially important source of inefficiency. The problem as stated in general by Williamson (1971) is that it may be prohibitively costly or even impossible to specify contractually the full range of contingencies and appropriate responses. He notes that "[o]n the other hand, if the contract is seriously incomplete in these respects but, once the original negotiations are settled, the contracting parties are locked into a bilateral exchange, the divergent interests between the parties will predictably lead to individual opportunistic behavior and joint losses" (1971, p. 117).

We have limited ourselves to the analysis of one of the many facets of contract incompleteness, namely the effects of the payment method on long-term investment projects. It has been shown that in commonly used payment methods there is a built-in incentive for the supplier to submit the product at a suboptimal date. Moreover, when payments are tied to work

[gg]That is, at the initial period prices.

progress, the contractor may find it profitable to produce in a way that does not minimize discounted costs, thus creating an additional social cost.

We have successively developed a payment method that eliminates all those difficulties and guarantees an optimal social solution for a constant as well as for a changing general price level. We believe this method to have several important advantages. First, it is relatively simple and applicable. Second, it requires no information on the part of the buyer about the contractor's production possibilities and cost structure or preknowledge of the rate of inflation by either side. Third, if production conditions change while the work is in progress, this method will provide the contractor with an incentive to adapt his actions optimally to the new conditions.[hh] Fourth, it can be adapted for situations in which the rate of interest varies over the project's execution and in which the undiscounted benefits to the buyer depend on delivery time. It is not, however, easily applicable to cases in which the undiscounted real benefits to the buyer vary in a complex way during the execution period.[ii] Thus the payment methods suggested here may be viewed as making only one, but relatively efficient step towards the solution of contract incompleteness between buyer and seller.

Notes

1. The problem of determination of the optimal price and delivery period by the contractor is analyzed by Zarnowitz for a given quantity of the product (1962, pp. 377 and 392-394). He considers the problem of a one-sided monopolist who for any given quantity sold picks along the demand curve facing him the profit maximizing combination of price (to be interpreted as present value) and delivery period and gets a unique determination of those two variables. The difference between his result regarding price determination and ours is caused by this difference in assumptions regarding market structure; price is indeterminate under bilateral monopoly, but it is uniquely determined when the seller is a monopolist faced by a competitive demand. In addition, Zarnowitz implicitly assumes that the actual delivery period is independent of the pattern of payments which is the main topic considered in this chapter.

2. See also American Law Reports (1952, Vol. 22, p. 1344). Evidence on

[hh]This does not mean that the contractor must necessarily bear all the burden of unexpected changes in production conditions. For example, it may be possible to stipulate lump-sum compensations for changes in certain input prices.

[ii]See footnotes d and aa. Also, it does not apply if there is uncertainty with respect to buyer's benefits at contracting time. While such situations are common in certain industries (e.g., ship-building), it is sometimes possible to determine the future value of certain projects, expecially in the public utility sectors, with a reasonable degree of confidence. For example, the demand for power plants, which grows much as population and income do, may be evaluated with sufficient accuracy, provided good forecasts of population and income growth are available.

the American government's practice may be found in McBride and Wachtel (1965, Vol. 7, Chapter 44, p. 51). Other examples of standard clauses used in civil engineering and ship-building contracts in Britain may be found in the *Encyclopedia of Forms and Precedents* (1965, pp. 352-353, 522-523, 583, 595). In these contracts some form of a distributed payment scheme arises. In most cases payments are tied to the completion of specified stages of production.

3. On this point see also Richardson (1960, p. 83).

4. For a suggestion of full escalation of various contracts, see Morag (1962).

References

American Jurisprudence, 2nd ed., Vol. 13, "Building and Construction Contracts," Rochester, N.Y.: The Lawyer Co-operative Publishing Co., 1964.

American Law Reports Annotated, 2nd Series, Vol. 22, Rochester, N.Y.: The Lawyer Co-operative Publishing Co., 1952.

Carlson, J.A., "The Production Lag," *The American Economic Review* 63, no. 1 (Mar. 1973):73-86.

The Encyclopedia of Forms and Precedents, 4th ed., Vol. 3. London: Butterworth, 1965.

Fellner, W., "Competition among the Few, Oligopoly and Similar Market Structures," *Reprints of Economic Classics*, New York: Augustus M. Kelley, 1965.

Fisher, I., "Appreciation and Interest," *The American Economic Association*, third series II (1896), pp. 331-442.

Gill, W.H., *Emden and Gill's Building Contracts and Practice*, 7th ed. London: Butterworth, 1969.

McBride, J.C., and I.H. Wachtel, *Government Contracts*, Vol. 7, New York: Matthew Bender, 1965.

McCall, J.J., "The Simple Economics of Incentive Contracting," *The American Economic Review*, 60 (1970):837-846.

Morag, A., "For an Inflation-Proof Economy," *The American Economic Review* 52, no. 1 (Mar. 1962):177-185.

Richardson, G.B., *Information and Investment: A Study in the Working of the Competitive Economy*, Oxford: Oxford Univ. Press. 1960.

Williamson, O.E., "The Vertical Integration of Production: Market Failures Considerations," *The American Economic Review* 61, no. 2 (May 1971):112-123.

Zarnowitz, V., "Orders, Prices, and Business Fluctuations," *Review of Economics and Statistics* 44, no. 4 (Nov. 1962):367-394.

18 On the Assignment of Liability: The Uniform Case

Peter A. Diamond and
James A. Mirrlees

18.1. Introduction

Where there are externalities, economists are inclined to recommend that agents should pay the marginal social costs of their actions. This is not always a very helpful prescription. The measurement and collection of social costs can be a costly business. Thus simpler ways of shifting costs among agents should be considered. Such simple shifting does not, generally speaking, result in a competitive equilibrium that is a Pareto optimum. It is natural, then, to ask whether the equilibrium with shifted costs is more efficient than the one when costs are not shifted. Specifically, we seek sets of conditions that are sufficient to identify the more efficient equilibrium.

A leading example of the kind of situation we have in mind arises when there may be accidents between an agent engaged in one activity (for example, a railroad) and one engaged in a different activity (a truck, for example, or a horse-drawn wagon). The question we pose is whether it is more efficient to have accident costs remain on the parties suffering these costs at the time of an accident, or to have one of the parties bear a given portion of the costs that have fallen on the other party. An example is whether efficiency rises if railroads pay the medical expenses of truck drivers coming from truck-train accidents. This question has been addressed in the legal literature as that of the assignment of liability for accident costs.

Our attention has been drawn to this question by the interesting book *The Costs of Accidents*[1] by Calabresi. He argues that liability ought to be placed where it will produce the more efficient equilibrium, and calls the person who should bear liability under this rule the "cheapest cost avoider."[2] In this paper we identify some sets of conditions which, if satisfied, are sufficient for identification of the cheapest cost avoider.[3] We find that these conditions are sometimes complicated and difficult to judge intuitively. We conclude that it may well be necessary to do substantial empirical work to identify the cheapest cost avoider.[a] The theorems presented can serve as a guide

 Reprinted with permission from the *Bell Journal of Economics*, vol. 6, Autumn 1975, pp. 487-516. The authors wish to thank Hugh Cravelle, Victor Goldberg, and Alvin Klevorick for helpful comments, James Hess for research assistance, and the National Science Foundation for financial support.

[a]The fact that it may require detailed information to identify the cheapest cost avoider need not imply that the identification is unimportant.

to the information needed for this identification. As an introduction to the analytical work, we briefly describe Calabresi's discussion of accidents so as to place our specific model in the context of this literature.

There are many rules for deciding whether to shift costs in a particular accident, other than deciding before the accident that certain classes of costs will be shifted in all such accidents.[b] In particular, the impact of negligence rules on allocative efficiency has been examined by several authors recently.[4] Any rule creates administrative costs which offset the efficiency gain arising from application of the rule. Calabresi has argued that, particularly in the case of automobile accidents, the negligence rule has become so expensive to administer that it would be preferable to use a strict liability[c] rule, like the one we examine here.

Calabresi has identified three types of costs associated with accidents. *Tertiary costs* are those that come from the administration of any legal/compensatory scheme set up to deal with people who have had accidents. Since the alternatives we consider do not differ too greatly in their complexity, we ignore tertiary costs, on the assumption that they are approximately equal for the two alternatives whose efficiency we compare. *Secondary costs* are additional costs arising from failure to deal promptly and adequately with the consequences of accidents. They include complications arising from delayed medical treatment and the costs coming from changing marginal utilities of income in the presence of risk aversion and imperfect insurance. We shall also ignore secondary costs, assuming that all utility functions are linear in income available to spend on other goods. This assumption significantly limits the applicability of our results, perhaps only to accidents between firms and, possibly, thoroughly insured individuals (i.e., those with the correct amount of insurance and with premiums varying with their expected benefits). *Primary costs* are the resource costs arising from accidents plus the resources used to avoid them. We do not ignore these costs.

In considering the cheapest cost avoider, Calabresi paid particular attention to two important elements. One is that incentives to avoid accidents can be greatly dissipated by insurance which shifts accident costs from a party without relating the premium he pays to his behavior. Calabresi calls this case externalization by transfer.[5] As an extreme example consider a blanket insurance policy that does not even enquire whether an individual is engaged in some activity giving rise to increased risk. Provided the other potential parties to accidents have not also had their incentives fully blunted, there is an allocative gain from shifting costs to the person whose incentives are affected.[d] A second element

[b]In practice, an exception to such a flat rule is generally made for intentional damage, as opposed to accidents.

[c]A strict liability rule is one which allocates costs to a party independent of particular behavior giving rise to an accident. Such a rule has been applied in many particular settings. Specifically, costs arising from accidents from hazardous activities like blasting are borne by person in the hazardous activity. See Prosser [9] Chapter 13.

[d]The fact that individuals would try to avoid accidents even when insurance coverage is unaffected does not alter the conclusion here unless the nonfinancial motives giving rise to this care are, themselves, affected by the shifting of costs.

Calabresi has considered is the frequent need to alter behavior of parties not involved in the immediate accident, like manufacturers or highway builders. Some individuals or groups may be in a better position to do this than others. He calls the group in the more favorable position to affect the behavior of others, the best briber.[e] We shall be considering models in which these issues do not arise.[f]

We shall focus on two issues that are relevant for identification of the cheapest cost avoider—the relative importance of accident avoidance measures by the parties engaged in the different activities for total (social) costs and for costs individuals bear themselves. After presenting the basic model in the next section, we consider the special case where the only externalities are in the costs for which liability is to be assigned. (This situation might arise in truck-train accidents if all costs are to be borne by one of the parties.) In this case, greater efficiency is achieved by placing liability on the party whose accident avoidance expenditures, above the minimum of self-protection, are more important for social costs. This case is special because some externalities generally fall outside the parties to the accident (some medical expenses, lost income taxes, and cleanup costs may fall on the government, for example) and because it is not generally practicable to identify all externality costs accurately. (For example, some might arise outside an accident context.) The single condition, that accident avoidance by one activity is more important for social costs, is not sufficient for identification of the cheapest cost avoider, once we introduce externalities in addition to those for which liability is being assigned. To analyze these more complicated and interesting cases we also examine the amount of care taken under the different liability assignments. In the case where the additional externalities fall outside the two activities, it is sufficient to add a condition which implies increased total care from a shift in liability to the party whose expenditures are more important for social costs. In a situation where only the medical expenses of truck drivers might be transferred after truck-train accidents, we have externalities which are nontransferable (damage to trucks, trains, and truck drivers) and which fall on one of the two activities. For this case of nontransferable externalities within the activities, we find several different conditions which (together with the previous conditions) are sufficient for identification of the cheapest cost avoider. The reader who would like a specific example to help with the formal statement of the theorems can find the results summarized in terms of an example in section 18.8. For this chapter we assume that everyone engaged in a particular activity is identical, and we assume large numbers of such individuals with no externalities between agents engaged

[e]Following traditional static micro theory, we shall not explore the effects of liability assignment on the level of research on improved technologies to avoid accidents. In addition, misperceptions of the consequences of different actions do not fit in the model as analyzed except for unusual misperceptions mentioned in footnote h.

[f]In a later paper, we do plan to deal with the case where insurance blunts some incentives, but not all, as when insurance costs do not depend on behavior once engaged in an activity, but do depend on whether the activity is engaged in at all. An example might be automobile ownership itself or the use of an automobile for commuting.

in the same activity. In later papers we plan to develop models with large numbers, but without the other two assumptions.

18.2. Basic Model

We assume that there are two interacting activities. In each activity there are a large (not necessarily equal) number of participants. The participants in each activity are identical, but the two types engaged in the two activities may differ. No one is engaged in both activities. We denote by x the level of accident avoidance by each participant in activity one. This might represent actual expenditures on safety equipment or efforts, like paying attention, which affect accident probabilities. It might represent a choice made for nonsafety reasons which affects safety, like an increase in the speed or number of miles driven. The variable x might simply represent potentially damaged items which are not subjected to the risk of accident. Similarly we denote by y the level of accident avoidance by each participant in activity two. We denote the total expected costs, net of the utility from engaging in the activity, of participants in activity one by $A(x,y)$. When A decreases in y we have a marginal external economy from those in activity two to those in activity one, in that the greater the accident avoidance level in activity two, the lower the expected costs of those in activity one. On the assumption that there are no externalities within an activity, the care level x is chosen to minimize A given the level of y. $x^0(y)$ is defined as the optimal level of care:

$$x^0(y) \text{ minimizes } A(x,y). \tag{18.1}$$

Given the large numbers assumption, we model individual choice as optimization taking the decisions of others as given.

Similarly, we denote by $\tilde{B}(x,y)$ the total expected accident costs and accident avoidance costs (net of utility) of participants in activity two. Their optimal level of care is denoted by $y^*(x)$:

$$y^*(x) \text{ minimizes } \tilde{B}(x,y). \tag{18.2}$$

There is competitive equilibrium with correct perceptions when the optimizing choices are predicted on a correct perception of the simultaneous choices being made in the other activity. That is, x^0, y^* is a competitive equilibrium if

$$\left.\begin{aligned} x^0 &= x^0(y^*) \\ y^* &= y^*(x^0) \end{aligned}\right\} . \tag{18.3}$$

We assume throughout the paper that there exists a unique competitive equilibrium for any assignment of costs.

Transferred Costs

Assume that there are some costs which are to be transferred from participants in activity two to the participants in activity one. Denote the expected value of these costs by $C(x,y)$. For example, the medical expenses of those in activity two might be paid by those in activity one. Since the model has a symmetric structure, the expected costs C might alternatively be the medical expenses of those in activity one which were previously paid by those in activity two and are no longer to be shifted. The question being analyzed is the implication of a shift in the bearing of some costs.[g] Those in activity one now seek to minimize $A(x,y) + C(x,y)$:

$$x^*(y) \text{ minimizes } A(x,y) + C(x,y). \tag{18.4}$$

The costs of activity two are reduced by $C(x,y)$, and are now

$$B(x,y) = \tilde{B}(x,y) - C(x,y). \tag{18.5}$$

The choice in activity two is described by $y^0(x)$:

$$y^0(x) \text{ minimizes } B(x,y). \tag{18.6}$$

We have a new competitive equilibrium with transferred costs, that is, with liability assigned to activity one, at the values x^*,y^0 satisfying

$$\begin{aligned} x^* &= x^*(y^0) \\ y^0 &= y^0(x^*) \end{aligned} \tag{18.7}$$

There are two equilibria to compare: (x^*,y^0) with liability assigned to activity one, and (x^0,y^*) with liability assigned to activity two. We are interested in discovering which equilibrium has lower aggregate costs of accidents and accident avoidance. In addition to the costs A, B, and C that fall on participants in the two activities, one should consider also expected costs $D(x,y)$ that fall

[g]To interpret the shift of C as a change in cost bearing, it is natural to think of C as positive. This assumption, however, is not made for the analysis, which focuses on the signs of the derivatives of C, which indicate the presence of a marginal external economy or diseconomy. Whether C represents a cost or spillover benefit does not affect optimal individual decision making, although it does affect the distribution of expected utilities.

outside the two activities. For example, they might fall on the government or on passersby. They could arise from misperceived costs, provided all participants misperceive in the same way.[h] We define the sum of costs S, by

$$S(x,y) = A(x,y) + B(x,y) + C(x,y) + D(x,y). \tag{18.8}$$

The problem is to find sufficient conditions for comparing $S(x^*,y^0)$ with $S(x^0,y^*)$ and thus to judge which assignment of liability is the more efficient: when $S(x^*,y^0) < S(x^0,y^*)$ it is more efficient to place liability on activity one.

18.3. All Externalities Transferable

We start with the simple case where all externality costs are to be assigned to one of the activities: A is a function just of x, B is a function just of y, and D is equal to zero. We assume that A and B are convex and continuously differentiable. Given these assumptions, the values x^0 and y^0 that minimize $A(x)$ and $B(y)$, respectively, do not depend on the choice of care in the other activity. Thus they serve as natural origins, being the level of care for self-protection. We say that *care in activity one is more effective* if for any (positive) amount of care above the self-protection level it is more efficient to have that care taken in activity one,[i] that is:

---

[h]If $A + B + C + D$ represent the true costs which fall on participants in the two activities and $A + B + C$ are the perceived costs, whoever bears the cost C, the model applies directly to this case of misperceptions. For misperceptions about A and B this creates no difficulty. Generally, perceptions about C differ between participants in the different activities and C and D (but not their sum) change with a reassignment of liability. It is also possible that perceptions of A and B change when liability is reassigned.

[i]For an analysis of effectiveness using (0.0) as origin rather than (x^0,y^0) see the Appendix. One might like to check assumption (18.9) without estimating x^0 and y^0 (particularly in the cases to be considered later where A depends on y and B on x). (18.9) holds for *any* (x^0,y^0) if and only if

$$S_1(x,y) \leqslant S_2(x,y) \text{ (all } x,y). \tag{18.9c}$$

Since

$$S_1 - S_2 = \lim_{t\downarrow 0} \frac{1}{t}\left\{S(x+t,y) - S(x,y)\right\} \quad \lim_{t\downarrow 0} \frac{1}{t}\left\{S(x,y+t) - S(x,y)\right\},$$

(18.9) certainly implies (18.9c). To prove the converse, we calculate

$$S(x+t,y) - S(x,y+t) = \int_0^t \frac{d}{d\theta} S(x+\theta, y+t-\theta)\,d\theta$$

$$= \int_0^t \left\{S_1(x+\theta, y+t-\theta) - S_2(x+\theta, y+t-\theta)\right\} d\theta$$

$$\leqslant 0 \text{ if (18.9c) holds and } t > 0.$$

(18.9c) is, it must be emphasized, a very stringent assumption, excluding in particular the interesting case where S has a global minimum at finite (x,y) with contours surrounding that point.

$$\text{For } t > 0, S(x^0 + t, y^0) \leqslant S(x^0, y^0 + t). \tag{18.9}$$

The assumption is that care above the self-protection level by those in activity one decreases total costs by more than does the same increase in care above the self-protection level by those in activity two. This assumption does not immediately result in a comparison of the efficiency of different assignments of liability, since it does not guarantee that at least as much additional care will in fact be taken by those in activity one. For the case analyzed in this section, no such further assumption is needed to obtain the efficiency comparison. The complications in later sections arise precisely from the difficulty of comparing the levels of care taken under different liability assignments.

We state the result for this simple case.

Theorem 1: With costs $A(x)$, $B(y)$, $C(x,y)$, and with $D = 0$, which are convex and continuously differentiable, it is more efficient to have liability placed on activity one, if activity one is more effective in cost avoidance ((18.9) is satisfied) and we are dealing with external economies:[j]

$$C_2(x^0, y^0) < 0, \tag{18.10}$$

where C_2 is the partial derivative of C with respect to its second argument.

Proof: Let $t \equiv y^*(x^0) - y^0$. Since $B(y) + C(x^0, y)$ is decreasing in y at y^0 (and convex), the minimizing level y^* exceeds y^0. Thus t is positive and we can use (18.9) to conclude that

$$S(x^0, y^*) = S(x^0, y^0 + (y^* - y^0)) \geqslant S(x^0 + y^* - y^0, y^0). \tag{18.11}$$

Since $x^*(y^0)$ minimizes $A(x) + C(x, y^0)$ (and so minimizes $S(x, y^0)$), we have

$$S(x^0 + y^* - y^0, y^0) \geqslant S(x^*, y^0). \tag{18.12}$$

This completes the proof.

Our assumption about the effectiveness of care is a natural one to make when care in the two activities is measured in comparable units. In many cases, expenditure for the sake of cost reduction is the chief element of 'care,' and in these cases the measuring rod of money allows us to make sense of the transfer of care from one activity to the other. In other cases, such as motorists and pedestrians, or authors and editors, it is harder to think of a natural way to measure care. Therefore, one seeks a formulation of the result that is independent of the calibrations of care implicit in the cost functions.

Extending our previous definition, we say that *care in activity one is more*

[j]The same conclusion follows for the diseconomies case, $C_2 > 0$, if we assume that (18.9) holds for all $t < 0$. In this case $y^*(x^0) - y^0$ is negative and the steps in the proof remain valid.

effective if for any additional care in activity two above the self-protection level, there is some level of care in activity one that would have reduced costs further:

For all $y > y^0$ there exists $\hat{x}(y)$ such that

$$S(\hat{x}(y), y^0) \leqslant S(x^0, y). \tag{18.9a}$$

With this extended definition, Theorem 1 remains true as stated, by essentially the same argument:

$$\begin{aligned} S(x^0, y^*) &\geqslant S(\hat{x}(y^*), y^0), \\ &\geqslant S(x^*, y^0). \end{aligned}$$

The argument is illustrated in figure 18-1, with care levels on the two axes. The effectiveness assumption means that any S-contour that cuts the vertical $x = x^0$ also cuts the horizontal $y = y^0$. In our present case, with $S = A(x) + C(x,y) + B(y)$, the points (x^0, y^*) and (x^*, y^0) are the points of tangency of S-contours with the vertical and horizontal lines as shown. The result is therefore immediate. We shall return to this approach in section 18.7 to show how the later theorems also have their measurement invariant versions.

There is another interesting special case of (18.9a), similar to (18.9), but contemplating proportional rather than absolute changes in care levels:

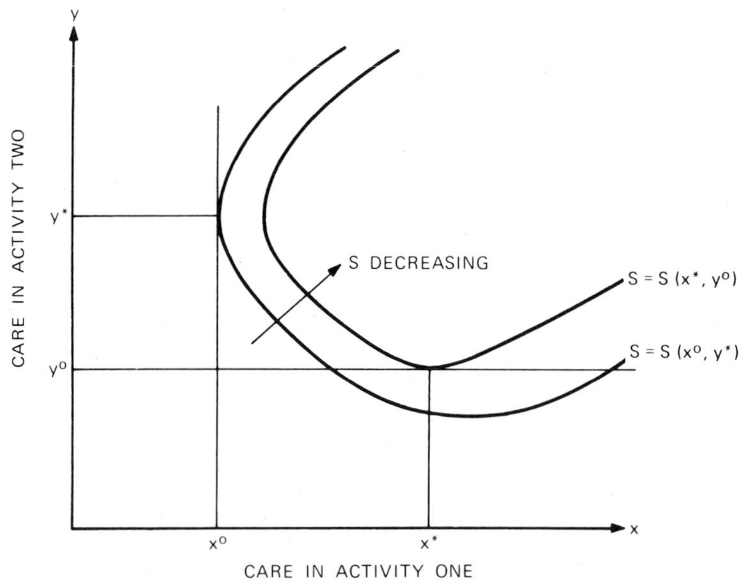

Figure 18-1. All Externalities Transferable.

$$\text{For } T > 1, S(Tx^0,y^0) \leqslant S(x^0,Ty^0). \tag{18.9b}$$

This says, for example, that twice as much care in activity one does more good than twice as much care in activity two. In situations where the care taken is the number of times some particular action is done (inspection of equipment, going on a journey, etc.), it is easier to interpret effectiveness as expressed in (18.9b).

While this result does little more than confirm the relationship between effectiveness (as defined in (18.9) or (18.9a) and efficiency, it is interesting how fragile the result is. From the proof, it is clear that the result will follow without requiring A to be independent of y. However, making B depend on care in the other activity or permitting D to be nonzero requires additional substantive assumptions to preserve the ability to identify the cheapest cost avoider. We shall see this as we examine next the case where D is not zero.

18.4. Outside Externalities

While preserving the assumptions that A depends only on x and that B depends only on y, dropping the assumption that D is zero ends the validity of Theorem 1 without further assumptions. This is true despite the fact that effectiveness is defined in terms of total costs, including the costs falling outside the two activities. The proof breaks down because $x^*(y^0)$ does not generally optimize $S(x,y^0)$ even though it optimizes $A(x) + B(y^0) + C(x,y^0)$, since S includes D. The problem is illustrated in figure 18-2, which can be contrasted with figure 18-1. At (x^0,y^*), $A' = 0$, $S_2 = D_2$, and at (x^*,y^0), $B' = 0$, $S_1 = D_1$. In the figure, it is assumed that $D_2 < 0$, $D_1 < 0$. (18.9) is satisfied in that every S-contour intersecting $x = x^0$ also intersects $y = y^0$. However, without further assumptions, it may be more efficient to have liability placed on activity two. In contrast to figure 18-1, x^* no longer optimizes S, given y^0. Thus the fact that the indifference curve through (x^0,y^*) intersects the line $y = y^0$ does not ensure that the equilibrium point (x^*,y^0) is better than (x^0,y^*).

Given that we are dealing with the case of external economies, it seems natural to add the assumption that $D(x,y)$ is decreasing in x. As figure 18-2 suggests, even this assumption is not enough, for $x^* - x^0$ might well be less than $y^* - y^0$, making $D(x^*,y^0)$ greater than $D(x^0 + y^* - y^0,y^0)$ and thus allowing the possibility that $S(x^*,y^0)$ is greater than $S(x^0,y^*)$.[k] This arises from the familiar difference between the total and marginal valuations. The relative sizes

---

[k]As an example that shows $D_1 <$ is insufficient, consider:

$$A = \frac{1}{2}(x - 1)^2,\ B = \frac{1}{2}(y - 1)^2,\ C = 10 - x - 3y,\ D = 15 - 4x - y.$$

For this case $(x^*,y^0) = (2,1)$, $(x^0,y^*) = (1,4)$, and $S(x^0 + t,y^0) - S(x^0,y^0 + t) = -t + 3t - 4t + t = -t < 0$ when $t > 0$; but $S(x^*,y^0) = 11\frac{1}{2}$, $S(x^0,y^*) = 8\frac{1}{2}$.

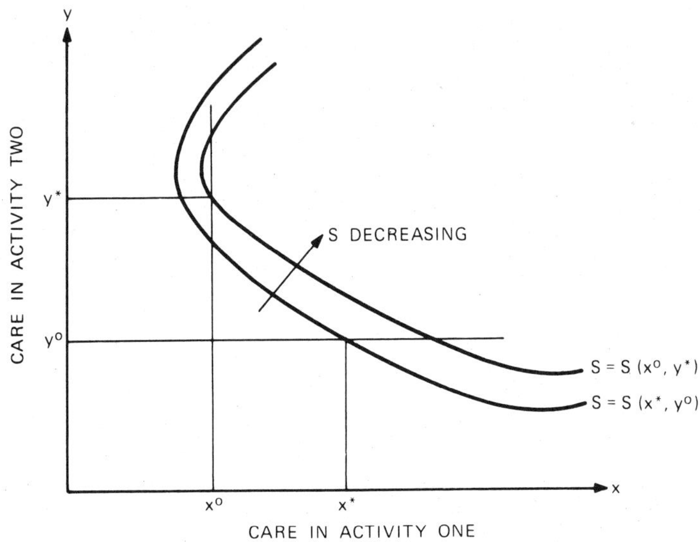

Figure 18-2. Outside Externalities.

of $x^* - x^0$ and $y^* - y^0$ depend on the values of the derivatives of A, B, and C while the assumptions entertained thus far consider only the level of total costs.

To complete an argument for this case, we add the following assumption:

$$\text{For } t > 0, A'(x^0 + t) + C_1(x^0 + t, y^0) \leqslant B'(y^0 + t) + C_2(x^0, y^0 + t), \qquad (18.13)$$

where A' and B' are derivatives. Thus the own marginal cost saving (of $A + C$ or $B + C$) is greater when first activity care increases above the self-protection level, rather than having second activity care increase above the self-protection level by the same amount. This differs from the effectiveness condition in that it looks at private costs rather than social costs and considers marginal costs rather than total costs. Since $A + C$ and $B + C$ are the costs borne by the bearer of liability under the different assignments, we describe assumption (18.13) by saying that activity one has a *greater incentive for care* when liable. To interpret (18.13) further, consider an imaginary market for care, with shadow price q so that care has a market price as well affecting costs. If $\overline{x}(q)$ minimizes $A(x) + C(x,y^0) + qx$, and $\overline{y}(q)$ minimizes $B(y) + C(x^0,y) + qy$, (18.13) is equivalent to

$$\overline{x}(q) - x^0 \geqslant \overline{y}(q) - y^0 \text{ for all } q \text{ such that } \overline{y}(q) \geqslant y^0. \qquad (18.14)$$

That is, at any price q those in activity one would increase their care levels (above x^0) by more than those in activity two would increase their care above y^0. To see this, put $t = \overline{y}(q) - y^0$ in (18.13). We have

$$A'(x^0 + \bar{y}(q) - y^0) + C_1(x^0 + \bar{y}(q) - y^0, y^0) \leqslant -q, \tag{18.15}$$

which implies (by convexity) that costs would be increased if x were reduced, i.e., $\bar{x}(q) \geqslant x^0 + y(q) - y^0$, which is (18.14).

In particular (18.14) holds for $q = 0$, when $\bar{x}(q) = x^*, \bar{y}(q) = y^*$, so that

$$x^* - x^0 \geqslant y^* - y^0. \tag{18.16}$$

Thus, placing liability on activity one results in a greater total of care taken, $x^* + y^0 \geqslant x^0 + y^*$. This condition and the assumed decrease in D with increases in x complete the argument. We state this formally.

Theorem 2: With costs $A(x)$, $B(y)$, $C(x,y)$, $D(x,y)$ which are convex and continuously differentiable, it is more efficient to have liability placed on activity one if activity one is more effective in cost avoidance ((18.9) is satisfied), activity one has a greater incentive for care when liable ((18.13) is satisfied) and we are dealing with external economies so that

$$C_2(x^0,y^0) < 0, D_1(x,y^0) < 0 \text{ for } x > x^0. \tag{18.17}$$

Proof: As in Theorem 1, $y^* - y^0 > 0$. Therefore, by (18.9)

$$\begin{aligned} S(x^0,y^*) &= S(x^0,y^0 + y^* - y^0) \geqslant S(x^0 + y^* - y^0,y^0) \\ &= A(x^0 + y^* - y^0) + B(y^0) + C(x^0 + y^* - y^0,y^0) \\ &\quad + D(x^0 + y^* - y^0,y^0). \end{aligned} \tag{18.18}$$

Since x^* optimizes $A(x) + B(y^0) + C(x,y^0)$, and since $x^* > x^0 + y^* - y^0$ and D is decreasing in its first argument, the last expression in (18.18) is at least as large as $S(x^*,y^0)$. *Q.E.D.*

Comparing Theorems 1 and 2, it is perhaps worth noting that the difficulty requiring further conditions comes from the dependence of D on x. Having D depend only on y would still permit the argument of Theorem 1 to hold. Of course the dependence of D on y must be considered as part of comparing $S(x^0 + t,y^0)$ with $S(x^0,y^0 + t)$ in the effectiveness condition.

18.5. Nontransferable External Economies

When expected costs of each activity depend in part on the level of care in the other activity, whichever way liability is assigned, we find it necessary to impose more severe restrictions if we are to be able to identify the more efficient assignment. In our previous arguments, we were using (x^0,y^0) as a fixed origin.

This was natural, because x^0 was determined by A,y^0 by B. In the more general case, (x^0,y^*) are determined simultaneously by A, B, and C, as are (x^*,y^0). This makes it more difficult to compare the magnitudes of the changes in care which occur with a shift in liability. It also makes the argument somewhat less appealing since the levels of (x^0,y^0) are more difficult to determine without calculations that effectively solve the problem. In the text we shall proceed on the same basis. Some results with effectiveness based on measuring care from (0,0) rather than (x^0,y^0) are presented in the appendix. Since conditions (18.9) and (18.13) may be true using a variety of origins, in some cases it may be reasonable to conclude that (x^0,y^0) lies in this range of origins, without knowing precisely where.

In the present section, and the following one, it is assumed that D is identically zero. The modifications required to incorporate a nonzero D into the results are indicated in footnotes. As before, we assume that the other functions are continuously differentiable and convex in control variables. We are primarily interested in cases where the value of x that minimizes A for given y, written $x^0(y)$, actually varies with y, and similarly for $y^0(x)$ which minimizes B. Notice that our last result (Theorem 2) yields as a corollary sufficient conditions for efficient assignment in the case where A and B are additively separable functions of x and y, and x^0,y^0 are consequently independent of y and x, respectively. Write

$$A = A^{(1)}(x) + A^{(2)}(y), B = B^{(1)}(x) + B^{(2)}(y). \tag{18.19}$$

Then it is clear that the situation is precisely the same as for a problem with $A^{(1)}$, $B^{(2)}$, C, and $D = A^{(2)} + B^{(1)}$. In this case, Theorem 2 assures us that (provided we are dealing with external economies) sufficient conditions can be obtained by combining the effectiveness condition (18.9) with the incentive condition (18.13).

To pursue the approach taken in Theorem 2, we isolate the heart of the argument used there in a Lemma, whose conditions will subsequently be derived from assumptions about the cost functions.

Lemma 1: It is more efficient to have liability placed on activity one if[1]

(i) activity one is more effective in cost avoidance, i.e.,

$$\text{for } t > 0, S(x^0 + t,y^0) \leqslant S(x^0,y^0 + t),$$

[1]If $D \neq 0$, we merely replace condition (iii) by (iii′) $B_1\,(x,y^0) + D_1(x,y^0) \leqslant 0$. The Lemma has a number of variants proved in the same way: the inequalities in (i) and (ii) can be reversed together: alternatively (or in addition) the inequalities in (iii) and (iv) can be reversed together.

(ii) people engaged in activity two will be more careful in equilibrium when liability is assigned to them, i.e.,

$$y^* \geqslant y^0,$$

(iii) when liable, increased care in activity one gives an external economy, i.e.,

$$B_1(x,y^0) \leqslant 0,$$

(iv) shifting liability to activity one increases the equilibrium care level there by more than the decrease in care in activity two, i.e.,

$$x^* - x^0 \geqslant y^* - y^0.$$

Proof: $S(x^0,y^*) \geqslant S(x^0 + y^* - y^0,y^0)$ by (i) and (ii)
$= [A(x^0 + y^* - y^0,y^0) + C(x^0 + y^* - y^0,y^0)]$
$+ B(x^0 + y^* - y^0,y^0) \geqslant [A(x^*,y^0) + C(x^*,y^0)] + B(x^*,y^0),$

because x^* minimizes $A(x,y^0) + C(x,y^0)$; and by assumptions (iii) and (iv). *Q.E.D.*

Parallel to the discussion of Theorem 2, the complication in Lemma 1 relative to Theorem 1 arises from the dependence of B on x, not from the dependence of A on y. If B is independent of x, y^* will exceed y^0 (with $C_2 < 0$), (iii) will be satisfied and (iv) unneeded.

To use Lemma 1 in the general case we need to find conditions to ensure that $y^* > y^0$ and that $x^* - x^0 > y^* - y^0$. Given the first condition, the second one is satisfied if we have the condition (18.13) that activity one has a greater incentive for care, which we restate here in the notation of this section:

$$\text{For } t>0, A_1(x^0 + t,y^0) + C_1(x^0 + t,y^0) \leqslant B_2(x^0,y^0 + t) + C_2(x^0,y^0 + t). \quad (18.13)$$

With x^0 and y^0 determined simultaneously with y^* and x^*, respectively, the intuitive content in (18.13) is lessened relative to the situation above. In some cases of this type it may be more intuitive to think in terms of aggregate care rather than the incentives for further care.

When B is independent of x, the condition $C_2(x^0,y^0) < 0$ is enough to ensure that y^* is greater than y^0. Under this condition $y^*(x)$ is everywhere above y^0. Thus $y^*(x^0)$ is also. This is illustrated in figure 18-3. When B depends on both x and y, the condition $C_2(x,y) < 0$ implies that $y^*(x) > y^0(x)$. But this alone does not guarantee that $y^*(x^0)$ exceeds $y^0(x^*)$. Two examples of possible difficulties are illustrated in figures 18-4 and 18-5. In the former we have $C_1 > 0$ and thus $x^0(y) > x^*(y)$. In the latter we have y^0 and y^* increasing functions of

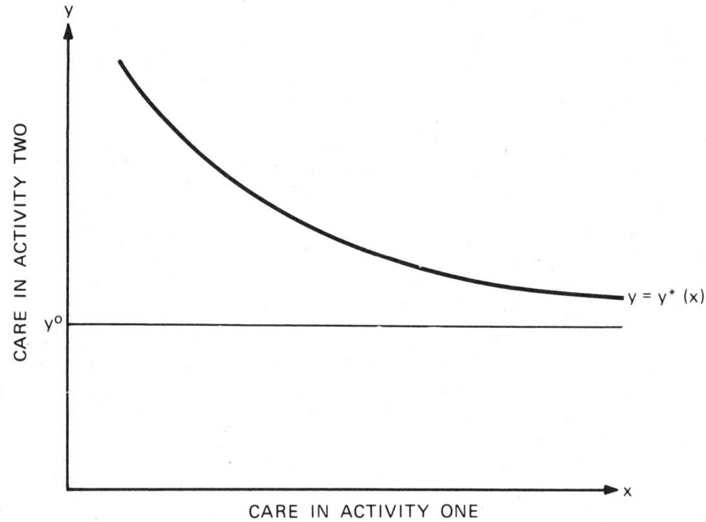

Figure 18-3. *B* Independent of *x*.

x rather than decreasing. Either of these circumstances can prevent y^* from exceeding y^0.

We prove below a theorem for the case that C is a decreasing function of both x and y, i.e., transferable costs decrease in both variables. This means that the four curves in (x,y)-space, defined by the reaction functions $x^*(y)$ (minimizing $A + C$ for given y), $x^0(y)$ (minimizing A for given y), $y^*(x)$ (minimizing $B + C$ for given x) and $y^0(x)$ (minimizing B for given x) lie with the y^*-curve above the y^0-curve and the x^*-curve to the right of the x^0-curve. One case is shown in figure 18-6, with all four functions decreasing in their arguments. The two points representing equilibria are ringed.

In the case shown, the x-curves decline more steeply than the y-curves. It is natural to regard this as a stable case. A sequence of points, obtained by having the two activities respond to one another successively, converges to the equilibrium. More generally, a sufficient condition for stability is that for all x and y,

$$\left|\frac{dx^*}{dy}\right| \left|\frac{dy^0}{dx}\right| < 1, \quad \left|\frac{dx^0}{dy}\right| \left|\frac{dy^*}{dx}\right| < 1. \tag{18.20}$$

The absolute slope of the y-curves should be less than the absolute slopes of the x-curves, as seen in the diagrams. We consider only cases with these properties.

In figure 18-6, $y^* > y^0$, and it is clear that this must always be the case if

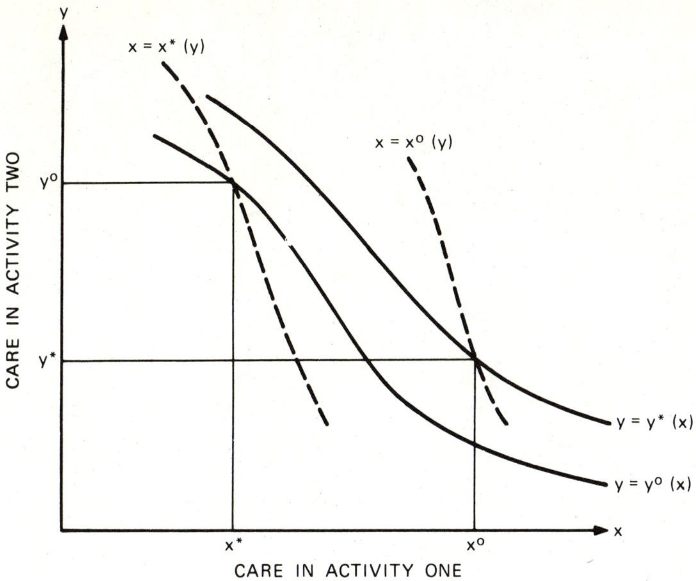

Figure 18-4. $x^{o}(y) > x^{*}(y)$.

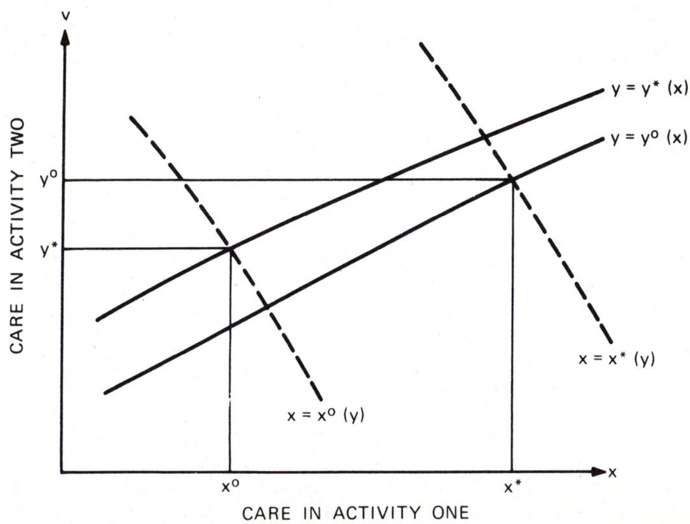

Figure 18-5. $y^{o}(x)$ and $y^{*}(x)$ Increasing Functions.

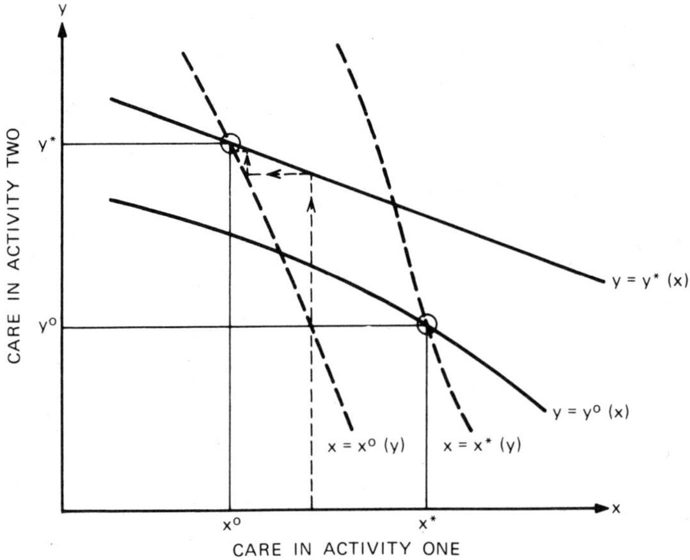

Figure 18-6. Convergence to Equilibrium.

the y-curves are downward-sloping: this is shown rigorously in the proof of the following theorem.

Theorem 3: When transferable costs are decreasing in both variables ($C_1(x,y) < 0$, $C_2(x,y) < 0$) and equilibria are stable, it is more efficient to have liability on activity one if activity one is more effective in cost avoidance ((18.19) is satisfied), activity one has the greater incentive for care ((18.13) is satisfied), increased care in activity one gives an external economy ($B_1(x,y^0) \leqslant 0$), and *one* of the following four conditions holds:[m]

(i) $y^0(x)$ is a decreasing function

(ii) $y^*(x)$ is a decreasing function

$$\text{(iii)}\ \frac{y^*(x^0) - y^0(x^0)}{x^*(y^*) - x^0(y^*)} \geqslant \frac{y^0(s) - y^0(x^0)}{s - x^0} \quad \text{for all } s \geqslant x^0 \tag{18.21}$$

(iv) $A_2(x^0,y) \leqslant 0$ and $B_1(x,y^*) \leqslant 0$ for all y,x.

Proof: We show that $y^* \geqslant y^0$ under (i), (ii), or (iii). As we have seen, (18.13) implies that $x^* - x^0 \geqslant y^* - y^0$. An application of Lemma 1 completes the

[m]If $D \neq 0$ the theorem holds if we replace $B_1(x,y^0) \leqslant 0$ by $B_1(x,y^0) + D_1(x,y^0) \leqslant 0$, replace $A_2(x^0,y) \leqslant 0$ by $A_2(x^0,y) + D\ (x^0,y) \leqslant 0$, and replace $B_1(x,y^*) \leqslant 0$ by $B_1(x,y^*) + D_1(x,y^*) \leqslant 0$.

proof for these three cases. To complete the proof we show that $y^0 > y^*$ and (iv) yield the result of the theorem directly.

By assumption, $y^*(x) \geqslant y^0(x), x^*(y) \geqslant x^0(y)$ and at the equilibria, the x-curves descend more steeply than the y-curves. Thus y^0, which is the intersection of $y^0(x)$ and $x^*(y)$, must lie below $y^*(x)$ and to the right of $x^0(y)$. If $x^0(y)$ does not enter the shaded region in figure 18-7, $y^* \geqslant y^0$. Since $x^0(y)$ is uniquely defined for each y, stability implies that $x^0(y)$ cannot enter the shaded region in figure 18-7. Similarly $x^*(y)$ (and thus $x^0(y)$) cannot enter the shaded region in figure 18-8, giving the same conclusion.

Now assume that (iii) holds. Since $y^*(x^0) > y^0(x^0)$ and $x^*(y^*) \geqslant x^0(y^*)$, the points $(x^0, y^0(x^0))$ and $(x^*(y^*), y^*)$ bear the relationship shown in figure 18-9. By hypothesis, the curve $y^0(x)$ lies below the line between these two points. For a stable intersection, therefore, $x^*(y)$ must cross $y^0(x)$ at a value of y below y^*. Thus $y^0 < y^*$.

If $y^* < y^0$, we can show, using $C_1 \leqslant 0$, $C_2 \leqslant 0$, that $x^* \geqslant x^0$. Suppose on the contrary that $x^* < x^0$. Then, we have the situation as shown in figure 18-10, with the y^*-curve eventually downward sloping, since it lies above the y^0-curve. By stability, it follows that the x^0-curve slopes downward more steeply, and must consequently lie to the right of the x^*-curve for the x^*-curve to pass through (x^*, y^0). This violates the assumption that $C(x, y^0)$ is a decreasing function of x. The contradiction proves that, as asserted, $x^* \geqslant x^0$. Suppose now that (iv) holds. Then, with $y^* < y^0$, $x^* \geqslant x^0$,

$$S(x^0, y^*) \geqslant A(x^0, y^0) + C(x^0, y^0) + B(x^0, y^*), \text{ (since } A_2 \leqslant 0, C_2 \leqslant 0)$$

$$\geqslant A(x^0, y^0) + C(x^0, y^0) + B(x^* y^*), \text{ (since } B_1 \leqslant 0)$$

$$\geqslant A(x^*, y^0) + C(x^*, y^0) + B(x^*, y^0) = S(x^*, y^0),$$

since x^* minimizes $A(x, y^0) + C(x, y^0)$, and y^0 minimizes $B(x^*, y)$. *Q.E.D.*

The theorem picks out three ways of ensuring that y^* is greater than y^0, so that Lemma 1 can be used. The assumption that care in an activity decreases with care in the other activity is easily checked and one that will frequently be valid. To go behind the conditions on $y^0(x)$ and $y^*(x)$, we would, of course, need to sign B_{12} and $B_{12} + C_{12}$, but it is more intuitive to focus on the supply conditions themselves. Condition (iii) compares the distances between supply curves of care with the average slope of one of them. In that sense it focuses on the importance of shifting the transferable costs (and going from $y^0(x)$ to $y^*(x)$) relative to the importance of the care level in activity one as a determinant of care in activity two. Condition (iv) shows that when all externalities are external economies, we can get the desired result from the two basic conditions of effectiveness and the greater incentive for care. Before considering the complexities of diseconomies, let us consider an example. The example will help to bring

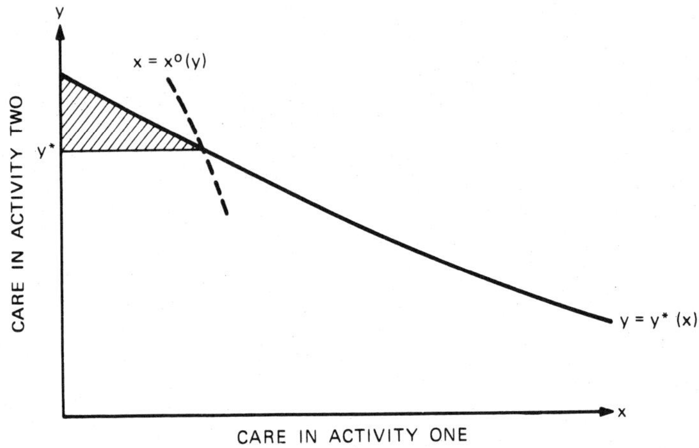

Figure 18-7. $y^*(x)$ A Decreasing Function.

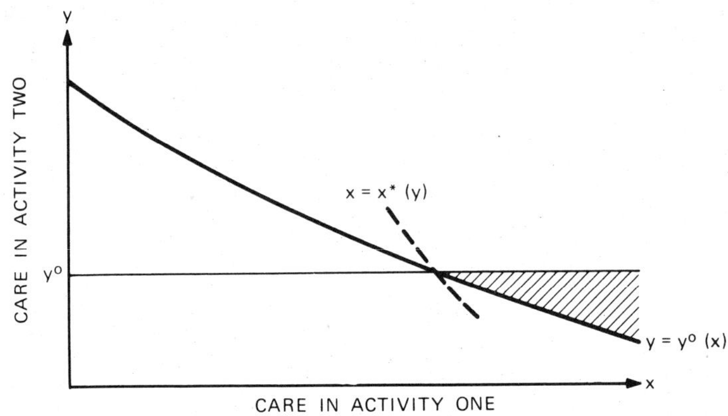

Figure 18-8. $y^{\mathrm{o}}(x)$ A Decreasing Function.

out the importance of the effectiveness condition and serve as an introduction to a formal consideration of the approximate validity of the effectiveness condition when nontransferable externalities are small.

Example:

Consider the following specific cost functions

$$A = x^2 - 2axy, \quad B = y^2 - 2bxy, \quad C = -2c_1x - 2c_2y, \; a,b,c_1,c_2 > 0, ab < 1. \tag{18.22}$$

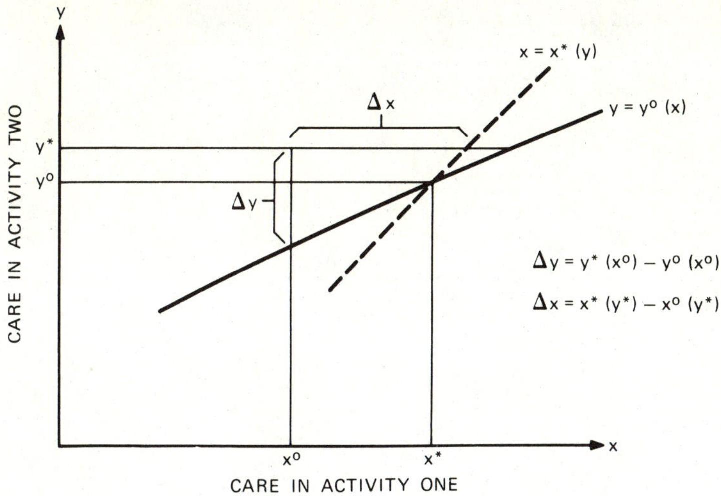

Figure 18-9. $\frac{\Delta y}{\Delta x} \geqslant \frac{y^{o}(s) - y^{o}(x)}{s - x}$.

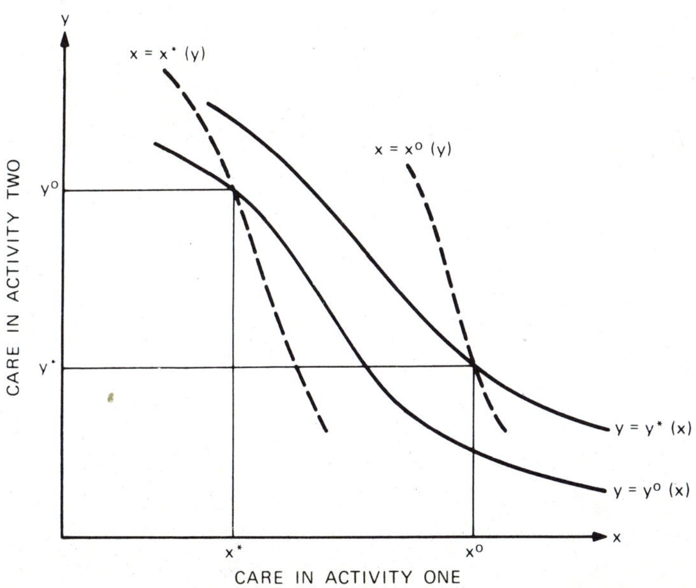

Figure 18-10. $y^* < y^o$ and $x^* < x^o$.

Minimizing A and B, we have

$$x^0(y) = ay,\ y^0(x) = bx. \tag{18.23}$$

Minimizing $A + C$ and $B + C$, we have

$$x^*(y) = ay + c_1,\quad y^*(x) = bx + c_2. \tag{18.24}$$

Solving the pairs of equations $x^* = x^*(y^0)$, $y^0 = y^0(x^*)$ and $y^* = y^*(x^0)$, $x^0 = x^0(y^*)$, we have

$$\begin{aligned} x^* &= c_1/(1-ab) \quad y^0 = bc_1/(1-ab) \\ x^0 &= ac_2/(1-ab) \quad y^* = c_2/(1-ab). \end{aligned} \tag{18.25}$$

Substituting in the definition of total costs, $S(x,y) = x^2 - 2axy + y^2 - 2bxy - 2c_1x - 2c_2y$, we get

$$S(x^*,y^0) - S(x^0,y^*) = -(1-ab)^{-2}[c_1^2(1+b^2) - 2c_1c_2(a-b)(1-ab) - c_2^2(1+a^2)],$$

which is negative if and only if

$$c_1/c_2 > (1+b^2)^{-1}[(a-b)(1-ab) + \surd\{(a-b)^2(1-ab)^2 + (1+a^2)(1+b^2)\}]. \tag{18.26}$$

By contrast we can calculate the effectiveness condition

$$S(x^0+t,y^0) - S(x^0,y^0+t) = 2t\left[(1+a+b)\ \frac{ac_2 - bc_1}{1-ab} - (c_1 - c_2)\right],$$

which is negative for positive t if and only if

$$c_1/c_2 > [1+a+a^2]/[1+b+b^2]. \tag{18.27}$$

It is an oddity of the example that activity one is more effective than activity two or activity two is more effective than activity one. With more complicated functional forms it may be true that for some range of parameters neither activity is more effective than the other. One can compare the regions on which each of the total cost differences is negative for some sense of how far the effectiveness condition alone gives a correct answer. Approximately, both criteria give the same answer in that both indicate a gain from assigning liability to activity one when

$$\frac{c_1}{c_2} > 1 + a - b + a^2 - ab + \text{higher order terms.} \tag{18.28}$$

It is worth noting that, even in as simple an example as this one, the strict criterion (18.26) is a distinctly messy formula. Fortunately, even when the nontransferable externalities are substantial, the difference between the exact criterion (18.26) and the effectiveness criterion (18.27) may be insignificant. If, for example,

$$a = \frac{1}{4}, \ b = \frac{1}{2},$$

(18.26) shows that liability should be assigned to activity one if and only if $c_1/c_2 \geqslant 0.763$, whereas the effectiveness criterion (18.27) yields $c_1/c_2 \geqslant 0.75$. If $c_1 = 3, c_2 = 4$ (so that $c_1/c_2 = 0.75$),

$$S(x^*,y^0) - S(x^0,y^*) = 0.653,$$

so that assigning liability to activity one rather than to activity two increases total costs by 0.653. In effect, this is a small increase; if $c_1 = 2$, $c_2 = 4$, the corresponding figure is 11.102. In the next section we explore the magnitude of error from applying the effectiveness criterion.

To apply Theorem 3 to the example we would also examine (18.13). (Since A_2 and B_1 are both negative, the remaining condition of Theorem 3 is satisfied.) Calculating (18.13), we find that activity one has the greater incentive for care when

$$c_1/c_2 \geqslant \frac{1+a}{1+b} \tag{18.29}$$

(which is precisely the condition for $x^* + y^0 \geqslant x^0 + y^*$). The application of the conditions of Theorem 3 to the example occurs in the direct manner that (18.27) implies (18.26) when $a > b$ and (18.29) implies (18.26) when $a < b$, as can be verified by lengthy calculation.

18.6. An Approximation Theorem

We shall now consider a formal argument that the effectiveness condition comes close to giving the right answer when the nontransferable externalities are not too large. Let

$$A = F(x) + \epsilon G(x,y)$$
$$B = H(y) + \epsilon J(x,y), \tag{18.30}$$

where ϵ is to be thought of as a small parameter. We shall show that *a wrong assignment as a result of using the simple effectiveness criterion cannot increase costs by more than the order of* ϵ^2. This result is much stronger than the plausible continuity conjecture that the error could be of order ϵ. We shall show that actual equilibria are close to those that would occur if the liable activities minimized social costs. The effectiveness condition correctly compares these two hypothetical equilibria. Formally, we have

Theorem 4: Assume $C_2 < 0$ and A and B as in (18.30). There exists $\epsilon_1 > 0$ and M such that for all ϵ with $|\epsilon| \leqslant \epsilon_1$,

$$S(x^*,y^0) - S(x^0,y^*) \leqslant M\epsilon^2$$

if activity one is more effective in cost avoidance than activity two.

Proof: Define ξ^*, η^0 by the equations

$$S_1(\xi^*,\eta^0) = 0, \quad B_2(\xi^*, \eta^0) = 0, \tag{18.31}$$

and ξ^0, η^* by the equations

$$S_2(\xi^0,\eta^*) = 0, \quad A_1(\xi^0,\eta^*) = 0. \tag{18.32}$$

The care levels so defined are continuous functions of ϵ. When $\epsilon = 0$, $H'(\eta^0) = 0$ and $H'(\eta^*) = -C_2(\xi^0,\eta^*) > 0$, so that $\eta^* > \eta^0$. By continuity, there exists ϵ_2 such that when $|\epsilon| < \epsilon_2$,

$$\eta^* > \eta^0. \tag{18.33}$$

If activity one is more effective in cost avoidance than activity two (for some particular value of ϵ with $|\epsilon| > \epsilon_2$), (18.9a) and (18.33) imply that

$$S(\xi^0,\eta^*) \geqslant S(\hat{x}(\eta^*),\eta^0) \geqslant S(\xi^*,\eta^0). \tag{18.34}$$

We estimate the difference between $S(x^*,y^0)$ and $S(\xi^*,\eta^0)$ by considering $x(u), y(u)$ defined by

$$S_1(x,y) = uB_1(x,y), \quad B_2(x,y) = 0 \tag{18.35}$$

as u varies between 0 and 1. Notice that

$$x^* = x(1), \quad y^0 = y(1)$$
$$\xi^* = x(0), \quad \eta^0 = y(0). \tag{18.36}$$

Differentiating (18.35) with respect to u, we have

$$(S_{11} - uB_{11})x'(u) + (S_{12} - uB_{12})y'(u) = B_1$$
$$B_{12}x'(u) + B_{22}y'(u) = 0.$$

Since, by (18.30), $B_1 = \epsilon J_1$ and $B_{12} = \epsilon J_{12}$, these imply that

$$[(S_{11} - uB_{11}) - (S_{12} - uB_{12})\epsilon \frac{J_{12}}{B_{22}}]x'(u) = \epsilon J_1 \tag{18.37}$$

$$y'(u) = -\epsilon \frac{J_{12}}{B_{22}} x'(u). \tag{18.38}$$

Let us choose ϵ_3 so that whenever (u, ϵ) is in the set E defined by $|\epsilon| \leqslant \epsilon_3$ and $0 \leqslant u \leqslant 1$, the expression in square brackets is positive. Since the set of $(x(u),y(u))$ for (u,ϵ) in E is bounded, it follows from (18.37) that there exists a constant M_1 such that

$$|x'(u)| < M_1 |\epsilon|, \quad (u,\epsilon) \text{ in } E. \tag{18.39}$$

Then, by (18.38) and (18.39), there exists M_2 such that

$$|y'(u)| < M_2 \epsilon^2, \quad (u,\epsilon) \text{ in } E. \tag{18.40}$$

By total differentiation,

$$\frac{d}{du} S(x(u),y(u)) = S_1 x'(u) + S_2 y'(u) = \epsilon J_1 u s'(u) + S_2 y'(u) \tag{18.41}$$

by (18.30) and (18.35). $J_1 u$ and S_2 are bounded in E, say by M_3 and M_4. Therefore, (18.39), (18.40), and (18.41) imply that

$$\frac{d}{du} S(x(u),y(u)) \leqslant M_1 M_3 \epsilon^2 + M_2 M_4 \epsilon^2 = M_5 \epsilon^2. \tag{18.42}$$

Integrating (18.42) from 0 to 1, we obtain (using (18.36))

$$S(x^*,y^0) - S(\xi^*, \eta^0) \leqslant M_5\epsilon^2, \quad |\epsilon| \leqslant \epsilon_3. \tag{18.43}$$

In a similar way, we can find $\epsilon_4 > 0$ and M_6, such that

$$S(x^0,y^*) - S(\xi^0, \eta^*) \geqslant M_6\epsilon^2, \quad |\epsilon| \leqslant \epsilon_4. \tag{18.44}$$

Set $\epsilon_1 = \min(\epsilon_2,\epsilon_3,\epsilon_4)$, $M = M_5 + M_6$. Then the inequalities (18.34), (18.43), and (18.44) imply that

$$S(x^*,y^0) - S(x^0,y^*) \leqslant M\epsilon^2. \tag{18.45}$$

where ϵ is any number such that $|\epsilon| \leqslant \epsilon_1$ and activity 1 is more effective in cost avoidance than activity 2. *Q.E.D.*

Notice that the ϵ multiplying G and the ϵ multiplying J both enter the proof, although the presence of nontransferable externalities from activity two does not affect Theorem 1. One might say, borrowing Malinvaud's terminology in another context, that our problem has second-order effectiveness-equivalence. Consequently, it seems right to emphasize the simple effectiveness criterion as a convenient and tolerably accurate test for determining the efficient assignment of liability.

18.7. A Measurement Invariant Approach

In the discussion of Theorem 1 we introduced an alternative definition of cost effectiveness which did not lean on the idea of x and y being in comparable units:

There exists $\hat{x}(y)$ such that

$$S(\hat{x}(y),y^0) \leqslant S(x^0,y) \text{ for all } y > y^0. \tag{18.9a}$$

Since many problems will not naturally be defined in terms of comparable units, it seems worthwhile to pursue this approach (which will also have an unexpected benefit). Condition (18.9a) is clearly independent of the units in which x and y are measured. This is a virtue not shared by (18.9).

To pursue a theorem like Theorem 3, we need to find a condition like the greater incentive for care condition, (18.13). It clearly would be sufficient to assume that for the function $\hat{x}(y)$ which satisfies (18.9a) it is also true that

$$A_1(\hat{x}(y),y^0) + C_1(\hat{x}(y),y^0) \leqslant B_2(x^0,y) + C_2(x^0,y) \text{ for all } y. \tag{18.13a}$$

Combining (18.9a) and (18.13a), we could describe the conditions as saying that for any increase in care above the self-protection level in activity two, there exists some increase in care in activity one which gives lower social costs and greater marginal benefits within the activity for further increases in care. But this condition does not share the virtues of this general approach since the magnitude of the derivatives depends on the units of measurement. To develop a condition which does not rely on the units of measurement we develop an alternative to comparing the marginal benefits within each activity from increased care.

Let us compare the impact of a change in care on costs within an activity to its impact on costs outside the activity. We define $\alpha(x,y)$ as

$$\alpha(x,y) \equiv -\frac{A_1(x,y) + C_1(x,y)}{B_1(x,y)} . \tag{18.46}$$

When activity one is liable, the numerator is the derivative of own costs with respect to care. The denominator is the derivative of costs elsewhere with respect to care. Minus their ratio is then the change in costs within the activity to create a unit change in costs elsewhere. Thus it is natural to refer to α as the *marginal cost of altruism.* This cost reflects the situation where activity one is liable. An alternative definition would be appropriate if liability were elsewhere. Similarly, we can consider the same construct for activity two[n] assuming liability on activity two,

$$\beta(x,y) \equiv -\frac{B_2(x,y) + C_2(x,y)}{A_2(x,y)} . \tag{18.47}$$

To avoid the obvious complications we assume that

$$A_2(x,y) \neq 0 \text{ and } B_1(x,y) \neq 0 \text{ for all } x,y. \tag{18.48}$$

Of course this rules out sign reversals on the externalities as well as an absence of externalities.

We consider now the situation where social costs can be lowered while lowering the marginal cost of altruism at the same time. We shall say that activity one is *strongly more effective* in cost avoidance if there exists $\hat{x}(y)$ such that

$$S(\hat{x}(y),y^0) \leqslant S(x^0,y)$$

and

$$\alpha(\hat{x}(y),y^0) \leqslant \beta(x^0,y) \text{ for all } y \geqslant y^0. \tag{18.49}$$

[n]In the case where $D \neq 0$ we can define α as $-(A_1 + C_1)/(B_1 + D_1)$ and β as $-(B_2 + C_2)/(A_2 + D_2)$ and obtain the results described in the text.

In applying this condition we get the pleasant bonus that it is no longer necessary to assume $B_1 \leqslant 0$. To have this result formally, we state and prove the analogy to Lemma 1.

Lemma 2°: It is more efficient to have liability placed on activity one if

(i) activity one is strongly more effective in cost avoidance than activity two, (18.49), and
(ii) $y^* \geqslant y^0$.

Proof: Apply the definition of strong effectiveness to y^*. Then

$$S(x^0,y^*) \geqslant S(\hat{x}(y^*),y^0), \text{ and } \alpha(\hat{x}(y^*),y^0) \leqslant 0 \text{ since } \beta(x^0,y^*) = 0.$$

$\alpha(\hat{x}(y^*),y^0) \leqslant 0$ means that $A_1(\hat{x}(y^*),y^0) + C_1(\hat{x}(y^*),y^0)$ has the same sign as $B_1(\hat{x}(y^*),y^0)$. Therefore $\hat{x}(y^*) \leqslant x^*$ if $B(x,y^0)$ is a decreasing function of x. $\hat{x}(y^*) \geqslant x^*$ if B is an increasing function. In either case,

$$B(\hat{x}(y^*),y^0) \geqslant B(x^*,y^0). \tag{18.50}$$

Therefore, we have

$$\begin{aligned} S(x^0, y^*) &\geqslant S(\hat{x}(y^*),y^0) \\ &\geqslant [A(\hat{x}(y^*),y^0) + C(\hat{x}(y^*),y^0)] + B(x^*,y^0), \text{ by (18.50)} \\ &\geqslant [A(x^*,y^0) + C(x^*,y^0)] + B(x^*,y^0) \\ &= S(x^*,y^0). \ \textit{Q.E.D.} \end{aligned}$$

Given the Lemma, the line of argument that resulted in Theorem 3 yields the same result with (18.9), (18.13), and $B_1 \leqslant 0$ all replaced by (18.49). In particular, if increased care in activity one reduces care in activity two, strong effectiveness is a sufficient condition for assigning liability to activity one.

°The following variant of Lemma 2 uses x^* and y^* as reference points:

Lemma 2': It is more efficient to have liability placed on activity one if

(i) For all $x \leqslant x^*$ there exists $\hat{y} = \hat{y}(x)$ such that $S(x^*,\hat{y}) \leqslant S(x,y^*)$ and $\beta(x^*,\hat{y}) \leqslant \alpha(x,y^*)$
(ii) $x^0 \leqslant x^*$.

The proof is similar to that of Lemma 2.

This Lemma assumes that activity *two* can compensate for reduced care in activity one without increasing its marginal cost of altruism above the level in the other activity.

18.8. External Diseconomies

We have focused on the case where the transferable costs decrease in both variables ($C_1 < 0$, $C_2 < 0$) and where nontransferable costs also decrease in the care of others. However, the first of these conditions is not a serious restriction in the analysis. Provided that transferable costs are monotone in each of the variables, we can define our variables so that this is true. (That is, if C increases, we measure the variables negatively.) This seems the appropriate measurement of what we call care. The complications arise in Theorem 3 when the transferable externality and the nontransferable externality differ in their signs, $C_1 \leqslant 0$, $B_1 > 0$ (and relative to condition (iv) in that theorem $C_2 \leqslant 0$ and $A_2 > 0$). In this case greater care decreases the transferable costs but increases the nontransferable costs. While this is not the case for care variables that affect the probability of an accident, it is not an implausible situation in some circumstances for variables which affect the severity of an accident, should one occur.

In the context of Theorem 3, the excess supply condition implies an increase in care from the level $x^0 + y^* - y^0$, but this involves a cost raising factor when B increases in x. The formulation in section 18.6 avoids this problem by focusing on altruism rather than on care. When increased care raises costs elsewhere, the altruism condition implies that care is decreased in the move from $\hat{x}(y^*)$ to x^*.

18.9. Some Remarks

In the simplest of settings the determination of the cheapest cost avoider follows the patterns one would readily expect. Having found the decisionmaker who has the more important effect on total costs, one has found the place to locate liability to achieve the more efficient equilibrium. Nevertheless this determination still requires some empirical verification that the expenditures of those in one activity are more effective than expenditures in the other activity. Once externalities are present in addition to those whose cost is being allocated, the situation becomes considerably more complicated. The conditions that we have found to be sufficient for identification of the cheapest cost avoider become more numerous and more difficult to verify empirically. This is not too upsetting, since it is rare that one can answer complicated policy questions without serious empirical work. When a general problem is complicated, one may have to be content with direct calculations for functions estimated in particular cases. But there remains value in more general results if they can be found, particularly when as in the present instance the number of possible applications is very great. Without general theorems, we are at the mercy of adventitious features in the estimated model, since we cannot say which aspects of the model are most important for the problem at hand. General theorems, and the arguments leading to them, ought to deepen understanding of the problem and thus cultivate some degree of intuitive appreciation in actual cases. They direct our attention to the empirical opinions that need to be articulated, the measurements that ought to be made.

Thus, while we might have stopped the analysis (and the reader may have ceased paying attention) when it became apparent at Theorem 2 that the situation became complicated, we believe that it was indeed worthwhile to pursue results which were not so neat as the first theorem. Our enthusiasm for continuing this line of work comes, in part, from a sense that there are many economic (and legal) problems which can be usefully considered in this framework, and, therefore, various elaborations of the basic model may prove useful.[p] First we shall restate the basic results in terms of an example. Then the remainder of this section will be devoted to describing another class of problems which may also fit into this framework and to considering some specific examples.

An Example

Let us consider accidents between trains and trucks at level crossings. The probability and severity of accidents decrease with the quality of the brakes that each has installed. Assume that trucks are damaged by these accidents but trains are not. Assume that truck owners bear all the accident costs and that we are considering shifting liability to railroad companies, with damages measured to perfectly compensate truck drivers.[q] In this setting, Theorem 1 is applicable. The shift in liability decreases expected social costs if for any level of expenditure to improve truck brakes (in excess of the level chosen when truck drivers bear no costs of these accidents) the resulting total of expected social costs exceeds that which can be achieved by some level of expenditures on train brakes, with brakes on trucks back at the level for self-protection (i.e., when these accident costs are not borne). In the circumstance where both parties are responding rationally to these changed financial incentives, this is surely the factual minimum that one would expect to need. Of course this is merely a sufficient condition and is not necessary for justifying a shift in liability.

[p]Some allocation decisions, like number of miles driven per year, are not subject to due care standards reflecting behavior at the time of a particular accident. Thus a negligence-contributory negligence system and a strict liability-contributory negligence system will differ in their impact on such a variable, even in the case where variables subject to a due care standard are unaffected by such a change in legal regime. Comparing these two legal systems will then require an analysis like that employed above.

[q]Since brakes are useful to avoid other types of accidents too, we would not assume zero expenditures for the party not bearing liability. We ignore externalities to others from these decreased accident possibilities.

Now let us complicate this story by assuming that there is a general revenue financed national health insurance. Thus in the original situation drivers do not pay their medical expenses (and ignore these costs in their decisions), but they do bear all other costs. Assume that with a shift in liability, railroads compensate drivers for the losses they experience, the government still paying for medical expenses. Now the situation corresponds to the one described in Theorem 2. To confirm that shifting liability increases efficiency we must check the effectiveness condition described in the last paragraph. In addition we must confirm the care incentive condition—that we can find a level of expenditures on train brakes which will reduce social costs to offset fully decreased brake expenditures by truck drivers and that at this level of expenditure railroads have a private incentive (given that they are liable) for further expenditures. This is indeed more difficult to confirm than the information we needed in the previous case.

Now let us assume that trains are also damaged by these accidents and that railroad companies bear these costs.[r] Now we are in the circumstance for which Theorem 3 has been developed. However, since we are assuming full compensation of truck drivers, should liability be shifted, we do not need to check any further conditions. Given full compensation, expenditure by drivers does not depend on the quality of train brakes. Thus we are assured that expenditures by drivers go down when they cease being liable since we are dealing with external economies (transferred costs decrease with truck brake quality) and are assuming a stable equilibrium.

To bring in the complications with which Theorem 3 is designed to deal, we need merely add the plausible condition that accident compensation is not precise (in expected value terms). This might occur because of systematic biases in damage measurement. Alternatively the shift in liability might be partial, with compensation for lost wages and out-of-pocket expenses but no compensation for pain and suffering. In the circumstance we are describing it remains reasonable to assume both that truck brake quality decreases when train brakes improve, whatever the assignment of liability, and that all externalities are economies. Either of these assumptions then permits the use of Theorem 3.

To bring in the complexities involving diseconomies let us shift our focus from brake quality to the design of the front of the locomotive. Assume there are costly design changes which decrease damage to trucks but increase damage to drivers. If the only costs we are shifting are the costs of property damage to trucks, then these design changes would decrease transferred costs but increase both lost wages (borne by drivers) and medical expenses (borne by the government). Now Theorem 3 will not apply, but if it is empirically confirmable, the condition of strong effectiveness would still give the result. Clearly the range of possible circumstances is very large and serious empirical study of different accident situations would be valuable in indicating the directions of theoretical advance which would be most helpful. Now let us turn to a rather different setting where these models might also be useful.

[r]If truck drivers compensated railroads and we were considering shifting liability for all of these costs, we would be back in the previous case.

Extensions

Even in situations where there is trade, it is often the case that allocation decisions are made before the trade opportunities are precisely determined. That is, allocation decisions are made on the expectation of trade opportunities' materializing. Sometimes markets are well enough defined so that trade opportunities can be viewed as independent of the behavior of any particular other individual. Sometimes trade is an ongoing relationship with repeated trades between the same parties. Otherwise an individual committing resources to produce for a future market is in an externality situation. By hypothesis, he is not negotiating in advance of making his trade, and is making resource allocation decisions in advance of trade which are important for other individuals. Any rules which alter the division of the gains from trade, alter the allocation decisions of the parties before trade takes place. Thus we may have a situation, as in the model, where it is not possible to get efficient *ex ante* allocation decisions on the part of all parties to future trades. The allocation of the gains from trade then serves to trade off incentives for some traders against incentives for others.

As an extreme example of this, consider the two activities of hiking in the desert and driving in the desert (both consumption activities). Assume that there is a probability of hikers' becoming lost and a probability for any lost hiker of his being rescued by some driver. The probability of a rescue thus depends on the frequency of both hiking and driving. (Assume that the probability of rescue is sufficiently small that we can ignore the possibility of two drivers' coming on the same hiker.) Assume that whenever someone is found he is in fact rescued. A rescue represents a large consumer surplus which results from the chance meeting. (This is the opposite of an accident.)

Since any contract which might be signed at the time of the rescue would not be enforced by the courts, the hiker keeps this consumer surplus. Thus we get the correct incentives for hiking, but incentives which are too small for driving in the desert. If such contracts were enforceable, the consumer surplus would go to the driver giving the right incentives for driving but too little incentive for hiking.[6] The efficiency implications of the allocation of this consumer surplus clearly fit the model described above.

This example is obviously an extreme case where the alternative to a particular trade is no trade at all. With perfect markets there is no consumer surplus from a particular trade, since the next best alternative is the same trade on the same terms with someone else. With imperfect markets where it is necessary to search for trade opportunities there will generally be a consumer's surplus associated with any particular trade. Legal rules which affect the division of that consumer surplus will then have allocative implications for behavior in anticipation of (and search for) trade.[s] By analogy, no rule just involving

[s]A similar analysis might be relevant in international trade where rules of access to the markets of a particular country may change.

transfers between parties will result in an efficient allocation. Models of the sort considered above may indicate the issues relevant for a comparison of the efficiency of different outcomes under different rules.

Notes

1. See reference [2].

2. Op. cit., p. 136ff. In a more recent paper, Calabresi and Hirschoff [3] have gone further in defining the cheapest cost avoider (p. 1060): "which of the parties to the accident is in the best position to make the cost-benefit analysis between accident costs and accident avoidance costs and to act on that decision once it is made."

3. One can be interested in efficiency without feeling that it alone should determine the assignment of liability. An alternative basis for assignment is advanced by Fletcher [6].

4. See, for example, Brown [1], Diamond [4, 5], and Posner [7, 8], as well as Calabresi [2].

5. In [2], p. 147.

6. These conclusions differ from those of Posner [7], p. 49, who considers the same situation.

References

1. Brown, J.P., "Towards an Economic Theory of Liability," *Journal of Legal Studies,* 2, no. 2 (June 1973):323-349.

2. Calabresi, G., *Costs of Accidents*, New Haven: Yale Univ. Press, 1970.

3. _______, and Hirschoff, J., "Towards a Test for Strict Liability in Torts," *Yale Law Journal,* 81, no. 6 (May 1972):1055-1085.

4. Diamond, P., "Accident Law and Resource Allocation," *The Bell Journal of Economics and Management Science,* 5, no. 2 (Autumn 1974):366-416.

5. _______, "Single Activity Accident," *Journal of Legal Studies,* 3, no. 1 (Jan. 1974):107-162.

6. Fletcher, G., "Fairness and Utility in Tort Theory," *Harvard Law Review,* 85, no. 3 (Jan. 1972):537-573.

7. Posner, R., *Economic Analysis of Law,* Boston-Toronto: Little, Brown, 1972.

8. _______, "A Theory of Negligence," *Journal of Legal Studies,* 1, no. 1 (Jan. 1972):29-96.

9. Prosser, W., *Law of Torts*, 4th ed. St. Paul, Minn.: West Publishing Co., 1971.

Appendix 18A

In the text, the approach taken to the asymmetry of S was to measure differences in care between a given point and the point (x^0,y^0), since (x^0,y^0) proves to be a convenient origin for the problem. However, in some cases it may be very difficult to determine the values x^0 and y^0. One way around this problem was noted in note i, by identifying a much stronger condition which was sufficient to imply the asymmetry condition used. An alternative approach, taken here, is to examine conditions using asymmetry relative to an arbitrary point which serves as origin. This will be particularly appropriate when the care variables represent expenditures and are measured from the point of zero expenditures.

The alternative definition of asymmetry is:

$$\text{For } s > t,\ S(s,t) \leqslant S(t,s). \tag{18.A.1}$$

(18.A.1) is implied by the condition (18.9c) in note i, but is substantially weaker. We present theorems which use this assumption among others to deduce the greater efficiency of assigning liability to activity one. As in the main text we have a simple result when all externalities are transferable.

Theorem 5: It is more efficient to have liability placed on activity one if A is independent of y, B of x, $D = 0$, and

(i) $A'(s) \geqslant B'(s)$ (all s)

(ii) $C(x,y)$ is a decreasing function of y

(iii) $S(s,t) \leqslant S(t,s)$ $(s > t)$.

Proof: (i) implies that $y^0 \geqslant x^0$, for it implies that $A'(y^0) \geqslant 0$. (ii) implies that $y^* > y^0$. Therefore $y^* > x^0$ and by (iii)

$$\begin{aligned} S(x^0,y) &\geqslant S(y^*,x^0) \\ &= A(y^*) + C(y^*,x^0) + B(x^0) \\ &\geqslant A(y^*) + C(y^*,y^0) + B(y^0), \end{aligned}$$

since $y^0 \geqslant x^0$, and y^0 minimizes B. Now x^* minimizes $A(x) + C(x,y^0)$. Therefore, we have

$$S(x^0,y^*) \geqslant S(x^*,y^0).\ \ Q.E.D.$$

When A depends on y, we have the same problem as before, that the last step of the above proof does not go through. We proceed by establishing first what inequalities between care levels can do for us.

Lemma 3: It is more efficient to have liability placed on activity one if

$$\begin{aligned}&\text{(i) } A + C, D \text{ are nonincreasing in } y \text{ and } y^0 \geqslant x^0,\\&\text{(ii) } B, D \text{ are nonincreasing in } x, \text{ and } x^* \geqslant y^*;\\&\text{(iii) } S(s,t) \leqslant S(t,s) \text{ when } s > t \text{ and } y^* \geqslant x^0.\end{aligned} \tag{18A.2}$$

Variants of Lemma 3: Any of the assumption pairs (i), (ii), or (iii) can be changed to the opposite sense without affecting the conclusion.

Proof of Lemma 3:

$$\begin{aligned}S(x^0,y^*) &\geqslant S(y^*,x^0), \text{ by (iii)}\\&= [A(y^*,x^0) + C(y^*,x^0)] + B(y^*,x^0) + D(y^*,x^0)\\&\geqslant [A(y^*,y^0) + C(y^*,y^0)] + B(x^*,x^0) + D(x^*,y^0), \text{ by (i) and (ii)}\\&\geqslant [A(x^*,y^0) + C(x^*,y^0)] + B(x^*,y^0) + D(x^*,y^0)\end{aligned}$$

by minimizing choices of the two activities. Therefore

$$S(x^0,y^*) \geqslant S(x^*,y^0) \quad Q.E.D.$$

To obtain a satisfactory theorem, one must find conditions implying the inequalities between the care levels. For illustration, we take the case of positive reactions, i.e., $x^*(y)$, $x^0(y)$, $y^*(x)$, $y^0(x)$ are increasing functions, with the stability conditions (20) satisfied.

In figure 18A-1 we compare y^0 and x^0, and y^* and x^* by reflecting the x^*- and y^*-curves in the forty-five degree line. The reflected curves are shown as broken lines. It is clearly sufficient for

$$y^0 \geqslant x^0, \; x^* \geqslant y^*$$

that the curves are related as shown, i.e.,

$$x^0(s) \leqslant y^0(s) \tag{18A.3}$$

and

$$y^*(t) \leqslant x^*(t). \tag{18A.4}$$

(18A.3) is implied by the following condition on A and B:

$$B_2(s,t) \leqslant A_1(t,s): \tag{18A.5}$$

for $A_1(x^0(t),t)=0$, so that with (18A.5) we have $B_2(t,x^0(t)) \leqslant 0$, and since $B(t,y)$ is convex with minimum at $y = y^0(t)$, $y^0(t) \geqslant x^0(t)$. Similarly, (18A.4) follows from the condition

$$A_1(s,t) + C_1(s,t) \leqslant B_2(t,s) + C_2(t,s). \tag{18A.6}$$

(18A.5) and (18A.6) specify certain asymmetries between the activities.

To establish $y^* \geqslant x^0$, the remaining inequality, we must find conditions that ensure the point (x^0,y^*) lies above the forty-five degree line. It is sufficient that

$$\text{For } s > t, \qquad A_1(s,t) \geqslant B_2(t,s) + C_2(t,s). \tag{18A.7}$$

This implies that for each t such that $x^0(t) > t$,

$$y^*(t) \geqslant x^0(t). \tag{18A.8}$$

In particular, if $x^0 = x^0(y^*) > y^*$, and $t = y^*$,

$$y^*(t) < y^*(x^0) = y^*, \tag{18A.9}$$

since the y^*-reaction is positive. Combining (18A.8) and (18A.9), we find that $x^0 > y^*$ implies $x^0 \leqslant y^*(t) < y^*$, a contradiction. Therefore (18A.7) implies $x^0 \leqslant y^*$, as claimed.

We state these conclusions as

Theorem 6: Let all reactions be positive. It is more efficient to have liability placed on activity one if the following conditions hold:

(i) $A + C$ and D are nonincreasing in y, and

$$A_1(s,t) \geqslant B_2(t,s); \tag{18A.5}$$

(ii) B and D are nonincreasing in x, and

$$A_1(s,t) + C_1(s,t) \leqslant B_2(t,s) + C_2(t,s); \tag{18A.6}$$

(iii) $S(s,t) \leqslant S(t,s) \quad (s > t)$

and

$$A_1(s,t) \geqslant B_2(t,s) + C_2(t,s) \quad (s > t). \tag{18A.7}$$

Corollary: If $C_2 \leqslant 0$, condition (18A.7) is unnecessary (because it is implied by (18A.5)).

Notice that $C_2 \leqslant 0$ implies, by (18A.5) and (18A.6), that $C_1 \leqslant 0$.

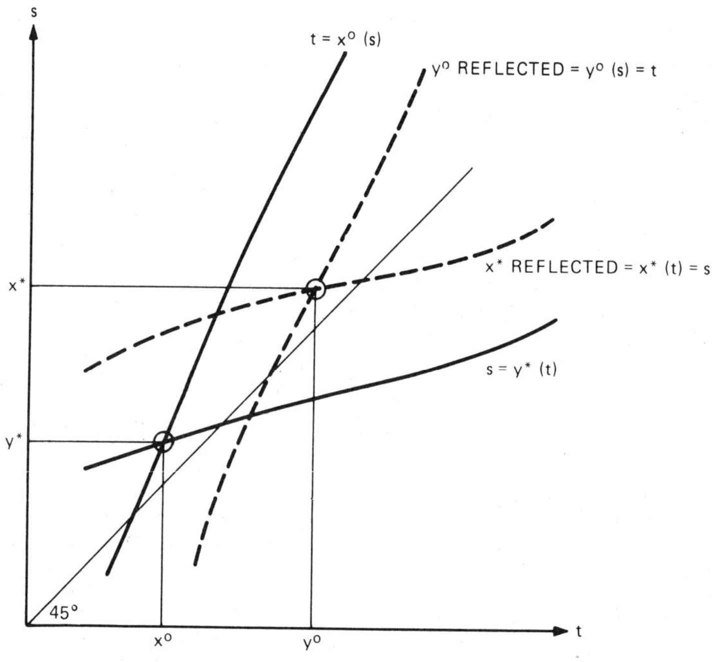

Figure 18A-1. $x^{o}(s) \leqslant y^{o}(s)$ and $y^{*}(t) \leqslant x^{*}(t)$.

List of Contributors

Robert J. Aumann, The Hebrew University, Jerusalem
Eitan Berglas, Tel-Aviv University and University of Rochester
Michael Bruno, The Hebrew University, Jerusalem, and Falk Institute
Alex Cukierman, The Foerder Institute for Economic Research, Tel-Aviv University
Peter A. Diamond, Massachusetts Institute of Technology
Martin S. Feldstein, Harvard University
John S. Flemming, Nuffield College, Oxford
Jerry Green, Harvard University
Joseph Greenberg, The Hebrew University, Jerusalem
Arye L. Hillman, Department of Economics and Foerder Institute for Economic Research, Tel-Aviv University
Ephraim Kleiman, The Hebrew University, Jerusalem
Serge-Christophe Kolm, School for Higher Studies in the Social Sciences and CEPREMAP, Paris
Mordecai Kurz, Stanford University
Jean-Jacques Laffont, l'Ecole Polytechnique
Joram Mayshar, The Hebrew University, Jerusalem
James A. Mirrlees, Nuffield College, Oxford
John Roberts, Graduate School of Management, Northwestern University
Agnar Sandmo, Norwegian School of Economics and Business Administration
Eytan Sheshinski, The Hebrew University, Jerusalem
Zalman F. Shiffer, Tel-Aviv University and University of Chicago
Carl Christian von Weiszäcker, University of Bonn

About the Editor

Agnar Sandmo is professor of economics at the Norwegian School of Economics and Business Administration, Bergen, Norway. He has had visiting appointments at the University of Louvain, Belgium, and the University of Essex, England. Professor Sandmo has published a number of articles in professional journals in the areas of economic theory and public finance, and he is a Fellow of the Econometric Society.